Authoritarian Apprehensions

Send questions beforehand

CHICAGO STUDIES IN PRACTICES OF MEANING

A series edited by Andreas Glaeser, William Mazzarella,
William H. Sewell Jr., Kaushik Sunder Rajan, and Lisa Wedeen

Published in collaboration with the Chicago Center for Contemporary Theory
http://ccct.uchicago.edu

RECENT BOOKS IN THE SERIES

*Deadline: Populism and the Press
in Venezuela*
by Robert Samet

*Guerrilla Marketing:
Counterinsurgency and Capitalism
in Colombia*
by Alexander L. Fattal

*What Nostalgia Was: War, Empire,
and the Time of a Deadly Emotion*
by Thomas Dodman

The Mana of Mass Society
by William Mazzarella

*The Sins of the Fathers:
Germany, Memory, Method*
by Jeffrey K. Olick

*The Politics of Dialogic Imagination:
Power and Popular Culture in Early
Modern Japan*
by Katsuya Hirano

*American Value: Migrants, Money,
and Meaning in El Salvador and
the United States*
by David Pedersen

*Questioning Secularism: Islam,
Sovereignty, and the Rule of Law
in Modern Egypt*
by Hussein Ali Agrama

*The Making of Romantic Love:
Longing and Sexuality in Europe,
South Asia, and Japan, 900–1200 CE*
by William M. Reddy

*The Moral Neoliberal: Welfare and
Citizenship in Italy*
by Andrea Muehlebach

*The Genealogical Science:
The Search for Jewish Origins and
the Politics of Epistemology*
by Nadia Abu El-Haj

AUTHORITARIAN APPREHENSIONS

Ideology, Judgment, and Mourning in Syria

Lisa Wedeen

THE UNIVERSITY OF CHICAGO PRESS
Chicago and London

The University of Chicago Press, Chicago 60637
The University of Chicago Press, Ltd., London
© 2019 by The University of Chicago
Published 2019
Printed in the United States of America

28 27 26 25 24 23 22 21 20 19   1 2 3 4 5

ISBN-13: 978-0-226-65057-9 (cloth)
ISBN-13: 978-0-226-65060-9 (paper)
ISBN-13: 978-0-226-65074-6 (e-book)
DOI: https://doi.org/10.7208/chicago/9780226650746.001.0001

Library of Congress Cataloging-in-Publication Data

Names: Wedeen, Lisa, author.
Title: Authoritarian apprehensions : ideology, judgment, and
    mourning in Syria / Lisa Wedeen.
Description: Chicago : The University of Chicago Press, 2019. | Series:
    Chicago studies in practices of meaning | Includes bibliographical
    references and index.
Identifiers: LCCN 2019006643 | ISBN 9780226650579 (cloth
    : alk. paper) | ISBN 9780226650609 (pbk. : alk. paper) |
    ISBN 9780226650746 (e-book)
Subjects: LCSH: Syria—History—Civil War, 2011–
Classification: LCC DS98.6 .W43 2019 | DDC 956.9104/23—dc23
LC record available at https://lccn.loc.gov/2019006643

Contents

Preface

When I returned to Syria in 2010 after an absence of over a decade, I was surprised to see how much had changed — and how much remained familiar. I intended to write a book that grappled with the seeming emergence of a kinder, gentler version of autocracy under president Bashar al-Asad (2000–). Among the issues I envisaged exploring were the forms of generational change that were both a product and a driver of market openings; the new aesthetic imaginaries of everyday life accompanying the marked embrace of consumption and departure from Soviet-era styles of insularity and asceticism; and the palpable support Bashar seemed to be garnering from communities that had hitherto withheld it from the regime, including former dissidents, artists, urban professionals, and members of the clergy. Then came the uprising in Tunisia, registering grievances and animating hopes for the end of tyrannies throughout the Arab world, inspiring subsequent large-scale protests in Egypt, Yemen, Libya, Bahrain — and Syria. I was still in Damascus when the uprising began in March 2011, leaving only toward the end of May, by which time indications of the regime's intransigence and the troubles besetting multiple oppositions had already become too glaring to ignore.

Authoritarian Apprehensions is the book that resulted. It remains keyed to my initial interests in authoritarian resilience and political change, abiding concerns to political scientists, while also exploring important issues currently under debate in political theory and anthropology. Focused from the outset on the complexities of ideological uptake and the processes of recruitment into what I had decided (pre-uprising) to call Syria's "neo-liberal autocracy," the book became increasingly inflected by the extraordinary rush of events—first by the revolutionary exhilaration of the initial days of unrest and then by the devastating violence that with terrible speed shattered hopes of any quick undoing of dictatorship.

The book's ideas thus speak to my decades-long engagement with Syria and Syrians, even as my expectations were also being transformed by unanticipated circumstances on the ground. Among the eye-opening aspects of doing fieldwork in such tumultuous times was the remarkable divergence in political views I encountered about what should/could be done. From friends, acquaintances, family members, colleagues, and interviewees, I heard people speaking out in favor of the immediate toppling of the regime, and others declaring persisting "love" for the leader. In between I found a range of opinion and emotion, experienced by people in moments of intensified excitement, anxiety, humor, anger, fear, and euphoria. The book registers my admiration for those who dared from the start to envision alternatives to the status quo and act in that spirit. As a social scientist attempting to understand what was quickly becoming a tragedy, I also benefited from interactions with Syrians who did not boldly take to the streets: the so-called gray people (*al-ramadiyyin*), the many who spent the heady early days of the uprising shifting between their desires for reform and their attachment to order. We will see in chapter 1 how the presence of this ambivalent middle proved critical at key moments to regime survival, affording the regime the latitude needed to recalibrate its relationship to rule.

As some readers know, my first book, *Ambiguities of Domination* (1999 [2015]), explored the transparently bogus rituals of obeisance characterizing the autocracy under Bashar al-Asad's father, Hafiz (1970–2000). My argument in that book was that the blatantly fictitious official rhetoric of the time operated as a means not of cultivating belief or emotional commitment but of specifying the form and content of civic obedience. Beyond the barrel of the gun and the confines of the torture chamber, as I put it then, Asad's personality cult served as a disciplinary device, generating a politics of public dissimulation in which citizens acted *as if* they revered their leader. By inundating daily life with instructive symbolism, the regime exercised a subtle yet effective form of power. The cult worked to enforce obedience, induce complicity, atomize Syrians from one another, and establish the guidelines for public speech and action. Even when citizens kept "their ironical distance, even when they demonstrated that they did not take what they were doing seriously, they were still complying. And compliance was what ultimately counted politically."[1]

Evidence of the distanced, irreverent attitude adopted by most Syrians toward regime rhetoric was everywhere to be seen under the elder Asad. Satirical cartoons, underground (and permitted) comedy skits, and discreetly shared jokes constantly poked fun at the regime's official claims to omnipotence in ways that laid bare the ambiguities of political domination and the incomplete but nevertheless potent effects of autocratic social control. Ambiguities remain under the son, of course, but this book focuses not on the chinks in domination but on the complexities of political attachment. As the ruling Ba'th Party relinquished its monopoly over the form, content, and dissemination of public discourse during the first decade under Bashar al-Asad, it became newly difficult in Syria to know for certain what even counted officially as support.[2] Gone were the excessively clear guidelines for acceptable civic conduct. In their place stood an invitation to a different kind of attachment where the tether was not so much political prudence as commodified desire.

Among the major beneficiaries in these emerging circumstances during the early 2000s were the Syrian television and advertising industries, both bursting with eager young professionals willing to press at the boundaries of the permitted by diversifying content and claiming a certain latitude as compared with the formulaic, party-oriented "correct line" of the previous regime. In chapter 1, we will see how a combination of influences, including the young president's own calls for "reform" in his first decade of rule and Syrians' growing access to an outside world (initially via satellite television and then the internet), shaped a generation of savvy and generally grateful (read: regime-friendly) professionals. And we will investigate how these professionals wielded their new rhetorical skills in helping create and manage the ruling family's updated image. The analysis in that as well as subsequent chapters is driven by the primary questions animating the book as a whole: How has the regime been able to bear the brunt of the challenges raised against it? And what does the Syrian example tell us about the seductions of authoritarian politics more generally?

My approach to this orienting puzzle identifies novel modes of ideological *interpellation* (borrowing Louis Althusser's term), new ways of "hailing" citizens into Syria's autocratic system. From various angles the book investigates the complicated, varied, often incoherent forms of address that secured the citizen buy-in the regime needed to survive.[3] In political science, questions about authoritarian resilience have tended to privilege materialist claims, detailing how patronage is used to garner instrumental support, and coercive mechanisms of control to generate obedience. By contrast, my work has always centered on what I call the disciplinary-symbolic modes of domination, rejecting the sharp dichotomy between materialist and ideational approaches from the outset and insisting on an analysis that theorizes ideology as "inscribed" in material practices, to borrow again from Althusser.[4] In resisting binaries, *Authoritarian Apprehensions* is no different. But unlike my previous work, this book presumes the unevenness of ideological reproduction, tackling head-on the complex forms of political attachment understood capaciously enough to describe both loyalty to the regime and a deep ambivalence toward it, as well as degrees of outright opposition.

The two books deal with three different forms of compliance inducement—and three different Syrias. *Ambiguities of Domination* captured the conditions of a durable autocracy whose reliance on single-party rule, an omnipresent security apparatus, and flagrantly fictitious claims had come to seem brittle and outmoded to observers and participants alike. *Authoritarian Apprehensions* examines two additional modes of compliance inducement. The first decade of Bashar al-Asad's rule ushered in an avowedly upbeat, modern, internet-savvy authoritarianism. Its institutions and rhetoric relied less on party mechanisms of social control and more on an array of cultural producers with their highly vaunted expertise as technocrats, along with regime-organized, market-inflected civil society organizations tapping into a spirit of youthful voluntarism. This all changed in the second decade with the emergence of a civil war autocracy, in which the means and mechanisms of mediation were no longer geared to perpetuation but rather to the restoration of a stability that had been radically challenged, first by peaceful protest and then by armed insurgency.

That challenge stemmed from a passionate commitment to an "it could have been otherwise" of political existence. The latter phrase echoes Theodor Adorno—and it speaks to this book's engagement with the possibilities of and impediments to social transformation—not so much "resistance" per se as the imagined alternatives opened up by the necessarily retroactive analysis of political potential in the present.[5] That may sound like a temporal impossibility, but what I am getting at involves an act of imagination in its own right, as articulated in a long philosophical tradition from Hegel, through Marx and contemporary Marxists, and on to Arendt, whose "between past and future" nicely captures this effort to theorize the in-between-ness of ordinary life, the ways in which the present is both always past by the time we narrate it and the source for creating something new.[6] And because we tend to inhabit ordinary life in multiple temporal registers, we can also retrace the steps by which ideology was made palpable, explore the paths not taken and the forms of knowing and resonance hovering around the edges of our multiple worlds. We can identify the potentialities that remain latent or seem to have withered away but which nevertheless haunt our contemporary situation and, in the right conditions, can be rediscovered and reactivated.

* * * *

As a scholar with ethnographic commitments, I write with a profound sense of solidarity with Syrians of various stripes. This solidarity includes the solidarity to disagree, to judge, to be surprised, angry, even repelled. Writing from a situated perspective in this way means not giving in to titillating curiosity about people who find themselves being violated and exploited by the conditions in which they are living. I do engage subjects as sources of ethnographic knowledge, but I do so while maintaining the ethical imperative to be vigilant about how we maintain respect for and stage interpretive encounters with others whom we seek to understand.[7] This orientation calls for cultivating curiosity, reflexivity, and *enduring* commitment.

Writing a book about Syria in these calamitous times has been heartbreaking, intellectually demanding, and confusing—sometimes gratifying and other times deeply frustrating, depressing, enraging, and simply exhausting. The pressure to produce a book quickly as the uprising began unfolding in 2011 was one to which I obviously did not succumb. But grappling with grief—my own as well as that of others much closer to the hopes and the violence than I was—and figuring out how to write about a devastating situation in ways that maintained fidelity to my social scientific commitments without either sensationalizing or seeming insensitive became an exercise in humility. As I noted in the 2015 preface to *Ambiguities of Domination*, I owe an immeasurable debt to Syrians of many different political orientations for their faith in me and for their patience, generosity, and insights, which have reliably expanded my thinking. I have learned from disagreements, even when they have pained me. It is difficult not to despair, or to wonder how any book could have merit at a moment like this. All the remaining political choices seem awful, with the direct and estimable pleasures enjoyed by revolutionaries and regime supporters alike at the beginning of the uprising seemingly lost. In light of such loss, it may seem odd that a major theme in *Authoritarian Apprehensions* is comedy (chapter 2)—but the lesson of Syrian activist comedians is that it is possible and perhaps imperative to find the humor in situations that are unbearable and yet must be borne. Like good scholarship, their challenge to the battering capriciousness of authoritarian violence demands both proximity to the object and a creative separation from it.

Grief, the Libyan author Hisham Matar writes, is not only a source of solidarity but "a divider; it move[s] each one of us into a territory of private shadows, where the torment [is] incommunicable, so horribly outside language."[8] Part of the difficulty in *narrating* grief is coming up with that language, even on the basic level of choosing the proper tense.[9] Loved ones as well as historical figures exist in the past, present, and future, as Matar also notes, for "we all live [as grievers and grieved] in the aftermath."[10] Writing in times of a catastrophe that has not yet ended raises important questions about how we as scholars are to capture lived experiences and what presumptions we make about the nature of experience. Life sometimes seems to be lived simultaneously in fast-forward and reverse, and interpretive encounters dramatize how we humans are never fully reliable even to ourselves. Recently, several important works have given voice to the experience of living under authoritarian rule in Syria, written by and about journalists, artists, refugees, migrants, activists, and former prisoners now living in exile.[11] This book, while crafted in appreciation of those writings, cannot be counted among them. Instead—for better and for worse—it is a work of interpretive social science, an effort to contribute to an ongoing theoretical conversation about authoritarianism. As will become apparent throughout, I do this by drawing attention back to the importance of ideology—to modes of interpellation, the complexities of political address, the fact of ambivalence, and the underlying investments in fantasy that are resistant to and even reinforced by criticism. *Authoritarian Apprehensions* also considers the openings for political judgment in the context of ideology as a structuring force. And it is an engagement with the potentialities inherent in proceeding through the long process of mourning, of gradually coming to terms with the enormity of the Syrian calamity.

In writing about love and loss, the novelist Anthony Marra puts his female protagonist at the kitchen table examining a glass of melting ice:

> Each cube was rounded by room temperature, dissolving in its own remains, and belatedly she understood that this was how a loved one disappeared. Despite the shock of walking into an empty flat, the absence isn't immediate, more a fade from the present tense you shared, a melting into the past, not an erasure but a conversion in form, from presence to memory, from solid to liquid, and the person you once touched now runs over your skin, now

in sheets down your back, and you may bathe, may sink, may drown in the memory, but your fingers cannot hold it. She raised the glass to her lips. The water was clean.[12]

Loss here is at once both nourishment and sorrow, an invitation to embrace the metamorphosis rather than the object lost. Easier said than done, perhaps — but also a possible way forward.

A Note on Transliteration

The transliteration method used in this book attempts to combine accuracy with technical simplicity. It is based primarily on the system adopted by the *International Journal of Middle East Studies*. However, diacritical marks indicating long vowels and emphatic consonants are dropped. Widely recognized Anglicized variants of place-names are spelled according to convention. Most names of persons are written according to *IJMES* rules, with the exception of those variants that are globally recognized and therefore easily searchable in English. In some instances where multiple spellings are used, I have tended to supply alternatives in parentheses. With regard to news agencies and production companies, names given in the Latin alphabet were transliterated in accordance with the media outlet's spelling. Otherwise, *IJMES* conventions were employed.

"I Know Very Well, yet Nevertheless . . ."

IDEOLOGY, INTERPELLATION,

AND THE POLITICS OF DISAVOWAL

If the Arab uprisings initially seemed to herald the end of tyrannies and a move toward liberal democratic governments, their defeat not only marks a reversal but is of a piece with new forms of authoritarianism worldwide. Liberal democracy seems to be unmaking itself in the United States and parts of Europe, where we find civil rights being curtailed and forms of ultranationalist populism emerging with little regard for due process or freedom of the press. In Russia, the short-lived experiment with genuinely contested elections that took place in the context of rapacious capital extraction has been eclipsed by the emergence of a charismatic leader whose apparent popularity among a majority comes at the expense of any number of dissident minorities. If in the 1990s pundits hailed the "end of history" and political scientists promoted theories of democratic transition, in the early 2000s they shifted their attention to studies of authoritarian retrenchment. Of course, scholars searching hopefully for the necessary conditions of democratic consolidation—all too often framed inadequately in narrow terms of electoral contestation—have always been alert to issues of "backsliding," elite rivalries, undemocratic power-sharing, variations in economic development and growth, inequality, and the institutional fragilities produced by colonial legacies.[1] But the current moment is rightly generating reinvigorated interest in authoritarianism as such, bringing us new accounts of phony elections and party co-optation along with a nuanced concern with the design of coercive apparatuses.[2]

Scholars are asking with renewed urgency why it is that citizens, and not only autocrats, so often seem to be attracted to autocracy.

This book is in part an effort to contribute to those debates by drawing from the Syrian context to rethink the political role and importance of ideology and of what Louis Althusser calls "ideological interpellation." It begins with the recalibration of authoritarian rule in Syria in the first decade of the twenty-first century, when the death of president Hafiz al-Asad after a thirty-year regime (1970–2000) seemed to prepare the way under his son for a kinder, gentler version of autocracy. The initial paradox, when the uprising broke out in March 2011, lay in how activists easily presumed that the regime would live up to the image of civility it had been cultivating for a decade, thereby bringing into bold relief how potent the ideological apparatus was, even at the moment when it was most threatened. The peaceful protesters' early demands for dignity and political reform assumed that rights could be granted rather than seized, that the regime could be persuaded to make good on its own hype—and that calls for political "freedom" and a "civil state" would be overwhelmingly popular and therefore capable of enactment.

Although certainly inspired by demonstrations in Tunisia, Egypt, Yemen, Bahrain, and Libya, the actual flash point for large-scale Syrian protest came with the brutal treatment of fifteen schoolchildren in the southern town of Dar'a, at the hands of security forces under the command of a close relative of the president.[3] Two women from Dar'a had been arrested in January, one of whom had allegedly been overheard discussing the likely overthrow of the Egyptian president Husni Mubarak on the phone, openly musing whether the Syrian regime would be next.[4] Prompted by the women's detention, a group of students ranging in age from ten to fifteen years and including the women's own children wrote anti-regime graffiti on the walls of a local school.[5] The regime arrested the students, turning the incident into a transformative moment, with residents responding by marching on the governor's mansion after Friday prayers and demanding the children's release.[6] Word then began circulating that the children were being tortured in detention. A week later, on March 18, security forces opened fire on a large crowd of protesters proceeding from Dar'a's main mosque after noon prayers, killing four. As the cycle of demonstrations and brutal crackdowns escalated, citizens from neighboring villages became engaged in the confrontation, until by March 25 solidarity protests had spread to Homs, Syria's third-largest city; the regime-identified coastal town of al-Ladhiqiyya (Lattakia); the notably pious area of Idlib; and drought-stricken al-Hasaka and Dayr al-Zur.[7] Later came mass protests in Syria's fourth-largest city, Hama, the primary site of the regime's war against Islamic opposition in the early 1980s, including the famous massacre of tens of thousands of residents, both political opponents and ordinary civilians, in 1982.

Outrage over disclosures that the children from Dar'a were being mistreated in prison, over the disrespect shown to elders attempting to negotiate their release, and over the sheer unaccountability of regime officials linked to the ruling family who were responsible for the children's treatment all tapped into a reservoir of dissatisfaction with authoritarian caprice, official corruption, ongoing brutality, and the government's inattentiveness to suffering. The slogan chanted by protesters—"With spirit, with blood, we sacrifice for you, ya Dar'a" (Bir-ruh, bid-dam, nafdiki ya Dar'a)—played on the regime's slogan of sacrifice for Syria's leader ("Bir-ruh, bid-dam, nafdika ya Bashshar"), substituting the tortured children for Bashar. This voicing of the national "we" in solidarity with the town where children had violated the norms of regime-sanctioned behavior made the abused students the focal point of new political intensities in which acts of collective citizenship coalesced around a determination to resist tyranny and disrupt the status quo.[8]

The regime's ability to adapt speaks to a broader set of ideological conditions related to political attachment. To be clear, I will not be arguing that ideology *caused* the Syrian regime to survive or that other factors were irrelevant to its success in doing so. The ability to limit army defections, exploit intra-elite rivalries, rely on devoted security forces and irregular troops, aggravate oppositional factions, galvanize business networks, and take advantage of regional divisions in order to court Iranian and Russian direct involvement all mattered. But the very fact of loyalty and pro-regime mobilization raises the question of what inclined people—and not simply the narrow group deriving obvious material benefit from the status quo—to stick to the kleptocracy they knew when the opportunity arose to (at least) entertain the idea of change. Fear was certainly part of the equation, but even fear must be made and remade, integrated into the warp and weft of everyday life, as we shall see. And fear did not deter everyone, for many others were in fact emboldened and enraged by the repression, often risking their lives and well-being to protest. Yet between fervent loyalists and political protesters resided a large population of ambivalent citizens— who might have made a difference in the uprising's tractive force had they tilted in its favor.[9]

Understanding this ambivalent middle is therefore key to our thinking about political outcomes, and, I submit, requires an updated account of how ideology intertwines with affect, in the context of war, to produce an atmosphere in which for many the exercise of creative political judgment becomes all but impossible. This atmosphere of epistemic and affective murk is politically efficacious, if not exactly optimal, for the regime. It is an atmosphere that continues to bear traces of neoliberal desires for the good life and its attendant forms of quiescence so central to Bashar al-Asad's first decade of rule (chapter 1). It is an atmosphere characterized by and reproduced through decades of ironic laughter (chapter 2) as well as new forms of media-inspired information overload—and the uncertainty about the truth itself that such conditions cultivate (chapter 3). Stipulating new and familiar forms of "as if" thinking, the regime produced guidelines for proper displays of mourning in wartime (chapter 4) and took advantage of circulating rumors to create fears of existential survival along sectarian lines (chapter 5). These factors in their interaction produced the seductive grounds for nonrebellion. They generated the ideological-affective mess that contributed to the remaking of Asad's political power—where atrocities by the Syrian regime found their revived conditions of possibility.

These circumstances also invited nonviolent, largely artistic challenges to the regime's aspirational control over image production. Puppetry lampooning the regime and, later, trenchant skits mimicking just about everybody (chapter 2), experiments in documentary reporting (chapter 3), and feature films countering authoritarian univocality with forays into what Hannah Arendt calls "representative thinking" (chapter 4) are all instances of daring to think otherwise. They lie not outside ideology but arise as critiques from within it. They are, in that sense, immanent—and therefore intimately aware of but estranged from contemporary circumstances in ways that tap into structural contradictions and devise means of bypassing or scaling the impasses of political life.

THE CONCEPT OF IDEOLOGY AS FORM

Old-fashioned Marxist notions about ideology emerging directly from class domination (expressed perhaps most prominently in *The German Ideology*) have been rightly superseded by more sophisticated analyses based on Marx's own discussion of commodity fetishism in *Capital*.[10] Drawing from Marx's account of the commodity form as the depository of labor, where labor is expressed in "value" and is thereby rendered abstract through social processes of exchange, some scholars have discarded the concept of ideology altogether in favor of analyses of form and fetishism.[11] Others such as Slavoj Žižek suggest a repurposing of the concept, inviting an understanding of ideology as homologous to Freud's "dream work." Instead of privileging explicit or latent content, ideology in this view is best understood in terms of its formal properties and function,[12] one of whose effects, as the cultural theorist Fredric Jameson has taught us, is to *contain* political contradictions and conflict.[13] And containment works through various practices of seduction, not all of them intentional or deliberate, as well as through mechanisms of incitement that channel affective energies and shape judgments. Ideology operates to manage desire in social rather than individual terms, so that repression and wish fulfillment operate together in what Jameson aptly describes as a "kind of psychic compromise or horse-trading, which strategically arouses fantasy content within careful symbolic containment structures which defuse it, gratifying intolerable, unrealizable, properly imperishable desires only to the degree to which they can again be laid to rest."[14]

Pace the Weberian understanding of ideology as a discrete doctrine, ethos, or worldview, ideology conceived in this way as form, entailing specific mechanisms of incitement and containment, is itself structuring. Within it are occasioned all the psychic, embodied, and imaginative processes that go into people's social and political experiences.[15] Žižek and Jameson here share the virtue of not falling into the trap of "false consciousness," for there is no such thing as a true consciousness to be held up against the false one as its definitive and salutary alternative. There is no social reality without illusion, fantasies, and their modes of mediation.[16] Instead, ideology renders abstract political anxieties and fantasies livable by exciting and managing them—sometimes through displacement (as we shall see especially in the discussion of sectarianism in chapter 5) and sometimes by filling in gaps and smoothing over what would otherwise be nagging and perhaps unsustainable inconsistencies (in ways that appear in various places throughout the book).[17] In this sense, ideology does more than offer a theorization of risk, interest, and pleasure; it organizes these concepts or is already presupposed in them. Far from existing outside calculation and desire, ideology structures how we go about calculating and desiring.

Of course, as Jean Comaroff points out, anthropologists and cultural Marxists have long used terms such as *value, habitus, discourse,* or *hegemony* in their attempts to capture such "dimensions of psychic colonization."[18] I prefer *ideology* if only because the term's own theoretical genealogy signals the incoherent, differentiated, ambivalent, and contradictory ways in which people are not so much colonized by ideology as drawn affectively and cognitively into the workings of multiple lifeworlds in ways it makes sense to call ideological. The term names an ensemble of prac- tices being undertaken by people at any given time—such as speaking, listening, feeling, emoting, believing, lying about believing (and/or not believing they're lying)—sufficiently in concert and with sufficient speci- ficity to be affixed with a label. And discrete labels (like *neoliberal* or *liberal* or *communist* or *capitalist* or *Christian* or whatever) give the impression of doctrinal coherence, simultaneously presupposing and putting on offer a sense of political membership. As Terry Eagleton has noted, the con- cept's capaciousness is both its weakness and its strength, indexing difficul- ties that give us traction on the critical theoretical questions raised under its rubric: why people submit to their subjection; why some practices of address are more resonant than others; how both addresses and responses by addressees vacillate between the propositional and the affective; how desires get mediated and social realities stabilized; how states of ambiva- lence that are consequential for political action can be generated by con- flicts between desire and attachment; how ideology operates as political mediation to orient citizens, specifying the terms of collective member- ship and the standards for judgment.[19]

Already implicit in this discussion of ideology is the understanding that the question of credibility in such an account is complicated. The compli- cations come in part because it is hard to know whether someone "really" believes something, as noted by both Timur Kuran, the game theorist who coined the term *preference falsification* (1995), and the anthropologist Wil- liam Mazzarella in his essay on "totalitarian tears" in North Korea (2015).[20] In fact, it seems easier ethnographically to capture blatant examples of unbelief, instances of dissimulation in which subjects act *as if* they believe, as my book *Ambiguities of Domination* (1999) demonstrated.[21] For Žižek, neither belief nor ideology refers to "an 'intimate,' purely mental state." Rather (following Althusser), both imply ritualized practices, habits, and thoughts that are *"materialized* in our effective social activity"[22]—an approach this book embraces. Social activity includes failures to act as well as failed action, instances of unbelief and of error, acts of resistance, and dissonances that do not get smoothed out, which then, in Žižek's crucial insight, offer not only possibilities for the initiation of a new world but also the positive conditions for reasserting the perpetuation of the old.[23] As we shall see in the case of Syria, ambivalence can be viewed fruitfully as one such instance of non- or partial integration, a product of ideology reproductive, albeit imperfectly and with slippage, of the social order. The very fact of incoherence within ideology, moreover, allows for political wiggle room while at the same time requiring the (impossible) imaginative work of making things add up.[24] Ideology's "function" as structuring reality is itself generative of further tensions, incoherencies, contradictions, and instances of uneven saturation—all the complexities and intensities that presuppose the political smoothing work needed for reproduction to continue.

Recognizing that these conflicts or dissonances exist both inter- and intrapersonally does not mean that anyone is required to act on, acknowledge, or embrace them. Instead, one hallmark of ideological uptake is the disavowal expressed in the famous line "I know very well, yet nevertheless . . ."[25] In Syria, as we shall be seeing in greater detail throughout the book, this logic of disavowal has worked in myriad ways: I know very well that the regime is systemically corrupt, yet nevertheless I act as if it will reform itself; I know very well that there is no return to the way things were, yet nevertheless let's act as if things can return to the way they were; I know very well that the opposition is hopeless, yet nevertheless let's act as if the opposition will make things right; I know very well that the commodity form takes a social relation among human beings and makes it into a relation among things, yet nevertheless I shall act as if the commodity form were a simple relation among things. The *as if* here is not the one of public dissimulation so crucial to my analysis in *Ambiguities of Domination*, but speaks instead to fundamental fantasy investments like the desire for an unattainable coherence or for an economic prosperity that comes at no one's expense.

The political implications of this difference are profound: even though we know better or are educable, our fundamental investments (in, say, comfort or order or the hope that change can happen effortlessly) prove resistant to ideology critique. Thus, we can "know very well" that a proposition is false or unjust or contingent *yet nevertheless* continue to act as if we believe in it because, at some level, we are still supported by fundamental fantasy investments in the very practices we nevertheless consciously want to repudiate.[26] Our underlying attachments, to express this in a slightly different theoretical register, can be in tension with our conscious desires and the propositional statements that communicate those desires to others. And this tension is what I am indexing as ambivalence, a situation in which the toggle between the attachment to order and the desire for change, for example, results (as it did among key populations in Syria) in the paralysis of political commitment, in the polarization of opinions and the gravitation toward existing comfort zones in some cases, and in a suspension of judgment in others (as we shall see in chapters 3 and 4).

To recap: *ideology* refers to a set of embodied, affectively laden discourses often conveyed acephalously through everyday practices. Understood not simply as content but also as form, ideology has identifiable structuring effects, the nature and function of which are to contain conflict and smooth out complexities that might otherwise make life unlivable. Undergirded by fantasy investments that prove sticky even in the face of knowing better, ideology structures a politics of "as if" that goes beyond enforced public dissimulation. More important than feigned belief or demonstrations of outward obedience—as critical as they may be for political compliance—are the common ways ideology's impact is reflected in and generated anew through ordinary moments of disavowal, in the "I know very well, yet nevertheless . . ." rationalizations that allow us to participate in and uphold existing orders. Accounting for ideology, moreover, will help us explore the seductions of status quo conventionality in the face of challenges to it (chapter 1); the varied work comedy does (chapter 2); the role "fake news" plays in unmooring political judgments from their frames of reference (chapter 3); the possibilities for appropriating the affective intensities around mourning (chapter 4); and the ongoing operations of sectarian Othering (chapter 5).

UPTAKE

Reviving the concept of ideology requires acknowledging the complexities of ideological address, some of which were famously theorized by Louis Althusser in his landmark essay, "Ideology and Ideological State Apparatuses" (1971). There he stages what has become an iconic scene in which a policeman calls out, "Hey, you there!" prompting a passerby to turn around, having recognized herself to be the one hailed by the call.[27] For Althusser, it is in this event of "interpellation"—this reciprocal recognition on the part of the policeman and the passerby—that the passerby becomes a "subject," someone subjugated to and the subject of political power. One familiar way to look at ideological interpellation is as a form of ritual affirmation, a set of discursive practices that with varying degrees of resonance secure and reproduce routine attachments.[28] The eventful moment in the allegory, from this point of view, is the retroactive fantasy produced by the ritualized behavior, which does *not* require that the individual undergoing subject formation believe in or credit such subjecthood in any particular way (although she may), but only that she enter into the routine or behave as if she inhabits a world in which that subjectivity is the one it makes sense to adopt.

Examples of interpellation as ritual affirmation are everywhere in our ordinary lives—in practices of citizenship like singing the national anthem (or enduring its being sung) at a sporting event, or signing a protest petition, or affixing a postage stamp featuring the nation's flag onto an envelope. The poster of Uncle Sam pointing at passersby and declaring "I want you"—that is, me, the anonymous citizen, the presumed spectator—to join the army offers a particularly succinct example of political interpellation in the US context. The pacifist's revulsion upon encountering such a poster, moreover, does not save her from being interpellated into the world of American patriotism, for it is through her very repugnance that she is being made into a peace-loving subject. Subjects in market economies are constantly being interpellated as consumers as well, in the drumbeat of advertising celebrating status distinctions, for example, or in succumbing to the allure of looking like a fashion model, without believing that any such transformation could or even should take place. Or, to take an overtly political example from Syria of the 1980s–90s: shopkeepers often rolled their eyes even while readily relenting to post the president's picture in their windows. And, as we shall see in chapter 1, as the regime initiated neoliberal reforms in 2005, market inducements became increasingly relevant to reproducing the political status quo—which for the well situated remains the case all the way through to the present.

A second feature of the allegory, as is clear from these same examples, is that interpellation presumes a degree of reciprocity between the two agents, in that the passerby must not only be called out by the policeman but also turn around in acknowledgment of having been hailed. This is a point that has occupied many commentators, among them Judith Butler, Mladen Dolar, Michel Pêcheux, and Slavoj Žižek. And for these theorists, the passerby's response to the address entails a *necessary* misrecognition, premised on what Žižek, citing Pêcheux, points to as an illusory prior "I was already there," a short circuit whose effects can be comical: "No wonder you were interpellated as a proletarian, when you are a proletarian."[29] In other words, there seems to be presumed in Althusser's formulation some unelaborated prior coordination, what Butler in an effort to specify the source of this addressability calls a "doctrine of conscience,"[30] explaining the seemingly precocious receptivity on the part of the subject-in-formation to the subject-forming hail. As Butler puts it, it is not simply that much can go wrong in the story, but that "the grammar of that narrative presupposes that there is no subjection without a subject who undergoes it."[31] Althusser's allegory thus seems to stumble on a temporal impossibility, in which the addressee is already presumed to have been constituted as a subject before the hail that constitutes the subject—for otherwise how could she have recognized herself in the moment of interpellation? Empirically oriented social scientists might respond that Althusser needs an account of socialization. But theoretically, the temporal impossibility is itself revealing of a tension in everyday life. For in relation to an ideological demand, we often operate without a specific originary moment. Ideological interpellation is, rather, secured through iterable linguistic conventions or language games (such as, for Butler, the conscience-stimulating reprimand implicit in the allegory[32]), which are observable independent of any identifiable initiating moment.

These two points tell us that ideology operates as a set of repetitive, sociopolitical interactions. But I want to argue that there is a third, little noticed but crucial dimension of interpellation, which came to the fore during my fieldwork: for interpellation to be complete, the issuer of the hail must also recognize the responder's recognition of it.[33] Subject formation, in the sense of becoming a jaywalker in the context of the police officer's "hey you" or a proletarian (or a consumer) in the context of capitalism or, returning to Syria, a citizen in the context of neoliberal autocracy, depends not only on people signing up for the system but also on the authority's response (or nonresponse) to the people signing up. In other words, the uptake of ideology (in this sense of the consummated exchange between the hailer and the hailed) is secured differentially—not simply because people are variously liable to recognize themselves as different kinds of hailed subjects (implying a kind of "coming alive" of individuals in the law) but also in the lawgiver's recognition of the citizen's response, which is critical to how the contours of inclusion and exclusion are drawn.

In the years leading up to the uprising, this third dynamic was frequently in evidence in the obvious unease some Syrians were made to feel when they did not fully live up to the regime's brand of modern commodified competence. Scenes like the following, in which worlds collided, became typical. A nuclear family of seven dressed in conservative clothing comes to town from the outskirts of Damascus to have pizza or ice cream at the Café Roma, an upscale establishment in the prosperous Malki district. Money as such is not an issue. But styles of comportment are.[34] In these settings, dress, bearing, dialect differences, and even the pronunciation of certain words invite invidious distinctions between citizens coded as "country bumpkins" (despite their newly acquired wealth) and the embodied dispositions or "habitus" of the regime's upwardly mobile professional managerial elite. The disdain was palpable in public places where people of different background conditions were brought together—the snickers of contempt audible, the comments on smells and styles of comportment part and parcel of a grappling with new forms of commercialized living. As Pierre Bourdieu writes, those who "presume to join the group . . . without being the product of the same social conditions, are trapped whatever they do, in a choice between anxious hyper-identification and the negativity which admits its defeat in its very revolt."[35]

Bourdieu describes working-class aspirations and aristocratic forms of "cultural capital" in Europe. By contrast, the image-making strategies opted for in the Syrian case combined a globally recognizable imprimatur of name-brand chic with a longtime, largely Sunni-bourgeois sense of urbane decorum, compensating for the regime's parvenu origins in the hinterland. The theoretical point is nevertheless the same: the collusion between regime and market in Syria produced a set of mechanisms for inviting and signaling membership, disseminating the standards through which alternative choices for everyday existence (such as conservative clothing, intensified practices of piety, and large family size) were deemed inferior. And this judgment—registered in the 2000s in the dissemination and enforcement of the new official aesthetic as opposed to the party pamphlets of old—operated, as the allegory of interpellation suggests, to dismiss, ignore, or disparage other ways of being in the world. What makes scenes like the one at Café Roma so cringeworthy and typical is their occurrence in the face of such efforts at hyperidentification. Adopted by the ruling family and purveyed through sanctioned glossy magazines, global PR firms, lifestyle-oriented radio and television programs, and local billboards, these signaling mechanisms exemplified the convenient alliance between neoliberal capital and autocracy. As we shall see in chapter 1, those whose styles of comportment, affective registers, and ordinary embodied habits chafed against the newer, glitzier, regime-oriented ones generated spaces for conflict, occasioned resentment, and ultimately created populations rife with dissatisfaction. Practices of rejection, including microprocesses signaling disdain and disrespect—being coded as backward—diminished what otherwise might have been earnest if sometimes embarrassed pursuits of inclusion into the existing system. As scholars of social movements and of civil war grievance note, it is not these conditions in and of themselves that cause change. But they do describe sites of disaffection disposed toward some degree of activism—often independent of parameters such as wealth or simple economic well-being. In Syria these scenes of encounter suggest the background conditions for what became a clarion call for dignity (*karama*; *karameh*), a political-ethical claim both castigating the regime (*nizam*) for its moral and material corruption (*fasad*) and demanding recognition (*i'tiraf*) of humans' non-instrumental, intrinsic worth.[36]

MOVING FORWARD

Like most of my work, this book tacks back and forth between theory and ethnographic evidence—the latter derived in this case from fieldwork conducted in Syria in 2010 and 2011, then in France, Germany, Lebanon, Turkey, and the United States as so many of my Syrian interlocutors were forced into emigration by worsening conditions at home. Chronologically, chapters 1 and 2 cover the first decade of rule under Bashar al-Asad and the unmaking of neoliberal autocracy after the uprising got underway in 2011. Chapters 3 and 4 focus on 2012–13, when the uprising devolved into a devastatingly bloody civil war. The concerns with judgment these later chapters foreground speak to a moment when alternative paths forward for Syria, while glaringly obvious, were proving increasingly elusive of pursuit, when intensifying discursive contestation and the beginning of armed violence ushered in what observers from every angle recognize as a turning point. Chapter 5 bookends the study by returning to the first months of the uprising, a retroactive exploration of the workings of ideology in a time when cracks in the system were opening, shedding light on regime efforts to shut things down.

Viewed from a more substantive angle, chapter 1 explores the uneven saturation of ideology and, in particular, the role of ambivalence in status quo conventionality by investigating the marked absence of large-scale protest in Syria's two most important cities during the first, predominantly peaceful year of the uprising. Whereas accounts of dictatorship describe the role of staunch loyalists or highlight opportunism in the operations of regime maintenance, my privileging of ambivalence in the Syrian context reveals how an ideological structure of disavowal can work politically to stifle transformation. And it allows us to examine how citizens flatten out the complexities and horrors of civil war to render bearable the present world-shattering reality.

Chapter 2 demonstrates both the reliability and the incompleteness of ideological reproduction by detailing how dramatic comedies were operating ideologically among Syria's television-savvy citizenry as Bashar al-Asad's market-oriented autocracy emerged. Here I take as emblematic the work of Allayth Hajju (Allaith or Laith Hajjo), one of Syria's best-known television directors, for it registers both the grim realities of the decade just past and the evident seductions of the neoliberal turn. At times uncannily prescient, at times poignantly bleak, Hajju's comedy, especially his highly popular series *Day'a daay'a* (*A Forgotten Village* [2008, 2010]), creates alternatives to its own most conservative impulses, demonstrating the potency and unevenness of ideological saturation. Or to put the same point differently, even his most biting comedy illustrates and helps perpetuate an ideology of neoliberal autocracy while providing openings for (and attempting to manage) an oppositional consciousness. In continuing to explore the complex workings of ambivalence under conditions of neoliberal autocracy, the chapter avoids the reduction of comedy to an either/or choice between its reproductive capacities in cultivating domination and its emancipatory qualities as resistance. Instead, I describe comedy as expressing a struggle between desires for political reform and attachments to everyday conventions, as prefiguring solidarities in acts of disruption that are themselves ambiguous—and politically relevant for being so. Those solidarities congealed, at least partially, in the righteous and notably unambivalent humor of the uprising's early days and have come to be refreshed in the open-ended minipublics of the contemporary period. Irreverent-toward-everything monologues of young activists— from al-Ghouta to Gaziantep—amid the devastation of 2016–17 do more than suggest resilience; their capacities for mimicry, their multiple registers of address, and their embrace of uncertainty draw attention to future possibilities in the paths not taken.

Autocracy has been conventionally theorized in terms of regimes maximizing power by withholding information from their citizenry. Chapter 3, in contrast, exposes the mechanisms enabling an excess of information and the sheer velocity of its circulation and consumption to be exploited for political gain. As the focus remains on Syria, the specifics relate to conditions of autocracy. But at the same time, the chapter raises questions about the changing meaning of the distinction between democracy and dictatorship in the context of what seems to be the eroding factual basis of political discussion worldwide (as tricky as the question of fact must be in an interpretivist account of ideology). Organized therefore around the thinking of Hannah Arendt and Ludwig Wittgenstein, this chapter explores the fragility and stubbornness of factual truth as well as the political-affective conditions of uncertainty and forms of discursive addressability these circumstances promote. Despite the seemingly democratizing aspects of such recent technological innovations as greater access to information on the internet, the regime in Syria has proved able to exploit the conditions of what I call "high-speed eventfulness" to the advantage of its counterinsurgency project. Yet at the same time, with factual truth and the conceptual systems they presuppose under attack, new forms of expression are brought into being. The chapter concludes with a look at the efforts of the artists' collective Abounaddara (Abou naddara; Abu Naddara) to stretch, even circumvent, the conventions of documentary film representation, hinting at ways in which judgments might be animated by a mode of reflection able to appreciate contingency without abdicating responsibility.

Chapter 4 deepens the analysis of political judgment in conditions of uncertainty, shifting attention to the appeals of national sentimentality — the various efforts undertaken by the regime and multiple oppositions to activate people's affective attachments ideologically. Putting theorists of melodrama, sentimentality, and affect into conversation with political philosophers of judgment, I look explicitly at the fantasies of repair that nationalist rhetoric evokes, the communities of empathic recognition that nationalist fantasies define, and the conundrums that arise for political reflection from taking refuge in the sentimental. Like chapter 3, chapter 4 ends with a consideration of work by Syrian artists: some newcomers to the field, such as Khalid 'Abd al-Wahid (Khaled Abdulwahed) and Ziad Kalthum (Kalthoum), but also the prominent filmmaker Ossama Mohammed (Usama Muhammad) from an earlier generation. The efforts at alterity examined in this case speak to the libidinal and epistemic seductions of national belonging; the familiar temptations to cultivate empathy by representing suffering Others;[37] the creative possibilities for and difficulties of instantiating alternative visions; the varying intensities of affective investment in nationalism, human rights discourses, and revolutionary change; and the necessarily fragmented way in which ideological recruitment works.

Rosy visions of economic prosperity and sentimental appeals to national sovereignty supply some of the content to the form of ideological containment, but so do stories about tolerating difference and getting along. By considering recent writings about sectarianism, chapter 5 investigates why sect, in particular, becomes a relevant category (when it does). In the Syrian case, this means explicating the extent to which sectarian fears about existential survival came to work in tension with fantasies of multisectarian accommodation. Highlighting a pair of rumors that both stimulated and exploited a sense of vulnerability justifying regime intervention, I explore what Raymond Williams calls the "structures of feeling," the affective residual and emergent socialities that operate implicitly beneath the radar, often organizing ordinary experiences of atmosphere and situation before they are recognized explicitly.[38] I offer an account of what happens when this form of "residual sociality," to borrow again from Williams, percolates to the surface. Eschewing the now tired debates between primordialism and social constructivism, I use Williams to advance the understanding of how interpellation works to produce attachments beyond the economic— forms of fantasy investment that, in the case of Syria, illustrate the affective gnarl and conundrums for judgment that result when the (relatively) impersonal claims of national identification chafe against sectarian communalism's ordinary intimacies.

Throughout the book, I make use of films, videos, television serials, comedies, and other works by regime- and opposition-oriented cultural producers, not simply as evidence to demonstrate a point, but also in order to think with and through these cultural products. Like Gabriele Schwab's discussion of literature in *Imaginary Ethnographies*, these artifacts are not mere representations or illustrations or affirmations of a theory. They not only attune us to the implied audiences of artistic products, as important as these aspects of cultural analysis might be, but they also generate possibilities for what Hannah Arendt calls "world making," the ability to begin anew, to think and act critically, to operate beyond or in excess of referentiality—to encourage the art's evocatory functions, speaking to a relationship of collaboration rather than simple ethnographic data gathering. The invitation is to treat some Syrian artists as political theorists in their own right, interlocutors rather than "informants," their artifacts productive of possibilities for expanding the space of interpretive encounter in order to diagnose (and see ways out of) the impasses—collectively.

CONCLUSION

Authoritarian Apprehensions challenges scholars to consider what the epochal, as well as ambiguous, set of regional events known initially as the Arab Spring means in larger historical and theoretical terms. Locating the Arab world within a world-historical frame is necessary for any adequate analysis of what these events betoken, and doing so raises certain central questions of modern critical thought. But this book also prompts thinking about what categories like neoliberalism or ideology or autocracy might mean—not only as grounded phenomena or as instantiated in historical moments but as theoretical constructs in need of parsing in relation to power, politics, aesthetics, subjectivity, and belief.

Retooling the construct of ideology for contemporary times therefore calls for an understanding of the concept not only in discursive terms (through the logics of everyday practices, policies, scholarship and so on), although these are important. Ideology must also be understood through recourse to the languages of seduction, affect, attachment, and the incitements of desire. In the pages that follow, we will be attending to the psychic and embodied processes that trigger mimetic identifications with persons and fetishized objects, whether they be the Syrian president and first lady for loyalists or SpongeBob SquarePants waving the pre-Ba'thist flag for children of activists.

Classic theories of ideology attempted to explain precisely why piercing critique was so often forestalled by governing ideas. Capitalism perpetuated hope, it was said, even among the dominated, in dangling the carrot of upward mobility. *Authoritarian Apprehensions* taps into this vein of scholarship, not in accepting the perhaps crude sense of ideological capture, but by looking instead at the contradictions and aporias internal to its approximation—without arguing that contradictions or other kinds of dissonance are necessarily the source of a democratic or any other kind of oppositional consciousness. The book's preoccupations are set against the backdrop of intensified collaboration between privatized consumer interests and authoritarian cults of personal governance, in the context of the globalization of a variety of authoritarian populisms that likewise threaten democratic participation. In these current circumstances, there seems to be an acceptance of an order reminiscent of the fascisms of old. This acceptance is visible and tangible in the personal autocracy of Asad in Syria, as it was in Zuma's macho-nationalist South Africa, in China's country-as-corporation, in the ultra-right nationalisms in Europe, or, for that matter, in the "law-and-order" governance of the United States.

Given this condition, where might we expect an affirmative politics to take root, if at all? Where, given the machinations of global capital, the maneuvering of regional powers, and the seductions of dictatorship itself, might we find openings like the ones that protesters who took to the streets in 2011 hoped to exploit? This book contains no definitive answers to these questions, but it does find, in some of the experiments with comedy and film during Syria's catastrophic war years (2012–), pathways for critical thinking—a necessary basis and resource for cultivating "an actualized next or new that is somehow better than 'now.'"[39] At their best, these works, discussed in chapters 2, 3, and 4, embody a kind of potentiality—in wrestling with the conventions of genre or the narration of loss or both. As self-conscious products of the political contradictions of the present and in generating critical distance from these contradictions, the works are avowals of creativity amid the overwhelming destruction of war, refusing—

despite their markedly different treatments of violence—to ignore the horror or be fully done in by it.

A final note about the title: *Authoritarian Apprehensions* is a triple entendre. *Apprehension* can be a synonym for *arrest* or *capture*. It also means "to understand or perceive." And it connotes ongoing anxieties. All three meanings are operative in this book—which, at its core, is an effort to convey the complicated ideological relations central to the maintenance of authoritarian power.

1

Neoliberal Autocracy
and Its Unmaking

Touted by its publishers as the "most prestigious lifestyle and luxury magazine in Syria,"[1] the English-language monthly *Happynings* enjoined readers of its January 2011 issue to accessorize with camouflage: "From combat cool to aviatrix chic, military style took the fall runways by storm. We show how to pledge allegiance to the season's hottest trend and work army accents into every look."[2] A music video by Husayn al-Dik, the brother of a regionally famous crooner, echoed this aesthetic imperative in Arabic, backed by performers dressed in black-and-gray fatigues, matching hats, and lace-up boots dancing to his sexually suggestive tune "Natir Bint al-Madarseh" (Waiting for the Schoolgirl).[3]

At odds with the ascetic, austere, tanks-in-the-streets reality of the 1980s, the image of military apparel shifting from a sign of autocratic control to an accoutrement of consumer choice proved ephemeral, undermined by the reappearance of soldiers in the streets when protests got underway in mid-March. As demonstrations gained momentum and the regime responded by attempting to crush dissent, the public prominence of consumer preoccupations with lifestyle and luxury gave way to anxieties about conspiracy and disorder—at least among Syrian supporters of president Bashar al-Asad's regime. For others dreaming of an end to authoritarian rule or worrying more about crop failure or lax morals than what to wear to the party, the return of the military to the streets laid bare the unvarnished essence of autocracy—its reliance on coercive power to squelch unrest. As the situation worsened, the glamour and glitz of Bashar al-Asad's first decade could no longer obscure the regime's violence or its evident refusal to respond to protest demands with anything more than empty promises. Yet among Syrians, the regime's marked willingness to destroy perceived threats to its survival was not met with anything near uniform condemnation. Particularly notable for our purposes is the apparent oddity that even as demonstrations mushroomed in various parts of the country, in Syria's two major cities, Aleppo (its largest city and key commercial hub) and Damascus (its capital), the population failed to mobilize in significant numbers.[4] The question posed by this chapter is, Why? Considered against the backdrop of the war's horror, the question of initial participation in protests may seem a remote one. But to move toward a precise understanding of the limits of the rebellion and the seductions of status quo conventionality, it helps to see how the Syrian regime managed to produce a silent majority of citizens invested in stability and fearful of alternatives.

I argue that what might best be described, following Lauren Berlant, as an ideology of the good life operated among key metropolitan populations to organize desire and quell dissent.[5] Syria's good life entailed not only the usual aspirations to economic well-being, but also fantasies of multicultural accommodation and a secure, sovereign, pride-inducing national identity.[6] It is these visions and inducements to compliance in the first decade of president Bashar al-Asad's rule, unevenly saturating and in flux, which defined the terms in which neoliberal autocracy was created, sustained, and, in the context of the uprising, ultimately reconfigured.[7] Neoliberal autocracy implies two contradictory *logics* of rule: the one cultivating desires for market freedom, upward mobility, and consumer pleasure, and the other tethering advancement opportunities to citizen obedience and coercive regulation.[8] This contradiction was mediated and managed in pre-uprising Syria in part through a local image world that wedded private capital to regime control in a way officially epitomized by the seemingly glamorous, urbane, and assertively modern "first family." A first-family mimesis worked to produce the celebrity president, his elegant, English-speaking first lady, Asma', and their young children as sites of an aspirational consciousness imbued with individual responsibility, refined taste, fashionable possessions, and domestic intimacy.[9] In this first decade of the 2000s, fantasies of upward mobility became tied to acts of personal initiative and a commitment to the status quo, replacing the quasi-socialist promises of state-initiated development or party cadre activism of the previous Asad regime (1970–2000) with a classier, "upgraded" autocracy.[10] By 2011, in the context of the region's growing unrest, we see the regime revamping its modes of ideological interpellation in service of a doubling down on the connection between the continuation of this good life and autocratic survival.

The chapter begins in part 1 by investigating neoliberal autocracy's forms of ideological address, chronicling the regime's success in the younger Asad's first decade of rule in producing this image of an enlightened, more benevolent dictatorship under the paradoxical sign of market freedom. Part 2 explores the onset of the uprising in some ethnographic detail, along with the broader discursive conditions that helped structure forms of *both* reticence *and* political participation characteristic of the first year of unrest. Neoliberal autocracy—built on the contradiction between promised freedoms and ongoing coercion while focusing the diffuse desires of Syrians onto centrally managed celebrity—began to unravel. As it happened, the system came undone in the absence of alternatives outfitted with the necessary programmatic vision and organizational wherewithal to mount a decisive challenge. Part 3 complicates the convenient but inaccurate picture, popular among scholars and journalists, of the uprising as largely a product of class conflict." Anticipating objections to my focus on ideology, this section insists on ideology's coimplication with issues of political economy, fear, sectarian difference, and generational conflict— marshalling both ethnographic and quantitative evidence to suggest that areas of protest and quiescence do not map at all neatly onto regions of relative deprivation and plenitude. The chapter's overall exploration of ideology's importance and its production of ambivalence—the specific contexts of neoliberalism, authoritarian rule, and their combined formation in experiences of neoliberal autocracy—requires a few clarifications, to which I now turn.

A NOTE ON AMBIVALENCE IN POLITICS

Scholars of the Left correctly note that neoliberalism produces "zones of social abandonment"[12] and disaffection, as safety nets disappear or are revamped in the context of growing inequality and the availability of perquisites like luxury goods. My intervention, in contrast, aims to explore the power of neoliberalism to seduce even those who recognize and condemn its injustices. For neoliberalism has also organized new forms of sociability, affective connection, optimism, and pleasure—explaining how and why neoliberalism generated the forms of ambivalence that helped sustain authoritarianism in the face of serious challenges to it.

Syrians with ambivalent positions on the uprising were widely referred to as the "gray people" (*al-ramadiyyin*), and unsurprisingly, they came in various shades. Some were coded by activists as *mutazabzib* (vacillators), people who swing back and forth between "wanting and not wanting change."[13] Their self-definition as ambivalent onlookers was symptomatic of neoliberal autocracy's success. Opposition activists dismissed this version of ambivalence from the start, calling the onlookers "opportunists" (*intihaziyyin*) who "every hour had a new opinion" (*kull sa'a bira'y*), who could not "commit to a point of view" (*ma 'andu mawqif*) or failed "to stabilize their position" (*ma yathbut 'ala ra'y*). And the number of citizens roughly fitting those descriptions put systemic limits on the uprising and constituted an ideological victory for the regime. Syrians self-describing as "moderates" (*mu'atadilin*, connoting equilibrium or balance) were another shade of gray. Early in the uprising they found themselves being lambasted by opposition activists but tolerated by the regime, with some even recognized as part of an "honorable opposition" (*al-mu'arada al-sharifa*). The characteristic disavowal among this group runs something like this: "I know very well that the regime will insist on holding on to its political power, yet nevertheless I'll act as if it won't"; or "Nevertheless, I'll act as if a civil state is possible within its confines." And finally, regular riders on the microbuses were heard declaring their indifference to what was happening, saying it didn't involve them (*mani 'alaqa*).[14]

Represented among these three varieties of ambivalence were two distinct demographics. One set comprised those fortunate enough to be already accustomed to the pleasures brought by new types of prosperity, sociability, and consumerism. Their communities formed the worlds of downtown Damascus and Aleppo, or what advertisers (expanding their thinking beyond strictly economic categories to practices of taste and distinction) rated the "A+, A, and A–" neighborhoods of the two cities.[15] The rest, if more in aspirational mode, were able to imagine at least a modicum of such luxury for themselves. For these, the payoff while unrealized remained a payoff. It was visible in the environment and palpable, worth waiting and working for. In the early days, these two populations were noticeably absent from the protests, evidently preferring quiescence to venturing into the uncharted territory of political resistance. So long as these ambivalent populations continued not signing up for the uprising, the regime had a much easier time responding to pockets of peaceful resistance by deploying scorched-earth tactics.

And this brings us to my invocation of "the good life." Despite its roots in Aristotelian ethics, usage (outside social theory) tends toward the trivial these days, as in a synonym for "consumer pleasures" or as a meme in

new to a belief subject

the pep rally version of American political values. To be sure, neophyte consuming subjects may be expected to act accordingly, but I have more at stake in deploying the notion—both theoretically and in relation to Syrian specifics. Part of what I have in mind is similar to what Jean Comaroff notes of advanced capital in its globally varied neoliberal forms in describing the "powerful fetishisms at work that relate not merely to commodities as consumable goods, but the commodity (and the whole structural order that secures it) as a hieroglyph of profound understandings of value, power, truth, and world-making."[16] These fetishisms are potent in their effects, reshaping in economized terms people's very understandings of and engagements in contemporary life. Itself reshaped by corporate forms of capital, the regime had become a quasi-clan-based corporation, fostering affinities between the idea of market opportunities and political conformity that are familiar from nominally democratic regimes as well. Such major or minor opportunism constituted a degree of outright support for the regime, but perhaps more important, it went along with enough political ambivalence to keep large-scale peaceful protest from developing in the two major cities.

In other parts of Syria (such as "first-mover" areas like Homs, Dar'a, Hama, and Idlib), any number of alternative commitments—ranging from styles of family upbringing to attendance at mosque-based study groups or ties to the Communist Party—provided a basis for a potential challenge to the regime's ethical, political, and aesthetic valences.[17] At the same time, regional particularities even within a province are considerable. Mohammed Jamal Barout tells us that so many police officers come from Idlib governorate that when a male baby is born, people exclaim, "It's a policeman!" Yet other areas of the same province are known for their Islamic anti-regime activism. And still other regions of Idlib, in the context of the uprising, became famous for their humor, such as Kafranbel with its inventive caricatures lampooning the regime, or for their well-known affiliation with anti-Ba'thist leftist parties. Explaining these variations in detail will ultimately require significantly more fine-grained sociological research and attention to regional specificity than this study allows. That work is already underway, with scholars beginning to grapple with such problems as gathering statistical evidence based on counting protests or having to rely on regime economic data. Barout has been especially attentive to the differences, similarities, and interdependences between the "Damascus metropole" and areas on the periphery of the city, or Rif Dimashq, showing that places belonging administratively to the periphery can be economically and socially very much a part of the city,[18] while the dynamics found elsewhere in the periphery can differ from both Damascus center and other parts of the periphery.[19] Kevin Mazur's work provides another example of important research underway. One of his findings is that the relatively few protest-related deaths that did occur in central Damascus were in areas resembling ones from the rural hinterland.[20] Scholars such as these, and others, like Kheder Khaddour,[21] are generating extraordinarily rich accounts of regional variations, with implications for why people were willing to rebel—when they were.[22]

It remains the case, however, that no one as yet has accounted compellingly for why the uprising erupted in some places and not in others, or why it became violent in some places with recent histories of violence but not in others (at least at the onset). My own view, stepping back a bit, is that the areas that did revolt would not have risen up had Egypt and Libya, the two authoritarian examples with which Syrians of various stripes most vocally identified, not witnessed massive protests previously. The regime's neoliberal autocracy was sufficiently possessed of efficacious compliance inducements to forfend rebellion had there not been regional demonstration effects. Given the uprisings elsewhere, however, my own argument would require that any answer to the variation question consider the salience of attachments to the good life and the complex relationships between ideological addressors and addressees, rather than reducing the analysis to statistically visible indications of, say, affluence. Citizens were similarly hailed but recognized differentially by the regime, whose hold on power was maintained by way of the production of neoliberal lifeways through autocratic means. Neoliberal autocracy required hiding those mechanisms in plain sight, both exciting aspirations for initiative and limiting their political potential. While this chapter is more about Damascus's and Aleppo's quiescence than that of the country as a whole, my general argument should encourage scholars to consider not only conditions of plenitude and deprivation but also citizens' fantasy investments. Attending to the coimplication of ideology and material practices allows us to see expectations shifting in the context of neoliberal autocracy. Citizens were differentially interpellated—unevenly addressed by the regime's seductive images of economic prosperity, discourses of freedom, and empowerment, and by varied experiences of migration.

As a point of clarificatory insistence: I do try to debunk existing explanations that reduce protests to economic grievances, but my immediate objective is *not* to explain the reasons for the uprising. Rather, to reiterate, I want to understand the importance of ambivalence in sustaining neoliberal autocracy despite major challenges to it. From the point of view of studying ideology's potency, understanding why people refrain from action is as important as explaining their participation.[23] By shedding light on the enticements of neoliberal autocracy in Syria, this chapter offers lessons both for students of comparative politics and for social and political theorists, showcasing fantasies of order and prosperity that are evident (in varying flavors and degrees) in other neoliberal autocratic countries as well.

In short, my focus on the neoliberalism part of neoliberal autocracy in this chapter designates an especially seductive, particularly insinuating, and largely implicit endorsement of market-mediated experiences such as those associated with risk and pleasure. As a particular ideological formation, neoliberalism is saturating without being fully naturalized, organizing lifeworlds in ways that can also structure dissent. Autocracy, despite its cruelties and caprice, offers the promise of order, a way of blanketing over or managing what might be made into incendiary differences (like sectarian affiliation or pious extremism). Neoliberal autocracy, then, delimits a diffusely bounded comfort zone in which staying safe seems possible and consumer aspiration desirable, on the condition that citizens harbor no dreams of even superficial political transformation. By analyzing the 2011–12 period, this chapter brings to the fore a concern that animates the entire book: the spectrum of affective dynamics by which support persists at the same time that ambivalence matters, and resistance — even repugnance — gets organized.

One final caveat: I use the term *neoliberalism* despite its problems, some of which I have pointed out elsewhere. The concept indexes at least four distinct political economy processes: (1) macroeconomic stabilization (via "austerity policies" encouraging low inflation and low public debt, and discouraging Keynesian countercyclical policies); (2) trade liberalization and financial deregulation; (3) the privatization of publicly owned assets and firms; and (4) welfare state retrenchment.[24] Sometimes these four processes work in concert, but often they do not, and their impact on population welfare varies from place to place.[25] Moreover, scholars have captured important variations not only between countries but also within them.[26] In Syria, many citizens never fully abandoned moral commitments or a sense of entitlement to some version of the welfare state, while differing sectors of the economy proved either more vulnerable than others to market competition or better able to exploit new opportunities for regime-business collusion.[27]

Too exclusive a focus on divergences among neoliberal regimes, however, forecloses what can be a fruitful consideration of the neoliberal order as a distinct ideological project, one with the specific capacity to suture together vastly different political-economic situations by enlisting citizen subjects into novel modes of regulation, intervention, and protest, all of which goes on in service of what Michel Foucault calls "the general art of government."[28] In this sense, "neoliberal" ideology refers to how everyday practices, scholarly works, official policies, and countless other characterizing instantiations invoke the language of efficiency, consumer choice, conspicuous consumption, cost-benefit calculations, and personal initiative in ways that "mark a shift in risk-bearing" away from governments and corporations and onto individuals and families.[29] By 2011, neoliberalism as a bundle of global, epochal phenomena had come to suffuse everyday life, "powerfully creat[ing]," to borrow Jean Comaroff's words, "the nature of late modern ontology—both in its explicitly discursive registers (in economic theory, human capital talk, casino idioms, etc.) and in the lived ontology of fetishism."[30]

PART ONE: THE MAKING OF NEOLIBERAL AUTOCRACY

Although authoritarian rule in Syria was long-standing and its stabilizing effects entrenched by the late 1980s, its neoliberal variant began gradually to emerge in the 1990s with "selective" economic reforms, followed by ambitious privatization initiatives culminating in the official adoption in 2005 of what was euphemistically termed a "social market economy."[31] Devised by an emerging professional managerial elite, sounding like the International Monetary Fund with its language of "good governance" and "stakeholders," this social market economy involved encouraging private sector investment, stressing the virtues of individual philanthropy, and making provisions for offloading risk and responsibility onto "civil society."[32] Cultivating private sector investment and celebrating the merits of private welfare, moreover, made for growing elective affinities between Syria's 'ulama (clergy), with its historical roots in the country's urban notable classes, and regime-oriented crony capitalists. The regime's turn toward the private sector by the 2000s helps explain the clergy's divergent and fractured responses to the uprising—and the relative quiescence of key religious leaders in both Damascus and historically rebellious Aleppo.[33]

In Syria in the 2000s, circles of privilege expanded and contracted at the same time, resulting in countervailing tendencies that congealed some differences—the gap between rich and poor widened, with more people appearing more prosperous in both major cities—while producing new bases for inclusion.[34] Access to information technologies, increased possibilities for travel, an expanding circle of financial and social networks reflected in the first family's exemplification of cosmopolitan living, and a growing familiarity with urbane tastes (if not necessarily the means to indulge them) — such quotidian novelties constituted an important shift from Hafiz al-Asad to Bashar. Introducing some measure of economic reform and playing catch-up with global trends in the glossies were only part of what changed. The professional managerial elite broadened to include global advertising's local subsidiaries and members of Syria's regionally successful and celebrity-conscious drama community. The latter, as we shall see, could be called on to produce messages extolling a modernity that performed — both on and off the screen — a version of the good life consonant with the one being exemplified by the regime.

The centerpiece in this celebration of first-family sophistication and urbanity, and perhaps the signal example of amped-up public relations campaigns in the decade preceding the uprising, was the vigorous effort to market the president and first lady as members of the moral neoliberal class — at once role models with whom to identify, exemplars to aspire to, and patrons to submit to — part of a growing cosmopolitan political elite that could represent a palatable privatization of the public sector. By disarticulating regime from state, the ideal of the moral neoliberal ruling couple provided a new basis for public dissimulation — for an acting *as if* the glamorous neoliberal autocratic regime was not personalistic, patronage-based, kleptocratic, and violent; for acting *as if* its lip service to individual voluntarism and civic empowerment could actually offer a civil, moral solution to the problems of governance that the corrupt, tired, crude, overtly brutal developmentalist party state of old did not.[35]

The first family's forays into consumption-oriented, morally laden image management began in 2000 with Bashar al-Asad's marriage to first lady Asma', but really got underway in 2008 with her heralded appearance in the weekly newsmagazine *Paris Match* and UNESCO's designation of Damascus as the "cultural capital" of the Arab world.[36] Three years later, the portrayal of the couple as modern, enlightened, reform-minded, and chic to its upper-class cronies as well as to a broad Syrian and global constituency aspiring to glamour and luxury culminated in a photo spread in a now-infamous *Vogue* article. In those pages, Asma' al-Asad, "a rose in the desert,"[37] became a walking, talking metaphor of the new moral order, elegant and yet down-to-earth. A former investment banker at J. P. Morgan in London whose purported love affair with Bashar, then studying ophthalmology, had propelled her into a world of celebrity, the first lady epitomized this image of philanthropic refinement—ministering to orphans and hobnobbing with the Jolie-Pitts. As both a businesswoman and a mother, Asma' personified neoliberal efficiency, her skills honed in banking "transferable" to running what she calls her NGO work—as if her projects were independent of the authoritarian regime's mechanisms of social control. Moreover, the *Vogue* article's now-disgraced author, Joan Juliet Buck, notes admiringly that the first lady "runs her office like a business, chairs meeting after meeting, starts work many days at six, never breaks for lunch, and runs home to her children at four." For, as Asma' herself points out, "It's my time with them, and I get them fresh, unedited—I love that. I really do." Far from being simply a technocrat with useful banking skills, the first lady is here positioned as an ordinary working mom and the carrier of an urbane modernity, her "central mission" being, according to Buck, "to change the mind-set of six million Syrians under eighteen, encourage them to engage in what she [Asma'] calls 'active citizenship.'" Bracketing the regime's authoritarianism, Asma' elaborates in the conventional language of neoliberal empowerment: "It's about everyone taking shared responsibility in moving this country forward, about empowerment in a civil society. We all have a stake in this country; it will be what we make it." In celebrating the first lady's Syria Trust for Development, with its youth programs designed to provide extracurricular activities and enhance employment opportunities, the article describes a scene in which Asma' visits children in the Saint Paul orphanage, reproducing the official version of the regime as the guarantor of multifaith coexistence.

Vogue's feature piece, which also lauds the Asad family for being "wildly democratic" and for wanting to give Syria a "brand essence," was pulled from the magazine's website a few weeks later at the first signs of the coming troubles, in a move reminiscent of Soviet strategies of forgetting.[38] But by then it had already been translated into Arabic and was widely cited across social media sites. For those supportive of the regime or ambivalent about its democratic deferrals, the timing of the article was unfortunate, but its celebration of Syria's *tanawwu'* (diversity) and the first lady's *anaqa* (elegance) was worthy of some sympathy. For others, it was the source of considerable derision, a blatant instance of hypocrisy and Western naïveté.

People who had not read the piece came to hear about it through others, with its anecdote about the Jolie-Pitts' purported focus on the first family's absence of visible personal security providing the grist for diametrically opposed readings. In the article, a lighthearted Asma' tells Buck about Brad Pitt's concern:

"My husband was driving us all to lunch, and out of the corner of my eye I could see Brad Pitt was fidgeting. I turned around and asked, 'Is anything wrong?'"

"Where's your security?" asked Pitt.

So I started teasing him — "See that old woman on the street? That's one of them! And that old guy crossing the road? That's the other one!" They both laugh.

The president joins in the punch line: "Brad Pitt wanted to send his security guards here to come and get some training!"

The story is remarkably ambiguous: maybe every single citizen loved the first family, and therefore no one needed protection. This is presumably the story the first lady was telling to calm Pitt's nerves. Or, as activists were quick to point out, every citizen was so fearful that no one would dare to challenge the regime. Or everyone along the predetermined route was part of the secret police, and that is why there was no need for a specific security detail. Even supporters of the regime recognized the official narrative's instability, its vulnerability to rapidly changing circumstances as uprisings broke out across the region. They had questions: How central to this seemingly cosmopolitan regime were its autocratic underpinnings? How far would it go to protect its monopoly on decision-making? These questions were, at this time, open and disputed, and from practically any angle grounds for disavowal and displacement, for a finessing of the situation that valorized the status quo. No one, except just conceivably *Vogue*'s naïve author, regarded Syria as "wildly democratic," but the regime's commitment to reforms (albeit endlessly deferred) and encouragement of its managed civil society activism remained the basis of articulated hopes and attachment for those who could not bear the unknown or imagine salutary alternatives. The regime's brand and the aspirational consciousness it broadcast were not confined to first-family celebrity or glossy English-language magazines. These were also dramatized in Arabic-language films, taken up in seemingly apolitical advertising campaigns, and generative of new forms of sociality. Take, for example, *Marra Ukhra* (*Once Again* [2010]), a Syrian film whose importance, it must be quickly said, is ethnographic rather than cinematic.[39] When it was shown at film festivals, including repeatedly at Damascus's own, as well as in the few commercial theaters that existed, capacity audiences were filled with individuals mirroring the aspirational glamour and hipness of neoliberal autocracy's urbane elite, their fashion choices inspired by trends in Beirut, Paris, and New York, and lending a pop-music atmosphere of youthful celebrity.

Centered on a love affair between a Lebanese Christian woman and a Syrian Muslim man, both children of the war years in Lebanon, *Marra Ukhra* purports to chronicle the life of an actual military officer posted in Lebanon and the obscure circumstances of his death.[40] Coincidentally, the officer portrayed in the film is the father of the director, Jud Sa'id, but more noteworthy for our purposes is the film's celebration of upward mobility and unbounded wealth. Championing the alliance between finance capital (the lovers, including a jilted third party, all work in a bank) and neoliberal autocracy, *Marra Ukhra* offers a fantasy made possible by generational change.

The main protagonist, Majd, resides in a deluxe apartment overlooking Damascus and equipped with all the latest gadgets—a large flat-screen television, video game equipment, and most important, a surveillance setup with which he monitors his fellow citizens' internet and Skype conversations. In typical neoliberal fashion, public surveillance in the film has become privatized, internalized, and in effect "outsourced" to the nouveau riche. Majd, clearly the director's alter ego, spies on others voluntarily, without any directive from on high, evidently in response to his need to maintain control.[41] He is a damaged soul, but one capable of redemption in the context of a love story that at the same time sutures the wounds of war in a new collaborative, post-Syrian occupation era. Syrians and Lebanese can work together, even love, across sectarian, historical, and regional divides. When Israel attacks Lebanon "once again," Joyce, Majd's love object, forgives him for spying on her, and it is through his connections and expertise that she can return home. The final scene is especially heavy-handed, showing the two lovers together on a suspension bridge linking Syria to Lebanon.

In general, though, the film's reportage is noticeably spare, at odds with the hagiographic imagery and inflated language of the Hafiz al-Asad era (1970–2000). Even the Israeli invasion of Lebanon in 2006 is noted flatly. What distinguishes the film is its relentless attention to lifestyle—its portrayal of the sophisticated well-to-do as connoisseurs of wine, whiskey, and fast cars who live in an ideologically neutral era devoid of class conflict, shot through with market openings and inflected by generational difference. Unlike the father, who "can't handle the new world" and understands that his "time has passed," the son literally wakes up (our hero had spent some years in a coma, conveniently underscoring the cognitive abyss that separates him from the old order) to an altered political climate in which military status has been displaced by purchasing power. Majd is part of a younger, wildly successful generation able to produce evidently unlimited wealth and consume it ostentatiously in a world where glamorous pool parties and countryside hunting excursions are the depicted norm. Majd also enjoys connections to high-ranking members of the old guard—officers from a previous era who have survived to embody the current marriage of finance capital and military might. Their careers spanned a transition to the regime-run banking sector, one that also welcomes the business-oriented, risk-seeking men of a younger generation, like Majd.

The fantasies on display in *Marra Ukhra* present in particularly stark terms a version of neoliberal accommodation of autocracy, one that seems to endorse the coalescence of class, political, and consumer inequalities—or that ignores the inequalities in a way that reform-minded Syrian television directors, even those longing for order, would not. Yet the film dramatizes subtler and more ambivalent renderings of how ideological interpellation operates in the present. It betrays the characteristic forms and intensities of the professional managerial class's investments in a now-lost but memorable sense of security, in the experiences of social freedom, in a commitment to a multicultural secularism protective of minorities, in the joie de vivre that market openings promoted, even in the promise of reforms endlessly put off. Affective investments are related to material enticements, not only for those who can afford them, but also for those who cannot, yet are persuaded to imagine themselves inhabiting a consumerist mirage of pleasure and status. The latter is well illustrated by groups of high school and college students with whom I worked, who despite divergent backgrounds and radically different ambitions—the careers they dreamed about ranged from yoga instructor to civil society activist to policeman and entrepreneur—nevertheless all shared the aspiration to own flashy, fast cars.[42]

Speaking the language of "entrepreneurship" (*riyadat al-aʿmal*) and championing the virtues of volunteerism, these students wanted to "develop themselves while helping society," affirming slogans like the one on a classroom wall that read, Negotiation Is Compromise. As one student put it, acquiring business skills allows a person to be "one's own master." In one exercise in which seventeen students were asked to describe who they were by making collages with glossy images clipped from Arabic- and English-language magazines, most of the girls highlighted fashion and shopping, while some also included sports and music. Most of the boys privileged sports. In one young woman's collage, a picture underscoring multicultural accommodation (young men and women of different ethnic backgrounds and an English-language caption reading, "Celebrating differences") appeared together with a photo of fashion goods bearing the

both seeming to like the regime

maybe a @ here?

tell her to talk about it from...

caption "Shopping 24/7" and the words "business," "passion," and "goal" (*hadaf*) rounding out her embrace of neoliberalism. Another female student devoted her poster to an affirmation of patriotism, putting a photo of the president front and center with the declaration "I love my president and I love Syria." But in her discussion, she added that she "hates war, loves food, children, restaurants like Costa Coffee," and was attracted to "fast, fancy cars." Others prised apart the neoliberal from the autocratic, opting for homages to either the leader or money, with the son of a police interrogator lamenting the paucity of pictures of the president in the magazines supplied for the project. As a make-do, he reproduced a familiar Ba'th Party slogan attesting to citizens' love for their leader: "Minhibbak ya hami al-watan" (We love you, O protector of the nation). A young woman was decidedly bored by the assignment, but with no discernible irony covered her entire poster with different representations of money—pictures of Syrian lira, dollar signs, and so on.

Cultivating desires for commodities, fostering new ambitions of upward mobility, and producing individual philanthropic programs envisioning citizens' empowerment in ways that presume their limitations—these were the sorts of disciplinary effects this market-oriented era tended to generate.[43] The appearance of supposed nongovernmental institutions that were nevertheless under the control of the first lady's office—devoted to aiding children with cancer, teaching youth business skills, and offering a range of extracurricular arts programs—explicitly encouraged volunteerism. Helping produce a philanthropic corps on the model of American and European nonprofits, GONGOS (the oxymoronic acronym for government-organized non-governmental organizations) displaced the strident Ba'th Party cadres of the developmentalist state with what the anthropologist Andrea Muehlebach calls a "third sector," an "affective and ethical field" that could put forward the "moral neoliberal" as the exemplar.[44]

These new, sophisticated techniques through which neoliberal autocracy's messages were aestheticized did not eliminate party rallies or cultlike practices altogether, but they did work to relativize them.[45] In 2007, four years before the uprising and amid neoliberal reforms, the regime staged a "presidential election," with the president supposedly garnering 97.6 percent of the vote. The spectacle seemed an especially blatant blast from the past, a reminder of the elder Asad's mechanisms of social control. But even in that instance, the requisite demonstrations of outward allegiance were confusing in a way that rule in the 1980s and 1990s had not been. The displays of enthusiasm for the son's (uncontested) victory suggested a wellspring of support and an excess of emotion—an attachment that continues to be asserted by committed loyalists and informs the distinct ambivalence experienced by others. As we have seen with the beginning of the uprising itself, this era also produced novel occasions for transgression and resistance, hitherto-unheard voices of fury, piety, and joyous camaraderie, inventive ways of staying safe, and the shifting of limits to what seemed reasonable, questionable, sayable — or maybe even thinkable.

PART TWO: ZONES OF PLEASURE/ZONES OF PROTEST

For the first two months of the uprising, it was common in Syria's two largest cities to hear citizens supportive of the regime or ambivalent about change repeating the diagnosis "Rah tinhal" (It will be resolved), an act of wishful passivity in the present, a fantasy of repair reflecting the attitudes of people who had benefited from or imagined prospering under the pre-uprising conditions of neoliberal reform. As events wore on and resolution proved elusive, the refrain among some of these same people tended to change to "Ma fi badil" (There is no alternative), a justification for continued nonopposition rooted in resignation or cynicism or both. Others, whether outright loyalists or simply averse to irresolution of any sort, began wistfully recalling the days of Hafiz al-Asad, noting that if he "were alive he would have finished the matter once and for all."[46] Yet even those who registered nostalgia for the father's straightforward authoritarianism could do so on grounds that reproduced the ideology of the son's urbanity, labeling protesters as rubes (in Aleppo, the word *day'ajiyyeh* was common) who were not yet ready for the freedom they were demanding, a subject to which we shall return.

Until protests began in March 2011, the operative contrast taken to summarize the then present had seemed to be between the Damascus of the 2000s, the city of plentiful restaurants and boutique hotels, and the ascetic, drab capital of the 1980s and early 1990s. In the "new Damascus," to modify Christa Salamandra's term,[47] the breadlines in its poor areas were shorter than they had been in the 1980s, while croissant bakeries were springing up in its prosperous neighborhoods. During the lean years of food shortages, "even Hafiz al-Asad had no bananas at home," or so urban legend claims — an example that became a familiar refrain among Damascenes from diverse social classes in their efforts to capture what had changed under Bashar. According to this narrative, what changed was not just the availability of bananas but also the value placed on doing without in times of scarcity.

In the 2000s, affluent and middle-class residents of both Damascus and

self disciplined, abstaining from indulgence

Aleppo, many armed with computers and iPhones, whiled away their evenings smoking water pipes (available also for home delivery) and chatting without the fear that was so pervasive during the rule of Hafiz. Citizens found themselves even mentioning the young president by name in public without anxiety. New forms of social life were brought into being by young Syrians who found no contradiction in performing bike stunts to the sounds of expletive-peppered hip-hop in the shadow of the Umayyad mosque. Once-scarce coffeehouses peopled by old men with endless time for backgammon gave way to new cafés serving Starbucks-like beverages to a bustling multigenerational clientele, heralding what residents of the capital themselves referred to as the birth of a "café culture." Whereas few in the early 1990s would have dared walk in many parts of the old city at night for fear of being feasted on by voracious Damascene rats, the historic district of 2010 boasted beautifully renovated Ottoman dwellings housing bars, clubs, and restaurants that were attracting locals and tourists by the thousands into the wee hours. Aleppo's old Christian quarter similarly became a site of renovated restaurants and boutique hotels while a luxurious Sheraton near the grand mosque accommodated a growing, globally oriented business clientele.

Although the demonstrations that began in March 2011 have been read by many scholars as expressing the divide between haves and have-nots, the actual contours of protests were more complicated than any neat economic picture of dawning prosperity amid ongoing privation. For "the good life" ultimately indexes the political valences citizens attach to being in their comfort zone, which includes not only consumer pleasures or the means or aspirations to satisfy them but also the structural-symbolic order that organizes everyday life. At issue, then, beyond the simple materiality of the commodity form were the values ascribed to order; the question of what counts as citizen obligation; the importance of piety (whether in support of the status quo or as a language of opposition to it); the dangers of communal affiliations; and leaders' commitments to authoritarian control. This is the bundle of commitments comprising Syria's good life. It includes secularist narratives insisting on the virtues of multisectarian accommodation, and nationalist ones celebrating Syria's geopolitical salience and the need to uphold "the nation's" sovereignty. In the changing context of the region's growing unrest, the regime and its purveyors of cultural capital were obliged to insist on the inextricable connection between this good life and regime survival. Thus, for example, the president's spokesperson Bouthaina Sha'ban, both in written form in a major magazine and in public statements (thereby capturing multiple constituencies), was at pains in

March 2011, with all eyes focused on the Egyptian unrest, to underscore the differences between Husni Mubarak's regime and Asad's, focusing particularly on Egypt's abandonment of an Arab nationalist project whose integrity the Syrian regime defended.[48] Her resorting to old-style rhetoric underscored the good life's multidimensionality, welding the magazine's concerns with lifestyle to the regime's longtime nationalist anxieties about losing sovereignty to Western imperialists and Israel. Other loyalists noted the difference between the Mubarak regime's hostile relationship to minorities and the Asads' favorable one. Still others who cheered broadcasts of uprisings in Egypt, Yemen, and Libya—and were not necessarily pro-regime in Syria—nevertheless found reasons to dismiss evolving events. Forfending anxieties of disorder and Syrian powerlessness in the face of global powers, they asserted that "Syria was different," the "Syrian people are peaceful," or "it isn't time here yet."[49]

And yet the time clearly had come for something to happen. In what became a battle to represent the future in the present, members of the professional managerial class engaged in the regime's politics of cultural production became galvanized. Perhaps they feared losing the privileges associated with their entanglement in regime-sponsored patronage networks, and/or perhaps they were concerned about being displaced symbolically by the activism—of no longer standing in for the exemplary public or producing the mimetic guidelines for an aspirational Syria pinned to orderly, modern progress. For our purposes the key point is that the regime not only moved to crush the resistance by force but was also able to marshal its ideological state-market apparatus—talk show hosts, actors, directors, and advertisers who were indebted (*mahsub*) to the regime—in the service of maintaining its rule. And this indebtedness was not simply about patron-client relationships and the livelihoods they secured; it also bespoke a potent elective affinity between the regime's notion of the good life and the cultural milieu it had nourished over the previous decade to communicate that image. From the standpoint of these new cultural producers, representing secular cultural interests could be both strategically sound and expressive of political commitments.[50] Whatever their motivations, these cultural producers became central purveyors of the good life and inciters of affective attachments to it—so much so that their identification with the regime when the uprising began had loyalists and ambivalent citizens defending the dominant culture industry's position while activists expressed surprise and outrage at these A-list celebrities' "shame" and betrayal.

With the onset of the uprising, radio programs devoted to "lifestyle" and the importance of applying mascara correctly gave way to elaborate talk shows and street interviews in which the initial idea seemed to be to deny that protests were going on (*ma fi shi*), even while simultaneously situating them in terms of orchestrated machinations by foreign governments, often with "America at the heart of the conspiracy." Famous Syrian actors were enlisted for countless television appearances in which fundamental disagreements were overridden by concerns for regime stability, coupled with demands for public displays of loyalty. The well-known actor Basim Yakhur, for example, looking frustrated with his colleagues during a televised roundtable discussion about a humanitarian petition being circulated by the scriptwriter Rima Flayhan, chastised his colleagues for focusing on such an insular issue instead of on "politics." By "politics," Yakhur meant the ways in which the demonstrations had been "orchestrated" (*shay' madrus*) from the start by foreign powers.[51] Flayhan's petition, appealing to the regime to allow passage of provisions for children in the besieged area of Dar'a, had incited considerable debate and a number of threats from both top regime officials and production companies. In McCarthy-esque fashion, signatories were warned that if they did not withdraw their endorsement of the petition, they would be blacklisted from work in Syrian drama. Flayhan and others who lent their names to the document found themselves players in a real-life drama in which livelihoods were threatened, cleavages made public, and retractions demanded.

Syrians identifying with the need for political reforms but stopping short of condemning the regime outright were inclined to claim that the petition exaggerated the situation. According to these folks, some of whom had visited Dar'a after the regime's attack on the area, basic goods were being allowed in, and contrary to rumors, children were not going without milk.[52] To be sure, these prominent Syrians conceded, some residents, out of distrust of the regime, might be unwilling to pick up the emergency milk supplies the army distributed. Given the unrest, however, they had no issue with the army being there as such. Indeed, the famous actor Durayd Lahham publicly defended the army's presence so fulsomely that it prompted a short segment from Al-Jazeera. The segment contrasted his current political stance with the one represented decades before in his film and theatrical portrayals of Ghawwar al-Tushi, the clown-like issuer of courageous political statements, that had made him a beloved actor.[53] A billboard positioned in key thoroughfares of Damascus further underscored Lahham's public commitment to the regime's version of the good life and questioned the patriotic intentions of those who might think otherwise. The actor is depicted declaring, "Syria is a beloved, brotherly, safe country. Who would want other than that?" His celebrity billboard was one of two that appeared on major roadways in the city at the time, replacements for market advertising campaigns that were dwindling as capital fled. The other regime-sanctioned celebrity poster had the veteran Lebanese-Tunisian journalist Bin Jiddu questioning those who questioned the regime's version of events. Trafficking in conventional metaphors of enlightenment to pledge his allegiance, Jiddu's likeness appeared over a caption that read, "The truth is like the sun. No one can extinguish it."

Official rhetoric under Bashar al-Asad never fully abandoned practices reminiscent of the old regime under Hafiz al-Asad, producing guidelines for public speech and action, enforcing obedience and inducing complicity in part by continually generating patently spurious statements. Only this time, celebrities were put on the spot. Many of them registered views of outright support and love for the president, perhaps payback for their access to the good life in an era in which Bashar al-Asad was cultivating his own celebrity status by acknowledging and bankrolling theirs. Others tried to carve out what they identified as a "middle ground" and so were chastised by opposition and pro-regime loyalists alike. This position—deemed "neither here nor there"—betrayed an important ambivalence, conjoining familiar calculations of socioeconomic opportunity and risk with a yearning for a vanishing order where some criticism was tolerated as long as outright political contestation was contained.

Whether intentionally or not, regime-oriented image makers seized on these contradictory feelings, affixing widespread anxieties over vulnerabilities to such abstractions as market-oriented progress, sectarian or rural backwardness, and/or national solidarity. In a more chilling vein, some reverted to old-style Ba'thist Party "Othering," in which those opposed to the regime were all labeled terrorists, smugglers, rural rabble, collaborators, armed gangs, or supporters of *fitna* (discord), carriers of a toxic dissension. A billboard depicting a handgun formed from the repeated phrases "sectarian *fitna*," "media incitement," and "conspiracy" appeared at downtown Damascus bus stops in April–May 2011, sponsored by a small group of advertisers demonstrating their loyalty to the official narrative about the rebellion. Those who refused to stand with the status quo were coded by the regime as subversive "traitors to the nation," even "germs" infecting an otherwise healthy body politic; they were deemed "lacking or excessive in some fatal way,"[54] as William Mazzarella puts it in his analysis of advertising in a different context. The return of billboards marketing the disinfectant Dettol seemed to some a direct communication from the regime, doubling as both an announcement of an affliction and a threat in its own right—likening unruly citizens to germs that must be exterminated.[55] More affirming, but in keeping with the regime's assertions of national solidarity, was the reprise of an old advertisement for Giordano's clothing, featuring attractive teenage soccer fans draped in the official version of what had become by now a contested flag. The familiar combination of red, white, and black in the advertisement contrasted with the uprising's preference for a pre-Ba'thist flag in red, white, and green, a move to distinguish its patriotism from the regime but which also cast the old ads as expressive of regime loyalty.

More complex than either of these variations on obeisance was the "I am with the law" campaign.[56] Using an open hand as the first letter in the pronoun *I* in Arabic to assert that individuals belonged to a diverse national "we"—"young men and young women," "big and small," "rational and sentimental"—this campaign embraced all who were identified as subscribers to the law. Addressed simultaneously in its status of individuals as members of diverse groups and as part of a national unity, the target audience was called on to practice moderation, recalling recent fantasies of a neoliberal nation-state where citizens (regime members included) undertook the obligation to uphold the rule of law in order to bring it into being. More billboards cluttered the streets, appealing to proper management practices, the importance of containment, and the curbing of excess— a pithy encapsulation of the good life broadcasting the virtues of national sovereignty and multicultural accommodation through the medium of advertising. Subject to many parodies on Facebook, Twitter, and other internet sites, the moderation campaign exemplified the workings of what Lauren Berlant calls "cruel optimism": an effort on the part of advertisers to create or tap into attachments to a system that is no longer doing affirmative work (if it ever did)—in this case, referencing one that was starting to come apart at the seams.[57]

The "I am with the law" campaign reflected an ambivalence among some in the professional managerial elite, particularly those in advertising, where commitments to an open market order did not necessarily imply unwavering belief in the regime's ability to secure it. And yet those anxious about stability, or with much to lose, could act as though the problem were not primarily the result of authoritarian rule, that the regime's kinder, gentler version of autocracy could be compelled to secure the rule of law, that the neoliberal could outrun the autocratic by way of the national. To believe so was to succumb to a politics of disavowal—I know very well that the regime will not commit to the rule of law, yet nevertheless let's act as if the problem lay with ordinary citizens. This wishful thinking, to put it in different terms, may itself have been a product of the collaboration between political and economic elites. Certainly, from the mid-1990s through the 2000s, this collaboration had bound business elites and other notables to regime politics as usual. And there is no doubt that the more affluent citizens of Damascus and Aleppo—as well as those aspiring to affluence and identifying with neoliberal standards of success—seemed content to forgo political freedoms in exchange for expanded social freedoms, such as tolerated access to the internet and the protection of spaces catering to the expression of urbane tastes and habits. Hopes for the rule of law could even be felt as genuine *and* imagined as conducive to profit, but they were not to be allowed to get in the way of neoliberal autocracy: economic opportunities generated by market openings had to remain tethered to the regime's secular vision of prosperity and security.[58]

Market liberalization likewise structured the terms in which some grievances and alternatives were put forth, so that we see, for example, philanthropic organizations identified with the opposition treating the plight of refugees as an opportunity to brand suffering. And here we encounter the contradictions of neoliberal autocracy in bold relief. For on the one hand, neoliberalism's circumstantial flourishing in the absence of socialist substitutes makes a visionary oppositional politics or a programmatic alternative to market-oriented capitalism difficult to imagine. On the other, the alliance between consumer/advertising-oriented capital and the state, unlike aspects of industrial or military capital, is endangered by the harm being done by the regime to its own citizen customers. The regime's penchant for defining enemies in broad terms and its failure to govern in ways that ensure or even enable popular aspirations for the good life may help explain why Syrians in Aleppo and Damascus began to register their moral outrage politically in relatively small yet growing numbers between May and July of 2012—before violence from all sides made the two cities part of what some have described as a "living hell."[59]

It is tempting to look to the contradictions of neoliberal autocracy to account for the system's particularly brutal breakdown in Syria, but they also exist in similar polities, such as China, Vietnam, and Singapore, which so far have remained stable. And neoliberal autocracy characterizes most cases in the Middle East, including those whose citizens took to the streets in unprecedented numbers in Tunisia, Egypt, Yemen, Libya, and Bahrain, and those where protests were contained or nonexistent. Thus, it is not the contradictions per se that explain either the peaceful protest or the country's devolution into catastrophic violence. Moreover, ordinary people operate within the contradictions of their intimate and political/collective lives all the time.[60] And those contradictions change—as does the political work that ideology does in smoothing them over. For our purposes here, the change in Syria's case runs from a time of autocratic stability undergirding visions of market-oriented prosperity to the period when challenges arose in the form of calls first for reform and then regime change, and the regime responded with violence and cynical efforts at stage management. As we shall see in the following chapters, the technocratic-managerial elite and cultural producers who remain in service in Damascus in 2017–18 are not navigating the same contradictions that they had to deal with before 2011—although they are still doing that navigational work while attending pool parties, peddling in bikeathons, and participating in volunteer efforts, such as cleaning up Damascus's Barada River.[61] Their counterparts from Aleppo, many of whom escaped the devastation of that city by moving to the now-booming coastal town of Tartus, continue to cling to aspects of the good life even while also experiencing its ongoing endangerment.

Instead of citing contradictions in explaining transformation, as if they were an extraordinary feature of an otherwise contradiction-free life, I want to underscore two more precise points. First, as protests got under-way, the legacy of neoliberal autocracy from the decade before the uprising helped immunize the Bashar al-Asad regime—muting outrage and deflecting attention from the regime's ongoing brutalities, and confusing people into thinking they had a choice between deposing the dictator now or disposing him later, or for that matter not having to depose him at all. This widespread disposition in the early months of the uprising came to frequent expression in the notion that "the Syrian people" were still too backward or not yet ready for transformation. Second, and relatedly, the subjectivity associated with neoliberal autocracy suggests in its affective dimensions that despite the very real contradictions noted above, *neo*liberalism is compatible with autocracy in a way that liberalism explicitly is not. This affinity is brokered ideologically for ambivalent subjects through the illusion of subjective choice, not in the form of actual opportunities so much as in terms of options to be exercised later. In other words, the ideological work being done by the regime as the uprising got underway was geared to incline people who might otherwise have been open to imagining that the time for rebellion was *now*, to see value in waiting until later.[62] Accustomed to the deferral of political reforms, and with the specter of violence looming large, citizens in Damascus and Aleppo chose quiescence, opening a gap between those who were newly discovering the pleasures of politics by acting in concert and those for whom civil society and the ballot box were not obvious "panaceas" for the ills of dictatorship.[63] The hallmark of these ambivalent subjects was their inability to entertain the possibility of a salutary alternative to what they could admit was a problematic status quo: think again of Octave Mannoni's account of ideological disavowal, "I know very well, yet nevertheless . . ."

PART THREE: A TALE OF TWO CITIES (OR, ANTICIPATING OBJECTIONS)

Expressed in the language of game theory, ideology as we see it operating in Syria carries out dual signaling functions, with the same vision of benevolent autocracy serving simultaneously to seduce opposition activists into imagining that their grievances would be addressed and to keep citizens who were ambivalent about the uprising anchored to a fantasy of deferral. Expressed in the language of social theory, ideology is polysemous and activates different addressees in myriad and divergent ways that change over time. But more precisely, as form, it works according to a push-pull logic, enjoining some subjects to desire—not simply accept—the status quo. Key to this desire is what Fredric Jameson calls a "utopian impulse" toward some imaginary social harmony or sense of plenitude or ideal leadership. The regime activated this impulse while simultaneously seeking to foreclose its excess.[64]

It could be objected that this emphasis on ideology underplays other important considerations that would help in understanding citizen ambivalence in Syria's two major cities. Chief among these is the fear of repression, and no doubt much coercive power was devoted to discouraging rebellion in Aleppo and Damascus. Nevertheless, efforts to suppress dissent elsewhere did not keep protesters from taking to the streets.[65] Moreover, when repression worsened in both cities in May and June 2012, resistance (although still relatively small) increased rather than diminished, evidently in response.

Another concern might be that protests were more common in these metropolitan centers, even from the get-go, than is often acknowledged. A show of solidarity with the people of Libya in front of the embassy as early as February 22, 2011, and protests after Friday prayers at the Umayyad mosque by March of that year meant that some Damascenes were indeed "early movers," with a group of secular-minded activists often leading the charge. Flash mobs and graffiti activism in both cities registered important, if small-scale, opposition to the regime. And occasional funeral marches in outlying areas of both cities threatened to overflow into the city centers, undercutting the regime's insistence to these populations that all was normal, that nothing out of the ordinary was happening.[66] Nevertheless, all told, and in comparison with other less metropolitan areas or protests in other countries such as Yemen or Egypt, the number of participants involved in these actions remained small.[67] The reluctance to get involved was especially notable in Aleppo, which in the late 1970s and early 1980s had been a key area of rebellion against the previous Asad regime.

One seemingly compelling but flawed objection to a focus on ideology points to the "economic geography" of the protests.[68] In this view, the conflict is between the haves and the have-nots, with the relative quiescence so apparent in the affluent parts of Damascus and Aleppo coinciding with the geographic distribution of wealth in the two cities—both in comparison with other cities and internally with regard to neighborhood. On the one hand, there is some evidence to support this explanation. Activists on the ground at the time reported that highly touted demonstrations in affluent parts of these big cities (such as the one in Mezze, in Damascus, on February 18, 2012) drew their crowds from adjacent poorer areas that had already been engaged in rebellion.[69] Moreover, citizens in drought-stricken areas of the countryside, in less well-to-do cities, in city outskirts where rural migrants had moved, and in the markedly poorer parts of well-to-do neighborhoods were remarkably resolute in waging opposition (both peaceful and armed), often at tremendous bodily risk.[70] In contrast, there is ample indication that old-money bourgeois families and the swelling ranks of the nouveau riche in the posh downtowns generally preferred wishing away the manifest need for political transformation over joining the struggle to bring it about.

However, the onset of conflict does not reduce neatly to this sort of economic determinism: economic data before the uprising show a more complicated picture of prosperity and hardship than economic reductionism would allow for, with important countervailing tendencies like continued subsidies for basic foodstuffs, economic growth, and a rise in foreign direct investment offsetting analyses focused solely on the bleak.[71] Nor were the places where the uprising began the hardest hit by negative economic developments. And economic indicators suggest a temporal lag between protest involvement and stresses like the ongoing mismanagement of drought conditions or the lifting of energy subsidies.[72] Moreover, in poor areas throughout Syria, the demands expressed in the early days of the rebellion were not simply or even primarily economic in character. Although economic determinants of discontent need not find expression in economistic language, repeated calls for the "downfall of the regime," "freedom," and "dignity," and increasingly as time went on, assertions that

"God is great," cast additional doubt on economic interpretations of the uprising.[73] Referring to the Syrian president's then-prominent spokesperson Bouthaina Sha'ban, people in a poor area in the coastal city of Lattakia chanted in March 2011, "O Bouthaina, O Sha'ban, the Syrian people are not hungry" (Ya Buthayna, wa ya Sha'ban, al-sha'b al-Suri mu ju'an).[74] The persistence of such slogans point to an *ideological* geography of protest—one embracing divergent patterns of consumption and commitment, suggesting a variegated relationship to market-oriented openings and the pleasures they afford.

A housing boom in the 2000s turned areas adjacent to the downtowns of Aleppo and Damascus into a font of wealth for inhabitants who had formerly lived modestly from farming or operating small businesses.[75] These families became well-to-do—but they nevertheless were understood by supporters of the regime in Damascus and Aleppo as Other, as country bumpkins, simple folk (*darawish*), and even nomads (*nawar*)—all derogatory terms that indicate how unreliably income maps onto political power or social status. Wealthy inhabitants in these areas of resistance tended to have large families and renewed commitments to pious practices, in marked contrast to the lifestyle choices exemplified emblematically by the first family. Their ideological interpellation was partial because their aspirationalism was often misrecognized—to recall the stark symbolism of Althusser's allegory—in that their wealth provided an unacceptable basis for more than superficial inclusion in the elite world of urbanity central to the regime's political aesthetic. Being wealthy, in short, did not necessarily imply identifying with the glitzy, assertively modern aspects of the "enlightened" (*tanwiri*) elite. And, of course, citizens attached to fantasies of the officially sanctioned good life were not necessarily capable of achieving it. Moreover, although some loyalists did claim that first-moving protesters were uncivilized rural or tribal folk, there were plenty of rural and tribally organized regime supporters in places like Dayr al-Zur and a significant number of urban families allied with resistance in cities such as Hama and Homs. The protests in the poorer parts of Aleppo, still counted as within its municipal boundaries, were small. Most of eastern Aleppo— although in many ways a different world from the affluent western part— chose not to rise up in solidarity with the small group of young activists on the ground there in 2011.[76]

Furthermore, it seems common globally that young people are amenable to risk taking, and judging from protests large and small, Syria was no exception. Many protesters were too young to remember the regime's suppression of rebellion in Hama and Aleppo.[77] Their partial interpellation into the neoliberal autocratic world meant embracing the value of liberal political "freedom" while avoiding an older generation's Communist Party– or socialism-inspired emphasis on the structural injustices of market capitalism. For some protesters in this post-Hama, post-Soviet era, a political focus on the elimination of tyranny implied sharing the regime's neoliberal fantasies of consumer freedom, but registered a loss of faith in the autocratic regime's ability or willingness to secure it. The regime's neoliberal image-making may have unintentionally fostered a generation of couch surfing Facebook enthusiasts, who in addition to being tired of regime-sponsored corruption were globally networked and fluent in the language of human rights, electoral contestation, "civil society" activism, and individual empowerment. The regime's efforts thus had two quite divergent effects on a similarly situated (young, urban, privileged) population: either the regime could attach these young people ambivalently to the status quo in a spirit of "I know very well, yet nevertheless . . ." or it could help motivate them to embrace oppositional politics in an effort to press for democratic freedoms that the regime promised but did not deliver. Even the small university protests in Aleppo and the youth activism in mixed-income neighborhoods of Damascus bore witness to the generational dimensions of the contention, which crossed class lines and made little recourse to slogans voicing explicitly class-based demands or grievances.[78] In short, we do not see a neat correlation between economic disadvantage and protest, and the protesters themselves did not consistently declare themselves as suffering economically.

The example of the area of Mu'addamiyya lays bare the complexities that make purely economic analyses inadequate to our understanding of political fault lines. Known for its auto repair shops, small transport businesses, and household farms, Mu'addamiyya is considered part of the Rif Dimashq, best translated in this context as the outskirts of Damascus, in what used to be the capital's agrarian hinterland. The inhabitants are generally poor or lower middle class, and they tend to identify as pious Sunnis. As early as April and May of 2011, the regime was in negotiations with the elders of the area to contain discontent: inspired by protests elsewhere, restive citizens had begun to demonstrate; and in an effort to manage conflict, the regime promised to compensate inhabitants for farmland bought by the state in the 1970s–80s at below-market costs—or outright expropriated. Historically, this land claimed by residents of Mu'addamiyya had been used for housing units for the regime's Defense Brigades (Saraya al-Difa'), led by Rif'at al-Asad, brother to the then president Hafiz al-Asad. Called Sumariyya, the brigades' enclave within Mu'addamiyya housed military personnel who self-identified as 'Alawi, wore special uniforms, and were known for their brutality, economic corruption, personal loyalty to their leader, and endorsement of an energetic, fast-paced project of secular modernization. Later, with Rif'at's failed coup attempt against his sibling in 1983, troops specifically loyal to the president and his sons were moved into Sumariyya and brought their families into the enclave, which remained identified (by residents and outsiders) as 'Alawi, security-driven, reliant on regime patronage, and poor.[79]

According to stories circulating in the first days of May 2011, the elders of Mu'addamiyya had conceded to a compensation deal with the regime, and for a week the area was quiet. Young people then returned to the street, either disregarding the agreement or doubting that it would be implemented, calling for the regime's downfall, staging demonstrations, and blocking a main artery leading into downtown Damascus. Mu'add-amiyya has been more or less under siege ever since. As the violence escalated, so too did retaliations and counter-retaliations, with the neighboring area of Sumariyya (still inhabited by staunch loyalists) also drawn into the fighting on the side of the regime and consequently made vulnerable to attack, especially to car bombs. The contrast between Mu'addamiyya and Sumariyya demonstrates how similar class positions can be trumped by sectarian divisions. But the initial willingness of some young people in Mu'addamiyya to violate an agreement secured by elders also suggests a politically relevant generational cleavage. Young people there were not won over to the regime's strategies of public affect management emphasizing the virtues of status quo stability. That the elders could not control their younger constituents was a harbinger of things to come.

The class dimensions of the conflict are also significantly complicated by the fact that certain merchants involved in the regime's brand of crony capitalism were reliably said to be funding the resistance.[80] Some of these businessmen became fed up with the rampant corruption—the requisite payoffs, protection-racket-like activity, and unfair advantages given to the regime's family members and closest cronies. Others continued to operate beneath the radar or play a double game from inside Syria. The success of a call for shopkeepers to strike in May 2012, as opposed to the resounding failure to get them to shutter their businesses when the same move was made in May 2011, is emblematic of a general point: class and other collective solidarities toward the conflict were—and remain—in flux.

Reducing the conflict to an economic struggle, moreover, would be to ignore the ongoing recruitment in large numbers of *shabbiha*, the rank-and-file thugs in the president's security forces who tend to hail from

lower-income families.[81] Many of them self-identify as ʿAlawi, and sectarian affiliations (as the juxtaposition of Muʿaddamiyya to Sumariyya
implies) have become increasingly salient as to when and where the violence takes place. It may well be that the regime's sectarian claim-making
worked to prevent protests from those Syrians anxious about their existential survival as minorities. The regime certainly galvanized these anxieties
by underscoring the affiliation of ʿAlawi leaders killed in battle (as early as
a televised funeral in Homs in May 2011), arming "popular committees"
that often identify as threatened Christian and ʿAlawi "minorities," and
sustaining a rumor mill by turning out seductive conspiracy theories that
tapped into long-standing (and in some ways real-enough) fears of external
threat and internal subversion. Images of the regime as the guarantor of a
sovereign, stable nation-state and an explicitly multisectarian order belong
to a recognizably decades-old, evolving nationalist repertoire that has also,
paradoxically, required the reproduction of sectarian difference and anxiety, a central theme of chapter 5. For now, the point is that these fantasies
of accommodation and order could be readily harnessed to figurations of
market-oriented prosperity—for people ranging from wealthy and upstart
neoliberals to poor regime thugs. In fact, the regime could mediate these
contradictions such that even those who might otherwise be excluded
from the dream of social mobility could feel that they had some access to it.

CONCLUSION

This chapter has focused primarily on the first year and a half of the uprising and the decade preceding it, an era in which market reforms were both
product and productive of new consumer-oriented aspirations. Investments in the ideal of economic prosperity became moored to familiar older
fantasies of national sovereignty and multisectarian peaceful coexistence
(see chapters 4 and 5, respectively, where the latter two themes are considered in depth). Only partially economic in content, the aspirational consciousness animating new forms of sociability in this period found iconic
expression in the Lady Di and Prince Charles–like imagery of "Syria's first
family." Idealizing the modern, urban, and urbane professional managerial
class, the first family offered one version of what it meant to be exemplary
of the good life in Syria: glamorous, entrepreneurial, individually responsible, and civilized. The veneer of a kinder, gentler neoliberal autocracy
glossed over the economic cruelties caused by the state's attenuation of
social provisioning (including widening inequalities and new opportunities for corruption), and as time went on the escalating use of coercive

control to handle unrest. Nevertheless, as we have seen, the uprising was more complicated than a simple class-based or economic-grievance narrative would suggest, addressing a broader imaginary of desire and attachment.

As authoritarian regimes in Tunisia, Egypt, Yemen, and Libya began to teeter, some Syrians, affectively invested in stability and consumer pleasure, voiced hopes that the seemingly popular young president would understand the need for reforms and manage an orderly transition to an electoral system. Instead, in apparent homage to the more overtly dictatorial practices of the father, old-guard political advisers came out of retirement like a recurrent nightmare, making the regime's fear of losing autocratic control glaringly apparent. This will to regime dominance found dramatic and unusually candid expression in a *New York Times* interview with Bashar's notorious first cousin and (fittingly, given the neoliberal context) paragon of corrupt entrepreneurship, Rami Makhluf. As early as May 10, 2011, even as the president went on promising reforms, Makhluf openly declared that the regime was determined to "fight to the end."[82] Meanwhile, security forces were rediscovering their raison d'être in their (re)expanded duties as the signs of disrespect for autocratic control became more manifest. And in an ideological struggle over who stands in for Syria, it was children who would come to substitute for the first family, offering up a vision of innocence and helplessness in the face of the regime's overweening display of political and increasingly military power. Whether it was the young students arrested in Dar'a, the more anonymous children who prompted anxieties about milk deprivation in the face of a military siege, or the widely circulated images of a sweet-looking, pudgy thirteen-year-old boy, Hamza al-Khateeb (al-Khatib), who was tortured to death by regime operatives in Dar'a later in 2011, children signaled the disruptions of generational change, unmet aspirations for political reforms and noncorrupt modes of socioeconomic access, and the various affronts to dignity (*karama*; *karameh*) that the neoliberal autocracy both effected and attempted to conceal.[83] The regime's idealized world was revealed as a fantasy with little chance of becoming an actual world to which the fantasy could be anchored. In this context, a younger generation's oppositional savvy in circulating images of brutality became a form of protest in its own right, a way of bearing the brutality by bearing witness.

2

Humor in Dark Times

In the dark times
Will there also be singing?
Yes, there will also be singing.
About the dark times.
BERTOLT BRECHT

Comedy is not singing, of course, and "the dark times" Bertolt Brecht references are not the same darkness that fell over Syria. Yet the riposte resonates—comically, as it happens—both with the first decade of neoliberal autocracy under Bashar al-Asad and subsequently with the regime's violent response to the uprising in 2011. Brecht's clever verse also serves as a reminder that creativity need not be stymied by dire conditions but instead can be inspired by them. The humor in the passage derives from the incongruity between song and suffering, or what the philosopher Henri Bergson calls the comedic use of "incompatibility," discontinuity, and contradiction.[1]

This chapter discusses the form and content of a selection of Syrian television comedies as a way of homing in on questions of uneven ideological saturation in authoritarian politics, citizen ambivalence, and the workings of ideology in general.[2] With regard to ideology, comedy both reproduces and places it at risk, operating through forms of immanent critique that are powerful because they are internal and proximate to the objects of (ir)reverence while also achieving a degree of clear-sighted detachment from them. Comedy attunes us to things we already know but are not attending to. It is also a profoundly social activity. As Bergson notes, "However spontaneous it seems, laughter always implies a kind of secret freemasonry, or even complicity, with other laughers, real or imaginary."[3] Laughter presumes a community but also remarks on it, and in this double action may also summon one into being. Lauren Berlant and Sianne Ngai argue similarly: comedy "helps us test or figure out what it means to say 'us.' Always crossing lines, it helps us to figure out what lines we desire or can bear."[4] Comedy is a form of mutual recognition that provides comfort in the solidarity of a collaborative disruption.[5]

In the context of authoritarian rule specifically, the political effectiveness of comedy comes from inducing alternative solidarities that counteract the atomization and isolation fostered by powerful mechanisms of social control.[6] Witnessing others go through the motions of gratuitous obedience can make subjects feel isolated, while a shared giggle in the awareness that an even slightly transgressive comedy skit or cartoon is broadly popular enables people to recognize that, paradoxically, the isolating circumstances are widely experienced. The effectiveness of comedy under autocratic rule, whether in permitted or prohibited form, depends in part on the extent to which it finds ways to reassert common experiences, puncturing official claims of omnipotence and moral righteousness. People sharing in laughter resounding in a room can cancel out the concrete isolation and atomization manufactured by the dynamics of fear and the need to maintain disciplining fictions,[7] with the resulting solidarities frequently operating in competition with official criteria of belonging or cementing forms of cohesion cultivated at the sovereign's expense. And, as we shall see, under the first decade of Bashar al-Asad's rule specifically, tolerated comedy did work as an incubator for oppositional consciousness, a testing ground for novel ways to experience and claim the "us" of collective action.

Even while potentially counteracting political atomization and isolation, comedy can work paradoxically to shore up another disciplinary mechanism—namely, how authoritarian politics rely, at least in part, on external obedience. As Slavoj Žižek points out, external obedience, unlike good judgment or conviction, depends on a self-conscious submission to authority: "The only real obedience . . . is an 'external' one: obedience out of conviction is not real obedience because it is already 'mediated' through our subjectivity—that is, we are not really obeying the authority but simply following our judgment."[8] Comedy can help advertise and reproduce a self-consciousness of routinized civic obedience, drawing attention to the ways in which many citizens lack conviction but are nevertheless willing to act as if they have it. Under Bashar al-Asad's neoliberal autocracy before the uprising, the relationships between compliance and support were subtler and more complex than they were in the waning days of his father's rule. We have already examined in the previous chapter how the ideological underpinnings of domination shifted toward sophisticated

Madison Avenue–like forms of interpellation. But the point about tolerated comedies remains: comedy may have counteracted the atomizing effects of autocratic politics, but it did so while at the same time supplying citizens with the guidelines for complying with an authority many were ambivalently related to. As this chapter will demonstrate, citizen ambivalence was keyed into the regime's self-presentation as a kinder, gentler form of autocracy, and the public presence of edgy political satire helped nourish that image of benevolent dictatorship.

In the biting, tolerated comedies popular in the first decade of Bashar al-Asad's rule, ambivalence resided in the conflict between attachments to order, on the one hand, and the desire for reform-minded political change, on the other. In the comedic fare of the first years of the uprising (the subject of the second section of this chapter), this affective struggle was displaced onto concrete political demands for dignity and the end of dictatorship. Once the uprising was underway, Syrian comedy ceased being as richly nuanced as it had been in relation to its objects as young rebels seized on their newfound freedoms to lampoon the very persons who had hitherto been represented in reverent terms. The first family, itself a copy of the idea of first-family celebrity, could become in comedic form a copy of the copy,[9] a source of collective derision — exposed like a version of the naked emperor staking all on the very brutality he claimed to be minimizing.

MARKETING DICTATORSHIP, INCUBATING ALTERNATIVES

In the encounter between two seemingly contradictory logics, the neoliberal and the autocratic, it is arguably the comedic television series *A Forgotten Village* (*Day'a daay'a* [2008, 2010]) that best exemplifies their reconciliation, situating the attachment to unfreedom in the rural backwardness of citizens unaccustomed to the urbanity of the good life. But the richness of the series comes from its ambivalences toward the objects of its critique. In this context, its over-the-top aspects can be seen to operate as a particularly in-your-face exaggeration of ordinary realities — a way of drawing (citizens') attention to citizens' habituation to them.

The series remains the most celebrated comedic work of Allayth Hajju (also transliterated Allaith or Laith Hajjo), one of Syria's most prominent television directors, whose contributions to Syrian drama include the pathbreaking comedy sketches of *Spotlight* (*Buq'a daw'* [2001–]), which launched his career.[10] Hailed as one of the most talented among a new generation of experimentally inclined and ensemble-oriented directors in the early 2000s, Hajju went on to create the caustic, darkly humorous sketches of *Hope—There Isn't Any* (*Amal—ma fi* [2004]) before embarking on *A Forgotten Village*. Like others encouraged by president Bashar al-Asad's inaugural speech of 2000, which promised a new era of political and economic liberalization, Hajju and some close colleagues began pushing the parameters of the possible, taking the young president at his word and using the promises of reform to inoculate cast and crew against recriminations for poking fun at socioeconomic and political life.[11]

With *Spotlight*, Hajju became the first of a number of directors to take advantage of new televisual forms derived from film and advertising to broadcast autocracy's open secrets: the regime partly relied on rituals of obeisance that were transparently phony; it enforced participation by threatening coercive violence for noncompliance; corruption was omnipresent and everyone vulnerable to its seductions; and citizens helped uphold a system that humiliated them, resigning them to taking advantage of opportunities that put them at odds with one another.[12] The series also supported the regime's vision of multicultural accommodation and secular modernity by satirizing practices of sectarianism and the region's Islamic revival. As discussions about reforms in Bashar al-Asad's first year grew into what came to be referred to as the "Damascus Spring" of 2001, arguably presaging the uprising a decade later, the regime's coercive apparatus moved quickly to snuff out political expression and disband fledgling organizations. Many in the culture industry rationalized the large numbers of people suddenly being detained as a temporary setback to the president's reform agenda, hoping that his oft-stated intention to overhaul the militarized, kleptocratic security state would yet find expression in concrete reform policies. The only commitment to change, as it turned out, was to change endlessly deferred.

The seventy-some sketches of Hajju's *Hope—There Isn't Any* emerged three years after the suppression of the Damascus Spring, in a moment of recalibration. The skits emphasize the characters' "stuckness," to use Berlant's felicitous term, but also seem cynically related to the condition, offering scenes easily understood as conducive to the reproduction of political lethargy.[13] The episodes all take place in a rundown, poorly lit shack where two tramps—shabbily dressed armchair intellectuals without the armchairs, played by the well-known actors Bassam Kusa and Fayiz Qazaq—sit facing the audience at a rickety table, sipping countless cups of tea. In Samuel Beckett fashion (think *Waiting for Godot*), their dialogues are conveyed in a tone of what Christa Salamandra rightly calls "existentialist gloom,"[14] their resignation to prevailing circumstances leaving no way out of their discomfort and skepticism but the reassertion of the status quo.[15] In the episode "Malignancies" (Awram khabitha [2004])—its title a play on swollen body parts and metastasized corruption—Qazaq is soaking his hands in one pail of warm water while Kusa, sitting alongside, has his feet in another one. Both are moaning. We learn that Qazaq, in obediently applauding the regime's panegyrics, has "clapped too hard," while Kusa's sore feet come from failing to have done so, and having his soles lashed by the security forces for noncompliance. The skit and others like it expose the fiction that the regime is inevitably popular, and that citizens' support is heartfelt. But it also conjures up the ever-present possibility of punishment, broadcasting the threat of violence independent of the regime's actual use of coercion and reinforcing the idea that all options are bad and painful.[16]

In "The Democratic Imperative" (Dimuqratiyya ilzamiyya), written in the immediate aftermath of the 2003 US invasion of Iraq and broadcast in 2004, the two tramps are conversing about democracy. Kusa, who claims to be defending democratic principle, constantly and bombastically interrupts Qazaq, who is constantly raising questions. "Shut up!" (literally, "swallow your words"), Kusa insists repeatedly, in a joke that depends on the lived incongruity between tyrannical ambitions and claims to democratic commitment. As a well-observed critique of the pedantry, smug self-satisfaction, and hypocrisy of "democrats," especially those supportive of US empire, this sketch, far from a condemnation of the Syrian regime's authoritarian politics, reinforces official principles of autocratic order and a familiar anti-imperial (and anti-US) version of national sovereignty.[17] In "Ali Baba and the 400 Thieves" ('Ali Baba wa al-arba' mi't harami [2004]), corruption has once again metastasized, but the tramps remain resigned to the new narrative, the recognition of thievery an acknowledgment of a problem that seems, through its metastasization, to have lost its agency.

Similarly, in "Pulse of the Street" (Nabd al-Shari') and "Revolution" (Thawra), also from 2004—skits that were repurposed by activists as the actual uprising got underway—the point was that there would be no revolution in our lifetime. The pulse is a simple drumbeat, rather than people alive to political change, with the title "Pulse of the Street" mocking the common metaphor that reads vitality into dead asphalt. In "Revolution," the title refers to a litany of movements in the past—standing in for dashed hopes of radical transformation and current disappointments. Kusa is "wandering" in his thoughts, "because there is no other place to wander." Qazaq asks what he is thinking about. Kusa replies that he is wondering "who is leading the revolution." "Which one?" Qazaq inquires. "The Great

Arab Revolt, the July Revolution, the al-Qassam Revolution, the Bolshevik Revolution?" Kusa exclaims, "God forbid, not the Bolshevik Revolution!" "The French Revolution?" "Not the French one either."

On the contrary, Kusa explains in mock seriousness—the camera zooming in on his face to emphasize the intellectual grandstanding: "The revolution that hasn't happened yet." He was musing over what would happen if "the revolution that hasn't happened were to happen . . . and under whose leadership" (al-thawra illi ma sarit, iza sarit, wa bi qiyadat min). The pause that follows is clearly meant to underscore the question's pretend profundity. "Sometimes," Kusa intones with escalating self-importance, he imagines that the leader is "already here among us." But "sometimes," he says with an air of feigned mysteriousness, he wonders whether maybe "he is in a place no one yet knows about." And sometimes, he thinks the leader may "still be a young boy in school." And sometimes, he reflects with mock perspicacity, "he hasn't even been born yet." Soberly, Qazaq advises him to stick with the latter hypothesis, and the skit closes on that note, a parody of political optimism steeped in an acceptance of despair.

The sketch's tethering of revolutionary activism to the presumed necessity of a strong leader further buttresses existing authoritarian assumptions, while the repetition so characteristic of comedy works to satirize leftist intellectuals (including ruling party Ba'thist ones) who ponderously pronounce on progress and cheerlead for social transformation. The ambiguity of the verb tenses used at the opening of the skit—in Arabic, "who is leading" could also be "who will lead"—allows the dialogue to become a recitation of past events before morphing into the conditional, open-ended, dreamy "It could be otherwise if/when a strong leader is born." But the skit can also be read, as it was during the early days of the uprising seven years later, as a registration of things to come: a dialogue which, despite its seemingly conservative aversion to an abstract notion of a universal history, nevertheless presages and taps into the desire—think again of Fredric Jameson's "utopian impulse"—for a better future. Its repurposing in 2011, and its widespread circulation to Syrians both inside the country and in exile, suggested how incomplete that ideological maneuver was as the message of resignation got prised apart from the criticism it also excited. And in most instances, the activists of 2011 no longer affixed that desire to a strong leader, but instead celebrated the collective potentiality of "the people."

In restaging these skits at the beginning of the uprising, activists made the otherwise implicit references concrete. In March 2011, one day after Bashar al-Asad's speech in parliament, dissidents organized under the moniker Shamrevolution posted a remix of another dialogue from *Hope—There Isn't Any*.[18] In the original, Kusa tells Qazaq that he has been busy clapping by himself just for practice. In the remix, Qazaq declares that clapping has gone out of fashion, and there is no reason to do it anymore. But Kusa disagrees: "You say this now, my friend, but when push comes to shove, everyone will applaud."[19] He starts to clap vigorously and is soon accompanied by a cacophony of applause in time to "The Radetzky March" by Strauss. Now it seems that everyone has joined in, the unseen Syrian spectacle with the martial soundscape triggering the automatic response. The remix also features scenes of crowds cheering and members of parliament standing in ovation (as they had the day before) interspersed with the dialogue, so that the ominous line "when push comes to shove, everyone will applaud" no longer signals resignation but becomes an incitement for revolutionary action. Similarly inspired by *Hope—There Isn't Any*, the anonymous youth collective With You produced *Freedom and Nothing But* (*Hurriyya wa Bas*), a program that aired on the oppositional Dubai-based Orient Media Network during Ramadan of 2011. The title plays on a familiar regime slogan, "God, Syria, Bashar, and Nothing But," while the graphics are directly borrowed from the Hajju series. In the context of the uprising, calls for unqualified "freedom—and nothing but" replaced the dismal negation "hope—there isn't any." And although the configuration and costumes are recognizable from 2004, this remix also registers the new moment by substituting two unkempt young men for the bad-tempered old tramps, with the scene transported from the dimly lit indoor shack to an outdoor junkyard.[20]

If *Hope—There Isn't Any* generally performed the same political resignation it diagnosed, *A Forgotten Village* threw into bold relief the general tension between the disciplinary and the emancipatory dimensions of comedy. These two striated possibilities may be especially visible in authoritarian contexts, in which humor can easily be seen to shore up a regime's ideology even while raising the potential for world-creating openings by pointing out quotidian absurdities.[21] Neither necessarily a vehicle for collective, therapeutic mobilization—a successful effort to counter what Walter Benjamin called the "beastly seriousness" of ongoing oppression[22]—nor a means, as Theodor Adorno writes, of coping with "fear by defecting to the forces that are to be feared,"[23] *A Forgotten Village* offers both a means of enduring the present and an invitation for people to free themselves from it.[24] The richness turns on the series' capacity to operate as a vehicle or laboratory for oppositional thinking, even as it helps reproduce attitudes central to politics as usual.

Arguably, no comedy in Syria has ever enjoyed the critical acclaim garnered by *A Forgotten Village*.[25] In 2010, the streets were empty during Ramadan, with a multigenerational audience celebrating the holiday by taking in Allayth Hajju's comic fare. Educated and uneducated viewers, regime officials and would-be opposition members, officers in the army and ordinary conscripts, all took pleasure in watching the series. Set in a fictional hamlet on the northwestern coast, *A Forgotten Village* uses situation comedy—employing elements of slapstick and caricature—to tackle issues of everyday corruption, regime capriciousness, poverty, and the incongruities of political rhetoric in dark times. Parodying the regime as well as citizens and the mechanisms of social control enmeshing both, the series pokes fun at authoritarian circumstances and lampoons political stasis in the hinterland—invoking a world that is both a critique of rural folk and a stand-in for backwardness more generally.

Well-informed viewers were impressed with the serial's agility in playing with linguistic incongruities. In homage to Syria's multiculturalism, the characters spoke an exaggerated blend of dialects from both the coastal city of Lattakia and the surrounding countryside, with subtitles translating colloquial Arabic into a modern standard, simultaneously making fun of subtitling conventions and ensuring a pan-Arab viewership. The series also presented a complicated picture of sectarian coastal dominance—many top officials, including the Asads, come from that area of the country and self-identify or are identified as 'Alawi[26]—and invited viewers of all stripes to laugh at themselves and at one another. A successful effort at community-building that temporarily produced the very collectivity it advocated, the insular village served discursively (that is, within the narrative's logic) to contain political difference and lament the absence of a functional modern nation-state.

Take, for example, the episode "In the Pitch-Dark of Night, the Full Moon Is Missed" (Fi laylat al-zalma', yuftaqad al-badr [2010]), the title an ironic appropriation from a poem on the theme that we appreciate what we have only once it is gone.[27] The familiar trope of pining for loves lost is perversely grafted onto a story in which the departure of the local snitch from the village triggers an unexpected appreciation of the service he provided, and ultimately a collective longing for his return. The episode documents how information, fear, and the social expectations surrounding them work to reproduce the conditions of authoritarian rule in such a context that everyone is wearing blinders—or to keep with the title metaphor, everyone is operating in the dark. In part 1, the village informer leaves town, offended by his treatment after his report to the authorities about his fellow villagers gets leaked—requiring the police to find a substitute snitch among the locals. Part 2 details the anxiety caused by the departure of the known snitch, for no one can know whether his successor is already working among them. It could be a friend or a neighbor, even a spouse. All claim to have refused the job, but no one can be sure that anyone else is telling the truth. Part 3 chronicles the villagers' solution to their own anxiety: they opt for the certainty of a coercion they know over the unbearable uncertainty of not knowing, so they decide to find the snitch and bring him back into service. If in Jean Genet's *The Balcony* the chief of police is the only one who doesn't know that everyone knows he wears a toupee, here the situation is reversed: it's the police who know that no one knows that everyone has refused the role. Citizens' lack of confidence in one another's goodness cancels out the possibility of any more promising form of collective action other than opting for a solution that maintains the status quo. Even the anxiety of waiting for the snitch to return becomes too much to bear, so the villagers collaborate with the police, each agreeing to share the duty of informer according to a publicly posted schedule. The decision simultaneously mocks the sham secrecy associated with a surveillance of which everyone is aware and underscores citizens' inability to do more than reinstantiate their own unfreedom.

On the one hand, then, this is a grim story. By making viewers feel hopeless, the episode may participate in the very conditions of oppression it brings to our attention. On the other hand, comedy, in its world-building dimensions, creates possibilities for solidarity and critical thinking. It invites imagining hypotheticals, a what-if-ness that takes pleasure in attunement and irreverence. This is not to romanticize permitted comedy skits. Nor is it to deny how they might operate as safety valves, providing both citizens and officials relief from the dreariness of prevailing conditions, thus aiding in their reproduction. But it is to stress comedy's ability to dramatize what we already know but may not recognize, inviting us to detach from aspects of ordinary life that no longer do affirming work.[28] It is this sensibility that helped motivate calls first for reform and then for the toppling of the regime—and did so among rural folk, members of the very population that Hajju's comedy suggests were incapable of this detachment, a supposedly "forgotten" population less taken in by the neoliberal autocratic good life.

At once a stabilizing form and an incitement to alternative visions, *A Forgotten Village* consolidates a shift in comedic strategy among Syrian cultural producers. Unlike the court jester/common man who mocks the government and demands that citizens be treated with dignity, the characters in *A Forgotten Village* are in no way exterior to the conditions oppressing them. Here it is the writer and the director who speak truth to power, not the characters representing everyday people. If earlier comedies positioned ordinary citizens as the ones acknowledging their own participation in the violence of which they were also victims, in *A Forgotten Village* the villagers are generally good-hearted citizens who know right from wrong. What they lack is the narrative capacity to reflect on either the broader conditions or the microdynamics of their oppression. The series is thus in part a class fantasy rooted in positioning the professional managerial and cultural elite (in this case not the characters but the writer and director as omniscient narrators) as harbingers of a slow but steady progress—one that celebrates modernity by contrasting it to the villagers' naïve, country-bumpkin-like efforts. The villagers here even devise creative ways to reestablish existing power relationships after becoming unsettled and finding their absence too anxiety inducing. In earlier series, the powerful were identified as the responsible parties and ordinary citizens as victims, but the powerful were simultaneously made so by a system upheld by supporters and victims alike. *A Forgotten Village* carries traces of this sensibility. But here both ruler and ruled have become buffoons, and the critique of the regime is matched by a diagnosis that situates "the people" at the heart of the problem.

This point is most elegantly made in an episode called "Tamalluq" (2010)—a word implying excessive flattery, fawning, sycophantic behavior, the practice of "sucking up." An order comes from on high that the villagers are no longer allowed to suck up to officials, which leaves folks completely at a loss. Few even understand the order, and most who do are too afraid to abandon their previous practices to express themselves freely. Made anxious by a policy requiring an embrace of unfamiliar ways of being, the villagers prove more successful in ceasing to flatter than they are at expressing their opinions. As in Hajju and the comedic screenwriter Mamduh Hamada's episode about the snitch, the villagers ultimately come up with an ingenious solution to manage their anxiety, although at the cost of reproducing their oppression: they turn themselves in when they cannot obey the injunction to speak their minds, thereby choosing the safe confines of the jail cell over the uncertainties of an outside world made newly treacherous. An incisive chronicle of citizens' habituation to the sycophantic fictions that sustain autocratic rule, the episode raises important questions about the nature and burdens of free speech, the atmosphere of distrust autocracies generate over time, the arbitrariness and absurdities of orders from on high, and ordinary people's coping mechanisms—that is, (rural) citizens' own attachments to compromised positions that undermine rather than enhance possibilities for rewarding lives.[29]

Like the episodes focused on snitching and obsequiousness, "The Night of the Arrest" (Laylat al-qabd [2008]) plays with the themes of guilt and innocence central to authoritarian modalities of social control. Employing the familiar comedic forms of repetition and snowballing, the episode works like a parodic version of the Althusserian allegory of ideological interpellation (discussed in the introduction). The sweet clown-like dunderhead, As'ad, is almost run over in the dark of night by a secret police agent passing through the village. Apprehended for crimes unknown, he is taken to the police station, where the chief, as usual, is literally sleeping on the job. On display here is the hierarchical relationship among functionaries. The secret police agent is an outsider, more connected to the powers on high than to the villagers. The policemen are sycophantically related to him, and not even the mayor, whose comic insistence on his elevated status is a regular feature of the series, is immune from interrogation.

The sadistic secret police agent and his corpulent partner assume that As'ad must be guilty of something (which he is), so they try to exact a confession, leading As'ad to admit to being guilty in general. Yet he fobs off responsibility (for what, we do not yet know) to his friend, Judeh, the local chicken thief and classic trickster, who then blames the mayor, who in turn accuses the grocer. The secret police agent presses each to confess; but as the episode gains in comedic intensity—with every villager professing a willingness to confess while implicating the next one—it becomes clear that the regime's representatives suspect an insurgency is in the works, whereas the villagers are complicit in something else entirely. Out of fear of being beaten, the villagers all take refuge in the local jail, ultimately to learn that these particular arrests resulted from a case of mistaken (village) identity. A call from on high clarifies the situation, and the agent takes leave of the wrong hamlet to pursue rebels in a neighboring one. In the meantime, the accused villagers packing the jail cell manage to escape so that they can redress the wrong they did commit. For it turns out that they had stolen diesel fuel from a broken-down tanker by the side of the road; returning the "government property," they reason, relieves them of the need to confess. When the snitch tells the police that the villagers are in fact guilty of a theft, the sleepy chief feigns exhaustion, and instead of arresting the villagers anew, he returns to the scene of the crime to reenact it by stealing the fuel himself. "The law," to borrow the Althusserian logic, is in this case corrupt yet innocuous and ineffectual, the episode both trivializing the fact of regime brutality and pointing to its ubiquity.

Allayth Hajju's comedies pose a case in which ideology is being both reproduced and at least partially placed at risk. His work offers both cynical conclusions and ways of seeing afresh, allowing us to attain a prohibited knowledge that we in fact already have (of how paranoia ramifies, for example). On the one hand, in its more typical moments of cynical frustration and, some would say, regime-oriented accommodation, the caricature of the village idiot seems to stand in for a generalized political backwardness that can be alleviated only via the tutelage of an enlightened, professional managerial elite. As noted in chapter 1, an elective affinity between Syrian drama and regime officials during the 2000s produced what Donatella Della Ratta rightly calls a minority community of *tanwiri* (enlightened) cultural producers, who in conjunction with regime officials envisaged ruling over a "backward majority," eventually enabling the majority's advancement through a process of secularizing, modernizing enlightenment.[30] Hajju himself has claimed repeatedly that Syrian television's mission was to "heal social backwardness through drama."[31] In this view, the television comedies were in a double sense restorative—of good humor in the face of dreary circumstances, and of a political order favoring the early rule of Bashar al-Asad and neoliberal autocratic citizen management.

On the other hand, *A Forgotten Village* provides more than a cynical account of the "people's" (in)capacities, and thus rises to the level of a critique of popular sovereignty and regime rule. For when comedies playfully mock the people, suggesting that they are not yet ready for political freedom, it is tantamount to arguing that the regime has failed to build state institutions capable of ensuring the education of its citizenry. Hajju's comedies can thus even be read as a substitute pedagogical enterprise, one that adumbrated what would soon become a newfound ability to express collective disrespect. For comedy is a mode of aggression, raising questions about how we discuss collective life and who the "we" is that gets to talk in the first place.

In Hajju's case, as with all tolerated comedy, the refreshing irreverence was also a way of containing the very hostility it acknowledged—even encouraged—reflecting the ambivalence on the part of the managerial class toward a system of rule celebrating this class's very presence. As a critique of prevailing circumstances, his comedy gave the impression of regime openness while underscoring citizens' attachment to and recognition of their own subjection. And that recognition is almost always dual, inducing complacency but also providing some ground for potentially new, disruptive publics.

If in pre-uprising Syria the edgiest television series put the responsibility for problems—of corruption, fear, surveillance, corporeal abuse, and rhetorical excess—on both rulers and ruled, it was left to the dark humor of the uncensored internet (embraced by members of the opposition) to broadcast parodies of official discourses in ways that called unequivocally for the regime's ouster. A video circulating on Facebook and other social media from late June through early August of 2011 featured three masked men wielding crutches and sticks as if they were guns. The men had garlands of okra, mimicking bandoliers, strung around their necks. One man even tossed a baby eggplant "hand grenade." The video mocked regime claims that protesters were armed gangs engaged in violent insurrection, using rhetoric from one of the president's speeches to point to the gap between official discourse about the protest and anything the protesters were actually doing: "These are the infiltrators and germs that Bashar al-Asad calls terrorist gangs," says a man pretending to be a reporter for Syrian television. "What's that? You're going to liberate the country with okra?" At once both anxiety-relieving and anxiety-inducing, skits such as this played to a global audience and to opposition-oriented Syrians capable of finding humor in the incongruity between the regime's toxic propensity to demonize the opposition and the opposition's relative innocence. But in the case of this spoof, the joke was limited to those who subscribed to an image of the opposition as untainted, reproducing versions of an "us" much more circumscribed than the earlier audience delighting in the comedy of *A Forgotten Village*. Indeed, subsequent internet comic fare has made frequent use of interspersed scenes from *A Forgotten Village*, in a move that marks as more generally Syrian what are otherwise increasingly particular publics. If, as the Lacanian theorist Alenka Zupančič argues, comedy is the expression of the universal in the concrete, then these comedies also made clear the difference between recognizable comedic form(s) and contextually specific content—setting the terms in which something was to be judged as funny.[32]

As the uprising got underway, the terms of what counted as humorous were clearly in flux. Clever remixes of the president's speeches and fast-paced parodies of regime thugs' machismo expressed a newfound creativity unbound from the censors. One of the most remarked on by scholars and activists was the YouTube finger-puppet series called *Top Goon: Diaries of a Little Dictator* (all episodes broadcast in November 2011) by the group Masasit Mati. The group's name comes from the straw used for sipping yerba maté tea, a popular beverage throughout Syria but especially among its soldiers and rural dwellers. According to a group member, the idea was to evoke the pleasures of getting together with friends and family, "drinking and discussing points of view."[33] But the name also suggests that imbibing regime rhetoric does not mean accepting it.

The puppet show was among the first performances of irreverence directed at actual celebrity figures in the regime, not caricatured anonymous functionaries. The president puppet is a callous buffoonish figure whose wooden head sports big ears, a high forehead, a widow's peak, and a beaky nose, which along with Bashar's characteristic lisp are exaggerated for comic effect. He is completely dependent on thugs, or "goons," to stay in power, and he is continuously being flattered by stupid sycophantic advisers—themes reminiscent of scenes from *A Forgotten Village*, now repurposed with a fundamental disdain for personalized authority at their comedic core. In the first episode, "Beeshu's Nightmares," Beeshu—a diminutive of Bashar, which reduces him, as diminutives do—speaks and otherwise acts like a toddler. It takes an entourage of caretakers to tend to his narcissistic needs, and notable among them is Shabih (*shabbih*, literally, "goon" or "thug"), dressed in a drab green uniform with bright military stripes sewn above the left breast. Shabih's job, it seems, is to soothe the infantilized leader through the night. Beeshu's nightmares revolve around his lost popularity: "Why don't Syrians love me anymore?" he wails. "Why do they want to put me on trial?"

Educative as well as humorous, the skit draws parallels between father and son to underscore the contrast. Beeshu is cruel but inept, haunted by a father he cannot hope to imitate successfully. Dressed in a ridiculous pajama set and nightcap, he is awakened by a nightmare that the regime has been toppled, even though he hasn't "killed as many people as my father did in Hama." Shabih reassures him that the regime is still in power and urges him to go back to sleep. For tomorrow is Friday, and they "have a lot of work to do" (referring to the biggest day of protest after the noon prayer). Shabih then sings a lullaby: "Sleep, sleep, I'll slaughter all of the people of Syria. Aleppo's businessmen won't rise up, even if the regime falls," thereby taking a jab at political quiescence in Aleppo, the Syrian business hub (discussed at length in chapter 1). Bashar is heartened by the thought that Aleppo's businessmen are as loyal as the famously obsequious Grand Mufti says they are—another reference to the alliance between formal clergy and capital so central to the regime's survival. In specifying the contours of insider-ness that make the skit funny to some Syrians, the skit also uses incongruity to expand on what counts as inside. "Beeshu,

Beeshu, little cutie," Shabih says preposterously. "One day you'll be able to pronounce the letter *sin* properly." *Sin* is the Arabic letter *S*, so the reference is, of course, to the president's well-known lisp, by now the frequent target of parody. "And the infiltrators [*mundass*] will be dealt with. A silver bullet is all they'll need."

Beeshu is lulled back to sleep, but is soon frightened awake by a new nightmare about protests in a strategically important area in the Damascus outskirts. Shabih, mistaking Beeshu's moaning about his nightmare for an announcement of an actual protest underway, begins shooting around indiscriminately with his puppet-sized machine gun. And now it is Beeshu's turn to allay Shabih's fears. Resolved to end his nightmares, Beeshu suggests that he step down. Enraged, Shabih asks whether the toddler president is "crazy"—harking back to the series' opening song, in which Beeshu is constantly saying he isn't crazy (*ana mani majnun*). Shabih grabs him impetuously by the neck as if to wring out the toddler/leader's delusions of grandeur: "Do you think this is your decision?"

After all, the joke seems to be, the leader is a puppet. But then so is Shabih, who smooths over his own aggressive moment by taking a common fiction of autocratic rule (that the leader is universally loved) and combining it with the demographic facts of the uprising: "I mean, Sir, it would be a shame, given that 99 percent of the people are with you. The businessmen of Aleppo are with you, Sir. The businessmen of Damascus are with you, Sir. Who do you think are paying the goons, Sir? Who do you think is going out partying on Friday nights?" In order to accomplish some political pedagogical work while shaming the professional managerial elite supportive of the regime, the skit charts some of the ways aggression is handled under dictatorship. Excessive flattery, for instance, is used to repress or channel what might otherwise spill over, even among regime operatives, into attacks on the leader's person.

All the episodes in *Top Goon* tack between the specificity of Syria and the generality of satire as a comedic form to convey a seemingly simple political message: the regime is brutal, and Syrians who protest will not have sacrificed in vain. The skits are at once an assertion of Syrian unity, an effort to produce the grounds for that unity, and an unwitting account of the challenges to its realization, but in this episode that triple operation is made especially apparent, situating Beeshu's nightmare as if it were the Syrian "people's" wish fulfillment. In the next scene, Beeshu is snoring away peacefully, Shabih having carried him back to bed after tickling the toddler and then singing, "We love you, we love you." But soon Shabih is compelled to wake up Beeshu with the news that the leader's bad dream has come true. The regime has indeed fallen. Beeshu thinks Shabih is joking, but the joke is on Beeshu. As Shabih flees the scene, the disembodied voice of the puppeteer sings, "Syria, don't be afraid, Bashar will follow [Libyan dictator Muammar] Gaddafi." (The slogan, a familiar one during the first year and a half of the uprising, rhymes in Arabic.)[34] The humor disappears at this point, as it will for most of season 2, giving way to a political messaging campaign that no longer appeals to ambivalent citizens or attends overly much to the regime's ambiguities.

Yet many of the remaining episodes in season 1 retain their comedic form, largely by presenting political and aesthetic judgments that do not try to cancel out the contradictions or incongruities of authoritarian rule. Episode 2, "Who Wants to Kill a Million?" twists the conventional game show *Who Wants to Be a Millionaire* into gallows humor. The episode imitates that show's familiar question-and-answer format and keeps its trademark suspense music; stymied contestants have the same options, such as "phone a friend." The questions revolve around regime brutality and inept leadership; Beeshu's responses, most of them correct, are sillier still. The juxtaposition of silliness to sovereignty makes the episode work, as when Beeshu needs to phone a friend, he realizes that he doesn't have any. Playful props, such as a podium made from a Rubik's Cube, add to the absurdity. In episode 3, "Prostitute Media," the puppets mimic the meretricious news coverage provided by official media outlets; in episode 4, "Dracula," Beeshu is a bloodsucking vampire who consumes even the very people who protect him. The first lady is "the Rose of Damascus," parodying *Vogue*'s untimely feature article that appeared right before the uprising (discussed in chapter 1).

In episode 9, "Beeshu's Reforms," Beeshu makes yet another speech promising change. The unseen audience is familiarly obsequious—laughing at the president's attempts at humor, applauding his stated commitments to reform, and ignoring his slips of the tongue. These slips, as opposed to his lisp, are instances of parapraxis, accidents that really aren't, moments when power speaks truth to itself. Beeshu mistakenly lauds the regime as "sadistic" and claims he'll become "God" rather than leave office. Actual actors, their faces concealed by *keffiyehs* (checkered scarves), appear, only to drop out of the frame when felled by machine gun fire. With no one left, the president rejoices: "It's over because all Syrians are gone." Now the toddler-tyrant is sovereign over no one—but his moment of pleasure gets interrupted by a Syrian rap song calling for revolution. Beeshu exits as hands making the peace sign emerge from where the actors have fallen. The revolution will be victorious, this episode assures the audience.

A tyrant cannot continue to rule in these conditions. Peaceful resistance will triumph over violence.[35]

In the final episode of the first season, "Last Days in Hell," much of the parody characterizing previous episodes of *Top Goon* has already been surrendered to revolutionary didacticism and the compulsion to reassure. Beeshu is giving another speech, this time confusing the names of martyrs with those of pop singers. He vows never to leave, reminding the audience that the world has abandoned the Syrian cause. As he prepares to withdraw from the stage, however, Beeshu is summoned back to confront his puppeteer, who announces, "I am done carrying the burden of you." Beeshu counters, "You agreed to let me speak for you, to take over for you, to exist in your place, to breathe for you, to eat for you, to make decisions for you, so go back down where you belong." The puppeteer has literally and figuratively become heavy-handed, no longer able to bear the puppet's weight. But then, in a classic instance of inversion, he makes Beeshu dance to the famous song of resistance, "Go on, leave, O Bashar!" (Yalla Irhal Ya Bashshar! [to be discussed in the next chapter]).[36] If citizens were the puppeteers all along, then they have the power to manipulate the ones in power, to make them dance to their own demise. Then the puppeteer grasps the puppet with his other hand, pulling off Beeshu's head to reveal the controlling finger underneath. The other puppeteers join him onstage, and they all make the peace sign. Next, instead of traditional credits rolling on the viewer's television screen, this last episode of the first season shows a dedication: to a neighborhood in Homs under siege, and to the "martyrs of Syria" more generally. "For all Syrians, freedom is coming," the closing words assure the viewer. A scholar of Syrian theater and film, Edward Ziter, glosses the episode's final scene this way: "There is no longer any reason to crouch beneath the stage while the tyrant struts above. The power to claim one's place in the open air has been secured by the blood of the people."[37] Yet none of the troupe's members can be credited by name—and little was, in fact, secure(d). More important for our purposes here, despite the courage and correctness of the positions repudiating tyranny, something key to the comedic cannot be sustained when the episodes become didactic rather than simply educative. The tensions between assertions of Syrian unity and the actual experience of class and regional fragmentation, for example, are themselves not open to parody here, obviating sources of the comedic that might otherwise play with incoherence and ambivalence.

Henri Bergson writes in an oft-repeated phrase that comedic laughter is prompted by the appearance of "something mechanical encrusted on the living," by "some rigidity or other applied to the mobility of life."[38] Puppets exaggerate this mechanical feature; they are in some respects pure mechanism—which may be why they are so readily adapted for purposes of parody. Alenka Zupančič extends and revises Bergson's account of the comedic in ways that give us traction here. She notes that at his best, Bergson invites us to see that "the mechanical element in the comic is not simply one of its two sides or compounds, but the very relationship between the two . . . (the relationship of reproduction/duplication, involved in imitation). What appears to be mechanical (habit) on the one side, and a pure fluid life, on the other, are effects produced in this movement in which a life is referred back to itself, confronted (by means of imitation) with itself as seen from the outside. The crucial question is thus not: Is life reducible to mechanism? The question is: Is life reducible to itself?"[39]

According to Zupančič's reading of Bergson, for him the answer is yes, it is. But for her, there is no such thing as a pure "immaterial life," no such thing as life as an "ever-evasive ungraspable leftover of everything that could actually be said to be":

Life is not (fully) reducible to itself, which is why it does not constitute transcendence to all there is, but, rather, a crack in all there is. It is this noncoincidence of life with itself that takes the form of a relationship, and it is this relationship that can occasionally strike us as mechanical. It is in this sense that the mechanical is intrinsic to life, and cannot be satisfyingly conceptualized in terms of exteriority as opposed and foreign to a vivid spontaneous interiority. As a matter of fact, comedy has always exploited the register of the following question: To what extent is mechanical exteriority itself constitutive of the very liveliness of the "inner spirit"?[40]

This coimplication of automatism and aliveness is central to the comedic form as such, but may be especially stark in puppetry. As Lauren Berlant and Sianne Ngai understand Zupančič here, "The question of what's living, what's mechanical, and who needs to know is what really haunts the comedic and makes it an uncanny scene of aesthetic, moral, and political judgment."[41] Puppet comedies bring these questions to the fore effectively in part because the mechanics of the medium are so exposed. And this exposure, as I suggested at the beginning of this chapter (following Mladen Dolar, who follows Zupančič here), invites an account of comedy's capacity to play with mimesis—copying the copy, as it were, in a redoubling that makes us see. And this comic capacity may be especially pronounced in satirical forms like parody—itself an imitative form by definition. Beeshu is the imitation of Bashar, who is himself imitating the idea of despotic rule.

This imitation, as *Top Goon* shows us so clearly, depends on the world of others who are imitating ideas as well—of sycophancy and of dissidence (the latter not subject to humor in the series), without which the fiction of sovereignty could not be upheld. *Top Goon*'s inability to sustain its comic bent over the long run has to do in part with its creators' fidelity to a revolutionary rigidity, at odds with something that Berlant and Ngai suggest may be internal to comedy: the way it is able, relative to tragedy, "to hold together a greater variety of manifestly clashing or ambiguous affects."[42]

This is not to argue that *Top Goon: Diaries of a Little Dictator* was good comedy until it became bad comedy. It is, rather, to point to the political complexities of comic mimesis, illustrated perhaps most pronouncedly in a popular rap video in the spring of 2011, "The Strong Heroes of Moscow."[43] The video offers an especially ironic parody of regime discourse, an imitation that is so much like the original that it risks being mistaken for it. (In the American context, think of Stephen Colbert's imitation of a right-wing talk show host on the *Colbert Report*.) Dolar, writing about comic mimesis, invokes Plato's cave, noting that the philosopher's fear was "not that the copy, the imitation, the mimetic double was but a pale and unworthy shadow of the real thing; his fear was that it was too much like the real thing, too close to it."[44] Thus, the model is tied to its "ephemeral double" in ways that confound the distinction.

In "The Strong Heroes of Moscow," something similar is at work. The video begins with images of newspapers from 2011 featuring real-life headlines supportive of the official narrative, in which demonstrators were part of a global conspiracy to destabilize Syria: "Armed Men Arrested at Jisr Al-Shughur [in the Idlib area of northwestern Syria] with Five Tons of Dynamite"; "Salafi Emirate Dismantled in Talbisa." The most outrageous: "Hamza Al-Khateeb Killed after Attempt to Rape Officers' Wives." (Recall that Hamza al-Khateeb is the uprising's iconic thirteen-year-old boy who died after being brutally tortured in Dar'a, his genitals removed.) These images are followed by elegant graphics in an abstract realist style while the rap lyrics spoof (for those who get the joke) the homoeroticism/ hypermasculinity associated with fascistic national desire. Overflowing prison cells are juxtaposed to the discharging or emptying of machine guns, the song's chorus paying parodic homage to sadistic-sexual delight:

We want to fill up the cells
We want to pack prisons
We want to empty Russian guns
For the Asad nation

The successive verses feature keenly observed aspects of Syria's dictatorship in catchy, rhyming four-line stanzas keyed to a thrumming bass line, the combination of destructive energy and erotic abjection made personal in declarations of surrender to the nation's sovereign:

> We're your soldiers, O Bashar!
> We're just dust on your shoe
> We'll destroy houses just for your eyes
> Democracy is you!

Unsurprisingly, loyalty requires the demonization of infiltrator-Others, who will be squashed like bugs by devoted lions/wild beasts. The comforting clichés of marketplace value (quality beats quantity, but quantity is good too), followed by lines about conspiracies from Mars, help signal the parodic irony of the otherwise plausible rhetoric:

> Wherever you walk and step
> We'll kneel before you and kiss the ground
> We'll squash every infiltrator
> Like wild beasts
> We're your lions, don't you worry
> We'll fill the square with blood
> It's not about quantity
> We have quality
> Enough about freedom and all this crap!
> There is a conspiracy coming from Mars!

Embracing the apparent values of self-, familial, and fiscal sacrifice to the leader, the song blends autocracy with neoliberal austerity:

> O one of high forehead [an idiom that means "proud" and may also
>   reference the Asad family's high foreheads]
> I sacrifice my soul and money for you
> For your eyes, precious one
> I'll slaughter my family with a dagger.

Or later, in the hyperbolic register so typical of the cult of personality under Bashar's father, but again with judgments (the sovereign is willing to let his people starve, for example) indicative of the song's irreverence:

Your name rises high
Your voice is heard in the sky
Even if your people die of hunger
We'll elect you for life
We don't have opinions
We have your lights blinding our eyes
You are our great and graceful one
You are the king of humanity.

Despite any number of signposts, the video's creators were sufficiently anxious about being mistaken for regime supporters that in closing they appended a clip of cell-phone footage of an elderly man being beaten by soldiers.[45] But their effort to forfend misreading misfired, as the video was understood in more than one instance not as a condemnation of the regime but as praise for "filling up the prison cells" and taking cues from Russia. The accompanying ditty was even reportedly picked up by some regime thugs as a ringtone for their mobile phones. And for those who took pleasure in the song—who were in on the joke, who recognized regime discourse being altered by the parodic copy—their enjoyment was brief: what began as a comedic gesture morphed into elicitations of disgust, moral outrage, and/or collective responsibility. None of this was funny in the context of intensifying abuse and suffering. The "Strong Heroes" experience came with a lesson that would be relearned repeatedly as activists struggled with comedic form. Irony always runs the risk of the subject of the joke failing to recognize himself as its object, or of outbidding the subject's own sense of the ironic. And efforts to work prophylactically against misrecognition are no guarantee that the interpretive encounter can be successfully managed.

If the revolutionary rigidity and pedantry that increasingly characterized *Top Goon* ultimately diminished its punch, it was the abandonment of irony that undermined pleasure in "Strong Heroes." Perhaps this is because the latter's comic mimesis relied on the risk of being misunderstood; it played with the discrepancy between the double and the original, putting them in relation by juxtaposing the preposterousness of actual regime rhetoric to the absurdity of conspiracies from Mars. Getting the humor, as I noted more generally in the introduction, required both proximity to the object and a creative estrangement from it.[46] Finally, the add-on of the man being beaten broke with the comic ambition, even while also not curtailing the enjoyment of thugs who saw in the celebration of violence a vindication of their own practices—or so the story of reappropriation would imply.

In a context in which encounters with loss are intensified by devastating carnage, it is noteworthy that Syrians have, in the 2016–17 period, made efforts to produce fresh accounts of daily life with ventriloquistic virtuosity. Young people, primarily but not exclusively men, are shifting from mockery centered on the person of Bashar al-Asad to exploring the sociological conditions and microprocesses of neoliberal autocratic rule. One set of skits, called *Nakzeh* (a slang word from Idlib meaning "little poke," which can be used to connote poking fun), features Sumar Barish from Saraqib, an area of Idlib known for its early demonstrations in 2011 and for its general history of activism. Relocating to Turkey as regime bombings and warring Islamic-oriented militias vied for control, activists from Idlib (including several people from the Barish family) engaged in a variety of important cultural activities, many of which showcased the region's well-known humor. *Nakzeh* features a young man whose most trenchant monologues draw attention to the key demographic categories emerging since the uprising began—poking fun at the loyalists, the ambivalent middle, or "gray people," and the opposition.

In an astute account of the "gray people" (*al-ramadiyyin*), for example, the episode so named differentiates among four different kinds: the sleazebag (*al-nisnas*), the windbag or farter (*al-fasweh*), the gecko (*abu brays*), and the motherfucker (or pimp, *al-'ars*).[47] The sleazebag is a coward who does not get involved, remains silent in front of thugs, and is even "scared of a mouse entering the home." A pathetic character preoccupied with eating and sleeping, he gets "very upset when the electricity goes out." The fart or windbag is, like his namesake, "silent but deadly," one of the most dangerous types of gray people "because he is opposition. He hates al-Asad and he hates the regime and he's not lying, but he sees that the presence of the regime is better than the destruction of the country." And when "cities are bombed, protesters are dying, and women raped, he says, 'oh brother, let's make sure.' And when you tell him that they killed your brother, he says, 'May God help you bear the burden, but you are overtaken by your emotions and you must think with your mind.'" His mantra is, "What did I tell you?" Windbags favor the news channels France 24 and the BBC because of these channels' reputation for neutrality and civility—as well as their pretensions to intellectual superiority. And they prefer the conservative casualty figures of the Syrian Observatory for Human Rights to the emotionally fraught accounts by the opposition news, their very recourse to reason an excuse to support the status quo—a point we shall explore in a noncomedic register in chapter 3.

As for the gecko, he is a hypocrite whose mottled skin and patches of lost pigmentation imply the absence of a strong, solid position, and he is the consummate pretender: "On Thursday he's drunk and on Friday he's at the mosque. He prays in the front row and his head taps the ass of the shaykh." When he sees an opposition Free Syrian Army soldier, he wishes him victory over his enemies. He does the same thing when encountering the regime's army. And then there is the pimp or motherfucker. He is the worst version of the windbag, because he disparages "the people" for being backward, incapable of proper revolution. His vulgarity makes him more grotesque but less dangerous than the farter, for he straightforwardly "rebukes the people and eats them." Like "gelatin," with no backbone, he experiences every military attack as testimony to the people's incompetence, saying, "There you go, you want a revolution! You want freedom." A consummate complainer, he sees the problem "ass backwards." He longs for the past, by which he means the 1990s under Hafiz al-Asad, "when having a supply of bananas at home was evidence of belonging to the middle class. The 1990s. (*Fake sighs.*) When we used to talk in North Korean."

Dressed in a green T-shirt depicting what appears to be a tooth clad in a suit and tie holding a coffee mug in one hand and a newspaper in the other, Barish's casual costume implies that the gray people are toothless, members of the managerial elite whose pretensions to knowledge (the newspaper) and to office-style professionalism (the coffee mug) belie an underlying cowardice — or worse. Simple cartoon graphics pop up during the monologue, in contrast to Barish's deadpan, including some words in English like "silent but deadly." References to well-known politicians and intellectuals, as well as jump cuts to Syrian television serials, address Syrians as insiders who can share in the specificity of the references. Speaking like an average funny guy from Saraqib, Barish also punctuates his monologue with an air of the educated pedagogue — making fun of the penchant for typology while also engaging in its practice.[48]

The ability to mimic various kinds of Syrians marks an effort to reestablish commonality without occluding the fact of difference. This kind of ventriloquism finds especially sophisticated expression in the YouTube video comedy series *Min Fawq al-Asatih* (*Over the Roofs*, a title that connotes something done in secret or indirectly). The young activists performing the episodes of the series, from the particularly pummeled area of al-Ghouta on the outskirts of Damascus (which we shall discuss in relation to the chemical weapons attack of 2013), demonstrate a remarkable irreverence not only for the regime but also for the organizations and practices that have cropped up in areas under opposition control. In chronicling ongoing conditions of corruption and fear, the small troupe invites the very kind of direct expression it also favors.

In one of the most noteworthy episodes, a young comedian enjoins the newly elected President Trump to borrow from Syria's authoritarian playbook in order to expedite the achievement of despotism in the United States.[49] In a monologue that code-switches from the bombastic rhetoric of a Ba'th Party apparatchik, to the language of the stereotypical hip, cool guy, to the recognizable expressions of intellectuals, to the popular classes, and to the traditional Damascene specifically, each sentence stitches together various stereotypes in a masterly way, with the parodic pretense of ensuring Trump's success. Clips from Trump-Pence rallies have excerpts from Syrian patriotic songs as the accompanying audio. A video clip of Robert De Niro calling Trump a pig, or of Scarlett Johanssen, Michael Moore, and Madonna revolting against the newly elected president at the alternative inauguration, allows the comedian to shift into typical popular-class colloquial speech to say, "Have patience, dude, have patience" (Tawwal balik ya zalami, tawwal balik) . . . as if talking directly to De Niro. And then, in the register of a patron or boss, "What's this unruliness?" And then there is the comedian's advice to the "American people," including the recommendation that they not give up their identity cards, as the Islamic preacher 'Ar'ur, exiled to Saudi Arabia, enjoined Syrian revolutionaries to do; otherwise, they would be unable to get through "checkpoints in New Mexico." The choice of this US state is suggestive of Trump's nativism, but also of how the domestic and familiar territories within a nation-state can become, as they have in the Syrian context, alien and subject to militarization. In the next sequence, familiar language from Syrian television and among loyalists at the beginning of the uprising downplays the demonstrations: "It's normal, very normal, I mean, so what if demonstrations surface? Don't let this disturb you or eat you up. Don't be mad (la tij'az halak [the latter expression switching to Damascene dialect]). Everything has a solution."

Among the recommendations for Trump peppering the monologue are suggestions for co-opting artists and punishing those who disobey by appointing a loyal director to the nation's artist's guild, one who would expel those refusing to support the regime, as happened in Syria. But toward the end of the monologue, the advice becomes more personal, with recommendations that, like the Syrian first lady's establishment of the Syrian Trust for Development, Trump's wife needs to be kept busy running a GONGO, some tightly controlled government organization that can seem independent and claim to have a broader social objective. "Stir the yogurt": that is, make something happen for her. But that is not all. To "guarantee your reign and little Barron's after you," there's a "recipe" to be followed: "You expropriate the land and you build a government institution on it. In order to put a deviant society back on the straight and narrow, make a small prison, and anyone who opens their mouths or breathes, you drag them out and skin them alive. Literally skin them." And then: "The thirteen thousand [a reference to the number of political detainees in the notorious Sidnaya prison] will give you trouble, but your hands will get good at it." The mood obviously shifts here. The music is no longer the patriotic fare favored by the regime but "Mawtani," a song popular among activists identifying with the "beauty of the nation" or homeland. The recourse to clips of American demonstrators, Trump rallies, and famous US actors castigating the newly elected president give way to black-and-gray animations of people incarcerated, people tortured, and people hanged in prison; the tempo of the monologue slows to reflect the gravity of what is being conveyed. In some ways reminiscent of the gallows humor of "The Strong Heroes of Moscow" but also like Henri Bergson's philosopher who succumbs to the omnipresence of loss, the humor in this sneakily profound piece turns out to be urgent—yet difficult to sustain.

Trenchant monologues such as in this episode of *Min Fawq al-Asatih* do not attract large audiences, unlike the Syrian pre-uprising comedies such as *A Forgotten Village*, whose popular appeal was overwhelming and avowedly national. They do not even produce the generalized buzz that early revolutionary comedies had, with their marked irreverence toward individual leaders and celebration of rebellion attractive to Syrian and global audiences alike. It is no accident, for example, that *Top Goon: Diaries of a Little Dictator* ended up being captioned in English—part of a short-lived upwelling of international solidarity in the name of what many hoped would be a full-fledged revolution. But the sheer variety on the internet these days and the hardships in wartime of managing such practical difficulties as funding even for modest YouTube programs, or indeed of having electricity to enjoy them, combine to produce what the next chapter identifies as "siloed publics." These populations signify polarized judgment, on the one hand, and the possibilities for suspending it, on the other.

CONCLUSION

Alenka Zupančič notes that comedy works when it "leads us away from the actual direction from which the punchline comes, emphasizing the effect of surprise, upon which the joke depends. Surprise is a key aspect of joke-telling." Zupančič also highlights the "specific temporal modality of jokes," writing that "the point [of a joke], 'the joke of the joke,' operates through the mechanism of what Lacan calls *le point de capiton*, the 'quilting point,' that is to say the point at which an intervention . . . retroactively fixes the sense of the previous signifying elements."[50] This element of surprise, the possibility that enjoyment or surplus satisfaction precedes demand, entails a "shift in temporality." Although Zupančič distinguishes between the temporality of the joke and other kinds of comedic effects, comedy in general "switches the supposedly natural sequence, in which we start with the demand and end up with more or less inadequate satisfaction."[51] Instead, comedy offers us the surprise of satisfaction before we even know we have the demand. The "comic sequence," then, is "always inaugurated by some unexpected surplus-realization," by the recognition of a failure or mistake or misunderstanding.[52] In the case of *A Forgotten Village*, this surplus realization stems from the villagers' prior underestimation of the snitch's role in securing their existential comfort, and the subsequent counterintuitive desire for reclaiming the oppression they know; their failure to grasp or their willingness to forfeit a more profound freedom; and their own misrecognition of one another's goodness. In the case of the regime puppets of *Top Goon*, the surplus in the "Who Wants to Kill a Million?" episode, for example, comes from the use of a conventional television serial to expose regime violence. The episode takes the silliness of a show whose hollow aspirations are about getting rich quick and stitches it to the fraudulence of authoritarian rule, thereby inviting us to detach ourselves from both the money-making values of the neoliberal good life and the fear generated by autocracy's coercive control. Putting neoliberalism and autocracy together in this way makes them seem especially absurd. Not knowing the punch line keeps us in a state of pre-surprise, and the eventual surprise retroactively fixes the situation, allowing us to be satisfied in our laughter before realizing we demanded such play. We see a similar sort of mechanism at work in "The Strong Heroes of Moscow."

The comedic form's reliance on the unexpected, its embrace of misrecognition, the temporal inversion of satisfaction before demand, the attunement to retroactive fixity, and the call to attend to aspects of ordinary life to which we are generally inattentive, as well as the spirit of open-ended play (the latter less highlighted by Zupančič) all point to the struggle between our desires and our attachments. Comedy, as Berlant and Ngai note, "enable[s] the very contradictions and stresses to which it also points."[53] At times, it invites us to think collectively in more open-ended ways, in part by cultivating an attunement to and irreverence toward conventions. It summons us to an "otherwiseness" of commitment—to theories and creative genres with the capacity to conjure the coming into being of political activity (if not necessarily a novel political program) in the present.[54] On other occasions, or viewed from the vantage point of accommodation with the status quo, tolerated comedies in particular seem to lament a stasis they also help secure.

Bergson once again comes to mind. Likening laughter to a child's encounter with the snow-white foam on receding waves along a sandy beach, he notes that a child grabbing a handful of foam finds himself a moment later with nothing more in his fist than surprisingly brackish water. "Laughter," Bergson writes, "comes into being in the self-same fashion. Like froth, it sparkles. It is gaiety itself. But the philosopher who gathers a handful to taste may find that the substance is scanty, and the aftertaste bitter."[55] In one reading of this passage, the beach scene registers a sense of the tragic impermanence of the comedic. In another related possibility, the passage suggests that the desire for affective spontaneity can be difficult to satisfy. People return to absentmindedness, a tendency that leads the child to forget to hold what he has been grasping, and thus to lose it.[56]

The dangers of inattention, as Bergson's example implies, are always present—as are opportunities to forfend it. Comedies in their irreverence may be an especially political site of judgment, for even small collectives of comedians and the audiences who get the humor provide testing grounds for broader collaborative disruptions. They can be ways of managing conflict, as pre-uprising comedies surely were, but they are also unpredictable and liable to repurposing, as we saw with both *Hope—There Isn't Any* and *A Forgotten Village*. Far from being any uniform offering of a redemptive politics, they are nonetheless a mode of detachment which, at its best, invites disengaging from aspects of life that are harmful and can be better imagined otherwise.

3

On Uncertainty

FAKE NEWS, POST-TRUTH, AND
THE QUESTION OF JUDGMENT

When in the winter of 2014 the social networking giant Facebook shut down pages devoted to the uprising, Syrian activists protested, pointing to what they perceived as the suspicious timing of the decision. Insisting that pages showing atrocities had been routinely posted before, they suggested that now, three years into the conflict, groups supportive of president Bashar al-Asad had mastered the art of "gaming the system" by "reporting on their rivals."[1] Noting that anyone can lodge a complaint with Facebook's user operations team without being revealed as the source, activists surmised that something like the pro-regime Syrian Electronic Army, already known for hacking major news sites, must have orchestrated the closures. Facebook, for its part, argued that the decision to shutter the sites reflected what Michael Pizzi, in an article about the affair in the *Atlantic*, glossed as "years of content breach" that "may have finally caught up to the pages" that had been in existence since the emergence of opposition groups in Syria in 2011.[2] In this view, Facebook's decision was not so much biased as slow in coming. But that still did not answer the question of what precisely was involved in the content breach. Was it the graphic images, the unverified allegations, and/or the incitements to violence? What counted as incitement? Or, as in some cases, was it an apparent endorsement of Al-Qa'ida or other militant groups? A Canadian NGO spokesperson responsible for several digital-security initiatives in Syria took the opportunity to underscore the difficulty of determining community standards: "You have, for the first time, a conflict entirely documented over social media.

Facebook is basically policing a large country and trying to do so without access to what's really happening. Even for us, [and] we deal with the conflict on an ongoing basis, there are a lot of actors who are popping up, changing, and it can be difficult to make a judgment call on what's going on."[3]

The proliferation of websites disseminating purported news; the ease with which digital photos can be doctored; the accelerated cycles in which "news" gets circulated, absorbed, and then superseded by the next catastrophe; the tension between rival discourses registering moral outrage from different angles—all play a role in how we are observing a condition of generalized uncertainty developing and metastasizing, not only in Syria but seemingly throughout the increasingly networked world.

Whereas the tragedy in Syria is extreme and particular in any number of ways, rhetorical strategies involving the deliberate sowing of doubt are unique neither to that country nor to situations of armed conflict.[4] We have only to recall the outcries about fake news in the wake of Donald Trump's victory in the US presidential election of 2016 (and the subsequent way in which lies became a defining part of his presidency) to recognize the salience of what journalists have increasingly dubbed a "post-truth" era. As Pagan Kennedy writes in the *New York Times*, citing BuzzFeed, "During the last three months of the election, hoax stories outperformed real ones on social media. Thanks to people enthusiastically sharing pro-Trump headlines cooked up by clickbait farms . . . the fake can be more profitable than the real."[5] The advantages of posting fabricated stories, however, can be political as well as pecuniary, and it is not only in Syria that ways have been found to manage political conflict and discredit opponents by sabotaging what Hannah Arendt calls "factual truths." This chapter deals with instances of direct manipulation, but it also focuses on a host of conditions underlying the proliferation of less overtly directed forms of uncertainty and doubt—forms that come into circulation acephalously, independent of propagandistic strategy. Competing images, rumors, and conspiracy theories, alongside the divisive testimony of "eyewitnesses" regarding real or purported events, all make for a consequential if sometimes unwitting collusion between commercial media outlets and political regimes.

In the Asad dictatorship in war-torn Syria, these dynamics appear in bold relief: we see the media's demand for sensational content driving both regime supporters and well-meaning citizen journalists from the opposition to massage (if not manufacture) purported evidence of all kinds, leaving Syrians at home as well as global observers doubting the validity even of what might be regarded as authoritative news reports or the claims of international fact-finding missions. These conditions of generalized uncertainty have significantly aided the frayed state's counterinsurgency campaign—not so much by helping it maintain credibility in its own version of events as by casting doubt on all reporting, enabling the regime to seize critical advantage in an oversaturated high-speed information environment.

My argument about ideology and its relation to judgment in this chapter is threefold. First, and this is a lesson that citizen activists learned at tremendous cost: too much information may generate the very uncertainty that circulating it is intended to allay. Over the course of the uprising, the Syrian state's ideological apparatus, no longer able to brand the regime as a kinder, gentler version of autocracy, learned how to use conditions of fear and insecurity to counter human rights activists' and citizen journalists' attempts to document "the truth." By disseminating its own claims and counterclaims, and exploiting the political inexperience of the fractious opposition, the regime has not always been able to establish its own authority over the facts, but it has been repeatedly successful in sowing doubt among a variety of addressees about the nature of evidence as such and the credibility of oppositional narratives.

Second, as scholars of American politics have pointed out, information overload and the uncertainty it generates may induce people to seek out opinions reaffirming their own, and this tendency toward balkanization can lead to polarization.[6] Internet users (taking an oft-used, contemporary example) tend to isolate themselves into echo chambers, relishing the sound of stories they are telling themselves anyway—and the stories they tell themselves about the stories they tell themselves. The documentary filmmaker Errol Morris, in his 2014 book *Believing Is Seeing*, draws from psychological and visual studies long preceding the internet to make a compatible argument. The historical images Morris discusses have the capacity to allow observers to see what they want to see, demonstrating how images can be doctored to produce misleading gestalt effects. People find comfort in what they think they already know, gravitating toward a comfort zone in which believing is seeing, and may have little to do with actual facts—even on the assumption that the latter are ultimately knowable.[7] The atmosphere of uncertainty cultivated by an excess of information can create what I shall call "siloed publics," where the confinement of debate within narrow communities of argument allows interlocutors to take pleasure in exclusively encountering views that confirm their own.[8]

Third is a possibility that Morris and others do not consider but the Syrian conflict illuminates in particular: conditions of generalized uncertainty make it easy for people to find alibis for avoiding commitment to judgment at all. In circumstances of information oversaturation, and perhaps especially when feelings of present danger extrude a "remainder of surplus threat" (borrowing Brian Massumi's formulation), uncertainty can provide a seemingly potent rationale for inaction in contexts in which action might otherwise have seemed morally incumbent.[9] In the context of the intensifying violence in Syria over the course of the uprising, reasons for hunkering down and staying safe overwhelm. But at the beginning, this recourse to nonjudgment mattered, as we began to discuss in chapter 1. It put what came to be referred to as the "gray people" (*al-ramadiyyin*)—moderates or those in the "silent middle"—at odds with activists, and ultimately with the project of political transformation. Here we see an atmospherics of doubt nurturing a self-satisfied ambivalence, justifying political paralysis and withdrawal, particularly among the professional managerial elite and a subset of cultural producers. This variety of political resignation was an issue in the early years of Syria's neoliberal autocracy, as we saw in chapter 2 in reference to sanctioned comedies serving both to uphold the existing order and to incubate an oppositional consciousness. In the context of outright protest, the professional managerial elite's silence helped the regime navigate and prevail (at least at the time of this writing) amid the changing circumstances of its rule.

As the product of novel technologies of information dissemination *and* the not-new circumstances of war, this generalized uncertainty exists in the Syrian context alongside certainties that are well entrenched—sometimes cleaving along demographic lines and sometimes registering something more on the order of a mood or position within a single person. Moving beyond a commentary on the paradoxical effects of the so-called digital revolution,[10] the effort here is to demonstrate how the opening to cumulatively reflexive questioning in Syria, the supposed hallmark of the liberal public sphere which defined experiences of civic solidarity at the beginning of the uprising, got shut down as a form of *revolutionary mobilization*. Syrian activists were under no illusions as to whether the regime itself was liberal, and they were adept readers of the structuring guidelines for public speech and action that characterize autocratic rule. A great many Syrians did, however, share the expectation that their own work would help bring into being a world of public debate and reflection. This chapter is about those expectations and how they were stoked and then extinguished, managed and then deferred—or in some cases recalibrated in exile. It is also about the logics of autocratic retrenchment and the manner of their convergence with market mechanisms of social control.

PLATE 1. Hundreds of thousands of protesters gathered in Assi square (al-'Asi) in Hama in July 2011, calling for the downfall of Bashar al-Asad's regime. Hama is Syria's fourth-largest city and was a focal point of the uprising. As such, it is known for having the largest sustained peaceful demonstrations in the country.

PLATE 2. An iconic photo of first lady Asma' al-Asad as an exemplar of moral neoliberalism.

PLATE 3. The infamous *Vogue* article of March 2011 featuring Asma' al-Asad as "a rose in the desert." Photograph of the magazine courtesy of Lina Sergie Attar.

PLATE 4. A poster showing the repeated phrases "sectarian *fitna*" and "media incitement" and the repeated word *conspiracy* forming the shape of a handgun appeared at downtown Damascus bus stops in April–May 2011. It was sponsored by a small group of advertisers demonstrating their adherence to the official narrative of the rebellion. (See chapter 1.) Photograph courtesy of Yves Gonzalez-Quijano.

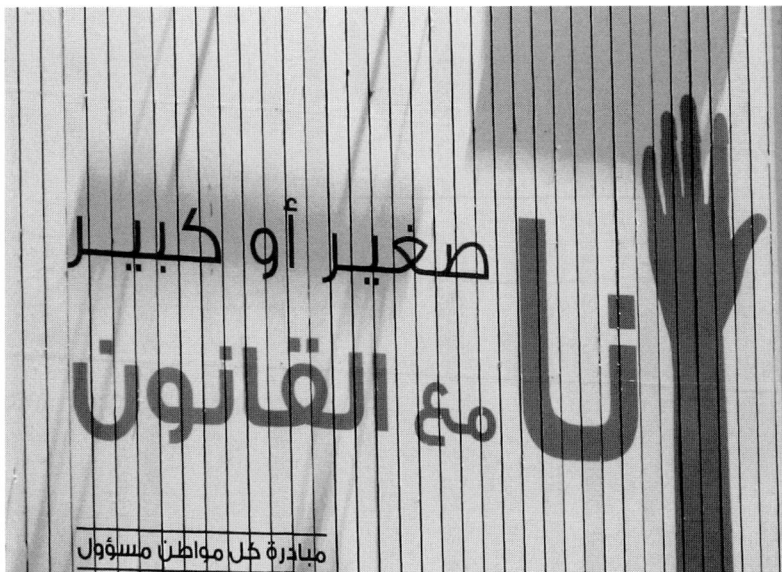

PLATE 5. "Big or small, I am with the law." A billboard in downtown Damascus that appeared in the spring of 2011 as part of the national "I am with the law" campaign. (See chapter 1.) Photograph courtesy of Donatella Della Ratta.

PLATE 6. One of 'Ali Farzat's most politically direct cartoons, depicting Bashar al-Asad hitching a ride from Libyan dictator Muammar Gaddafi (Mu'ammar al-Qaddafi) with the suited Syrian foreign minister Walid al-Mu'allim by his side. After it was published, Farzat was kidnapped, beaten, and left by the road-side on August 25, 2011—an act many believe was the regime's response to the cartoon's recognizable representation of Asad and the obvious suggestion that the Syrian leader's fate was linked to the Libyan's. (Gaddafi was already on the run at the time but was killed soon after, in October 2011.) Farzat survived the attack and now lives in exile. Reprinted with permission from Farzat.

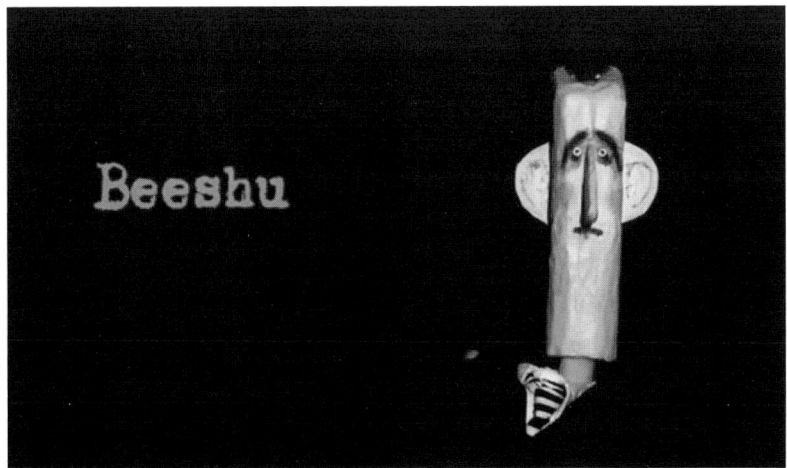

PLATE 7. Title frame from the televised finger-puppet show *Top Goon: Diaries of a Little Dictator* by the group Masasit Mati. The series was a favorite among opposition-oriented Syrians and foreigners. "Beeshu" is a disparaging nickname for Bashar al-Asad. (See chapter 2.)

PLATE 8. A typical classroom wall at a school for Syrian refugees in the Turkish province of Hatay, near the Syrian border, December 2013. In addition to the photos of a swan and a kitten are children's drawings of the flags of the Syrian uprising and of Turkey. Also on the wall: images of the nationalist hero and minister of war Yusuf al-'Azma, who died during the French invasion in 1920; the "martyred" Free Syrian Army soldier, Abu Furat; and thirteen-year-old Hamza al-Khateeb (al-Khatib), whose death under torture in Dar'a became a rallying cry for protesters. Photograph by the author.

بالصور.. عرسٌ سوري وسط الدمار يثير الجدل
hespress.com

... دمروا حمص وجلسوا
zamanalwsl.net

مشاهد عرس وسط الدمار- إحياء للأمل أم ...
dw.com

بالصور.. ضابط وعروسه على أطلال الدمار ...
enabbaladi.net

مشاهد عرس وسط الدمار- إحياء للأمل أم ...
dw.com

... i24 - فنانون سوريون يستوحون اعمالهم
i24news.tv

PLATE 9. Wedding photographs taken amid the destruction in Homs became popular among regime loyalists from late 2012 onward.

PLATE 10. The *shabbiha*, or regime thugs. (See chapter 5.) In the background is a picture of the regime-favored version of the Syrian flag behind images of a young Bashar (*left*); his father, Hafiz, the previous president (*center*); and his notorious brother, Maher al-Asad (*right*), current commander of the Republican Guard and the Fourth Armored Division.

PLATE 11. The Arabic in this image reads: "the time of manliness and men"; *rujula* (manliness) can also be translated as "bravery" or "courage." A woman can be courageous but would not be described as having *rujula*, which comes from the word for "man," *rajul*. The Russian at the bottom of the image has a slightly different valence: *muzhestvo* means "courage" and can be used for both sexes, although it can be deployed narrowly to connote manliness or manhood. So the Russian seems to underscore the manliness of the situation by adding the adjective *real* to *men*: "the time of courage and real men" (*nastoiashchix muzhchii*). The image, with a recognizably old-style Ba'th Party aesthetic, appears to have been originally affixed to a wall, but it has subsequently circulated in digital form on social media websites and in online newspaper articles. (See chapter 5.) Thanks are owed to Anya Bernstein for help with the Russian.

PLATE 12. An online image posted by the loyalist website SyrianFreePress.net conveys a familiar Ba'thist Party aesthetic and celebrates Syrian patriotism in a more encompassing way than *shabbiha* allegiance. The Arabic reads: "Syria: the army and the people together, hand in hand, fighting terrorism and building the Syria of tomorrow."

In contrast to one common conception of authoritarianism, in which it is the withholding of information that enables domination, Syria exemplifies an excess of information and accelerated conditions of dissemination being exploited for authoritarian political gain.[11] But the Syrian case does more than that. It invites a renewed exploration of the always fragile relation between truth and politics, exposing in particular how the specter of immediate danger works when danger has in fact become immediate. By way of getting at these matters, I want to unpack two exemplary moments. The first involves a controversy that arose concerning the mystery of who might have been responsible for the murder in Hama of a prominent local singer whose mutilated body had been left on the bank of the Orontes River, presumably as a warning to activists—unless, that is, the victim was someone else entirely, or, as was conceivable at one point in the narrative's unfolding, no one had been murdered at all. The story marks an important turn in the uprising, when it became apparent that activist expressions of countrywide solidarity, outrage, and creativity were starting to encourage forms of rhetorical overreach, exaggeration, a willingness to rush to judgment, and the bringing to expression of clear political positions with only the murkiest of facts.

The second moment is the seemingly incommensurable example of the chemical weapons attack in eastern al-Ghouta in August of 2013, a devastating event in which the "evidence" seemed to be pointing in different directions, stirring a global debate among politicians, activists, and scientists weighing in on what actually may have happened and who was to be held accountable. These conflicting accounts in the Western press also circulated in Syria, where they were often translated into Arabic or excerpted in Arabic on Twitter and Facebook. At the same time, local eyewitness accounts, rumors, and images appearing on Arabic websites were being translated into English and circulated accordingly. The result was to polarize Syrians whose positions were already firm, even while intensifying uncertainty for others less sure of their commitments. Bringing these two examples together allows us to see in events local and world historical the ongoing speculative reproduction of an affective and epistemic insecurity, the operation of which conduced to favor the beleaguered Asad regime's counterinsurgency project—or at least its survival.

Throughout, the chapter is informed by the thinking of Hannah Arendt and Ludwig Wittgenstein. In the closing pages, I put Syrian artists whose current work unsettles the conventions of documentary representation into conversation with these two theorists, drawing out mutual points of relevance for our understanding of politics in the local Syrian as well as the more global present. I argue that these artistic efforts bypass the impasse produced by an intensified atmospherics of doubt. In an overly saturated information environment, no preponderance of evidence becomes credible enough to convince those whose minds are already made up that an alternative account is the right one. Nor does more or better information serve to allay the ambivalence of those in the "gray area," whose ideological investments become framed by forms of nonjudgment encapsulated by the phrase "I know very well, yet nevertheless . . ." My contention here is that by working orthogonally, artists like those of the Syrian collective Abounaddara acknowledge uncertainty without succumbing to political paralysis—allowing ambiguity, contingency, and competing views to thrive, and thereby reopening possibilities for political judgment—for the considered reflection and ongoing assessment of complex political circumstances.

ATMOSPHERICS OF DOUBT

In the early days of the uprising, an anti-Asad song emerged that became a political phenomenon, recorded on cell phones and uploaded on YouTube. Marked by a catchy rhythm, the song, "Yalla Irhal Ya Bashshar!" (also noted in chapter 2), had simple rhyming lyrics enjoining Syria's president to step down and leave the country.[12] Stanzas opened and closed with the repeated chorus "Go on, leave, O Bashar" (Yalla irhal ya Bashshar), invoking familiar allegations of first-family corruption. The song also referenced such events as the deployment against protesters of an elite military formation led by the president's brother, Maher. In reproducing slogans from other parts of the country (including "O Bouthaina, O Shaʿban, the Syrian people are not hungry" [Ya Buthayna, wa ya Shaʿban, al-shaʿb al-Suri mu juʿan]), the song conjured up historical references of betrayal by the regime, as when, under Hafiz al-Asad, soldiers were abandoned in the Golan during the October War of 1973. And it offered rejoinders to the president's own public declarations: Bashar's actions after his speech to parliament on March 30, 2011, made him "a liar"; contrary to a statement by the president, citizens were not "germs" (*jarathim*) infesting the body politic. Exhilarating in its irreverence, with crude insults leveled directly at Bashar, his notoriously brutal brother, and his venal cousin, the song was at once angry and joyful, challenging the self-evidence of tyranny while paying homage to lives lost. By performing a newfound sense of solidarity, the lyrics invited popular participation, which came in the form of extemporaneous add-ons expanding and adapting the song—giving license to each singer, writer, and listener to act in concert with the acoustics of revolutionary change. The proliferating stanzas surpassed the abstractions of the typical, more elitist political songs, not only perpetuating defiance but working to air publicly what had hitherto been predominantly private grievances.[13] They also beckoned diverse areas of the country to share emerging details, alerting others to specific injustices and making them common knowledge. Moreover, the repeated recourse to the straightforward imperative ("Go on, leave") and to the proper nouns of failed leadership summoned into being cross-class identifications, a soundscape of national solidarity untethered to the regime's official discourses—literally giving voice to the potentiality of the protesting crowd.

Initially, it was widely thought that the song's original singer had been one Ibrahim Qashush, a firefighter in Hama thought to perform occasionally with another local, 'Abd al-Rahman Farhud, or, as he was more popularly known, Rahmani (or Rahmuni).[14] On July 4, 2011, Qashush reportedly turned up dead, his corpse left on the bank of the Orontes River with the larynx carved out. Many understandably interpreted the murder in terms of the crude symbolism, presumed at the time to have been the work of regime thugs bent on punishing the subversive singer in the most graphic way possible.

In making these assumptions, people were probably wrong. First of all, the singer of the song was likely Rahmani, not Qashush; and Qashush, far from being a beloved singer of subversive tunes, may have been a police informant. In likely being mistaken about who Qashush was and what role he may have played in the events in question, a multitude of Facebook postings, featuring new songs and videos made after his supposed demise, ended up paying tribute to a possible double-crosser—whose body it may or may not have been that was found by the side of the river missing its larynx. Moreover, as suspicions spread that Qashush was guilty of traitorous complicity, whether responsibility for the mutilated corpse lay with regime thugs was also cast into doubt. Stories quickly emerged claiming that vigilante activists had executed Qashush (or someone else) for collaboration.[15] Finally, as if scripted, sightings of Qashush surfaced in 2013, accompanied by articles and Facebook photos attesting to his continued well-being in exile and culminating in a *GQ* article in 2016. This piece, reported a few days later in Arabic, purported to reveal that the "real singer" was not Qashush but Rahmani—the latter still alive and well in Spain. The article stated that Qashush had, in fact, been slain on the bank of the Orontes River, and had been a guard (not a firefighter) at the fire station. He was not the singer of revolutionary songs or, for that matter, any songs at all.[16] The article dealt with issues ranging from the circulation of rumors to sins of omission (by both Rahmani and opposition outlets); an effort by the late Anthony Shadid of the *New York Times* to report the factual truths; and tellingly, the failure of Shadid's story to "stick" in the context of the "avalanche of new media propaganda."[17] The Qashush story thus exemplifies a conflict in which truth claims, rather than accumulating in a collection of established facts, recall something more like a shifting kaleidoscope of putative alternatives—registering both the uprising's complexities *and* the multiple efforts to paper over them.

The regime not only helped produce these conditions of uncertainty— for example, by barring professional journalists from entering the country—but also repeatedly capitalized on them, seizing on moments of exaggeration and misrepresentation to discredit opposition positions, polarize communities of argument, and disorient worlds in which truth claims might have led to action. That is, the regime's advantage lay not in its exercise of strict control over an ideological state apparatus but in *not* having to be believable in order to be powerful. From the inception of the uprising, the burden of proof lay always on activists taking the moral high ground—in calling for an end to tyranny and advocating for dignity and a civil state. Citizen journalists bore the onus of offering a discursive corrective to autocratic dissembling, whether in the blatantly fictitious terms reminiscent of Hafiz al-Asad's cult of personality or in the subtler forms of market-oriented spin characterizing the urbane élan of the son and the glamorous first lady.

Especially illustrative of this structural asymmetry is a short interview aired on the Arabic-language television show *The Truth about Syria*, broadcast in 2012 by the regime channel Al-Suriya. Entitled "The Truth about Ibrahim Qashoush," the segment featured a young man from Hama, Fadi Zurayq, whose look—longish hair, full beard, and stylish T-shirt—signaled hip. Clearly knowledgeable about media and about the situation in Hama, Zurayq described Qashush as just an "ordinary" person, not the heroic crooner-activist martyred for singing revolutionary songs. Bemoaning the media's "exploitation" of events, he repeated the claim that Qashush had nothing whatsoever to do with the songs, that he was the murdered man but not for any revolutionary activism. Rather, it was "armed" men in the opposition who did the deed, motivated by Qashush's association with security forces.[18]

Rewind to autumn 2011. It turns out that this same Zurayq had already appeared on the same regime television channel a year before the murder, speaking (in what may or may not have been a forced confession) about his own contributions to the "lies and fabricated videos" being broadcast in opposition media with funding from Qatar and Saudi Arabia. In a technologically amped-up, more intimate talk show version of the classic show trial, Zurayq reproduced the regime's position that the uprising stemmed in fact from a conspiracy by "Wahhabis and Zionists to destabilize Syria."[19] That the Zurayq spectacle was orchestrated was never in question, but whether it had been compelled was another. As one Syrian analyst-activist puts it, "These interviews were staged for sure. This guy Zraik [sic] could be someone who works for the Syrian intelligence and he volunteered to confess to the camera. So he was paid to say these things. Or he was threatened like many others to say these things on camera."[20] The interviewer, 'Ala' Al-Din Al-Ayyubi, was already known to Syrian viewers for his long-running weekly series, *The Police in the Service of the People* (*Al-shurta, fi khidmat al-sha'b*), an homage to the regime's version of national order, in which the interchanges were scripted—and widely understood to be.[21]

Zurayq's confession (if that's what it was), as well as countless other ones like it, also dealt in resonant historical images of alleged conspiracy in Hama, where in 1982 the regime had massacred anywhere from five thousand to twenty thousand people, thereby putting an end to a rebellion led by the Muslim Brotherhood. These public confessions signaled anew the regime's strategy of using fictions to enforce obedience. And here, too, as in the past, the regime and its purportedly errant subjects could be reunited under a ruling ideology in which the guiding ideal of modernist progress entailed lip service to historical reason, such that the accused's admission of betrayal was the condition of being accepted back into the collective folds of the nation.[22] But now the circumstances of resistance were different, not least because the regime was battling both a technologically savvy opposition and the broader appeal of the 2011 protests, in contrast to resistance organized through clandestine cells in the pre-internet days of the late 1970s and early 1980s.[23] This surplus of revolutionary exuberance in the present had to be quashed. Or to use Émile Durkheim's phrase, the "collective effervescence" of the crowd had to be flattened.[24] In pursuing this task, the regime deployed its media resources to resecure national unity, in idealized terms if not in fact, through the recognition of and address to multiple audiences, including loyalists worried about changes to the status quo and ambivalent citizens of various stripes (including nationalists and secularists)—anyone anxious about the erosion of national sovereignty in the form of outside intervention.[25]

The show also served as a warning to would-be opposition-oriented viewers who could be discouraged from joining the protests by imagining the consequences—all too embodied in the image of the distressed young man confessing to his involvement in terrorism. In giving the impression of a throwback show trial, the interview operated in excess of a show of force, underscoring how the regime could get away with the hoax, whereas the opposition continually faltered in its inability to construct a common world based on factual consensus, a democratic counterpart, if you will, to the obsolete version of modernism's historical reason.[26]

Ludwig Wittgenstein teaches us that "the *truth* of certain empirical propositions belongs to our frames of reference. When we first begin to believe anything, what we believe is not a single proposition, it is a whole system of propositions. . . . It is not single axioms that strike me as obvious, it is a system in which consequences and premises give one another *mutual* support."[27] What we are seeing in Syria is the collapse of these frames of reference, and with it the annihilation of truth, in Wittgenstein's sense— not the truth of philosophical a priori principles but the political truth of empirical propositions, by which I mean what counts for purposes of politics and political discourse as matters of fact. Wittgenstein's insistence that what allows our beliefs to make sense is the relational system in which they are embedded points to the difficulty involved in judging evidence or ascertaining the nature of truth claims circulating in Syria's "media wars" since the uprising began in March 2011. In this respect, the story of Qashush is more than an isolated incident of mistaken identity. The mystery about who might have murdered a well-known singer or indeed whether he was a well-known singer or even killed, his contradictory deployment as a symbol of oppositional courage and regime brutality, and then later as a symbol of regime co-optation and opposition revenge—all this is but a single complex example, both symptomatic of and contributing to an entire economy of uncertainty, which works to dilute moral outrage among addressees who otherwise might be available for political activation. This economy of uncertainty causes political judgments to come unmoored from the very conceptual systems in which they are situated.

In this context, the curious lack of follow-up articles and interest by opposition activists initially so invested in the song and in the purported singer's purported murder could be read ungenerously as indicating a cover-up of journalistic failings. Or it could be seen as symptomatic of reading and writing habits cultivated in conditions of high-speed eventfulness and information overload. But this silence relative to the commotion caused by the initial discovery of the corpse by the river also speaks to a collective disappointment born from the uprising's ongoing-ness, the forms of depredation that have squelched revolutionary exhilaration. The song had originally beckoned ordinary people to take part in something momentous, to participate in events charged with the embrace of political responsibility, to sing what they meant. New forms of sociality made possible in the moment, the resonances embodied in the musical invitation to action, and the fleeting sense of political promise worked together to summon into being what Kathleen Stewart in a different context calls "a solid ephemerality," a sense of something graspable, temporary, promising—a potential something.[28] This potentiality is precisely what had dissipated even before questions of mistaken identity or sightings of a healthy Qashush made their lackluster appearance. The revolutionary *idea* of Qashush had already "been assassinated," as one activist put it, taken down not only *in* conditions of uncertainty but, I want to argue, in part *by* them.[29]

POLITICAL IMPASSE

Few would disagree that the chemical weapons attack in eastern al-Ghouta on the outskirts of Damascus was a devastating event. My purpose in revisiting the incident of August 21, 2013, here is to extend our exploration of the work uncertainty does by considering a case that dramatizes how the whirl of excessive information interfered with revolutionary forms of political activation, calling into question prevailing relational systems and their frames of reference. A pared-down time line of the attack looks like this: In the early morning of August 21, Syrians on the ground began to report mysterious deaths in that area. Stories of children whose faces had turned blue, who were foaming at the mouth, or who had stopped breathing; entire families discovered dead; and still other civilians who suddenly fell ill began to circulate on social media, with eyewitness accounts proliferating as the day went on. On August 24, Doctors without Borders confirmed that on the twenty-first, staff had observed at least 355 deaths from "neurotoxic symptoms" at three medical centers in eastern Damascus. On August 25, regime forces agreed to a cease-fire to allow inspectors from the United Nations, already in Syria examining cases of an earlier alleged use of chemical weapons, to conduct on-site investigations; these took place during a series of five-hour periods from August 26 to 29.[30]

It was during this period of cease-fires that US secretary of state John Kerry issued a statement seeming to commit the United States to some form of direct military intervention against the regime, which in Kerry's narrative was the undoubted perpetrator of the atrocity. Unsurprisingly, given recent instances of high-level US officials lying to the American public and in testimony before the UN Security Council, Kerry's statement would itself generate doubts and speculation about cynical US motivations. It was in attempting to forfend just such a reaction that Kerry appealed to moral conscience and common sense as evidentiary supplements to empirical facts "on the ground":

> Anyone who can claim that an attack of this staggering scale could be contrived or fabricated needs to check their conscience and their own moral compass. What is before us today is real, and it is compelling. So I also want to underscore that while investigators are gathering additional evidence on the ground, our understanding of what has already happened in Syria is grounded in facts informed by conscience and guided by common sense. The reported number of victims, the reported symptoms of those who were killed or injured, the firsthand accounts from humanitarian organizations on the ground like Doctors without Borders and the Syria Human Rights Commission [sic]—these all strongly indicate that everything these images are already screaming at us is real, that chemical weapons were used in Syria. . . . And with our own eyes, we have all of us become witnesses. We have additional information about this attack, and that information is being compiled and reviewed together with our partners, and we will provide that information in the days ahead. Our sense of basic humanity is offended not only by this cowardly crime but also by the cynical attempt to cover it up. At every turn, the Syrian regime has failed to cooperate with the UN investigation, using it only to stall and to stymie the important effort to bring to light what happened in Damascus in the dead of night. And as Ban Ki-moon said last week, the UN investigation will not determine who used these chemical weapons, only whether such weapons were used—a judgment that is already clear to the world.[31]

This statement was translated into Arabic and circulated widely through multiple media, within Syria and across the Middle East.

Despite Kerry's insistence on certainty, or perhaps in some instances because of it, what was supposedly "already clear to the world" became increasingly difficult to discern amid the inundation of claims and counterclaims prompted by the secretary of state's statement. And the more information that emerged, the more uncertainty it seemed to generate both in and outside Syria. Some reports basically confirmed Kerry's allegations—using eyewitness accounts, relying on the circulation of information and images on social media sites, and producing a plethora of articles translated from Arabic into English and vice versa.[32] Other reports attempted to complexify what counted as the Syrian regime. An example here would be Phil Sands's article in the Abu Dhabi daily *The National*, claiming the following:

There were indications that some of the army officers involved had tried to distance themselves from what happened, and insisted they were not told the rockets they were firing were loaded with toxins. "We have heard from people close to the regime that the chemical missiles were handed out a few hours before the attacks," said a source from a well-connected family, with contacts both with the opposition and with regime loyalists. "They didn't come from the Ministry of Defence but from air force intelligence, under orders from Hafez Makhlouf [a relative of President Asad's]. The army officers are saying they did not know there were chemical weapons. Even some of the people transporting them are saying they had no idea what was in the rockets—they thought they were conventional explosives."[33]

Similarly, *Foreign Policy* registered both the Asad regime's culpability and its simultaneous fragmentation in a blog post entitled "Exclusive: Intercepted Calls Prove Syrian Army Used Nerve Gas, U.S. Spies Say." According to the article, "In the hours after a horrific chemical attack east of Damascus, an official at the Syrian Ministry of Defense exchanged panicked phone calls with a leader of a chemical weapons unit, demanding answers for a nerve agent strike that killed more than 1,000 people." That conversation was reportedly intercepted by US signals intelligence and then leaked to the press.[34] References to this article made the rounds in Arabic-language publications even five years later.

As early as a week later, however, a counternarrative began to emerge, one that placed ultimate accountability with the opposition.[35] As 'Adnan 'Ali in the opposition-oriented magazine *Al-Jadid* pointed out in a 2016 article looking back on the massacre, the regime typically operates in ways consonant with such a dynamic: it first denies that anything has happened; then, when news stories attesting to the occurrence of an event overwhelm, it fabricates evidence and manipulates images to blame the opposition for what has occurred.[36] Although early reports accusing the opposition of the chemical attack seemed to lack the authority or credibility of sources like the ones holding the regime to account, they nevertheless became increasingly susceptible to uptake. These latter reports were less a way of anchoring an alternative certainty than of questioning the empirical propositions on which existing frames of reference relied. One article, appearing on the strident, conspiracy-oriented MintPress News website, was supposedly penned by frequent Associate Press contributor Dale

Gavlak and Yahya Ababneh, the latter a self-professed Jordanian freelancer and actor (!) identified as on the ground in Syria. It claimed Saudi and, by extension, opposition involvement in the attack. Perhaps because it was relying on exchanges in internet chat rooms that were also foregrounding conspiracies, key details were left obscure in the MintPress story, but the allegation seems to have been that Prince Bandar bin Sultan, the Saudi intelligence chief, provided weapons to a Saudi militant named Abu Ayesha. Rebels, whose factional identification was not provided, were supposedly unaware that it was chemical weapons they were storing in tunnels in al-Ghouta.[37]

The story circulated widely, discussed in Arabic on "global research" websites and on additional ones that provided translations of Russia Today (RT) internet articles,[38] as well as on Military.com, Voice of Russia, Consortiumnews, and in the Spanish newspaper *ABC*, to name a few news outlets. Further obscuring matters, the pro-opposition media phenomenon and amateur scientist known initially under the pseudonym Brown Moses (and subsequently as Eliot Higgins, his actual name) later published on his blog Gavlak's denial that she had been involved in writing the article; the *New York Times* followed up with an account that also raised questions about MintPress's journalistic practices and the source of its financial backing.[39] Yet despite Gavlak's disavowal and the suspicions about MintPress's agenda, the report of the Saudi conspiracy continued to spread, picked up (and Gavlak's Associated Press connections exploited) in additional parts of the Arabic-language press and in conversations among ordinary Syrians—both inside the country and in exile.[40] Some expressed uncertainty about who was behind the attacks; others engaged in heated exchanges of polarized beliefs; and still others justified inaction or suspended judgment on the grounds that the truth of what happened was impossible to know.[41]

The story took a technical turn on September 4, 2013, with the publication of an article in the comparatively reputable (if sometimes wrong) *New York Times*. Entitled "Rockets in Syrian Attack Carried Large Payload of Gas, Experts Say," the report drew on a study by Richard M. Lloyd, an "expert in warhead design," and Theodore A. Postol, a physics professor at MIT.[42] The study promised a scientific resolution of the accountability question by addressing a previously unnoted problem at the heart of the investigation: how could what were initially thought to be rockets with minimal carrying capacity deliver enough gas to kill so many people over such a large area? Like Higgins in basing their analysis on photographs publicly available on the internet, Lloyd and Postol drew the conclusion that the munition in question was designed to carry "about 50 liters (13 gallons), not the one or two liters (about half a gallon) of nerve agent that some weapons experts had previously estimated."[43] The question of the quantity of gas involved in the attack was significant, because it raised technical issues about prevailing US government assertions of clear-cut culpability. Lloyd claimed that the opposition, not just the regime, had the capacity to manufacture the rockets used, while admitting that it remained unclear (at the time) how the rebels might have acquired that much nerve agent (again, as reported in the *Times*). Other experts interviewed were explicit about their doubts that the opposition could have acquired so much gas, thereby advocating on behalf of the opposition but producing an even greater sense of uncertainty that largely benefited the regime.[44] Subsequently, Lloyd and Postol published a second report, this time casting doubt on UN and US calculations of rocket trajectories rather than carrying capacity, and further generating skepticism about the regime's role in the attack. Based on photographs of the remains of what appears to have been the wreckage of rockets that had delivered the toxic nerve gas to al-Ghouta on August 21, Lloyd and Postol argued in this second report that *had* the rockets been launched from regime-held territory, they could not have flown far enough to have reached the target. All these findings appeared also in Arabic translation. As C. J. Chivers of the *New York Times* wrote in a sober update in December 28, 2013, "The new analysis [of Postol and Lloyd] could point to particular Syrian military units involved, or be used by defenders of the Syrian government and those suspicious of the United States' claims to try to shift blame toward rebels."[45]

Memorable among those participating in what became a lively discursive jostling, with high-stakes consequences bearing on foreign direct military intervention and thus on regime survival, was the Syrian presidential spokesperson Bouthaina Sha'ban. In a statement given on September 4 to Sky News (in English and then reiterated on many Arabic-language sites), Sha'ban held the opposition responsible for the attack.[46] "They kidnapped children and men from the villages of Lattakia and they brought them here, put them in one place, and used chemical weapons against them. That's the story that the villagers in these villages know." In this narrative, the ones killed were by implication 'Alawis from areas supportive of the regime, not the opposition. By concocting a narrative that transports pro-regime victims to opposition territory, Sha'ban accounted for what would seem to be the central problem the regime had in telling its story: why opposition forces would victimize civilians in territories they controlled. Especially interesting in our context, however, is how Sha'ban, who had just offered "the villagers in these villages know" as definitive evidence for her claims, concluded: "But why don't you leave it to the UN Commission to investigate, to analyze?" Or again: "Western countries are always very scientific, they go by the law, they investigate. Why when it comes to something concerning our countries, they say 'it is believed that the Syrian government used chemical weapons'? Why don't you wait for the specific, scientific results of a neutral UN committee that is investigating?" The incoherence of her appeals and the sheer outlandishness of the story nevertheless produced its own rejoinders, including reports noting that the regime's kidnapping scenario would require a five-hour trip by a large caravan of buses passing unhindered and unnoticed through many checkpoints. In other words, the story could be simultaneously dismissed and addressed, with each new interpretation producing its own extended labor of fact-checking, efforts which themselves contributed to the work uncertainty does in turning what could be the object of ethical-political judgments into confusion—with implications for global actors as well.

One more aspect of Sha'ban's preposterous statement is worthy of note—namely, her appeal to science. And here, too, science worked less to establish truth (or falsify fallacious claims) than to convert what might have been provisionally consensual knowledge into entrenched political conviction, including the conviction that we can never know what happened. The scientific democratization of expression personified by Higgins could not override the views of experts like Lloyd and Postol, but those MIT-authorized scientists could do nothing more than produce knowledgeable speculations in a world saturated by claims at work reinstantiating communities of agreement already in place. These were not conspiracy theories of the caliber that Sha'ban and others brought to the fore, but their very existence as disagreements enabled those whose minds had been made up in advance of circulating evidence, which was itself confusing, to stay that way.[47]

US president Barack Obama's prime-time speech on September 10 and Russian president Vladimir Putin's *New York Times* op-ed the following day looked like a matched-set throwback to Cold War politics in which political posturing trumped all curiosity. Facts, already hard to adjudicate, became pared down to an acknowledgment that something bad had happened—a chemical attack—while attributions of responsibility broke along classic political fault lines, with Obama assuring the American people that the regime was behind the attack and Putin recommending caution by placing the blame on the opposition: "No one doubts that poison gas was used in Syria. But there is every reason to believe it was used not by the Syrian Army, but by opposition forces, to provoke intervention by their powerful foreign patrons, who would be siding with the fundamentalists. Reports that militants are preparing another attack—this time against Israel—cannot be ignored."[48] Putin's invocation of Israel may have been a cynical attempt to curry favor with American readers and their particular Middle Eastern commitments and anxieties. More interestingly, his closing rhetorical gambit provided a more plausible motive than Sha'ban's for why the rebels, if they were the ones accountable, had timed the attack when they did. In doing so, he demonstrated how privileged access to state knowledge (even when the specific knowledge of a case does not exist or is not supportive of the claims being made) can be used to convert uncertainty into an anxiety that then reproduces another set of certainties—that is, these militants must not be supported.

The UN's own authority as a fact-finding team and its careful language regarding what it could and could not ascertain was undercut by past mistakes. Its reputation as a partial international body, as opposed to an objective arbiter of truth claims, produced doubts about its conclusions—as tenuous and as carefully worded as they were. And in some cases, appeals to science and skepticism about the UN's neutrality could converge, as in MIT researcher Subrata Ghoshroy's September 26 analysis, "Serious Questions about the Integrity of the UN Report."[49] Ghoshroy charged that there had been "communication between the UN team and the analysts outside, which prejudiced the UN's report." That report supposedly confirmed various aspects of the divergent analyses by Lloyd and Postol and by Eliot Higgins. Additional expert assessments were released after the end of the UN inspection but before the publication of the UN's report, suggesting some sort of leak. Ghoshroy continued, "Secretary of State John Kerry dismissed the UN inspectors as irrelevant because they would not bring to light any new information that the US did not already know. He was right. The purpose of my analysis is not to prove or disprove anything. The sole purpose is to raise questions about the integrity of the UN team's report. Decisions on war and peace depend on it." He also accused Higgins of "interspersing" photographs and video from another area where a chemical attack had occurred with images of the massacre in al-Ghouta, not to demonstrate that the same sorts of munitions were used in both cases, but to deliberately "mislead" the reader.[50] Ghoshroy's accusation should recall for us Errol Morris's insights into how "seeing is believing": because we know imagery is manipulated, because we can imagine it to be, or because we have difficulty accommodating cognitive dissonance.

The December appearance of "Whose Sarin?" in the *London Review of*

Books raised additional doubts. In this investigative report counteracting Obama administration claims, Seymour Hersh contended that the president "failed to acknowledge something known to the US intelligence community: that the Syrian army is not the only party in the country's civil war with access to sarin, the nerve agent that a UN study concluded—without assessing responsibility—had been used in the rocket attack." Faulting various studies circulating online and through conventional news channels, Hersh maintained that it was known that the opposition force and Al-Qa'ida affiliate Jabhat al-Nusra had access to the necessary ingredients to make sarin and had demonstrated interest in using it.[51] In a follow-up piece published in April 2014, Hersh went further, suggesting that Turkey was in fact behind the al-Ghouta attacks.[52] These claims then showed up in Arabic-language media, and made up the bulk of what a reader received when she Googled in Arabic (in Chicago but also Beirut), "Who is responsible for the Ghouta chemical weapons attack?"[53] This remained the case until April 2017, when arguably, the attack on Khan Sheikhoun (Khan Shaykhun), the most devastating one since 2013, supplanted queries about responsibility for the earlier massacre. And importantly, a similar logic of regime denial characterized this attack—sowing doubts about the timing of chemical spread, alleging doctored images of damage, and shifting ultimate responsibility to the opposition by claiming that the devastation was not caused by an "air launched chemical attack."[54] Aided in pronounced form by Russian allies claiming that the deadly chemicals were dispersed as a consequence of a preemptive strike on a munitions factory controlled by the opposition group Hay'at Tahrir al-Sham (previously known as Jabhat al-Nusra), the regime could reproduce ambivalence among those who remained uncertain about the murky facts while stoking loyalist claims. Ardent supporters, like official Russian statements, came to justify the attack on the grounds that the opposition would have otherwise used these weapons against innocent civilians. Reliance on a form of hypothetical, anticipatory reasoning to explain state violence, as we shall see in different form in chapter 5, has been a strategy of regime management from the start.[55]

Moreover, the still-popular question of who is responsible for these attacks and so many others like them is made to order for conspiracy theories. Conspiracy theorists view seemingly disparate happenings as connected, as intentional products of a force whose interests are ultimately served by and organized through another's victimization or ruin.[56] And they are not always wrong. Hersh's investigation into the 2013 attack was potent because it was plausible. So, too, were reports suggesting that Hersh was hoodwinked by his contacts in the Pentagon—to help avoid direct military intervention or to limit the US mission to eliminate the Islamic State.[57] In structuring arguments in terms of what some scholars have termed a "paranoid" functionalism that posits effects as the product of purpose,[58] the question Who is responsible for the chemical weapons attack? is easily harnessed to a familiar regime narrative of national vulnerability and threat—in which the "national" becomes, once again, coterminous with regime oriented.

Questions of "who is behind" a specific act need not reduce to a conspiratorial narrative, of course. For others, the very posing of the question conveyed a sense of collaborative unknowability, in which doubt could modulate affective registers like outrage and disgust along with the political judgments that might ensue. Phrasing like the following was typical: "The chemical weapons attack was sickening. But who was responsible? Was the regime really worse than the opposition? They were both awful, of course." The regime and opposition groups could plausibly deny responsibility—at least for those open to skepticism. It was not simply that camps were polarized, with staunch loyalists and people in the "gray area" following regime-oriented sites and tracking investigative reports such as Hersh's, while official opposition sources called for US intervention because the regime clearly had "crossed [Obama's] red line." As young people identified with the uprising became increasingly disillusioned by both regime and opposition, as the impossibility of adjudicating truth claims came to apply to virtually continuous acts of unspeakable cruelty, some in exile sought to redefine and radicalize the terms of debate, conceding to a situation in which facts were especially vulnerable—and everyone might lie. A surplus of information, even better information, did not necessarily lead to truth, it turned out. Circulating truth claims were vulnerable to counterspin from the get-go, generating difficulties of adjudication that augured poorly for the establishment of anything like a democratic or revolutionary consensus. A combination of autocratic politics, outside intervention, and high-speed news dissemination had worked to cultivate forms of uncertainty that were unlikely to be resolved by any amount of reporting that accords with standards of journalistic evidence suitable for political deliberation. In conditions of violence and discursive disorientation, the very conceptual projects of verifiability, eyewitness reporting, and objectivity had themselves become grist for the mill. And meanwhile, more people had died—impervious to the technical debates and political posturing of all involved.

The loss in Syria of what Hannah Arendt calls "a common world" is drama-tized by the relentless, soul-crushing violence, but it is also characterized by an atmospherics of doubt in which recourse is made to forms of cer-tainty that polarize some people based on what they think they already know while providing others with the grounds for disengagement and disavowal—in that they know that they do not know. Such a situation pro-foundly complicates possibilities for political judgment. We see in Syria today the constellation of mutually related rules, propositions, experi-ences, techniques of reasoning, everyday practices, and mental images through which we are "trained" to judge—in Ludwig Wittgenstein's sense—having been undermined by a world in which information is para-doxically both incomplete and overwhelming.

The Syrian experimental filmmaker Khalid ʿAbd al-Wahid captures this loss of a common world in his unreleased 2015 film, *Qanadil al-Bahr* (*Jelly-fish*), about four citizen journalists reflecting on their work covering the Syrian civil war. ʿAbd al-Wahid converses with them on camera about los-ing their reluctance to twist the truth, to stage scenes of disaster, victory, and solidarity, even to lie outright in the service of getting at what they understood at the time to be a more profound political truth—namely, that tyranny is wrong and must be abolished by any means possible. Now no longer certain that the ends justified the means, these citizen journalists recount how they learned to pander to donors in the United States and the Gulf, as well as to satellite television channels. Al-Jazeera, Al-Arabiya, and CNN, to name the obvious examples, were likely to ignore mundane oppo-sition experiments in municipal government, while they could be counted on to air dramatic images of suffering or a protest turned bloody. Some demonstrators in turn felt obliged for the sake of newsworthiness to carry signs thanking a network, and the citizen journalists zoomed in on the gestures of appreciation in hopes that doing so would cause their footage to be selected for broadcast.

The point of ʿAbd al-Wahid's film is not to "out" his interviewees as bad journalists but to depict a disorienting environment in which the factual has become so tenuous that the activist journalists whose sense of self-worth was once derived from responsibly disseminating facts lose the con-nection to what they want to say, winding up after many months in the field unable to recognize who they have become. This is not simply von Clausewitz's proverbial "fog of war," where military commanders know exactly what they would say given perfect information, which is made impossible by the fog. Rather, this is a condition in which what is lost is faith in the efficacy of what until then had been understood as valid informational currency. As Arendt acknowledges in her rich essay "Truth and Politics," the "politically most relevant truths are factual"[59]—and they are, as Linda Zerilli underscores, also the most imperiled, the most vulnerable to "human mendacity" and to the "pursuit of [narrow] political interests."[60] Politics is a domain of plural contingent opinions, argues Arendt, where the understanding of freedom is rooted in an appreciation of the human capacity for speech and other kinds of action. Intriguingly, even lying for Arendt is expressive of a kind of freedom, although it cannot be the freedom of an affirmative politics; for prerequisite to the political in a salutary sense is a contingent, open-to-revision factual truth-telling that helps establish a common world.[61] Wittgenstein shows us how such a world is made up of frames of reference that are subject to collapse. ʿAbd al-Wahid shares this appreciation, showing us the death of politics that occurs when a common world in formation is crushed by dissimulation and violence, leaving his once-committed journalists robbed not only of their message but of their sense of themselves as political actors.

The work of the anonymous film collective Abounaddara, made up of "self-taught and volunteer filmmakers" engaged in "emergency cinema," likewise suggests that when the conventions of the documentary are challenged, something radical or at least out of the ordinary might happen in their stead.[62] For the most part, the collective's short films hint at prospects that are left vaguely defined, gesturing toward experiences of self-assertion as well as of self-dissolution and unpredictability, offering accounts of events or situations in which there may be room for reclaiming judgment as a political activity. Take, for example, *In the Name of the Father* (2013), in which a woman whose aesthetic style recalls Syrian television stars, whose accent is Damascene, and whose sectarian affiliation is notably unclear invokes kinship to consider domestic political affairs anew. Drawing from people's presumed shared experience of intimacy, she tries to make the politically abstract meaningful by analogizing the politics of unseating leaders to what goes on in family life, using the idiom of kinship against its authoritarian invocation. As difficult as it is to risk severing connections to a father, she argues, ordinary families have arguments all the time. Carrying through on disagreements in the family tends to facilitate a generative forgetting, for in the context of a dispute between real fathers and children, the patriarchal dimension of the relationship can disappear:

Consider the family . . . I want to get to my father, to overthrow him. There are things I don't like . . . I can do that. It's not a question of father and daughter. When you disagree, you forget he's your father. Things come up and you forget that he's a father. I try my best with him so that he listens, understands, compromises. But maybe I end up overthrowing him. I'll tell him, "I no longer want you," and turn my back on him and leave. And with time, I've lost him. But he's finished; he's overthrown. Of course a father is always a father, but still, he's overthrown. And in a state, I can go to the polls and say, "I don't want you." I'm sure it will succeed. Why wouldn't it succeed? Why are they so confident that fear would lead people to elect [Asad]?[63]

Such moments of forgetting—willful or otherwise—raise possibilities. The woman beckons us to suspend our connection to authority in a way we already know how to do. Her metaphors of family life provide the viewer with an example of an iterative, ordinary context within which a scenario for enacting a new future of electoral contestation is imagined. Her invocation of familiar tropes of family are not harnessed to status quo stability, nor do they exactly justify rebellion. Indeed, elsewhere in the clip she is critical of the revolutionaries for not planning properly or failing to consider the ramifications of their actions.

In political theory as well as in various regime rhetorics, family metaphors are often invoked to represent idealized relations of domination and membership.[64] Groups of people are understood to be imagining themselves more or less unconsciously in a relation of kinship fealty to the leader. The woman in the film works with the complications introduced into fealty by bringing family into it—so that the metaphors serve equally to envisage the toppling of authority or the bolstering of it. She then adds, somewhat abruptly, that in the context of Syria, where the expectation is that people will vote for Asad out of fear, Syrians might be expected on some other basis to overcome their fear rather than act on it: just as a daughter can choose to set aside her filial role in the context of a disagreement, so, too, do elections allow voters to replace the father/leader. In this view, elections become the mechanism for a political "family romance," to recall Freud's felicitous term, rather than for revolutionary patricide; a medium for collective maturation.[65]

Appealing to the example of an ordinary family squabble on the one hand and to the extraordinariness (in the context of dictatorship) of liberal electoral proceduralism on the other, the woman's declaration is simultaneously one of self- and of political reinvention. But her appeal is also paradoxical, requiring a fantasy in temporal excess of the immediate substitution of better parents in the family romance while seeming more moderate than the radical patricidal one. The father figure in Syria's symbolic universe used to be Hafiz al-Asad, the now-deceased (but for activists revenant) patriarch who continues to haunt the uprising. She, by contrast, evokes the image of the son who (in that it is possible for him to be *advertised* as fatherly) was incorporated into a first-family mimesis that valorized celebrity shared parenting and modern intimacy. There is no national father exactly—and certainly there are no fair and free elections, so the woman's fantasy is a doubled one—announcing its impossibility formally (the leader is not the father; the elections that do exist are bogus) while at the same time insisting on its commonsense plausibility. Likewise, her fantasy of forgetting the father seems fantastical. Does her statement "Of course a father is always a father, but still, he's toppled" even make sense? Does it have to? It could, of course, mean that the figure of the father—as in Freud's parable of parricide—is fully internalized. Overthrown externally, reinstalled internally. The film invites this kind of reflection, demanding an interrogation of the family metaphor as an adequate stand-in for politics.

Formally, the film works to convey the same messages—with all their complications. The close shot confines all movement to within the female protagonist, for nothing else competes for the viewer's attention. There is no cut, no profile shot, and her forward-looking gaze is sovereign—already filmically displacing the fantasy sovereign leader: the daddy figure with whom an individual's disagreement can "over time" lead to a new political order, one in which, to pursue the metaphor, the unequal relations between adults and children are replaced by a collective of equal voter-siblings, as in the Freudian story. And although Abounaddara maintains the subject's anonymity, everything about her in the way of appearance and attitude suggests her identity as one of those termed *mu'atadilin*, or moderates. This was the term that for activists had pejorative connotations as belonging to the gray zone of officially tolerated, perhaps even sanctioned, "honorable opposition" (*al-mu'arada al-sharifa*). For activists, the third-way political positions, between loyalists on one side and activists on the other, whether registering ambivalence or confusion, was akin to a cop-out. But with this short film, the Abounaddara collective presents us with a portrait rather than an argument, a study in the incoherence of this woman's middle-of-the-road position *and*, at its most stretched, an invitation to seize a freedom we already understand how to enact.

By contrast to this brief, (provocatively) confusing portrait of moderation, *The Trajectory of an Unknown Soldier* (2012) is a four-part series of films chronicling the evolution of a soldier fighting for the opposition—his decomposition in the face of gruesome wartime intensities and his ultimate struggle (in part 4) to recalibrate his relation to the world.[66] Filmed showing the soldier in silhouette, the visual in-shadow effect not only protects his anonymity but underscores, like a photograph's negative, how light reveals darkness and darkness light. The clanging of unseen pots and pans contributes to a low-key, ambient ordinariness, the sound an invitation to reinhabit the familiar in marked contrast to the soldier's story of violence and, until part 4, despair. Part 1 establishes the soldier's first realization that he is capable of killing. Faced with the need to take another's life, he was scared, but he felt he had no choice. That refrain—that he had no choice—provides the central animating theme of the first part, a testimony to judgment's suspension or at least compromise, to the simultaneous recognition and evasion of responsibility, to an emotional catastrophe that leaves the social fabric torn. He had to protect his family. He knows it is wrong to kill. But he had no choice. He fears God, but he had no choice. The regime left him with no choice.

Part 2 describes his experience of entering a home and finding children who had been lying dead for some days. There is no obvious cause of death. The soldiers were looking for food and water and just happened into the dwelling. In describing his search through the house, he bears witness to a mother's love for the son she "holds against her"—both dead. He tells us that the buildings behind the house, where he and others had been fighting, were besieged by the regime army, and he cries as he recalls the terrifying experience, part of a relentless nightmare in Syria's central city of Homs. It is a war that is both disorienting and suffocating. The remaining inhabitants of that embattled area were "as afraid of us as they were of the Syrian [regime] army," he admits, wiping tears from his eyes and noting how "truly frightening" it was. Residents could not open a window for fear of being shot; there was literally and figuratively "no breathing allowed."

These two segments lead us to part 3, in which the soldier has become self-consciously "dissociated" or "split" (his word, inqisam, means both in Arabic) from himself. Here he recounts killing "someone" by cutting the person's throat. In the soldier's retrospective lamentation, he notes that while his body slaughtered the victim, his soul was crying. Later, in the film's present tense, he can scarcely imagine having done it. No level of resentment or desire for revenge can make that "legitimately right." We see here what in US parlance might be called "moral injury," in which violence does not offer cathartic release but damages the perpetrator, even one who can be seen to be rightfully pursuing revenge for wrongs done.[67] The filmic strategy is to narrate the dissociation while at the same time diagnosing it as such, to suture the diegetic and the extradiegetic in an effort to repair filmically what cannot be healed practically. Politically, the soldier begins by saying that he does not want to be like the other soldiers in the Free Syrian Army, an opposition military force. But then he confesses that he has indeed acted like them. This acting of the body in violation of the soul suggests a specific horror of wartime, an experience of splitting in which an otherwise moral self is cleaved from his orienting ethical world. His anonymity, like that of the victims he encounters, or the ones he kills—or Abounaddara's insistence on its anonymity as a collective, for that matter—suggests a kind of national substitutability, in which each soldier or victim is both fungible and exemplary, as is each director. This gesture of interchangeability also suggests an interpretive generosity in which the soldier appeals to multiple audiences, perhaps including regime soldiers themselves.

Part 4 shows the haunted soldier's effort to regain a sense of the world that might make politics possible again. He prays to God for a secular state, the seeming contradiction not really one at all but rather an assertion of the right to private piety and a public "civil state." He identifies himself as Sunni but champions a multisectarian Syria, claiming half-jokingly even to like "Christians more than Muslims." He is careful, when speaking of 'Alawis, to qualify his willingness to generalize by underscoring that it is only "some" 'Alawis that oppress. And he treats as ludicrously unpatriotic the idea that Syria would be "dismembered," carved up into sectarian enclaves. In short, he recovers himself by imagining politics that make good on the regime's vision of national integration and multisectarian accommodation—indulging in the hope that despite the bloodshed, or perhaps because of all the sacrifice, dictatorship can be, indeed must be, replaced with a liberal, tolerant, Asad-free nation-state. This hope is not offered in the register of the uprising's early days of exhilaration. The soldier is deflated, but not fully destroyed. And in his worries and wishes for Syria's future, there is something tentative and stale, exhausted.

But not only that. There is also an acknowledgment that any politics going forward will necessarily involve mutual engagement between those who fought for the regime and those who fought for the opposition. Broadcast in 2012, the soldier's address is shockingly early, for members of the opposition tended not to register criticisms of their own actions until 2014–15. That prescience is part of what makes the soldier's gesture of self-scrutiny so important. And although like the rest of the Abounaddara corpus its circulation was initially limited—the audience made up mainly of Western and Syrian intellectual types sharing an interest in activism and film—the short films live on, accessible on the website Vimeo to anyone who wants to watch and reflect. In making unfashionable judgments about the conflict, the soldier, like the collective, is therefore reproducing not only an ideology of multicultural accommodation. Both the film's protagonist and the filmmakers are modeling interpretive generosity toward adversarial counterparts (among activists and regime soldiers) in the apparent hopes of inducing reciprocity. In this effort at reciprocity is adumbrated an aspect of what Hannah Arendt calls "representative thinking," to be explored in detail in chapter 4.

For now, suffice it to say that as in the work of other filmmakers (particularly Khalid 'Abd al-Wahid, as noted above), an important aim in this film is to depict how the experience of war has caused the protagonists to cease to recognize themselves. Theirs was initially an ethical war, a war against tyranny; but in living it, their hopes have been mangled. They have become Other to themselves, having been forced to make choices their real selves would never have made. The promising possibilities of a common world put forward in the early days of the uprising have by now been crushed by violence and all its accompanying distortions. And the soldier, like the director, seems to be involved in a project of repair, reclaiming the human capacity for politics by turning to speech and repudiating violence. In a situation reminiscent of Isak Dinesen's purported observation (cited by Arendt), "All sorrows can be borne if you can put them into a story or tell a story about them."[68] And this quartet of films seems to be the soldier's attempt at restoration, at making himself whole once again in a context in which, as Wittgenstein writes, "consequences and premises have ceased to give one another mutual support."[69]

Experimenting with viewers' expectations about what documentary representation entails, Abounaddara's short film *Aïcha* (2014) highlights a theme that has appeared frequently in Syria's uprising: in the ideological struggle over who stands in for Syria, children are offered up as a vision of powerlessness and innocence in the face of the regime's brutality and cunning.[70] Since the uprising's inception, children have signaled the disruptions of generational change, unmet aspirations for the good life, and the affronts to dignity (*karama*; *karameh*) that the regime both committed and attempted to conceal. As a form of protest, Abounaddara has recently made an issue of opposing the circulation of images of overt cruelty. Films like the three discussed here are an alternative way of bearing the brutality by bearing witness—without conforming to the evidentiary logics of conventional documentary or portraying violence in a way that distracts from the possibility of politics.[71] The collective's campaign for the "right to the image" is its effort to recognize the fragile relation between images and political action, advocating on behalf of what it calls "dignified" depictions so as not to generate a pornographic-like pity that either takes unacknowledged pleasure in the suffering of others or invites viewers to become desensitized to violence through overiteration.

In the case of *Aïcha*, we are secondhand witnesses to the plausible reality that those who have lost the most are the displaced children, but here as well the film collective manages to avoid the kind of maudlin sentimentality (a theme discussed at length in chapter 4) that it generally repudiates. The absence of a soundtrack (save for the beat of drums), the grainy footage, and the correspondingly opaque political messages help forfend charges of melodrama and didacticism. Through the camera we see first a girl's back and then her face, and then we glimpse her in profile, watching her watch buskers drumming in Istanbul. Like her, we are bystanders to the event. But of course unlike her, we are free to lament her situation (or not) and go home, while she remains on the streets, marginal, unintegrated even into the ranks of the dispossessed. That she is Kurdish is one of the few bits of identifying information to be gleaned from the film's brief moments of dialogue, and the lack of integration has partly to do with that. For Syrians and others knowledgeable about the region, she can easily be read as being what Syrians call *dumari*, "gypsies" whose lives, even before the uprising, were those of itinerant workers—based on selling water and gum on the streets, doing day labor on farms, and begging. Or, among the semiskilled, offering services such as tooth extraction at a discount.[72]

Aïcha thus betrays another hallmark of Abounaddara's filmic strategy: to reproduce a sense of Syrian-ness reliant on a division between those who are in the know and those more casual viewers, between those with the knowledge to interpret the few signals provided and those who would need more context to fully understand. The scholar Edward Ziter argues that Abounaddara's "curating of hundreds of fragmentary portraits is itself a project of national becoming," an act of performativity whose aspiration is to summon into existence a national community. He writes, "The project would seem to announce, 'Follow our Friday uploads, not so as to discern who we are but to help imagine who we might become.'"[73] In this sense, Abounaddara's short films are also experimental—trying out forms of national representation that are fragmentary and incoherently related to one another, in sharp contrast to the regime's muscular insistence on national indivisibility and a discursive "correct line."

There is something refreshing about this effort, but it is not without its limitations. Any viewer can appreciate the aesthetics and variation in Abounaddara's corpus, but much of the nuance of any of its short films' content requires a local knowledge that only Syrians or Syria specialists are likely to possess. At a 2015 event at the New School's Vera List Center for Art and Politics celebrating the collective's contributions to human rights, unknowing film scholars repeatedly lauded the collective's capacity to generate "mystery," but the scenes invoked were hardly as mysterious as the uninitiated contended. They simply betrayed some viewers' ignorance of what most Syrians would easily recognize.[74]

The collective's efforts do not disrupt the viewer's local affiliations or question the merits of national belonging as such. But by breaking the frame of official national discourse, these films function like debris that can be repurposed, shards that cut through the impasse by bypassing the very structure of journalistic publicity and claims to objectivity. And some films, like the *Unknown Soldier* series, provide an especially resonant critique of violence in which victims become perpetrators—and violence need not be overt to be seen; in which our vocabulary of victimization and perpetration seems inadequate to the war's ongoing horror; in which political commitments become tainted by the efforts to enact them. And life's ordinary dwellings become incubators of death and destruction—a profound sense of disrepair that dissociates bodies from souls, makes the air unbreathable and political commitments themselves seem stifling.

In such a context, what is to be done? Abounaddara offers no answers. But like Arendt's use of Dinesen to underscore the political potential of storytelling, the film collective attempts to find a salutary alternative to violence in the visual language of short films, sidestepping the evidentiary logic of news stories and conventional documentary genres by occasioning new possibilities for reflection in a context in which the usual grounds for judgment have been undermined. In distinction to official opposition and regime proponents alike, with their polarizing answers always at the ready, the collective embraces the ambiguity of the situation—extending even to questions of what the national community might look like, given what the war has done to what could conceivably be Syria. In doing so, Abounaddara gives up on a certain kind of knowing, without giving up on judgment and political intervention as such.[75] Whereas both the regime and the multiple oppositions demand that people take sides for or against, the collective's commitment to complexity is not the same as the frame-breaking uncertainty that provides an alibi for nonjudgment. On the contrary, the recognition of the fragility of subject positions allows viewers to embrace a temporal lag between perception and action without abandoning the latter, to counter the temptation toward ideological disavowal, to be humble and befuddled without being abject—an invitation to revitalize judgment with the full albeit paradoxical knowledge that nothing is ever fully known. This temporal lag is also evident in how the films are disseminated, with a single short film uploaded to Vimeo every Friday. As if to counteract the speed that makes sustained attention so difficult, Abounaddara's works give viewers time to absorb, reflect, and observe with a discriminatory eye—enabling what the historian Max Weiss calls, celebrating the unhurried pace of the novel as form, "slow witnessing."[76]

CONCLUSION

The forms of discursive oversaturation described in this chapter come from what I have called the temporality of "high-speed eventfulness," or the sheer velocity with which information is transmitted and apprehended in the internet age. The unceasing whirl of (over)information makes it easy for people to move on to something new the instant a favored narrative fails. The Ibrahim Qashush controversy brings into bold relief the conundrums for judgment posed by these new conditions, showing how the Syrian regime's media manipulations—a shorthand here for both direct propaganda efforts and an ability to exploit issues put into circulation by others (whether Russian diplomats, investigative reporters like Seymour Hersh, or scientists such as Richard M. Lloyd and Theodore A. Postol)—interfered with activists' capacity to maintain or develop a revolutionary narrative. This means that stories were easily knit into the narrative fabric of stories people were already telling themselves or that political exuberance was flattened, the latter ending up, like 'Abd al-Wahid's journalists or Abounaddara's unknown soldier, mired in doubt and disillusion. This disenchantment can be read as revolutionary activism's narrative counterpart to neoliberal autocracy's capacity to produce citizen ambivalence and loyalty. In the context of heightened uncertainty, both ambivalence and oppositional deflation thrive. Such an atmospherics of doubt is part of what Slavoj Žižek calls "systemic violence," which in the Syrian case operates in cahoots with other forms of overt regime brutality to extinguish or dampen what began as incendiary political excitement. In this context, artistic efforts such as the ones surveyed in this chapter are like embers: a trace of light and heat, a past-bearing invitation to begin anew.

4

Nationalism, Sentimentality, and Judgment

If chapter 3 explored how fake news interferes with the capacity to make political judgments, this chapter focuses on the aesthetic-political practices through which feelings around mourning are absorbed and organized. It explores commercial as well as regime- and opposition-identified ways of grappling with the devastation of civil war by looking at some of melodrama's specificities as a genre of ideological management whose logic in the Syrian case is to excite fantasies of collectivity, contain mutual hostilities, and absorb persisting anxieties surrounding national sovereignty. In doing so, the chapter addresses how mass sentimentality comes with a sense of (implicit or explicit) *moral* assertion, which, I argue, complicates possibilities for *political* judgment so necessary for ideology critique.

Beginning with a brief discussion of melodrama as a genre of sentimental expression, the chapter proceeds to analyze how melodrama gets combined with realism in the morally regulative regime-oriented discourses of longing and suffering. I then investigate an alternative political aesthetic expressed in two Syrian videos and two Syrian films. As experiments with cosmopolitanism (Khalid 'Abd al-Wahid's two videos), ethnography (Ziad Kalthum), and situated universalism (Ossama Mohammed/Usama Muhammad), these works exemplify the wrestling with political judgment that takes place in the intensified emotional context of ongoing mourning. The films chosen are especially illustrative of artists' attempts to generate modes of epistemic and affective address while resisting the pieties of nationalism, the pressures of a globalized, commodified human rights discourse, and other varieties of sentimentalized sorrow.

In this chapter, as in the previous one, my analysis is influenced throughout by Hannah Arendt, here by her understanding of political judgment as a distinct activity—one bearing similarities with aesthetic judgment while not being coterminous with the latter. Political judgment for Arendt involves evaluation and world-building simultaneously. Drawing from Immanuel Kant, she elaborates a process in which engagement and deliberation come together in a way that both derives from and cultivates our ordinary human powers of imagination.[1] What Arendt calls "representative thinking"—operating without any settled rules to guide adjudication and lacking the regulative impulses of moral judgment—allows for a commitment to curiosity without its tending to narcissism or over-identification with suffering. As we shall see, the concept of representative thinking also encompasses the coimplication of affect and cognition, the ambivalences that characterize ordinary life, and the contradictions, miscommunications, and indeterminacies that complicate standpoints, as well as our capacities to imagine these standpoints in the first place. As applied here, "representative thinking" helps us understand how potent national sentimentality can be, without succumbing to the seductions of either sentimentality itself or national collectivity per se. At the same time, Arendt's term, brought to bear in the context of the Syrian conflict, raises some otherwise underexamined problems for political judgment, ones that Syrian artists will help us navigate.

The chapter takes as its focal point the year spanning the summers of 2012 and 2013 (before the chemical weapons attack in al-Ghouta, discussed in chapter 3), when cultural producers were feeling an urgent need to speak on behalf of Syria to national and global audiences, and when transformative responses were still believed to be possible. Among the many plausible ways that the uprising could be periodized, one would be according to the bloody turning points that changed the contours of political struggle. These include the regime assaults on Homs and Hama in July–August 2011; the regime's siege of Homs, beginning with the aerial bombardment of February 2012; the massacre at Houla in May 2012; the bombing of regime headquarters in July 2012 and the ensuing intensified militarization of conflict in both the outskirts of Damascus and Aleppo; and, of course, the chemical weapons attack in August 2013. As Syria devolved into civil war, much of both regime- and opposition-identified cultural production sought to control what counted as experience (collective and otherwise)—with some instances of oppositional aesthetics proving more open to political contestation and more willing to embrace unpredictability than others. As in chapter 3, the emphasis here is on shared conditions of violence in which people find themselves no longer in possession of an intelligible world within which to make judgments. As the featured filmmakers demonstrate, however, this very unmooring can be used as a vantage from which one reliably re-cognizes oneself. And in this vein, the chapter explores what alternatives to nationalism might look like, and how to envision a creative otherwiseness (to channel Theodor Adorno) on which collective solidarities and political potentiality might be grounded.

AN EDUCATION IN NATIONAL SENTIMENTALITY

A scene from the 2013 television series *We'll Return Shortly* opens to the sound of thundering bombs. Two longtime friends, neighbors living in the old city of Damascus, are chatting peacefully about current events in Syria when one refers to the bloody war echoing in the background as "the crisis." His friend angrily responds, "It's called a revolution! If you're one of those people who believes it's all a foreign conspiracy, get out." It turns out that the second speaker's son has been detained by regime security forces for participating in the protests, so he is understandably upset by his friend's choice of words.[2] The series proceeds to narrate the fate of a family that has fled to Lebanon to escape the violence. Relying throughout on soap opera staples like frayed family ties, betrayal, and lust (the latter already indexed by the setting in licentious Lebanon), the series ends with the death of the forever-disappointed, displaced patriarch whose fantasies of repair seem destined to be buried with him. *We'll Return Shortly* was one of two television series broadcast during the 2013 Ramadan season that took the Syrian war as its backdrop. The other, *Birth from the Waist, Part Three*, likewise treated viewers to a quasi soap opera, this time involving corruption, sadism, and intrigue inside the regime's security forces.[3] Alternating action-packed suspense sequences with scenes of maternal sacrifice and grief, *Birth from the Waist* culminates in a tearful closing scene in which two long-suffering mothers—one whose neighbor has been murdered by the other's son—recognize the need for redress to end the cycle of violence. In this fantasy version of Syrian truth and reconciliation, conflict is resolved. The one mother consents to a terrible yet necessary decision, agreeing to sacrifice her perpetrator son.

Hackneyed themes aside, the brouhaha generated by the two series is worthy of note. Ramadan television shows are eagerly awaited by citizens and advertisers in the Arab world.[4] Families often break the fast while watching television together—and the season generates an expansion of the permissible in public conversation, centered as it is around popular-culture production. War and its hardships, including extended electricity outages, as well as the emergence of the internet, have changed viewing practices and reduced the importance of the coveted time slots in terms of overall consumption. But in the summer of 2013 the internet may well have allowed more people to watch at their own convenience—producing more debate outside the family setting in the atomized publics that nonetheless agglomerated into a broader public sphere. And it is arguably the case that these two series were the last ones to cultivate a general public discussion: audiences continued to fragment under the pressures of war, and subsequent Ramadan programming lacked the fresh, explicitly political content witnessed here.

Praised as a "stark departure from the past" and a demonstration that Syrian drama was "still alive and [enjoying] record viewership," the television shows were celebrated by some for "breaking the rules of polarization on the ground."[5] Others were outraged, calling for boycotts of both shows and lambasting them for their "superficial" treatment of events and for portraying identifiable public figures in simplistic or caricatured ways. Of interest here is how the controversies surrounding these two standout Ramadan dramas contributed to the sense of community within which Syrians' feelings of nostalgia, sorrow, anger, despair, and even mutual disapproval could be temporarily shared. As the film critic and curator Rasha Salti noted at the time, "In spite of the mediocrity of [the] performances, direction, and craft . . . , [the series] did something outstanding in terms of proposing a 'mediascape' beyond reality TV . . . that allowed for 'projections' and 'belongings' at a time when the national territory/social fabric/public sphere are embattled."[6]

These series, in other words, operated as performatives: they enacted the diversity of opinions and feelings comprising the collectivity called Syria, yet confined the exchange within the familiarity of genre. Or to borrow the words of the film and literary theorist James Chandler, these narratives work in the first instance to "epitomize or allegorize" a specifically nationalist sensibility, while styling themselves also as a "means to *activate* [it] by affective movement, and thus to shape it amelioratively."[7] Both series worked ideologically to incite solidarity while managing it, in this case producing a community of Syrians in which differences existing at large could be contained by being entertained—without demanding recourse either to hostilities or to any positive efforts to undo the status quo.

The debates, hype, and controversies surrounding the two series stimulated affective attachments to Syria as a nation even as the country itself unraveled. By representing divergent views, political positions, and resonant feelings, the television dramas provided a mode of identification, beckoning ordinary citizens from various backgrounds to see their own lives reflected in the storytelling. Although there are no reliable surveys of viewer response, in reception interviews people recounted experiences of being "recognized," expressing pleasure in identifying with some characters and disappointment in the shortcomings of others.[8] The appearance of exemplary differences onscreen elicited the airing of parallel disagreements among viewers in public, hailing them into a world where arguments could be entertained safely, acknowledging and buffering particular vulnerabilities by generalizing woundedness into a common, avowedly nationalist strain of sentimentality.

The series themselves were likely forgotten as the war raged on, but for a moment they occasioned a collective focus, inviting a general consideration of the dual dimensions of national sentimentality. For on the one hand, national sentimentality can be plausibly viewed as a short circuit in the hard work of mourning, simplifying the political by smoothing out people's experiences of incoherence or ambivalence. Through the intensification of feeling in and through television melodramas, something important about experience may be lost—or overmanaged, legislated, even cheapened. On the other hand, as Lauren Berlant points out, "sentimentality is not just the mawkish, nostalgic, and simpleminded mode with which it's conventionally associated." It also represents "a mode of relationality in which people take emotions to express something authentic about themselves that they think the world should welcome and respect; a mode constituted by affective and emotional intelligibility and a kind of generosity, recognition, and solidarity among strangers."[9] Or to make the point somewhat differently, sentimentality has to do with making certain emotions intelligible on the assumption that the feelings involved are generalizable, that others can and do share them. In scenes of exaggerated or simplified emotional expression, the overwrought characters model for viewers their vulnerability to others, setting the stage for a charitable reception by strangers—whether other characters in the drama or the individuals comprising the viewing public.

Much work has already been done on how melodramatic conventions in particular are used in the service of national sentimentality.[10] Scholars have noted, for example, that melodrama is a specifically modern literary and theatrical genre, in which emotions are intensified for the purpose of advancing a morally laden pedagogy of progress and national fellow feeling.[11] The classic literary work on melodrama, Peter Brooks's *The Melodramatic Imagination*, linked the development of the genre to the French Revolution (arguably the birthplace of nationalism) and to what he called a specifically "modern sensibility."[12] Drawing from the writings of Balzac and Henry James, Brooks used the term *melodrama* to draw attention to the "extravagance of certain representations, and the intensity of moral claim impinging on their characters' consciousness."[13] Subsequent writers, despite disagreements, have largely continued to invoke the term in this sense, referring to a hyperbolic genre designed to elicit strong identifications with protagonists, including visceral, embodied reactions. Characters, as Ben Singer notes, tend to be emotionally "overwrought," with actors depicting "heightened states of emotive urgency, tension, and tribulation."[14] Distinguished from classical narrative through its evasion of any simple structure of cause and effect, melodrama accommodates an "inordinate abundance of situation"[15] as well as a "greater tolerance, or indeed a preference, for outrageous coincidence, implausibility, convoluted plotting, *deus ex machina* resolution, and episodic strings of action."[16] Melodrama, although not always about moral polarities, is almost always moralizing, and it relies on sensationalism and intensified relations among characters to communicate messages largely expressing distress, suspense, sadness, and surprise. Yet despite the familiar acting codes of overstatement and associated camera work of, say, soap operas, Singer goes on to explain how melodrama can also contain moments of "credible diegetic realism" in which the drama being enacted is designed to be believable and to express an experience of actual events.[17] This combination of melodramatic overstatement and purported objectivity may be why so many debates during Ramadan 2013—on Facebook, in newspapers, and at social gatherings—turned on whether "reality" was being adequately portrayed in either *We'll Return Shortly* or *Birth from the Waist, Part Three*.[18] The clear expectation was that portraying reality was what the dramas were supposed to do, indeed politically obligated to do, so that failing in this task meant falling fundamentally short.[19]

If the serials of 2013 combined conventions of melodrama with techniques of realism, using the blend to enact national community by both specifying the guidelines for acceptable disagreement and generating it, then the regime's *direct* public relations efforts involved condensed versions of a similarly complex affective, moral universe. The same mix of genres is evident here, but with an important difference: overt regime projects devoted to the image of consensus and continued multicultural accommodation *brooked no dissent*.[20] It is in this light that we must read the regime's film commemorating Mother's Day in 2013. Running fourteen-plus minutes, its target constituency, aside from staunch loyalists, included sundry nationalists whose ambivalence toward the regime could be at least temporarily suspended.

In *With Your Soul You Protect the Jasmine*,[21] as the commemoration was titled, the regime's over-the-top sentimentality is of a piece with its claim to moral authority, an authority premised on the fantasy that the only suffering that takes place is on its side, that only its side experiences proper solidarities, that only it can ensure the maintenance of national sovereignty through sacrifice and therefore be representative of the nation. The film thus tethered aspects of melodrama to a cynical realism, producing a notion of the "we" that excluded anyone whose loss could not be folded into the regime's definition of what counted as such. The version of appropriate politics it generated was less inclusive than the one of the commercially oriented serials, attempting, as one Syrian citizen eloquently suggested, "to seize ownership of the pain."[22]

Dedicated to "the Syrian mothers who sent their sons . . . , all of their sons, to protect the nation, its pride and its unity," the film begins with a voice-over by the director, purportedly the very same Jud Sa'id whose 2010 feature film, *Once Again* (discussed in chapter 1), celebrated ostentatious consumption, new technologies of security, and long-standing figurations of national belonging. Here the director applies his skills to the commemoration of motherhood, connecting a generalized abstraction of national sacrifice to the intimacy of his own supposed memories of filial devotion: "When I go out, O my mother, I kiss the pride of your morning." The visual is a close-up shot of an older woman, hair covered in a white scarf/shawl (*sharshaf*) indicating a "traditional" woman from the countryside or recent migrant to the city. The camera then cuts to the same woman walking slowly down the banisterless, uneven cement stairs of her home to a sink where she performs her ablutions. "When the doors open, your soul engulfs me, your spirit protects me," continues the voice-over. "Those who protect Syria [are] like the sun, [they] never die, O mother." Onscreen, a text in Arabic reads: "With your soul [also translatable as "spirit"] you protect the jasmine."[23]

Mothers as protectors and caretakers and as inextinguishable as the sun—a well-known metaphor for hope and endurance, among other things—come in for altogether conventional treatment in this Mother's Day film. Yet the extradiegetic explanatory moments still work to remind viewers of a complex set of mimetic relationships in which mother protects son, mother protects Syria (and its capital, Damascus, the city of jasmine), son protects Syria, and Syria is the mother "of all." The film then cuts to the actual mother reading the Qur'an, evidently deriving solace from its spiritual wisdom in the privacy of her bedroom—not in public, where her piety might be mistaken for desecularized oppositional politics. The same woman is pictured in other moments of privatized ordinariness, drinking her coffee, watering her garden—in other words, tending to life against the backdrop of war's deathly encroachments. A close-up back in the palace of a second woman, her lined face evocative of grandchildren— maybe even great-grandchildren—underscores generations of maternal sacrifice.

Then the camera zooms out for a shot of the interior of the presidential palace, offering a telling and explicitly stately contrast to the scenes of ordinary domesticity with which the film opens. The palace's windowed walls, pristine floors, and decidedly modern aesthetic jibe well with the first family's stubbornly persisting official image as a stand-in for the good life, whose version of modernity tolerates privatized religion while continuing to prize multisectarian accommodation. The film's enactment of sovereignty in times of peril turns on visuals of actual mothers cathecting onto sovereign power—the first lady Asma', Syria, the slogans of Ba'thist Party rule—as a way of demonstrating the righteousness of their sacrifice, a displacement of love away from ordinary family life onto the abstraction of the national collective, thereby rendering the latter less abstract. "I have eight sons, and all eight are in the army," narrates a woman dressed in black. "Like any mother, I wish my sons were with me, but right now I'll sacrifice all of them for the country. On Mother's Day, like every mother, I tell him: my son, stay with your country and keep defending your country." Testimonies of maternal loyalty to the supramaternal nation go on and on: "I have three sons in the army, and today is Mother's Day, and I gifted them to the nation, to Syria, because Syria is the mother of all, and may God protect this nation, protect Syria, protect its sons, and protect the Syrian Arab Army." Another female voice-over recalls the intimacies of smell, a blanket and a pillow carrying the scent of a son in service, while others recount the actual loss of a son and implore God to protect the rest, rehearsing the familiar tropes connecting Syria to motherhood and playing on the fact that in Arabic, *mother* (*umm*) and *nation* (*umma*) share a common root.[24] Nationalism is conjoined here to state sovereignty, and both are protected by, indeed enjoy the moral authority of, God's good grace. There is no nation-state outside the regime's supporters here—and no other rightful relationship to God or the political in this time of war.

The camera work and soundscape establish what is to count as the commonsense limits to official nationalism by linking passionate drama to experiences of "intimate community":[25] as the voice-over switches from the director to a mother, the camera shifts to the palace. Starting with a long shot capturing the empty, stately room, the camera zooms in closer, in a tried-and-true device for establishing a familiarity between spectators and the characters or situation onscreen, as a new voice begins recounting another story. The first lady comes into focus, appearing with her back to the audience, looking out the window at the city below. She is both a mother among mothers and a leader burdened by weighty decisions. Her chic designer clothes have given way to an unassuming, tasteful T-shirt and peasant skirt. The sole concession to the glamour of yesteryear is a walk down the red carpet, connoting both the familiar political pomp of heads of state and the glitzy world of models and runway pageantry. She hugs one mother, caresses the face of another, and even wheels a disabled woman into the area where she will give her speech. In slow motion, to the accompaniment of a plaintive soundtrack of stringed instruments, the first lady and her entourage of mothers make their way to the hall where her speech commences.

The film's content and form operate together to produce the guidelines for proper mourning. With the women gathering around Asma', the shot now comes from above. Her reassuring presence combines empathy with a decidedly unmelodramatic self-restraint, the dignified center of an otherwise melodramatic field. Her physical proximity, her repeated touching of the women, and her speech in their midst work to make intimate and personal the public, abstract nation form. Her self-control and poise exemplify personal mastery. She is national sovereignty incarnate, at once a mother herself and a model leader, a person of both warmth and control: "A mother's heart yearns for her missing sons, yearns. The presence of his brothers may lessen the agony, but the missing one remains." And the women respond like a chorus: "A child is precious, but the nation [*watan*] is more precious."[26]

Passionate drama and intimacy here are conjoined to a pedantic rhetoric: the first lady asks in the empathic interrogative, when sons "are all absent, to whom will this heart give affection?" Acknowledging both mothers and grandmothers, she insists on how important caretaking is to a stalwart patriotism, which is both inculcated through the family and secured anew through public steadfastness and sacrifice: "These same hands are the hands that raised, cared, and taught, and in each moment . . . they raised them [their children] to love the homeland [*watan*]. With each heartbeat, fear and terror for them [the children], there's another beat of challenge, insistence, resolve, and strength." Inverting the mimetic relationship between leader and subjects, she insists on these women's exemplarity even as she produces the guidelines for the publicly acceptable standpoint of mourning: "In this position of yours, you're an example to me and to each Syrian mother . . . that giving should be big and that for sacrifice to be considered sacrifice, it should be greater."

While the tone is restrained, the poetic embellishments in the script imply an extrusion of feeling: "Each year on this day [March 21], spring begins," Asma' continues. "This year you are the spring. Your giving will make the roses, wildflowers, and jasmine bloom, the jasmine you protected and are protecting with your souls, your sons." And in a rhetorically ritualized refrain, the first lady makes clear that their exemplarity is also reassuring for the rest of the nation, for their sacrifice may mean that others will not have to:

> True, the son is precious, but you've shown the entire world that the homeland [*watan*] is more precious. True, the son is a piece of the soul, but you've taught us, in acts not only in words, that the soul is expendable for the sake of the nation when you sent all your sons to protect it. True, a mother is precious, very precious, but you taught us that the soil of the homeland is more precious. Instead of fearing for yourselves and your lives, you feared for all of Syria. Instead of your sons fearing for you only, they feared for all mothers of the country. They went to protect the nation, to protect you, knowing that the nation is a mother and Syria is the mother of all. Today, they, myself included, and yourselves, and many mothers with us, we came to tell her: the nation is precious, our mother Syria. May God protect you, and if all the mothers of your young men are like this, each year you [Syria] will be fine.

In addressing Syria as if it were a mother, the text personalizes the abstraction while also eliding the proclaimed defense of national sovereignty with regime survival. Next, a song performed by a young girls' choir reinforces the first lady's words while abandoning the tone of solemnity and restraint by moving into what might be called a transcendental melodramatic register in which pride becomes allowable through sacrifice to the proper collective:

> You're precious, you're precious my homeland, we belt you with fire
> High and high my forehead is high [an idiom of pride]
> Crowned with a wreath of laurel

Your voice coming from afar and your fragrance diffuses
Our sighs of love rise up wherever you go
Your name is the most beautiful poem and your love is a new song
Your glory's lightning shimmers, writing your glory with fire
You're precious, you're precious my homeland, we belt you with fire.

The soundtrack accompanies images of the first lady being filmed once again hugging her mothers/admirers in what becomes a series of slow-motion shots, followed by other shots of her being photographed with various guests. At this moment, the director has introduced a metamedium—almost as if the film's rhetorical extremes, matched by the extreme sacrifices of these women, must be tempered, not only by the first lady's restraint but by the director's own distancing mechanisms. The soundtrack itself indicates a shift in genre, with elegant piano music reminiscent of a dinner club announcing the change of scene: the first lady presides over a lavish luncheon even while personally serving her guests, her poise reprising the theme that she is one among equals, a mother who can also be ordinary and one whose logos, to use a literary term for the power of speech, she can easily exchange for a ladle. Here the film once again eschews melodrama and provides reassurance in the very containment of emotions, Asma''s composed warmth is a far cry from the excessive patriotism displayed by other mothers around her.

This differentiation of Asma' from other mothers is, I want to contend, structurally necessary to the film's assertions of sovereignty, her restraint less a repudiation of the mothers' affect than a means of harvesting it. The filming of the obligatory group picture taken after lunch, as well as a subsequent scene in which the modern city below is revealed through the vast palace windows on high, reasserts the sovereign's dominance and distance—the latter image by children singing the national anthem offscreen as the camera pans across the landscape to rest on the monumental tomb of the Unknown Soldier: the defense of national sovereignty has a long and respectable history, and the film is daring in its insistence on analogizing the current civil war to righteous wars of the past.

The director's voice, ventriloquizing a son in the army, closes the film on a melancholy note:

I'm returning, my mother, wait for me.
And if I forget my way back don't cry,
My eyes turned into two stars in my country's flag
Always remember me like that.

Having celebrated the virtues of the neoliberal autocratic good life in his 2010 feature-length film, in *With Your Soul You Protect the Jasmine* Saʿid pays homage once again to the surveillance state—no longer outsourced to entrepreneurial bankers with technological acumen, but rooted firmly in the army and the flag, whose stars, once a symbol of the pan-Arab union between Syria and Egypt, have come to signify a dead soldier's eyes.

The film's idealization of the nation-state underscores the importance of social difference even as political difference is excluded. Women's accents denote the variety of their regional affiliations; their attire suggests relative degrees of piety; the young girls dressed in uniform on the sidelines remind us that the regime has child devotees as well, a version of the Baʿth Party's vanguard units and testimony to the regime's steadfast commitment to the daughters of the nation too—not only as future mothers but as potential warriors. The regime-nation may be under siege, the film suggests, but it remains devoted to the defense of a world in which diversity is protected through multicultural accommodation predicated on maternal devotion, making even abstract collectivities proximate through personal pain. The soundtrack further intensifies these feelings while assisting in the offering up of a decontextualized "theater of empathy."[27] Operating in the mode of maternal mimesis, the film puts forward the idealized image of female behavior to be imitated, yet skirts the regime's own responsibility for the violence that is otherwise in plain view.

The Mother's Day film *With Your Soul You Protect the Jasmine* exemplifies the regime's ongoing efforts to define and police the parameters of membership. It offers a glossier, glitzier, and decidedly nationalistic reversion back to the future, one in which children stand in for the nation (as innocent victims) but can also be sacrificed (as quasi-agentive soldiers) on its behalf. This future is also one in which women suffer as mothers, wives, sisters, and cadres—while also connecting the intimacies of their individual experiences to the nation as form. The first lady's own gendered specificity finds abstract activation in this symbolic coupling of nation to regime. This move is made possible, not only by the bare fact of her appearance and its signaling functions (as mother, as national icon, as stand-in for the maternally figured nation as such), but by the film's mix of genres—its recourse to strategies of both melodramatic excess and realist restraint. The film thereby licenses viewers to feel intensely as long as these feelings operate within the reassuring parameters of mixed but recognizable genre conventions. By forcing sadness into a decidedly militarized national fantasy of sacrifice and order, it smooths out the complexities and ambiguities of collective experience. And, as with most regime propaganda,

the film calls to mind what Jacques Rancière terms "the stultifying pedagogue, the logic of straight, uniform transmission: there is something—
a form of knowledge—a capacity, an energy in a body or a mind on one
side, and it must pass to the other side. What the pupil must *learn* is what
the schoolmaster must *teach* her. What the spectator *must* see is what the
director *makes her see*. What she must feel is the energy he communicates
to her."[28] Viewers who refuse to learn or to embrace the regime's message
are written out of the official national narrative—there is no such thing as
non-regime-oriented sacrifice, or if there is, it deserves no recognition. In
this telling way, the two Syrian television series with which this chapter
opened differ from the Mother's Day video—they may be every bit as pedagogical and stifling, but their commitment to a market logic makes them
more inclusive, more open to a world of indeterminate consumer-citizens
whose spectatorship depends on their being somehow taken into account:
engrossed instead of simply grossed out.

As the war goes on, with prices rising and displaced families struggling
to find even basic foodstuffs, fuel, and clothing, appeals to the regime's version of the good life ring hollow. And yet, private instances of the kind of
luxury we see in the Mother's Day film's depiction of the grand but understated opulence in the palace continue to appear. People upload images
on Facebook and Instagram of festive pool parties hosted at hotels and
lavish residences, as if insisting that those on the right side of the conflict,
from the regime's point of view, were not to be deprived of their enjoyment while others were subjected to chaos and cruelty. An audacious ad
campaign for tourism in 2016 even tried to market the Syrian coast as a
plum destination for jet skiers and sunbathers—advertising a vision of the
persisting well-being of those living on the side of the regime. Also intensified in these lean wartime years are images of national camaraderie and
heightened anxieties about nonsovereignty, to borrow Lauren Berlant's
term, about coming collectively and individually undone.[29]

The first lady continues to be key to regime efforts to seize semiotic control of collective pain. Captured meticulously on social media sites pursuing good works, in October 2016 she granted her first interview for a global
audience since the war began, and in that same month was the subject of
a celebratory documentary. That both appearances were produced by
Russian television is a sign of the times, of course, registering the regime's
international alliances and the media complicities they generate. Yet in
the internet age these performances are simultaneously available to the
global community, with the interview on Russian television conducted in
English, presumably to galvanize commentary throughout the world; the

Russian-language documentary with its Arabic subtitling addresses Syrians more specifically. In both the film and the interview, Asma' embodies the regime's trademark modernity and sovereignty, broadcasting a confidence and worldliness pitched to "all Syrians"—a simultaneous harkening back to Bashar al-Asad's first, seemingly inclusive decade and code for the glaring qualification of *Syrians* to mean "regime-oriented" during his second.[30]

The interview in particular caused something of a ruckus in contradicting statements made by her husband, who was on an interview roll of his own, having sat for two in the same week. Whereas the president proposed that the now-iconic image of 'Umran—the bloody-faced child strapped into the orange seat in an ambulance—had been fabricated, the first lady acknowledged the tragedy.[31] She expressed her sadness at the deaths of "innocent children," specifying by name not only 'Umran but Aylan (also spelled Alan), the three-year-old whose lifeless body washed up on the Turkish shore in 2015 and inspired an earlier bout of global sympathy. Asma' makes a point of calling the deaths a "loss to Syria, irrespective of which side of the conflict we support."[32] Opposition media networks and Facebook commentaries were quick to point to the discrepancy, reading it as a sign of disconnect or an estrangement between the two. But his bravado and her compassion also reflect a familiar gendered division of labor, one that in the context of the uprising has become more marked, and usefully so. Bashar's forthright denial of the evident facts upholds old-style Ba'thist politics of public dissimulation, now combined with the doubt-inducing sensibility discussed in chapter 3. Asma''s 2016 appearances recultivate the image of internationally acceptable civility so well performed in the 2005–11 period, while continuing to put forward tales of maternal sacrifice and moral superiority, as dramatized in the 2013 Mother's Day film.[33] Her sanitized appearances and preternatural calm, indeed her unflagging elegance, provide an eerie continuity between the neoliberal autocratic past and the war-torn present, becoming ever more surreal as the war progresses. She epitomizes at once a measured compassion and a strange unflappability, performing in the interviews with none of the melodrama of her 2013 video.

Subsequent regime-orchestrated Mother's Day videos are also organized around melodramatic forms of sentimentality, but they lack the audacity or sense of novelty of *With Your Soul You Protect the Jasmine*. Nor have they generated the same sort of interest, if Facebook and ethnographic evidence is any indication. Similarly, Syrian television dramas have not incited the widespread conversations that the 2013 ones did. Nor did the arguments circulating in the wake of Asma''s 2016 interview trigger the same kind of social media frenzy as the 2013 video. In part, this relative inattention speaks to a general exhaustion born of the devastations of war and disillusionment on the part of regime supporters and opponents alike. In 2013, the video had multiple addressees—stoking the regime's base while offering a pointed affront to Syrians whose sacrifice was dismissed, excluded from the regime-defined national community being celebrated. The 2016 interview, by contrast, offered another variation on the politics of public dissimulation, one in which the first lady could act *as if* she were speaking on behalf of all reasonable Syrians, as if the war were a sad but minor perturbation that had distracted her from the "challenges" of her preconflict civil society work. To be sure, this sense of the war—as if it had come on like bad weather and were not the regime's direct responsibility—also reprises one of the regime's go-to registers of response, exemplified in 2012 by the bizarre television broadcasts of the president visiting the besieged city of Homs after the aerial bombardment, miked up like an athlete during a game and talking to people (engineers, architects, ordinary citizens?) about plans to hurry up and repair the damage. The first lady, meanwhile, was shown doling out provisions to survivors. This is natural-disaster relief as wartime photo op, as if through the token alleviation of citizens' suffering the regime could evade responsibility for being the cause.

Oppositional narratives have offered alternatives to the regime's constructions of national identity by disarticulating regime from nation and entreating Syrians to imagine themselves as a collective without a brutal dictatorship as its steward. Many also address a global constituency of would-be supporters, enjoining citizens everywhere to identify with the enormity of Syrian suffering.[34] This call for identification sometimes resembles regime films in using a similar blend of melodramatic intensity and what Ben Singer terms "credible diegetic realism." In other words, opposition-oriented nationalism implies a heightened, moralizing sense of emotive urgency combined with purported objectivity. Outrage at Western nonintervention and generalized callousness, pain at the extinguishing of both life and revolutionary promise, and an overall sense of powerlessness drive calls for lasting amelioration and rescue. In both artistic work and ordinary reportage, regime opponents often rely on sensationalism—easy enough to conjure up in this abysmal context—to generate moral polarities and exclusions or to insist on a resolution that has become increasingly difficult to fathom. In doing so, their works can be said to evade the hard work of *both* mourning and reflection on political contradiction, ambivalence, and uncertainty.

Yet there are others who have attempted to avoid the emotional short-circuiting of nationalist sentimentality proffered by both regime and some parts of the opposition, instead considering how, in the cases examined below, the cinematic form specifically can be used to mediate, integrate, and trouble the relationship between internal states of mind and external observation. The artistic efforts to which we now turn urge an open-endedness to interpretation without eschewing judgment, and they acknowledge loss without reducing complex affective registers to comfortable clichés and stock emotional phrases.

CRITICAL ALTERNATIVES

It may well be that mass politics is impossible in the absence of sentimentality.[35] Nevertheless, some Syrian artists, as we saw with incipient oppositional comedy in chapter 2 and in the example of the collective Abounaddara's short films in chapter 3, have distanced themselves from either melodramatic fare or the temptation to elicit overidentification, empathy, or pity from the spectator. The artists' works to be discussed below register the power of national fantasy in conditions of nation-state decomposition, while also operating in excess of conventional patriotism, allowing for redefinitions of political life to appear outside a simple nationalist frame.[36] One example is the video artist Khalid 'Abd al-Wahid's *Tuj* (2012), which synchronizes the bouncing of a ball off the wall in an interior space with the sound of explosions from outside.[37] The play is disrupted by a much louder explosion, and the light goes out. And then the light returns, and the ball is bouncing again—the repetition a reminder of the possibilities for play and the forms of light and aliveness that perdure, even in times of horrific violence.

More powerful to my mind is his *Slot in Memory* (the English translation of *Shaqq fi Dhakira* [2013]; better would be *Crack in Memory*),[38] which reiterates the theme of children's resilience, the importance of play, and repetition—along with an insistence on ordinariness despite the disruptions of war. Here we see children playing on a makeshift swing set, its back-and-forth creaking sounds a contrast to those of panicked, disembodied voices yelling. Light comes through what appears to be a door crack, like a camera aperture, offering us a single vantage point, and a narrow one at that. The scene captures a contradiction of war, the swing bearing the children up and down an instance of predictability amid the explosion-punctuated atmosphere of arbitrary shelling.

'Abd al-Wahid's efforts are easily dismissed for infantilizing citizenship, offering yet another vision of children as sentimental stand-ins for the nation. The relative helplessness of actual children always makes attempts to symbolize them liable to caricature—threatening, arguably, to evacuate the political via a sentimentalized attachment to an innocence at odds with adult world-building. But importantly, there is nothing *necessarily* national or sentimental about the collectivity envisaged in his videos, and the war has, in fact, made children vulnerable in particular—with an entire generation already lost to the violence adults have made.[39] The insistence on children's resilience may itself convey a sense of heroism in the ordinary, but there is nothing excessive or expressly maudlin about ʿAbd al-Wahid's work. It hints at possibilities going beyond the simplifying strategies of sentimentality, while also drawing our attention to some of its conventional seductions. And these short films remind us that along with the war's anguish, disappointment, and terror, there remain enclaves of affirmative possibility—instances of play suggesting an outlook that is not situated in a specific place. In contrast with others insisting on Syrian specificity, these works gesture toward what I am labeling a cosmopolitanism or supranationalism—an everyplace of war, offering an opening, which in the case of *Slot in Memory* consists in a view of the world through a barely open door. In *Tuj* that opening up to the world is, paradoxically, made possible through the lens of a closed room.

A similar but more expansive view characterizes Ziad Kalthum's (Kalthoum) autobiographical documentary, *The Immortal Sergeant* (*Al-Raqib al-Khalid*), released in 2014 but filmed and set in 2012–13.[40] It opens with an oblique angle onto a scene of domesticity, depicting askew the world of reliable ordinariness. The film reprises themes we already saw in Abounaddara's *The Trajectory of an Unknown Soldier* (2012) in that the central character, in this case the director, is split. A conscripted sergeant housed in army barracks by night, Ziad works by day as a cameraman for the well-known art film director Muhammad Malas. He is also internally divided, evidenced by repeated images of division—the split screen like a children's butterfly painting made by folding a piece of paper in half, as well as scenes shot professionally with a proper camera juxtaposed to ones shot surreptitiously on a handheld cell phone. From the professional camera, we get footage of downtown Damascus, where cast and crew of the fictional movie are filming on location, offering us a window on the world of quotidian work and artistic collaboration in wartime's disruptive circumstances. From the cell phone, we get grainy, unstable, stealthily captured footage of military life, largely from the barracks on Mount Qasiyun overlooking the capital, but also sometimes from unspecified areas of the country. The film is thus, among other things, a multi-sited metanarrative about filmmaking by a director taking advantage of his job(s) as both cameraman and soldier, resulting in an ethnographically rich, unusually prosaic, and unsensational account of skewed ordinariness and the profound damage done by violence, even at a distance, to the people suffering it.

On the set with his camera, Kalthum films the warplanes flying overhead, which make it impossible for the sound technician to record dialogue—he bizarrely caught up in technical details while the planes, like any other commonplace annoyance, interfere with his work. Members of the cast and crew converse with Ziad about the security police wreaking havoc, taking relatives away, even incarcerating a member of the staff for alleged collaboration with "terrorists." A lighting technician drinking the local liquor, 'araq, breaks down in tears, overcome by worry for his family. Another crew member, clearly high and already having been arrested once for drug possession, tells of his father being tortured to death while in detention. These last two stories underscore the pain of their intoxicated narrators without enlisting viewers in a structure of empathic overidentification.

One illuminating scene involves an extra on the set of the fictional film whose actual husband is in the air force. Trying to come to grips with what is happening and her husband's role in the escalating carnage, she assures the film crew in no uncertain terms that pilots can tell the difference between ordinary Syrians and terrorists. She tells a cockamamie story about technological advances that allow pilots to home in on the people who want to do harm to the country, avoiding ordinary bystanders. She is the butt of bitter laughter behind her back, while her presence nevertheless reminds us of the world in which people go on subscribing to regime discourse as usual—whether they believe it or not. And in her case, despite the outlandishness of the story, it is hard to know what she believes. The film collaboration brings together loyalists and dissidents, presenting a model, at once discomfiting and illuminating, for how difference can be navigated through work on a shared creative project. These scenes also afford Kalthum the ethnographic opportunity to acknowledge some of the less dramatic injuries of war, the damage wrought by the daily thrum of constant low-level fear as opposed to the spurts of high-intensity terror.

Kalthum devotes considerable time to filming a mentally disturbed man on the street who sits near a dilapidated well-known cinema which was already in a state of disrepair before the uprising began. The man's own memories of the theater's magnificent past contrast markedly with the stills decorating its walls, displays of cheap, dated commercialism, soft-core pornography, and other exemplars of vulgar moviemaking. A close-up of a woman's breasts is juxtaposed to the man's laments for "Syria, the mother." Kalthum plays with these discontinuities, using the camera to "quilt" (to invoke once more the Lacanian image of the *point de capiton*) the obscenities of nationalist rhetoric and aesthetic commodification together.

The disturbed man is mourning his son's death at the hands of "criminal gangs," as he puts it, echoing language the regime used early on to describe the opposition. In responding to a question about the regime's politics, he continues to demonstrate fluency in the official rhetoric, if not any ability to reflect on it. And for Kalthum, the violence here is also dual: the overt conflict of wartime makes the systemic, banal falsehoods of dictatorship more starkly delusional. Close-ups of the man—his face ravaged by time, his mouth missing teeth, his fingers stained with nicotine and nails encrusted with dirt—give these scenes an uncomfortable intimacy. He clings to regime pieties the way he clings to his cigarettes—his madness made palpable by the way he addresses himself and by his zany codeswitching. "Who are these flowers for?" Kalthum asks, pointing to jasmine in a jar. "For Karawan," the man responds. Then he adds: "Karawan is me." The karawan bird is a type of curlew or lark inhabiting riverbanks or the seashore. By invoking the bird, the man is making direct reference to the golden age of Egyptian music and of pan-Arab nationalism under Gamal 'Abd al-Nasir. The hyperidentification on the part of the self-anointed Karawan (with national coherence, authoritarianism, and celebrity) is both a registration of a common nostalgia among men of his generation and a painful witnessing to narcissistic attachment in which the fan and the object of adulation have become one. At times the man mimics the speech of an intellectual in an elevated, formal Arabic. At other times, he sounds like he is reciting from a school textbook, his language laden with nationalistic clichés. At times he claims to be friends with famous celebrities, his grandiosity akin to the regime's. And his own invocations of fatherhood are, in Kalthum's rendering, suggestively synecdochic: in his delusionary world he can stand in for the national father, openly imputing that he is no more mad than the president himself. In another scene, the man addresses his dead son in the second-person singular—posting a picture on the wall, the image a copy of the dead son's identity card, mimeographed onto a sheet of paper containing text commemorating his life, the image a duplicate of a duplicate, not dissimilar to how Kalthum's film is grafted onto Malas's.

These themes of doubling and splitting find expression in the handheld cell-phone sequences as well, in the martial, party-oriented iconography and Ba'thist sloganeering so familiar from an earlier era of autocratic rule. Audible on radio broadcasts throughout the barracks and attesting to the party's immortality, these staples of 1950s–80s propaganda stand in jarring contrast to the shabby, dilapidated army buildings. Kalthum's dark humor is evident here, as is a sense of time as both fixed and moving—the disembodied broadcast's assertions of immortality contradicted by stark images of material degradation. The wobbly cell-phone camera records the peeling paint, the posters hanging askew on the wall and curling up at the corners, as well as close-ups of the army's own film archives, reel piled on reel collecting dust. Nothing could be more contrary to the alleged glorious eternity of Ba'thist rule than the chronic state of neglect visible everywhere. The depictions of army life (a diet of eggs, bread, and caffeinated maté tea), the audio of the stale panegyrics, and most dramatically, a scene of soldiers riling themselves for battle by recalling other autocracies' martial preparations all raise (unanswered) questions about what could be sustaining soldiers' commitment. This open-endedness is one of the film's strengths, its avoidance of melodramatic predictability and didacticism allowing for the experience of loss without giving up on the messiness of politics.

Kalthum announces his own recalibrated relationship to authority by filming with his cell phone a sign declaring that cell phones are prohibited. He is no longer (if he ever was) the obedient soldier but rather a chronicler of political contradiction: sounds of bombs exploding, images of boots on the ground, smoke, trees splitting, anxiety mounting, a sense of menace overlaid with president Bashar al-Asad's speech calling for the return to security and enhanced sovereignty. The familiar chant "With our soul and blood we sacrifice for you, O Bashar" is disrupted by Kalthum's intercutting of people calling for the downfall of the regime. And then we meet Karawan, or whoever he is—the man mourning the loss of his son, a bundle of incongruities who embodies the madness of the moment.

The nervous giggling on set is audible as cast and crew discuss the everyday horrors of war—such as a colleague being taken away in the dead of night or the proliferation of checkpoints and the inability to move freely around a city that until recently was lively into the wee hours of the morn. Laughter seems to help people bear the unbearable, as we have discussed in chapter 2; but here the giggling comes in an attempt to cover up a noticeable discomfort while also working in Kalthum's film to draw the audience's attention to it.[41] The gigglers in the film are often (but not only) women identified with the regime or at least not in opposition to it, their mirth a gendered reaction to moments of cognitive dissonance, a corrective meant to render the terrible merely difficult. Kalthum juxtaposes action on the set to the activity of setting up for the scene; setting up is juxtaposed to news accounts on satellite television. And the news, at least in 2011–12, provides some anchoring for Kalthum to the world of vulnerable facts. His on-set interviews reproduce this fidelity to a sense of factual truth—its fragility, contingency, and reliance on a referential system which, as Hannah Arendt points out, recalling chapter 3's discussion, "is always related to other people" and "depends upon their testimony," while not being reducible to collective consensus or opinion.[42] Kalthum's ethnographic sensibility registers not only Ba'thist stridency but also opposition attempts to cancel out complexities. For him, possibilities for reimagining collectivity come out of a shared acknowledgment of Syria's diversity. Collapsing the wide array of views into a binary, he seems to be saying, is as harmful in its classificatory dualism as the affective splitting is to the individual. Factual truth—and indeed a renewed sense of the political—depends on capturing the messiness.

Far from denying ambivalence, much of *The Immortal Sergeant* is devoted to exposing and grappling with it. At least up until the penultimate scene, the film even avoids a musical soundtrack—unusual for Syrian film. But the moment of music's interjection and the film's consequent shift to a melodramatic register are themselves significant, coming immediately after an exchange between Kalthum and an elderly woman from Bab al-Saba', a popular quarter identified with the opposition in the besieged city of Homs. The woman is there as an extra in the fictional movie, and Kalthum takes advantage of a break in filming to find out who she is—treating her respectfully, but as an interview subject, in a way that reminds us of the ethnographer-cameraman's structural intrusiveness into the intimate lives of others. His seemingly anodyne question, "How many children do you have?" is itself fraught, gesturing toward loss and the relentless violence in Homs. She hesitates in response, finally asking, "Me?"

Is the pain momentarily too much, the question complicated for her because coming up with a number requires a decision about how to commemorate the dead and treat the missing? We do not know. At Kalthum's gentle insistence, she tells us that one of her sons died with his daughter, and another son has gone missing. In her case, it is reasonable to assume from context that her children are victims of the Asad regime—and her understated grief contrasts sharply with the grandiosity of the regime's portrayal of collective sorrow we recall from the Mother's Day film *With Your Soul You Protect the Jasmine*. This mother's initial inability to process the question is a touching testimony to the power of what can be said in silence. As if Kalthum himself could not bear his own turn to reportage or to the suffering it unearths, he layers on some heavy string music and runs the film in slow motion, undermining the movie's "countersentimental" impulses, as Lauren Berlant would call them,[43] as well as its otherwise notable ability to sit with discomfort and loss. The camera work here reproduces the very discourse of all Syrians bundled together—children, soldiers, and civilians—that his previous critique of martial culture and political uniformity brought into question.[44]

Ziad Kalthum's film chronicles loss, not as a particular occurrence but as an ongoing experience of war. His effort to come to terms with it, to do the work of mourning through ethnographic filmmaking, is why the recourse to the sentimental, at the moment it occurs, is so revealing of how difficult it is to reconnect with the external world while continuing to suffer unspeakable loss. Loss here is about loved ones, of course, as well as homes, property, and the pleasures of a secure ordinariness. But for Kalthum, at least, the film is also a requiem for Syria, one that as he suggests in his juxtaposition of tawdry soft-porn pictures to the obscenity of nationalist rhetoric was always illusory, an elusive "object-cause of desire," to use another psychoanalytic term, a constitutive lack, an absent presence, an object the very desire for which is motivated by its ungraspability.[45]

The Immortal Sergeant concludes by returning to the wobbly handheld cell-phone and grainy YouTube clips of his soldier self. Depicted as a larger-than-life shadow in military boots making its way on an unpaved path, an image used by other filmmakers and citizen journalists as well, he appears as the negative of the embodied soldier, a study in expurgating his own negativity by renouncing violence—both his own personal complicity in the war and the structural conditions that have demanded it. A series of jump cuts—involving a mushroom cloud explosion and lights in the darkness over the landscape of Damascus—proceed in staccato rhythm, suggesting the experience of living in a world in which psychic integration has been made so difficult. The camera clips come rapid fire: the army barracks viewed through the green-hued lenses of military goggles; televised announcements of heavy fighting in Aleppo; footage of men enlisting in the military; a voice calling Bashar al-Asad a vampire (literally "blood drinker"); news channels reporting different scenes of carnage as the war intensifies in 2012–13.

And then the camera goes askew. We hear the noise of the projector and the reel of film, then Kalthum gives us fast-forward images of the sky. Then the scene switches to a mass of male soldiers, suggestive of that potent blend of power and surrender. Next, another explosion and people running. Cut. The phone rings and he is identified by name: "Hello, sergeant recruit Ziad Kalthum." Images of men cheering the fighting. Empty hallways. Men dead. Clouds of smoke. Soldiers in uniform, then a close-up from the back of a bloodied head (footage used in other films too), then a close-up of a wasp on a lamp, an insect that stings but is also drawn to a light that can kill. The sound of labored breathing. And then the final words captioned on a dark, imageless background: "Based on this, I, sergeant recruit Ziad Kalthum, proclaim my rebellion against the army. The only weapon I shall carry in this life is my camera." Tellingly, the use of the referentless *this* in the phrase "based on . . ." implies that the referent can be presumed, the movie's previous scenes freighting the declaration with an acknowledgment of what is unspeakable in the violence, the contradictions of war and the agony of intense self-alienation no longer bearable to this sergeant. The political message is clear: Kalthum's, like the *Unknown Soldier*'s in chapter 3, is a repudiation of violence—regardless of whether the regime or the opposition is giving the call to arms.

More complex both aesthetically and politically is Ossama Mohammed's (Usama Muhammad) feature-length film, *Ma' al-Fidda* (*Silvered Water, Syria Self-Portrait* [2014]), a study in the process of mourning and an avowal of *cinema*'s evolving revolutionary capacities.[46] Unlike relative newcomers 'Abd al-Wahid or Kalthum, Mohammed was a prominent director before the uprising, known for his practice of drawing attention to cinema's specificities as an art form. His three prior films—in very different registers—pointed to the affinities between patriarchal violence and rural disrepair, on the one hand, and authoritarian control, on the other. Hailed for bringing to his cinematic object a sense of distance born paradoxically of knowing a place extremely well, Mohammed was forced into actual exile in 2011. *Silvered Water* chronicles his efforts to wrestle artistically with this displacement and the shift from peaceful protests to catastrophic war.[47] A product of a new estrangement, the film recalls to viewers those first exhilarating months in which Syrians demanding an end to tyranny and injustice crossed the threshold of fear. It also testifies to the subsequent carnage. And it intriguingly complicates Mohammed's long-term preoccupation with cinematic form by incorporating footage taken by ordinary citizens.[48] Unlike filmmakers who demand of the camera that it tell the truth, Mohammed has always been self-conscious about how decisions about locations and shot selection shape what we see. *Silvered Water* relocates this recognition, taking a massive archive of raw amateur footage and transforming it into cinema. Mohammed has precedents in this—

Godard's cinema verité comes to mind—but in this film the artfully composed cinematic collages highlight the director's role as archivist, curator, and poet, as arbiter of multiple points of view.

Silvered Water appears to be divided into two main parts. The first draws from Syrians' cell-phone footage—scenes of peaceful mass demonstrations and of the regime's ruthlessness in response—to capture those heady first days of protest and repeated acts of courage, and the relentless drive to crush them both. The second part narrates the director's interaction with a young Syrian-Kurdish woman, Wiam Simav Bedirxan, who appeared suddenly in the form of a Facebook friend request on Christmas Day 2011. A period of exchanging messages follows, resulting in an agreement to collaborate on a project. Simav, as she is called, is to film the ongoing destruction of her city of Homs—with the siege by this point already underway—and upload the footage for Mohammed to curate as director. Her footage registers not only the inhumanity of war but also her attempt to cling to the revolution's promise. Like the shots Mohammed uses of a clothespin clasped to a makeshift line, Simav is hanging on—to the memories of her family, to the pleasure of music she happens upon in an abandoned home, to a sense of the everyday that comes with washing the laundry as the destruction mounts, to hopes of a better future for the city's remaining children, and to her urgently felt duty to bring the images of war to the attention of the global public. Maimed and burned animals, bloodied bodies retrieved from rubble-strewn streets—scenes of irretrievable loss are only some of the horrendous images that appear in the film, drawn from her footage as well as clips from anonymous others in Homs, all woven in masterly fashion into Mohammed's whole.

Silvered Water has garnered controversy in addition to acclaim, in the process stimulating a critical and much-needed debate about the role and obligations of cinema in times of devastation, bearing on the representation of victimization and the relationship between aesthetics and politics.[49] Mohammed himself probes some of these issues extra-diegetically, asking questions directly in his own voice that exceed the frame: What is beauty? What is cinema?[50] Drawing our attention to the artifice of the medium, to the beauty lurking in the grotesque, Mohammed is all the while recovering stories of human resilience and connection in the face of annihilating violence. This is ultimately a film that can be reduced neither to its shocking scenes nor to a romance of resistance. It is, as the English-language subtitle suggests, a "self-portrait" of myriad Syrians and the director, a film whose poetry resides not least in its unwavering insistence on the human capacity to make something new—as well as to destroy.

Like Ziad Kalthum's account in *The Immortal Sergeant* but in considerably more graphic detail, *Silvered Water* depicts the struggle to maintain and take pleasure in ordinary life as violence progressively destroys the simple conventions affixing us to familiar worlds. This is true not only for Simav living and filming in the besieged city of Homs but also for Mohammed, who castigates himself for the "cowardice" of his French exile. The repeated juxtaposition of his world to hers expresses a difficult-to-bear contrast between the invigoration of life that takes place under fire and the guilt and corrosion that set in under conditions of privilege. His previous cinematic preoccupations with natality, birth, and new beginnings find expression in this film too—registered in repeated jump cuts to a newborn being washed, an umbilical cord being cut, and many shots of openings and camera apertures through which familiar worlds can be seen anew. Potentiality, a favorite theme of Mohammed's, reduces in one scene to an egg rotating in his Paris microwave. The shot encapsulates the director's sense of death in exile: "At night, I say: tomorrow I'll go back. In the morning, I buy a microwave." For viewers familiar with Mohammed's oeuvre, the irradiated egg poses a deadening substitute for the various signifiers of birth in his other films. Acknowledging his pain and vulnerability, his "stuckness" both physically and emotionally, he narrates a dream he had of his own death over a static shot of a dead man having been tortured in the *furuj* style, like a chicken bound to the spit, his contorted, balled-up body arranged to expose his bare feet to the torturer's beatings: "I dreamed that I was dead . . . in a static shot. I saw myself dead in the shot and I heard the voice, 'Such a pity, he was still strong, but he couldn't bear the distance.' I died."

The scene, in the closing sequence of part 1 of the film, is not the only one drawing criticism from some Syrians for self-indulgent melodramatic sentimentality. But that self-indulgence—if that is what it is—is also an invitation, an exemplary working through of a situation that would otherwise be intolerable, beckoning us to acknowledge weakness as well as strength, to see the humanity not only in heroism but also in fear, failure, and inconsequence. Unlike some opposition filmmakers, moreover, Mohammed is at pains to show the humanity of regime soldiers—at least when they are at rest. One soldier is able to operate his extraordinary voice like a plucked string instrument. Others we see energetically dancing the *dabke*, a vision of intense male solidarity and expert footwork. From Mohammed's narration it is clear where he stands politically, but his position does not require him to dehumanize others or neglect other points of view. Nor, in his mind, does it require shying away from war's atrocity.

The film stitches the horrifying images of mangled bodies to the spirit of revolutionary change, to the internal suffering of an exiled director, to the systemic violence that has made men into soldiers for the regime. Over footage of a man in the confines of an army tank, he narrates, "His tragedy as a soldier. He kills when he doesn't want to. He's killed when he doesn't want to be."

The same humanity is found in the friendship that develops between Mohammed and Simav: her bravery in filming the siege of Homs under unfathomable conditions, his reliance on her for connection to a world to which he can no longer return. Referring both to an Arabic reading exercise from an old textbook and to the Syrian uprising's irreversibility, the film notes repeatedly, "Darʻa's train has departed"—it has left the station. And where the train is heading, the film seems to be saying, is not under any one person's control. Patchen Markell has noted, in discussing Hannah Arendt, that "because we do not act in isolation but interact with others, who we become through action is not [simply] up to us; instead, it is the outcome of many intersecting and unpredictable sequences of action and response, such that 'nobody is the author or producer of his own life story.'"[51] In the film's recognition of our interdependence and non-sovereignty, Mohammed has found a way of affirming life, even in dark times.

With a Terrence Malick–like appreciation of life's mystery—the images of blue skies and sun-drenched cumulus clouds that make the heavens so spectacular on earth—Mohammed celebrates the possibilities for human connection with none of the mysticism we find in Malick. Shots of water, light, the skyline of Paris, a pyramid edifice seen through the aperture of a window, are about what Mohammed himself refers to as "universal" (*kawni*) thinking, a kind of contemplation that operates inside a connection to nature and human artifice and extends beyond the limits of nation-state solidarities. According to Mohammed, cinema's capacity to play with form and grapple explicitly with the world of appearance makes it distinctly amenable and perhaps vulnerable to tensions between sentiment and realism. Ideally, that makes it productive of new political possibilities, enabling an embrace of both the specificity of local experience and a version of situated universalism. Bearing witness—and indeed insisting on that situated universalism in relation to the Syrian catastrophe—entails acknowledging the discontinuous, heteronomous ways in which structural conditions of authoritarian injustice and devastating violence also motivate novel forms of collectivity. Mohammed renders this insistence on solidarity both in content and through form, composing a single collage from a thousand points of view, using moments of rhythmic intensity, images such as tumbling kaleidoscopes, and repetition (repeated shots of a baby being born and the recurring figure of a young man curled up and being tortured) to generate that effect. These image strands are not mediated through the first person, and they do not belong in the same register. Indeed, the film can be interpreted here as working performatively to bring into being its own register, in which juxtapositions can but need not be experienced as simply discontinuous.

When Simav enters the picture in the second half of the film, the point of view stabilizes in conventional terms, becoming more homogeneous both narratively and visually. Yet at the same time, between the woman on the ground with the camera and Mohammed is constant dialogue, so that the director never fully surrenders control. Instead, he experiments with what it means to be engaged differently by containing their dialogue in his monologue. Montage governs his efforts more than hers—when he announces he feels as if he were dying emotionally, it enables her to rescue him by generating a rawer filmic perspective, one that permits him to recompose the project by representing her simplified surety—her proximity to the object being represented, the revolutionary struggle, the war—while remaining faithful to art's capacity to create political distance. This distance is underscored both in the segment titles (in one section, the days of the week: Monday, Tuesday, Wednesday, and so on; in another, references to known epics, such as Herodotus's Marathon or Douma Mon Amour [a place on the outskirts of Damascus referencing the famous Alain Resnais film, *Hiroshima Mon Amour*]) and by a voice-over tying the images to essay-like rubrics: "cinema of the murderer," "cinema of the victim."[52]

In an unflinching account of death and destruction, the colossal tragedy of the situation is confronted, moreover, by Mohammed's insistence on openings, his aliveness to the beauty of a raindrop on the windowpane, to the capacities of a camera to venture closer or create distance, to see through apertures into worlds to which we are otherwise blind—to imagine what he has called "a universal place, a place for everyone."[53] The camera is at once a witness to the human capacities for destruction and for connection, the contradictions brought to the fore by the image of the word *freedom* in Arabic inscribed in blood in startlingly white snow. Simav has been teaching him words in her father's native tongue of Kurdish, as she has throughout the film. "Teach me 'human' in Kurdish," he says. She responds with a word and he repeats. "Color?" She responds again. "Red?" "White?" The camera closes in on the snow. Their conversation concludes on the anniversary of its beginning, on Christmas as it happens. He says,

"Merry Christmas. A year ago your first message came. I will celebrate both anniversaries, Jesus's and the Messiah's. It is our day, my friend. It was just like this day, a year ago, that we met." And she responds in Kurdish: "Roj Bash," which evidently means "good morning." She asks, "How did you know I was online now?" He responds, "How not?!" This is not to say that at other times in the film there were no scenes of disconnection, no need on his part to search for her presence. She is often unavailable. He worried about her, and about his ability to keep her interested in him, as compared with the intensity of the siege; he who is bored and frustrated and self-doubting in exile.

Silvered Water is dedicated to a little boy called Omar who wanders around with Simav—and whose name coincidentally is also that of Ossama Mohammed's dearest friend, the well-known documentary filmmaker Omar Amiralay, who died suddenly in February 2011, shortly before the uprising began: "To Omar, from Simav Bedirxan, 1001 Syrians, and me." Critics have noted the orientalizing impression it is possible to have here, as well as the excessive optimism implied in the reference to a thousand and one nights, given the war's ongoing-ness. But the dedication also underscores the film's status as a collective enterprise, one this auteur film-maker embraces both creatively and by necessity, while remaining at the same time somewhat discomfited by it.

Lauren Berlant notes that "cases of vulnerability and suffering can become all jumbled together into a scene of the generally human," replac-ing "the ethical imperative towards social transformation" with "a passive and vaguely civic-minded ideal of compassion."[54] This is the danger that Mohammed risks in *Silvered Water*. Its lavish use of graphic scenes of suf-fering, especially in the second half of the film, conceivably rides rough-shod over complex affective registers, including the need to mourn the loss of the political sensibilities calling for peaceful change that characterized the first half of the film. But Mohammed's insistence on multiple points of view, his own fidelity to montage (and his willingness to experiment by abandoning montage's contrasting rapid-shot sequencing) elevate the film far above any maudlin account of amplified feelings. The visual and audio use he makes of a complex pronominal universe, in which the first-person singular and plural are overlaid with second and third persons, helps create an imaginative "multiplication of perspectives."[55] The dialogue between Simav and Mohammed becomes a long and not entirely successful effort at artistic and political collaboration—all transpiring inside his monologue, which in addition to his first-person standpoint is also a channel for the contributions of anonymous others. Berlant rightly points to how a multiplication of perspectives can itself allow for melodrama, for an "expressive emotional self-integration,"[56] which in Mohammed's case would be friendship and partial healing of the fractured self for which cinema itself can be responsible. My point, *pace* the critics, is simply that the film can in no way be reduced to an exploitative narrative. Nor is the promised vision of alternative connections to be forged (whether on national grounds or as commodified human rights) ever worked out. The film toggles interestingly between issues of justice and a need to feel and solicit empathy with suffering others, perhaps producing too much feeling as a defense against ambivalence, confusion, or numbness.[57]

Although the efforts to express a common humanity found in the works of Khalid 'Abd al-Wahid, Ziad Kalthum, and Ossama Mohammed sometimes fail to exceed a kind of mawkish compassion, they also hint at the revitalization of a complicated, politically vibrant, and situated universalism. I mean by this something altogether different from the liberal universalism we have on offer these days, which has been forged, troublingly, through an international human rights regime trafficking in market-oriented, sentimentalized narratives of trauma. That genre has allowed people to take unacknowledged pleasure in overidentifying with actually suffering individuals while busily reproducing the very social order they delude themselves into imagining they are upending with their charitable gifts, their public displays of compassion, and so on.[58]

By contrast, these films help in the pursuit of an alternative basis for political solidarity, one recalling Hannah Arendt's appreciation of the "human capacity for freedom."[59] Unlike liberal solidarity, with its focus on individuals, institutions, and the law, Arendt's take on freedom privileges a politics of collective action. As distinct from solidarities based on nationalist collectivities, moreover, an Arendtian politics celebrates indeterminate forms of fellow feeling, refusing to specify any Othering content like race or territorial location. And for Arendt, exercising this human capacity presupposes intersubjective relations of a sort that depend on political judgment—what she calls, as noted at the beginning of this chapter, "representative thinking."[60] She writes:

> Political thought is representative. I form an opinion by considering a given issue from different viewpoints, by making present to my mind the standpoints of those who are absent; that is, I represent them. This process of representation does not blindly adopt the actual views of those who stand somewhere else, and hence look upon the world from a different perspective; *this is a question neither of empathy, as though I tried to be or to feel like*

somebody else, nor of counting noses and joining a majority, but of being and thinking in my own identity where actually I am not. The more people's standpoints I have present in my mind while I am pondering a given issue, and the better I can imagine how I would feel and think if I were in their place, the stronger will be my capacity for representative thinking and the more valid my final conclusions, my opinion.[61]

This is what Immanuel Kant called "enlarged mentality" or, more precisely, as described by Linda Zerilli, "an enlarged manner of thinking whose condition of possibility is not the faculty of understanding, but imagination."[62] And imagination entails in part what Wittgenstein describes as "persuading people to change their style of thinking,"[63] a practice that relies less on the introduction of new facts than on acknowledging what we already know by drawing attention to multiple points of view, resonances, and ways of saying and apprehending things about the world. We saw in chapter 2 how humor helps us acknowledge what we already know. And we saw in chapter 3 how, when facts fall victim to mendacity, other genres of aesthetic intervention such as the Abounaddara collective's short films bypass the world of conventional documentary fact-making by opening up styles of thinking that embrace ambiguity and foster curiosity, supplying what Kant called a *sensus communis*, or "common sense," that is contingent, indeterminate, open to revision, and a product of ongoing exploration and disagreement.

The films in this chapter, despite major political and aesthetic divergences from one another (and from Abounaddara's corpus), mark the most sustained efforts at the kind of imaginative modes of judgment Arendt terms representative thinking—or so I want to suggest. In 'Abd al-Wahid's short videos, an open-minded cosmopolitan sensibility finds expression in closed spaces. In Kalthum's ethnographic film, disagreement is portrayed in all its visual and cacophonous richness, and feelings of terror and boredom get mixed up with "viewpoints," and giggles, and crazy narrations, and tears, and charged silences. The director's ultimate decision to defect facilitates the previously split participant-observer's psychological reintegration, made possible by his embrace of cinema and of political judgment. Most dramatically, Ossama Mohammed's metacommentary on cinema's structural capacity to offer multiple perspectives and to envision dissonance as radical potential situates the director as representative thinker, putting him in various places where he is not—among protesters, amid the rubble of Homs, in the regime's barracks, dancing *dabke*. In doing so, his film avowedly commits to the image, not so much to supply additional facts as to reveal what we already know by changing the meaning of what we see.[64]

The Syrian films evoke possibilities as to what representative thinking might look like. They also hint at the concept's inconclusiveness. For despite the salutary provocations of representative thinking, Arendt's term does not give us much to go on. But the concept does imply a commitment to reciprocity and interpretive generosity that is disallowed by tyranny and rejected by Syria's first family—and President Trump, for that matter. The kind of imaginative thinking toward the regime soldiers we see in Ossama Mohammed's film, in showing us how the soldier is stuck in profound contradictions, does not apply to authoritarian rulers whose structural position by definition disallows the very reciprocity and mutuality the device of representative thinking requires. And indeed, Syria's first family from the beginning of the uprising has consistently denied any moral authority to the perspective of its critics. Nor does "representative thinking" presuppose an a priori standpoint of good judgment on which the person judging must rely in taking into account the situation of others.[65] Representative thinking, moreover, interrogates assumptions that educated, self-reflective people necessarily have good judgments or that human beings need specific rules or criteria for judging. Anyone who is willing can engage in the practice. And the "I" doing the imagining is changed in the context of interpretive encounters—that is what politics is about.

The concept's inconclusivity *does* suggest two supplements, fully consonant with Arendt's thinking but left unelaborated. First is an acknowledgment of the prior provisional commitments by which all of us are moored respectively to our multiple worlds and which guide us in judging. Not all judgments are equally valid, and Arendt does not suggest they are. But representative thinking can help us try to develop and complexify our standpoints—without self-satisfied complacency. Second is an appreciation of affective, sensorial experiences operating in excess of opinion or established "viewpoints." As the Syrian films discussed above have helped us see, the capacity to imagine alternative worlds—unbounded, public, indeterminate, skeptical, and discomfiting—means acknowledging loss, affirming solidarity, and registering ambivalence without abandoning judgment. In the case of Ossama Mohammed's *Silvered Water*, in particular, it means contending with what it means to stretch if not break aesthetic conventions whenever we find them reproducing the modes of relating we seek to challenge.

Nationalism has proved to be an exceptionally potent and adaptable way of imagining community. It is congenial to liberalism and fascism and to capitalist economies and forms of socialism. It fastens effortlessly onto genres such as melodrama that are designed to intensify feelings—in our case, of solidarity—while muting the possibility and promise of deliberative, agonistic, collective engagement. Nationalism's sentimental modes can work to impede judgment, obviating the exertion of representative imagination that is potentially conducive to structural transformation, as we saw in the television serials and in the first lady's Mother's Day spectacle. In the films of 'Abd al-Wahid, Kalthum, and Mohammed, the temptation to resort to sentimentality betrays a desire to acknowledge the suffering of others while at the same time short-circuiting experiences of loss that otherwise might be too difficult to bear. Sentimental modes of address assert commonality and forfend isolation, reassuring individuals, in this case Syrians, that they are not alone in their struggle. These artistic products are thus important both for their vulnerability to convention-sustaining forms of commodified sentiment and because they show us how people can renegotiate belonging. The ambiguous promise in these efforts, as well as their limitation, constitutes their political character in that they make it possible to address others in terms that connect actors' diverse and contentious interests to a common venture.[66]

The divergence between regime fare and these experiments in oppositional mourning suggests a crucial contrast between two economies of suffering. For the regime's version of sentimentality demands that only "we" experience grief and that only "they" inflict it. Predictable emotions operating within conventional structures of melodramatic nationalist sentimentality are heightened so that other unruly emotions and an alternative process of mourning can be refused acknowledgment, even if these emotions remain stubbornly present.[67] The regime version displays social difference, but only in ways that disallow all but officially managed kinds of difference, packaging diversity aesthetically within the abstractly accommodating sovereign confines of the palace. Difference here is tolerable only when disciplined and made tidy. It can in no way be disruptive or conflictual (aside, of course, from the a priori exclusion of "Others" from the "we" of righteous sufferers). It is in their acknowledgment of difference and conflict, of *nonsovereignty*, that Kalthum's and Mohammed's films in particular raise possibilities for politics, as distinct from a sentimentalized moral didacticism. Representative thinking, with the supplements noted here, can also be fruitfully understood as a mode of judging politically through the exercise of nonsovereignty—in which an "enlarged mentality" is open to radical differences in thinking and feeling, including desires for control. And in this light, the films can be seen as training spaces for political otherwiseness, as incitements to do the imaginative work entailed in ongoing processes of political judgment.

5

Fear and Foreboding

In the early days of the Syrian uprising, rumors of an impending massacre circulated among residents of various villages in the coastal province of Lattakia, warning local members of the 'Alawi sect that they were going to be murdered by Sunni "armed gangs."[1] The next night, some cars had their tires slashed. Although no people were harmed, as the rumors had warned they would be, something nefarious had in fact occurred. Common to a number of the versions I was told by interlocutors was the added point that villagers did not really believe that Sunni armed gangs had come in the night, suspecting instead that regime thugs associated with residents' own 'Alawi community had been responsible for both the rumors and the vandalism. The rumor nevertheless had the effect of framing anti-Sunni feelings in the language of moral justification, as if the important point was that the tire slashing *could have* been perpetrated by Sunni gangs.[2]

There are multiple ways to read the story, four of which underpin this chapter's efforts to consider the workings of ideology by analyzing the hardening of sectarian attachments. The account can be understood as (1) an invitation to interrogate temporality in conditions of affective excess, in which the present is displaced by *anticipatory* fears—a reaching for worst-case scenarios in advance of catastrophe; (2) exposing the violence at the heart of in-group solidarity; (3) underscoring a theme central to this book—namely, how a politics of what Octave Mannoni calls disavowal—*je sais bien, mais quand même . . .* (I know very well, yet nevertheless)—can be crucial to the maintenance of status quo conventionality, perhaps particularly in moments when order is profoundly threatened; (4) opening questions concerning the credibility of the report itself and the implications a lack of believability has for ideology.

Part 1 of this chapter unpacks these readings. Part 2 narrows the focus from the workings of ideology to the thugs themselves, considering how the political imaginaries and forms of addressability characteristic of thug loyalty are cultivated in excess of material incentives. Part 3 discusses what Raymond Williams calls the "structures of feeling," for him a concept associated with two others—"residual" and "emergent" forms of sociality—that together help us theorize some of the ways that sectarian identifications get activated, and in doing so displace other transformative possibilities for political solidarity.[3] As we shall see, the logic of preemption that proved so important to regime survival tapped into an existing set of hierarchies, some of which were sectarianized, and others carried acephalously through everyday practices like rumors.[4] In the context of the uprising, the regime's efforts to recalibrate its rule required it to take advantage of social practices already in evidence, but it also actively cultivated a situation in which existential survival was of paramount importance. Stories of sectarian conflict thus had to exist alongside ongoing (albeit incoherent) claims of multicultural accommodation and sovereign national order. Disruptions to the status quo could be officially coded as an assault on the collective per se, which ironically required specific sectarian identifications to stand in for the general national public.

PART ONE: IT COULD HAVE BEEN DANGEROUS OTHERS

The story about the nonexistent armed gangs and the real slashed tires invites us to revisit the question of how ideological interpellation operates—charting in this case the making of loyalist subjects in the context of neoliberal autocracy's unraveling and retrenchment. First, the fear among the villagers relied on a temporal structure privileging a hypothetical future over an experienced present. Perhaps especially in instances where national security seems threatened, ideology works in terms of what the cultural theorist Brian Massumi calls the "political ontology of threat," where both the threat and threat management depend on "what might come next" rather than "what is actually real."[5] "Fear is the anticipatory reality in the present of a threatening future,"[6] operating grammatically as the compression of the conditional and the future in the active present: it *could have been* those who pose a threat who slashed the tires (and could be the next time), as opposed to those who actually did the deed—the future being experienced as affective anticipation in the present.

The regime responded to the uprising by constructing security in terms of combatting terror, which entailed the fashioning of vulnerability in sectarian terms. Yet it did so, not simply by "Othering" dissidents (some of whom, despite stereotypes to the contrary, were 'Alawis), but by producing a sense of threat (in the possibility that "armed gangs" of foreign-funded Sunnis might terrorize the hinterland), which then seemed to justify the regime's deployment of a wide range of militarized practices against the citizenry. Or rather more precisely: over the period of time between the onset of the uprising and the opposition's turn to violence came the observable cultivation of what Michael Taussig calls a "nervous system"[7] (pun intended)—in this case, a complex circuit of ongoing apprehensions rooted in resonant claims about existential survival on the part of citizens who identified with minority sects such as the 'Alawi one. Rumors, not unlike Michel Foucault's "strategy without a strategist," were of service to this nervous system independently of demonstrable intention or purpose. They fed on what Massumi glosses as "the uncertainty of the potential next," which "is never consumed in any given event." For "there is always a remainder of uncertainty, an unconsummated surplus of danger."[8] This logic is "autopoietic" in the sense that its power is "self-causative" or self-reproducing.[9] In Syria, this "superlative futurity of unactualized threat"[10] helped produce what became actual violence: the regime protected itself by constructing an enemy—with the effect that the enemy became a reality. Moved by the iterative experience of protest and repression, battered protesters and defecting army conscripts were ideologically hailed into being as armed, foreign-supported actors after all. The compressed conditional—it could have been dangerous Others—worked as a double performative, helping create an in-group by demanding solidarity in anticipation of a menacing outsider whose existence had also been actualized in part by efforts to forfend it.

And this gets us to the second reading of the story, in which the rumor indexes the violence lurking at the heart of in-group solidarity itself. The philosopher René Girard, in *The One by Whom Scandal Comes*, argues that when "human beings either cannot or dare not take their anger out on the thing that has caused it, they unconsciously search for substitutes."[11] In our case, this would suggest that the rumor enables both the thugs and the villagers who uphold the fiction to bear the regime—and their own complicity in its reproduction—by projecting the violence onto "Sunni gangs." Or, in a different formulation, as Girard puts it in his celebrated account of in-group violence in *Violence and the Sacred*: what we see operating here may be mimetic desire (shared by thugs and villagers in the desire to be like the glamorous ruling family).[12] For Girard, mimetic desire ultimately leads to rivalry and conflict over goods and status. Stability is only achieved, in Girard's narrative, through the repetition of acts of collective violence against a scapegoat, which in our case would be the surrogate outsider on whom to displace the conflict that would otherwise be destructive of the intimate collective. In the rumor itself, this displacement is twofold: in-group membership is achieved not only by scapegoating Sunni Others but also in the guarding of the in-group secret, namely, that everyone (supposedly) knows that no Sunni gangs actually visited the village in the night.

Looked at in less Freudian, more rationalist terms, the rumor remains similarly revealing. The villagers would be making the calculation that while the thugs are hoodlums, they are *our* hoodlums, and their power to protect us depends on our willingness to guard the secret and imagine a prospect even more alarming than they. In this reading of the story, in actually slashing the tires the would-be "rescuers" of the 'Alawi villagers also displayed themselves as able purveyors of violence in their own right, whose control over the means of violence was not to be questioned. The initial anticipatory threat posed by Sunni armed gangs is thus followed by the token threat of additional violence, both demanding and exposing villager complicity in the structure of authoritarian maintenance. This complicity and the political imaginary it presupposes eclipsed possibilities for alternative solidarities. It is to be noted, for example, that most of these villages, impressions of 'Alawi privilege notwithstanding, remained poor and underserved by the welfare state. So solidarities based on class, *had* they been salient, might have given the uprising's revolutionary aspirations more traction.

Third is the politics of disavowal we see operating in the rumor. In a universe of heightened apprehension, being complicit called for the active bracketing of what villagers purportedly knew but failed to acknowledge—that it was their own thugs who did what they must dutifully imagine could have or would have been the act of dangerous Others. The ideological structure of disavowal, the "I know very well, yet nevertheless . . ." of this situation goes something like this: "I know very well that Sunni gangs did not vandalize the village in the night, yet nevertheless they could have—and given the opportunity, they would have done it." The rumor works to justify both hypervigilance and state-sponsored violence, with order ensured by having been violated preemptively. This reasoning process, to call it that, seems to call for a theory of public dissimulation in the sense of my earlier work on Syria in *Ambiguities of Domination*,[13] in that the villagers act *as if* it was Sunni gangs that slashed the tires, even while knowing otherwise. Only here, this doubling down on a belief the villagers did not hold in the first place points to the small forms of complicity activated by a residual us-versus-them orientation that then gradually congeal into entrenched differences or solidified connections. Or, to put the same point somewhat differently, a complicity born of prudence becomes over time a kind of loyalty. We see ideology operating here on a microlevel in the maintenance of a dissonant affective state. Through repeated calls to bracket what others are also bracketing, individuals are hailed as sectarian subjects, drawn by small acts of participation into a structure of disavowal that justifies silence. The villagers in the above story gradually become culpable for upholding an autocracy whose demands, at first limited, end up generating a more complete identification with the regime. The deeper a person is implicated, the harder it is to imagine extrication.

Fourth, other plausible readings of this story bear on the vexed matter of claim-making and further refine our discussion of belief. The frequent observation by interlocutors that no one believed the rumor, or that the villagers knew what was really going on, might itself misdescribe the situation.[14] Perhaps some people did believe the story, or at least were able to maintain themselves in a state of not doubting that Sunni vandals had somehow managed the attack. And this situation underscores a key point: People are capable of knowing something and not knowing it at the same time. This is a variation on the theme of ideological disavowal which would go something like "I know very well that it is implausible that Sunni gangs are in the area now, *but they might be, even though it is unlikely*, and even if they are not, they will be in the future." The temporal jump establishes the possibility of an imagined future as a warrant for the current reaction, as we have already seen. And this reaction not only accommodates contradiction but sidesteps veracity. And there are still other possibilities: generalized anxieties about the uncertain future, experienced in both epistemological and affective terms, can be real enough to cause groundless rumors to resonate. If the fears they index are real, uncertainty alone may make the threat credible simply as something worth hedging against. The feelings of solidarity presumed in and produced by listening to rumors and passing them on may serve to anchor these free-floating anxieties in easily imagined narrative details in which fears are allayed or possibly stimulated further. In either case, the rumor works, as Joseph Masco puts it, as a form of "affective recruitment."[15]

If the good life avoided a crass materialism by connecting economic prosperity to the moralizing registers of multisectarian accommodation and the defense of national sovereignty, regime cultural products such as the first lady's Mother's Day film (discussed in chapter 4) performed a circumscribed, less inclusive version of difference in a similar moralizing register. The Sunni gangs rumor, like the film, needs to be seen as a recalibration of rule in which in-group loyalties come to stand in for a broad, morally righteous nation. But in the rumor's case, the recalibration was not necessarily deliberate or initiated from the top down, and it served to protect the fantasy of toleration by drawing, paradoxically, from sectarian affiliations for solidarity. That paradox required a rhetorical displacement of sectarian extremism onto Others such as Sunni gangs while positioning increasingly sectarianized regime supporters (such as the thugs and complicit villagers featured in the rumor) as allies of national order.

PART TWO: LOYALTY RECONSIDERED

Regime thugs, like the ones sowing rumors in the village, have their own relationship to false stories, presumably typical of the staunch loyalist for whom there is no real dissonance involved in lying for the sake of the cause. Unlike the ordinary villagers, such loyalists operate without the same fears, ambivalence, or confusion. Their imaginary, at least in ideal typical terms, is not characterized by the temporal maneuvers of apprehension and related displacements discussed above. The *shabbiha*—as these thugs are called in Syria—are said to have taken their name from the Mercedes S600 car (the Shabah) that was popular among some of them in the 1980s. That *shabbiha* means "ghosts" is also fitting, of course, given the thugs' spectral presence haunting the coastal areas and ports, participating in a variety of protection rackets linked to smuggling, extortion, and, in the interior city of Homs, real estate. Self-identified as 'Alawi, shabbiha became a force to be reckoned with in the 1980s–90s, when they were controlled by close cousins of the ruling Asad family. Marginalized in the early days of Bashar al-Asad's reign, they remained in place, to be repurposed and empowered as the uprising got underway.[16] They were deployed by the regime, but also willing to take advantage of regime vulnerabilities—namely, army defections and growing protests in response to repression—thereby generating the conditions of their own indispensability.

This reliance on an 'Alawi-specific security force required ideological work to negotiate the discursive contradictions between sectarian specificity and national generality. Similarly in need of smoothing over, however, were socioeconomic contradictions, which had they been recognized might have inclined poor people of all stripes or rural inhabitants in particular to align against a corrupt, kleptocratic elite. A heightened awareness of sectarian difference—both generated from the top down and driven from bottom-up ordinary practices—also helped define shabbiha zones of influence and obligation, producing the anxieties necessary for regime survival. Sustaining neoliberal autocracy entailed the production of an ambivalent middle, as we have seen, but it also needed staunch loyalists—people whose feelings of existential threat could override such incendiary political potentialities as class-based solidarities or human rights demands (recall protesters' calls for *karameh*, "dignity").

Political economists who have focused on the shabbiha report regime-funded members earned as much as 7,000 to 10,000 lira (100–140 dollars) on Fridays, the initial flash point day for protest, and at least 2,000 lira (35 dollars) for their services on other days intimidating civilians in general and potential protesters in particular. Additional funding came from key businessmen allied with the regime.[17] And shabbiha found supplemental remuneration by taking advantage of new smuggling opportunities and increasing occasions for plunder.[18] Included in the latter category was the selling of household wares, jewelry, clothing, even underwear, at second-hand markets called *suq al-Sunna* (Sunni suqs)—not because the sellers were Sunni but because the wares had been taken from Sunni households. Shabbiha also enjoyed special privileges like skipping the breadlines at local bakeries, operating as rogue traffic police collecting bribes at select thoroughfares, and bypassing bureaucratic red tape.

Despite the perquisites, as the prominent Syrian intellectual and activist Yasin al-Hajj Salih has argued, a simple materialist explanation keyed to compensation falls short of accounting for the high levels of fidelity to the job routinely observed among shabbiha. An instrumentalist emphasis also neglects the sheer excess that seems to be a hallmark of their devotion—the hierarchical, almost cultish dimensions of hero worship animating these militias. By likening the organizational structure of these patronage networks and the affective intensity of leader-follower relations to the mafia, al-Hajj Salih draws our attention to the important blend of intimacy and reverence that characterizes shabbiha loyalty. This loyalty required ongoing work of a nonmaterial kind—a quasi institutionalization of a previously haphazard riot system, rousing these men to violence while valorizing the pleasure they were observably experiencing in dispensing it.[19]

Such excessive devotion is likewise found in a similar, still irregular but more formal formation of forces headed by Suhayl al-Hasan, the famous Syrian Nimr (Tiger), the high-ranking commander of special operations troops made up largely of 'Alawi-identified units known for being deployed in "scorched-earth" campaigns. In addition to his unquestioned loyalty to the regime, the Tiger is said to display a legendary fearlessness in protecting the Asads (lions), yet betraying no ambition to supplant them, thereby making him the ideal heroic figure in this feline menagerie. An object of adoration by his feared and generally effective troops, he is also the personification of national sacrifice in which nation elides regime, and regime increasingly elides sect.[20] And, as in many instances of propagandistic mimesis, his exemplarity for devotees is correspondingly a source of derision and irreverence for opposition-oriented citizens.[21]

The Tiger's figuration as at once ferocious and loyal recalls the nationalist aesthetics and bombastic prose of 1970s–80s Ba'thism. His staying power as a hero for staunch loyalists reveals how certain addressees in Syria's neoliberal autocracy were susceptible to that aspect of the promised good life that drew on an older nationalist repertoire underpinned by anxieties of nonsovereignty—of a nation and its protectors in peril. Conjuring up rhetorics of existential threat and martial solidarity, videos and songs paying homage to the Tiger amplify the patriotism of proper Syrianness. Consider this typical song:

> God bless the Arab Army, protector of Syria.
> God bless the Syrian Army, the symbol of national unity.
> You, cherished one, of the noble brow [denoting a proper kind of pride].
> (*Army official to the Tiger*) I carry greetings from our heroic leadership and
> 	our commander of the army and the armed forces to you and the men
> 	who are true to the great Asad. Asad who assigned you this mission
> 	giving you complete responsibility, as you are all heroes in exactly
> 	the way our leader Bashar Hafiz Al-Asad has always known you to be.
> 	Always forward is our hopeful goal!
> (*Song resumes*) God is great. God is great. God is great. God is great.
> Strike and you will find victory in your swords
> And you soldiers, forever heroes.
> Stand in defense of the land of your ancestors
> And your flowers will be the glory of generations.
> Hell awaits those who would cross your borders.

Your Navy is glory in action.

And your brow, cherished one, is noble.

Your flag, O Syria, hangs high.

You are my hope, my pride, and my destiny.

With your blood my honor is protected.

We are the Syrian Arab Army. We are the Syrian Arab Army.[22]

To be noted in particular is the elision of the second-person singular and plural, where the soldier addressee is merged with an army that both protects and stands in for Syria; where the "my" could be the personalized register of a single citizen soldier, or it could be ventriloquizing Syria as a whole. The song culminates, unsurprisingly, in the voicing of a national "we" and the invocation of fascistic blood-and-soil imagery.

This return to, indeed the regeneralization of, a rhetoric that before the uprising had been increasingly confined to party rallies and the barracks signaled the (at least temporary) end of a compelling fiction—in which autocratic rule could be kinder and gentler, a benevolent despotism focused less on conspiratorial narratives of disorder and sedition and more on aspirations to economic well-being and fantasies of multicultural accommodation. In other words, this song and countless others like it (posted on Facebook and representing small towns and villages throughout the country) are instances of citizens being hailed back to the future—partially unmaking the market-oriented aesthetics of neoliberal autocracy while drawing attention to the violence that sustained it.

Soldiers both embody anticipatory violence and rely on it, deriving their coercive and symbolic power from the higher authority of the nation. Here the nation is ruled exclusively by males—the loyal Tiger and his boss, the president, where Asad's own masculinity is no longer imagined in the corporate, cosmopolitan imagery of a modern peacetime leader but in the military fatigues of a hypermasculine warrior. Bedecking public walls and posted on the internet when Russian troops were expanding their presence in 2012–13 was a photo highlighting Asad's martial credentials, pairing him with Russian president Vladimir Putin, also in military fatigues, over a caption reading in Arabic and Russian: "The era of masculinity and of men."

If Asad and Putin, and the Tiger and his soldiers, symbolize this era, then the shabbiha are its extreme figuration, a pumped-up embodiment of violence that speaks to a paradoxical discipline and unruliness. Testosterone- and steroid-fueled male bodies fill the gyms in security-oriented places like Tartus, the heart of Syria's intense bodybuilding movement. Images on Facebook and Instagram celebrate grotesquely engorged muscles and male camaraderie. Tattoo parlors offer everything from etchings of Bashar al-Asad's face to elaborate engravings of the Shi'i hero Imam 'Ali for decorating backs or arms.[23] In putting themselves on display, thugs are broadcasting a capacity for coercion both disruptive of the social order and reproductive of it. They are the mirror image of the "armed gangs" against whom the regime initially claimed to be fighting. They are anticipatory violence incarnate, a living symbol of fraternal enjoyment and death-drive desires, distinguished from the army, at least in principle, by their only tenuous commitment to regulation. Allied with the Tiger's special forces by a nationalism encapsulating both an intimate, easily personifiable love of country and a morally resonant appeal to patriotic principles, their unruliness, in the service of the regime, allows the regime to seem especially strong—the only actor to which this outsized force is willing to submit.[24] The shabbiha, the Tiger's special forces, and civilian loyalists could thus be lumped together in a vision of the proper national collectivity, with dissidents figured as part of an enlarged and threatening outside. The trick lay in making sectarian specificity work to galvanize a generalized loyalty while channeling excess, lest it overwhelm claims to the official common good.

PART THREE: THE RESIDUAL AND EMERGENT DIMENSIONS OF SECT

My attention to threat potential and its deployment is not meant to suggest that Syrians' anxieties about sectarian backlash were baseless or that sect was merely an invented category. Nor is it the case, of course, that sect-based identities are in any way fixed or inevitable. Lauren Berlant, in her invocation of Raymond Williams's concept of "structures of feeling," highlights a "space of affective residue that constitutes what is shared . . . but circulates beneath the surface of explicit life," creating "atmospheres and environments that are occupied before they are apprehended."[25] Williams uses the idea to refer to "meanings and values as they are actively lived and felt," to "elements of impulse, restraint, and tone; specifically affective elements of consciousness and relationships: not feelings against thought, but thought as felt and feeling as thought: practical consciousness of a present kind, in a living and interrelating continuity."[26] These elements constitute structures of feeling in forming a set of "specific internal relations, at once interlocking and in tension," while at the same time existing as a social experience "which is still in process."[27] For Williams, these structures are never fully formalized or institutionalized, but are "social experiences in solution," not reducible to belief systems but lived and experienced in the present in line with specific "rhythms" and "kinds of sociality" that are characterized by their potentiality.[28]

Sect counts as residual in this sense, because although as a phenomenon it was "formed in the past," it persists "as an effective element of the present . . . lived and practiced on the basis of the residue . . . of some previous social and cultural institution or formation."[29] As residue, in other words, sect can be lived implicitly before it is embraced explicitly. Latent at any given time, sect remains available for political activation, operating as the beneath-the-surface Other to official claims of multisectarian accommodation and national unity. As residue, it exists as the underside to neoliberal autocracy's good life, capable of bubbling to the surface in the context of changing conditions. Both the "residual" and the "emergent" complicate any simple analysis of domination. But the "emergent" for Williams carries connotations of a specifically oppositional or alternative potentiality, of a break from prevailing norms and the appearance of "radically new semantic figures." This working "beyond or against a dominant mode" is what activists in the uprising were required to create and make stick if they were to mount a successful challenge to neoliberal autocracy.[30]

Understanding sect as a residual sociality capable of becoming activated avoids reifying the category or inviting arguments based on "primordialism," on claims of innateness or ahistorical, time-immemorial affiliations. The residual and the emergent are always social and historical,[31] something interpretivists and constructivists, with their attention to the dynamic and made dimensions of identity formation, have been aware of at least since Michel Foucault. They have focused fruitfully in particular on the historical and political processes by which categories (such as sect, or ethnicity, or race, or nation) get produced. And, indeed, Foucauldians do an especially compelling job of considering the role states play in creating classifications that work to manage and regulate populations.[32] In considering the dynamics of conflict in particular, the social theorist Rogers Brubaker urges us to recognize that "violence becomes 'ethnic' (or racial or nationalist or sectarian) through the meanings attributed to it by perpetrators, victims, politicians . . . , researchers, relief workers, and others. Such acts of framing and narrative encoding do not simply interpret the violence; they constitute it as ethnic."[33]

Nevertheless, thinking in terms of "structures of feeling," with the attendant concepts of the residual and the emergent, has the advantage as opposed to other constructivisms of drawing our attention to the importance of phenomenological experience, treating sect as something more than mere epistemological apprehension. People sign up for and communicate, and indeed experience, their affective commitments unevenly and incompletely in myriad ways, through stigmatization, joke telling, assertions of gendered norms of propriety, practices of piety, and divergent leisure patterns, to name but a few examples. Williams's approach gives us traction on these matters while also attuning us to how attachments to sectarian difference can be lived simultaneously in contradiction and in felt service to multisectarian accommodation and national unity. The concept of structures of feeling thus avoids reduction, while allowing "the known complexities, the experienced tensions, shifts, and uncertainties, the intricate forms of unevenness and confusion" to enliven our analyses, so that we do not presume the substance of sect but look at the ongoing processes of, and contradictions central to, its activation as a dynamically lived concept.[34]

Less clear is how Williams's emphasis on residual socialities explains what prompts one instance to bubble up while another does not. The answer to this question requires retrospection, which is to say a historical account explaining the significance of the past from the vantage point of the present. Rumors about sect have the traction which we have observed in part from antecedent patterns of inequality and the peculiarities of administrative classification, traceable to practices in existence before decolonization. Scholars also point to Ottoman reforms and outside intervention, emphasizing the importance of changes in property laws that came with the Ottoman Land Code of 1858, which was manipulated in various ways by landowners at the expense of ordinary peasants. In some areas, the most vulnerable and destitute of these peasants were poor ʿAlawis, some of whom, reportedly, were able to survive only by selling their daughters into indentured servitude to local landlords or urban notables, mainly Sunni identified. Administrative practices under French colonial rule (1923–46) arguably exacerbated sectarian difference by dividing what had been "Greater Syria" into domains of rule based on French notions of the salience of sect, carving out ʿAlawi and Druze ministates. The French mandate period also targeted minority populations to staff the military and lower echelons of the colonial bureaucracy, opening avenues of upward mobility that would shape the contours of minority and majority categories for decades to come.[35] Under the circumstances, the Baʿth Party, never an organization enjoying mass support, was able to gain a crucial foothold in the armed forces. And with its declarations of pan-Arab unity and "socialism," as well as its capacities to organize, the Baʿth's appeal could extend beyond the barracks, gaining sympathy among some: especially non-Communist leftists concerned with issues of land reform, autonomy from US empire, and "inclusion" of minorities into a broader national community. Those commitments would find expression in the establishment of a far-reaching welfare state in which goods and services were exchanged for allegiance and obedience. At the same time, popular social policies were continuously undermined by patronage and corruption, including inclusive forms of crony capitalism alongside a robust security state that became increasingly sectarian in character. In times of tumult, the regime has typically relied on elements within the security state that identify largely as 'Alawi—particularly by connections to the inner circle of the ruling family. In the current conflict, these attachments are reflected in and strengthened through a process of "militiafication," as the security analysts Charles Lister and Dominic Nelson note, in which the regime, in good neoliberal autocratic fashion, has subcontracted the state's military and internal security efforts to loyalist (overwhelmingly 'Alawi) militias.[36]

The idea here is not to rehearse this history in detail—something well done by historians and political scientists with area specialist knowledge. Nor is my aim to foreground instrumental reasons for sectarianism's uptake in the context of challenges to the regime's right to rule, although these are also important. It is, rather, to consider how it is that sectarianism, as one among many residual forms of sociality, would be the one percolating to the surface, becoming experientially salient in glaring contradiction to the regime's stated aims of multicultural accommodation. Although the importance of prior historical patterns of attachment has already been noted, the point is that these prior patterns are likewise multiple, so that the categories continued to have the resonance they did only because of the security state's reliance on sect and minority as idioms of attachment capable of displacing fears of the regime's own brutality onto other brutalizing forces—such as external intervention. The historicity of the fears speaks to an ongoing-ness of a world of imperial interventions (such as the US occupation of Iraq), regional rivalries (such as conflicts pitting Iran against Saudi Arabia), and fears of local blame and backlash (such as those generated by ordinary citizens' perceptions of 'Alawi privilege and worries about majority Sunni payback). The structure of violence that emerged in the context of this ongoing-ness had multiple feedback loops and generated powerful recursive interactions, in which suspicion, anticipatory fear, and cynicism all found expression. So, too, as we saw in chapter 4, did a militarized, sentimentalized nationalism undergo a resurgence which, as I am suggesting here, converged with what would otherwise seem like contradictory opportunities for sectarian sedimentation. That these contradictions could be smoothed over testifies to the workings of an ideology that re-tethered 'Alawis to the regime, occasioning the reproduction of individual and collective complicities with it. That sect, among latent structures of feeling, would become privileged does not derive in any obvious way from utilitarian gains—'Alawi areas remain surprisingly underdeveloped economically—nor can these structures be reduced simply to historical formations in the past, as important as these are. The emergence of sect as a newly salient category must therefore be seen also in the active, flexible forms of experience that are never either wholly accidental or wholly deliberate. A product of overt regime manipulation along with ongoing local and regional hierarchies of violence, these structures of feeling were also self-reinforcing, evolving as they were felt into an explicit (rather than implicit) defense of the status quo.

The rumor with which the chapter opens, in all of its variations, is of a piece with others circulating in Syria at the time in exposing this process by which residual forms of sociality—such as sect—can percolate to the surface and congeal there into active experience and thought. To be sure, these rumors draw from category-based knowledge, but they have the quality of being affective as well as epistemic statements. They are structured in relation to feeling as well as cognition, a product of historical formations and likewise of experience in the active, processual present. To see this more clearly, let us examine another striking rumor, also in circulation during the first months of 2011 as the uprising was getting underway. 'Alawi residents of Jableh, a stronghold of the regime and home to many of its loyal security forces, were alarmed to discover that X's had been painted on the doors of their homes. In biblical fashion, 'Alawis had been marked for slaughter, so the rumor went, by the son of a well-known Sunni businessman with a private militia. The rumor quickly spread from purportedly terrified 'Alawis in Jableh to relatives and friends in Damascus, with the effect of hailing them additionally into the nervous system with a story that, while scarcely credible, did provoke anxiety. Related stories soon followed, with the regime exploiting fears of hypothetical danger as an occasion to recruit people into vigilante committees and neighborhood watches, distributing weapons to trustworthy peasants and townsfolk based on sectarian affiliation. This rumor, in other words—like the opening one—was part of a discursive arsenal justifying the regime's actual coercive presence in terms that stimulated people's sense of vulnerability and responded to it at the same time. It subjected a present-oriented (and anxiety-ridden) sensorial sprawl to some kind of order, both activating and exploiting anticipatory fears.

Paradoxically a mechanism for structuring and acknowledging the inchoateness of feelings, these rumors register and (inadequately) alleviate uncertainty. Their circulation is evidence simultaneously of a story's potency and its questionable veracity, if only, as rumor, in having no discernible source. Similar stories tapped into historically embedded apprehensions of a nation invaded by foreigners by warning of dangerous Others already lurking amid the largely 'Alawi population in the coastal towns of Jableh, Banias, Lattakia, and Tartus. Said to be funded by the CIA and the "Zionists," although hailing from "Wahhabi" Saudi Arabia, the spectral presence of foreign actors established through such narratives helped "externalize"[37] the conflict, to borrow the words of the Lebanese analyst Fawwaz Traboulsi (Trabulsi), lending additional substance to free-floating anxieties of nonsovereignty.

Stories alleging external funding for the internal disorder not only circulated in rumor form but were also openly disseminated through official and quasi-official media. Chapters 1 and 3 highlighted examples from television and radio talk shows devoted to the "confessions" of Syrian "instigators," along with similar instances on Facebook, in newspaper reports of cached weapons, and on billboards warning of religious dissension (*fitna*). Together these discourses helped produce and maintain the Syrian nervous system by identifying future threats from foreign-backed "armed gangs," signaling, too, the regime's ability and willingness to use violence to preempt them. Rumors seem in retrospect to be an integral part of this logic of preemption, one of the ways of promoting styles of affective reasoning which in an exacerbated state of insecurity and suspicion privileged imagined fears over actual observation.[38]

Admittedly, even the most far-fetched rumors of threatened existential survival had some empirical grounding, providing grist for the ideological mill whereby the regime could justify its practice of preemptive violence. Incidents were there to be pointed to that raised doubts about the opposition's credibility, as noted in chapter 3. In addition, as discussed in chapter 4 in the context of anxieties about sectarian backlash, examples could be used to reassert the regime's position as the guarantor of Syria's fragile multisectarian "mosaic" and of national cohesion. Another liability the opposition had to deal with was its own fragmented character, with its various factions likely to be working at cross purposes. Democratic activists intent on demonstrating unity often found themselves caught up in compensatory moves that undermined their own credibility (in downplaying everything from incidents of violence to internal rivalries, foreign meddling, the glaring problem of incoherent policy messaging, or the use by a particular group of sectarian language). And while these activists did find unity in refusing to sectarianize protests, other members of a capacious opposition were not so restrained—resulting in suspicion, fear, and even violence in ways that advantaged the regime while drawing fringe opponents into the center of the struggle for opposition dominance. As democratic activists began to get cold feet in the face of mounting threats, and with historical residues of sectarian feeling hardening into fervent attachments, many who had dreamed of a democratic, multicultural Syria left the country, while those who stayed to fight had every interest in escalating the conflict, accelerating a process of polarization that doomed, at least for the moment, any possibilities for salutary social transformation.

In this light, three additional points need to be made about the Syrian nervous system in action. Looking in some detail at first, the sectarianization of the opposition; second, the issue in both material and discursive terms of foreign intervention; and finally, the vulnerability of minority groups (such as Christians) already primed for narratives of besiegement will allow us to identify the most important factors contributing to the solidification of sectarian attachments, thus bringing ideology into focus as it unfolds and evolves. In doing so, we will see in action the multiplicity of hailings coming from all directions that characterized the inception and progression of the uprising, creating a situation in which judgment was both urgently demanded and made all but impossible.

As regards making the protest sectarian, there is compelling evidence that the regime was not alone in this effort. Fringe groups in the opposition were known for depicting the ʿAlawi regime as heretical, as opposed to the pious Sunni majority, in ways that hijacked democratic activism by undermining oppositional claims to represent Syrian unity. Circumstances were often unclear—difficult for observers and participants alike to judge. An early example followed the extraordinary protest of February 17, 2011, the first show of potential reformist opposition to the regime. The protest came before the official start of the uprising and was one of the largest demonstrations Damascus was to witness. It erupted in al-Hariqa market (near the main entrance to the main Hamidiyya market) after a policeman struck a shopkeeper during an altercation. In what easily seemed at the time an unexampled show of public outrage, nearly a thousand people immediately gathered in the street, chanting, "The Syrian people will not be humiliated." The protest was not reported on official Syrian news, but social media sites—already attuned to uprisings in Tunisia and Egypt and alert to possibilities inside Syria—conveyed the news in detail. Among the postings was a YouTube video, produced by the hitherto-unknown

Islam4TV. It covered more than six minutes of the demonstration and was notable, at this early date, for the overtly sectarian language it had superimposed onto the images of the crowd. The indignation filling the crowd was identified as proper to "Ummayad Syria," a direct reference to Sunni Islam. The entire security apparatus, according to the titles, was peopled with 'Alawis or "Nusayris" (another word for "'Alawis," signaling their "heretical" relation to Sunni Islam). And Bashar was a "Nusayri hyena." Identified as coming from the Movement of Youth for a Free Syria (Harakat al-shabab li-Suriya al-hurra, translated with the English handle Youth Free Syria), the video was also overlaid with the sounds of people chanting and audio of men singing "God is great" in a style associated with Sunni preachers. To be sure, the actual crowd had not entirely eschewed religious slogans, alternating "there is no God, but God" with defiant exclamations that "the Syrian people will not be humiliated." But there was nothing sectarian about the protest's politics, as more straightforward reportage from any number of other sites made clear.

I encountered the Islam4TV clip at the home of a dear friend in Damascus later that same day of the dramatic unexpected protest. We were surfing online for accounts of what had transpired. My friend—we'll call her Dima—was well informed and sympathetic to oppositional politics, in line with her long-term desires for a democratic Syria. The clip's overtly sectarian veneer was surprising enough in the pre-uprising discursive atmosphere to prompt speculation. Certainly, it was possible that an unknown opposition group with the handle Youth Free Syria might have emerged on the spot or been poised to seize the moment—riding the coattails of the demonstration by glossing events to depict the protests in sectarian terms. Precedents for such sentiments remained in living memory from the late 1970s and early 1980s, when Syria's Islamic movement resorted to overtly sectarian language and targeted members of the 'Alawi elite for assassination. But this relatively straightforward account was not the only possibility. Without using the term, Dima began wondering whether the posting might have been a false-flag operation. She was in no way committed to this view, but the idea was that the regime might have fashioned the sectarian overlay to instill fear in people who otherwise might rally in favor of change.[39] There were many democratic activists who voiced similar concerns. And indeed, it was plausible in the circumstances that the regime's efforts to manage the unpredictable events could involve trying to sectarianize it, thereby undermining a nascent opposition by tapping into anxieties over a shadowy Islamic militancy ready to pounce at the first sign of weakness. But there is also evidence that parts of the country were already using this sort of sectarian language as early as March 2011, and it takes little planning to set up a YouTube account and caption a cell-phone video, making it at least plausible that a committed person or group did this spontaneously.[40]

We just did not know in February 2011—and still do not. What Syrians and observers alike do know now is that Islam4TV, and many sites like it over the course of the uprising, went on to report basic news events in ways that did much to exacerbate fears. Combined with broadcasts of sermons by such dissident Syrian preachers as the famous 'Adnan 'Ar'ur from his exile in Saudi Arabia, it became easier to believe that the alternative to Asad was a theocratic state, and therefore for secularists of many stripes to subscribe to the view that "there was no alternative" (*ma fi badil*) to Asad. Despite the efforts of many opposition activists to underscore the importance of democracy and a civil state, despite the slogans asserting citizen cohesion at various protests, and despite the forceful instances of well-known 'Alawis defying the regime by calling on it to step down, outlets like Islam4TV, alongside the steady supply of rumors in circulation, helped turn anticipatory fear and isolated instances of sectarian violence into a generalized condition of foreboding. The consequence was that loyalists and the gray, ambivalent middle heard chants of God and 'Ar'ur and Islamic militancy everywhere—with each instance, real or imagined, ratcheting into increasingly polarized politics. Ambivalent Syrians gravitated toward loyalists pitted against a fragmenting opposition that seemed often enough to be denying troubling aspects of the uprising that were in plain view. Among the disturbing signs were the emergence of actual Sunni-identified gangs; rhymes of intolerance such as "al-Masihiyyin 'al-Bayrut, al-'Alawiyyin 'al-tabut" (the Christians to Beirut, the 'Alawis to their caskets); and well-documented threats of sectarianized violence being made in places like Binnish, an area of Idlib's countryside: "Bil dhubah jaynakum" (We came to slaughter you). There also were and continue to be more prosaic statements of an increasingly sectarianized Sunni "we" that will "not forget and not forgive" (la ninsa wa la nusamih). The Islamic State's emergence in Syria in 2013 was one amalgamation of horrifying excess, its brutality against "infidel" minority sects, such as 'Alawis, the realization of the very nightmare regime fantasists had imagined and helped bring about. It is likewise with the regime's repeated claims of foreign interference. Though cynically deployed, these claims ended up generating what might be glossed as a self-fulfilling prophecy. And other states were at the ready—with Qatar, Saudi Arabia, Turkey, the United States,

Great Britain, France, and Israel united for the most part on the one side and, of course, Hizballah, Iran, and Russia joining the fray on the other.

And this brings us to the second point about the Syrian nervous system in action, the rumors and realities of foreign intervention. We have seen some ways in which the Asad regime was responsible for creating the enemy that then needed to be fought. This activity went as far as actually releasing Islamic activists from prison in the early days of the uprising, and perhaps in a less deliberate move, easing up on border policing, which revived smuggling routes for transporting arms and fighters in and out of the country. These circumstances allowed Syria to become, in part, what Asad had warned that it would—namely, a fertile ground for imperial and sectarian proxy wars. The regime could envelop its own struggle for survival in the rhetorical and material conditions made possible by the global war on terror. This is a project specific in some ways to the post-9/11 era, with the Syrian regime able to fold its ongoing imperative of regime survival into militaristic undertakings against diffuse Others, constructing a vision of national collectivity in which dissidence could be conflated with terrorism and the regime's violence valorized or ignored—or displaced onto the insurgent fighter. Recall that in his interview with Russian television in 2015 (noted in chapter 4), Asad maintained that for an opposition group to be considered a worthy party to dialogue and the peace process, it had to agree first to the paramount significance of the campaign to eradicate terrorism. The cynicism, of course, was blatant, given the equation between opposition and terror. But the point is that the claim itself can hardly be surprising, given the current historical conjuncture or, for that matter, the similar point made by Hobbes: all modern states require their citizens to renounce what the state defines as unauthorized acts of violence.[41] Moreover, this call for citizens to anticipate violence suggests a particular form of buy-in and dependence, which at once ascribes value to and specifies the contours of proper sacrifice—channeling the coercive force of martial nationalism, thug libidinal energy, opportunism, and imagination by conflating the survival of the sect with regime and nation, again a maneuver enabled by post-9/11 norms.

In the context of this dynamism and flux of judgment-making, some internationally renowned leftist writers, such as Seymour Hersh and Robert Parry (noted in chapter 3) or the pro-Palestinian reporter Robert Fisk, may have unwittingly helped the regime by reporting on these matters in ways that revealed less a sectarian gloss than secularist anxieties congenial to the regime's own. The regime could capitalize on this reporting too in its efforts to depict the uprising as radical Islamist insurgency, a product of Western and Gulf interventions such as the ones that had produced Al-Qa'ida in Afghanistan and the Islamic State in Iraq. Pro-uprising activists, in turn, became critical of "the Left" writ large, demonstrating a reasonable frustration with how reporters associated with democratic and redistributive causes in the past could nonetheless sign up by default for Asad, preferring the ordered brutality of a secular dictatorship to the threats of a Sunni theocracy or global instability.[42]

As for the third point, the congealment of sectarian differences also entailed enlisting minority fears—Christian fears primary among them—of nonsovereignty and multicultural dissolution. Whereas some Syrians were exhilarated by uprisings elsewhere—"We thought the Libyans were simple-minded [sakhif], but they turned out to be revolutionaries [thawri]!"—the situation in their own country was allegedly different for these same interlocutors. The Syrian conflict was likely to be "sectarian" (ta'ifi), noted many members of minority groups, primed from the beginning to fear the worst. One Christian woman, in discussion with an 'Alawi friend, insisted that the "Christian community totally backs the regime and is afraid of the alternatives," that it is reasonable for Syrians to be more cautious because of the "wars of the past" (referring to the uprising and subsequent massacre in Hama). At once too violent and too peaceful, the "Syrian people" were easily construed as both sensibly waiting out the moment of regional turmoil from the sidelines and harboring a destructive energy that would lead to terror and theocracy. Within the same conversation and with no acknowledgment of the contradictions, the statement "The Syrian people don't like wars" (Al-sha'b al-Suri ma bihibb al-hurub) could be followed by an account of the sectarian strife in the late 1970s and early 1980s.[43] In countless conversations, fears of an Islamic takeover collapsed the Muslim Brotherhood's bid for power four decades ago with secular activists' calls for democracy in 2011. It seemed simply too difficult to imagine the demand for democracy, and by implication majority rule, without sectarianizing it, displacing the problem of transformation onto uncivilized Muslim masses, rather than on a regime intent on staying in power at all costs—or in Raymond Williams's terms, turning the residual into a dominant form of expression and understanding.

As the journalist Alia Malek writes in chronicling the attitudes of her friends and family in Damascus, there were oft-repeated points in a logic of Christian besiegement: "Christians were here centuries before Islam; the continued presence in their homeland had to be protected; only this regime could protect minorities from a majority that didn't really want them."[44] Aided in these views by current events local and regional, Christians could point to the success of the Muslim Brotherhood and "Salafi" voices in Egypt, Tunisia, and Libya as well as to incidents of terror inside Syria.[45] The first large explosion in Damascus right before Christmas 2011 is a case in point. Two suicide bombs exploded outside Syrian military intelligence agency buildings, killing more than forty people and injuring 166. This incident may have been a false-flag operation or a symptom of the regime's own vulnerability; but whatever it was, its proximity to the Christmas holiday rattled Christians in general,[46] and gave those actually complicit with the regime what Alia Malek calls the "twisted ablution of chaos."[47] The regime immediately blamed Al-Qa'ida and brought Arab League observers to the site. Priests appeared on official TV, urging calm and offering their support to the regime. Unlike in Egypt, where the regime of Husni Mubarak had surreptitiously encouraged violence against the Coptic Christian community, in Syria Christians could plausibly view the regime as a guarantor of their safety. This is not to argue that all minorities backed the regime, but simply that the regime in affectively recruiting minorities as a social category, citing real and imagined dangers of intolerant, Gulf-inspired Sunni extremists, gained in many Christians a critical source of support.

CONCLUSION

There is significant debate in political science about the role sectarian or ethnic identifications play in the onset of civil war. Some scholars argue that such attachments are the main cause or among the key causes of conflict, while others see these identifications frequently coming to expression in conflicts that are otherwise motivated—reinforcing investments in a narrative (of victimization or imminent threat, for example), with the effect of further congealing solidarities in the occasioning of shared complicities.[48] In one reading of the first rumor opening this chapter, in accepting the pretense that the threat came from Sunnis rather than from the regime, the villagers' acting as if Sunni gangs had terrorized them in the night worked as a backdoor motivator of ongoing acquiescence and attachment, if not necessarily fervent loyalty. Ardent loyalty, by contrast, figured critically in the activities of regime thugs, with their displays of camaraderie and routine surrender to male leaders, thereby producing the conditions for ongoing, recursive forms of anticipatory violence. Aided by local and regional events, these different kinds of affective investments could coalesce to turn contingent, indeterminate, historically resonant, (and for some) vaguely experienced solidarities into consensually shared hardened attachments.

Central to Williams's approach is an invitation to provide a phenomenology of anxiety in times of tumult by chronicling the anticipatory fears, contradictions, and displacements of a careening practical consciousness under duress. But, as Williams's notion also implies, there were forms of "emergent" sociality available for activation as the uprising got underway that did not end up bubbling (powerfully) to the surface, and all the less so as the violence continued. Despite obvious differences in content, the hailing into being of democratic activists across divides such as ethnicity resembles being hailed into forms of sectarian attachment, insofar as neither is inevitable and each takes ongoing work. Here as in previous chapters, what we see in Syria is a nervous system in formation producing speculations and counterspeculations that solidified over time into fixed oppositions as individuals sorted out their relation to events in increasingly siloed communities. Ideological work was indispensable to the creation and maintenance of these conditions—in this chapter, to the deployment and counterdeployment of socialities in real time in ways that favored the regime. In this sense, the precise summary is not that Syrians were incapable of political judgment, although sometimes, as we have seen in previous chapters, conditions of uncertainty produced alibis for nonjudgment. Instead, circumstances also conduced to judgments that need not have been made.

CONCLUSION

At a Loss

At the time of this writing, the Asad regime looks as if it has won the war, but whether it will be able to govern again is open to question. Large swathes of territory remain secured only with the help of Russian and Iranian military might. The headlines in July 2018 chronicle car bombs in the south, deals between regional powers for reconstruction in the north, and residents in Idlib gearing up for what promises to be horrifying payback for their anti-regime allegiances. The fictions that governed the neoliberal autocratic order in the first decade of Bashar al-Asad's rule have come undone, with images of a kinder, gentler regime forever undermined by its overt brutality. And yet the language of the good life can be found again in reconstruction projects; in the contradictions between the regime's protection of minorities and its sectarianization of loyalty; in the revitalization of a vocabulary celebrating "civility" in terms that locate it in a modernized urbanity; in a vision of national sovereignty that depends on its ongoing endangerment. Citizen subjects in this new era will be, as they always are, internally split and complex—and thus available for all the varieties of interpellation or address. Ideology remains at work everywhere, of course. It is like the proverbial water to a fish: we see it in loyalists who confine themselves to dogmatism to the extent they are willing to entertain ideas at all; in opposition activists across the range, from the lost to the most astute and creative observers of life and war; and in the ambivalent middle whose continuous waffling registers ideology's most saturating successes.

Ideology works through seduction, arousing fantasy content while simultaneously defusing it and smoothing out contradictions. It helps manage collective anxieties and sociopolitical incompatibilities by providing mechanisms that allow dissonances to be contained, disavowed, and displaced. Let me take each separately. As *containment*: from the first family's exemplary images of enlightened despotism to the comedies of resignation in the initial decade of neoliberal autocracy, from the market-oriented melodramas of 2013 to the Mother's Day video of collective mourning—ideology operates with images as symbolic vehicles, making what are essentially social and historical anxieties seem natural and inevitable, gratifying desires largely to the extent that they are kept in check. This containment also works through modes of hyperidentification. Discussing ideological interpellation in the introduction, we saw how easily someone can fantasize about images of celebrity glamour (or elegance or composure or whatever) without necessarily believing that it will ever be adequately mimicked. In the words of one activist from the countryside who came to the city of Aleppo in the early 2000s: although factors like the drought were real, the urbanity of neoliberal autocracy "intrigued." Young people flocked to the city for opportunities—including the opportunity to couch surf, get educated, and enjoy the pleasures that neoliberal autocracy had begun to afford.

As *disavowal*: from the "I know very well that the regime is incorrigibly corrupt, yet nevertheless we can build government-sponsored civil society organizations that truly empower citizens" to "I know very well that there is 'no going back' to the way things were before the war, and yet everything will resolve itself as easily as 'biting into a zucchini' [*'addit kusayeh*]." Or, taking an example from the final chapter: "I know very well that Sunni gangs did not visit our village in the night, and yet nevertheless I shall act as if they did"; or, among secular activists: "I know very well that there *are* violent Islamic militants, but nevertheless they are not really a problem or I shall act as if they don't exist." Disavowal goes beyond denial in that the problem calling for judgment is posed. In disavowal the power of ideology comes into especially bold relief, with subjects hailed into a position where the realities that can no longer be denied can still be dismissed. In this sense, disavowal expresses the contradiction it simultaneously repudiates.

As *displacement*: in which unbearable fears are relocated onto a new object, allaying anxieties by transferring unacceptable attributes onto a fantasy Other. Conspiracies of national undoing that put "terrorists" at the heart of the problem or projections of in-group violence—these are some processes of displacement which, in tandem with disavowal and containment, were frequently at work helping organize collective life in Syria's authoritarian circumstances. This is not to say that the Islamic State or the various militias that blended opportunism with practices of piety did not exist or were solely a creation of the regime (or the United States—or Qatar or Turkey or Saudi Arabia)—although outside interveners and regime strategists all share responsibility for an overall ecology of violence in which these groups could flourish. The potential for the activation of militant group solidarities and the actual presence of such groups in some areas made the process of Othering easier everywhere, just as under nominally democratic regimes like the United States the existence of real communists enabled political demonization in the 1950s.

As we have seen throughout, images are central to the operation of ideology as form, whether in the context of the incongruous neoliberal autocrat or in the quick resort to state-sanctioned violence. And in ideology's neoliberal variants, sociopolitical life is economized in the marketing of authoritarian order as the palatable substitute for what would otherwise be chaos. As the specificities of the Syrian uprising showed us in its early days, this collusion of dictatorship with the market was only partially successful, for at the same time it generated demands for justice and dignity that stretched the limits of what Asad's version of neoliberal autocracy could manage ideologically—at least without the war. This is not to argue that the regime was behind all the violence or that it had everything under its direction or control. But it was able to take advantage of circumstances both local and global, whether new like the high-speed eventfulness of internet news cycles or old as in historical and sociological patterns of prejudice and injustice. It was able to put forward its own version of civility in a bid to represent rebel parts of the countryside as the ones that were uncivilized, hardening sectarian sentiments and stimulating fears of reprisal in the process. The regime convinced enough addressees that it alone could rule, exploiting ambivalent citizens' shift between the desire for freedom and the fear of disorder to turn what was for most a vaguely lived atmosphere of impending violence into a devastating conflict. Drawing from a professional managerial elite, including members of the Syrian drama community as well as those keyed to the advertising arts, Syria's ideological apparatus broached social contradictions and anxieties in the service of symbolic resolution, urging addressees to bury dreams for human dignity and a civil state and to embrace a nationalist re-tethering of community to the regime—a fantasy "bribe," to quote Fredric Jameson,[1] in which some form of collectivity is reestablished, but at the expense of political judgment and democratic action.

In these circumstances, pathways back to political judgment can be found in comedy's capacity for irreverence; in artistic efforts such as Abounaddara's to bypass the impasse of fake news by unsettling the conventions of documentary representation; and in the cultivation of interpretive generosity through representative thinking demonstrated by films such as Ossama Mohammed's controversial *Silvered Water*. These are all important attempts to perform an incandescent otherwiseness to the bleakness of the present moment. They are instances of creative estrangement that operate inside ideology but at a distance, opening imaginative possibilities for reclaiming some kind of ameliorative agency in the world. Such agency will come embedded in structures (of capital, dictatorial rule, and new combinations of the two) that can prove extraordinarily dynamic, agilely self-recomposing, and capable of almost organic rejuvenation. In avoiding the romanticization of resistance or the celebration of aesthetic politics as necessarily redemptive, my insistence on locating political judgment at the center of ideology critique remains an effort to discover, in the openings produced by reproduction, a wedge.

Looking at Syria, what the wedge requires is a commitment to world making in the face of disaster, acceptance of the exhaustion that accompanies failure — of the ways in which all of us are flailing in some way most of the time. In these circumstances it means doing the hard work of mourning the loss of revolutionary promise (for now) and the devastating death of human beings who were loved, cared for, and are irretrievably gone — transforming those who survived. How to narrate a Syrian present that incorporates those who cling to the past, those who fantasize its easy restoration, and those who worked hard for a political transformation that failed? This book is an early and provisional effort.

Acknowledgments

This book could not have been written without the help of many Syrians, some of whose names must go unmentioned. My fieldwork included the 2010–11 period in Damascus and extended in subsequent years to Beirut, Paris, Berlin, Budapest, Istanbul, and the Syrian-Turkish border. The hospitality shown to me by my hosts during these years was more than kind, as well as remarkably illuminating and thought-provoking, and at times devastatingly sad. The grief we all felt both united and divided us—sometimes running in parallel, not shared. I am not Syrian and do not know what it is like to lose my home. I am not a nationalist and will never know what it is like to feel sentimentally related to that political abstraction. But Syria was my happy place, the country I loved more than my own. Despite the different ways in which all of us found ourselves flailing, while witnessing and from a variety of distances experiencing the Syrian disaster—the heated political disagreements that sometimes had us at loggerheads, the various networks of friendship and enmity that kept us separate and together—we managed to find modes of solidarity and in some cases enduring connection. Thanks are owed to Dana Omari Berg and Jesper Berg for their warmth, wit, and hospitality—first in Damascus and later in Beirut. Also in Beirut I had the pleasure of learning from the extraordinarily talented Muhammad al-ʿAttar, Ziad Kalthum, Khalid ʿAbd al-Wahid, Golan Haji, and Kheder Khaddour. Among my Lebanese friends Nada Accaoui is a continuing source of joy and warmth. Nadia Bou Ali's fierce intellect and knowledge of all things Lacan opened up my world. Fawwaz Traboulsi's patience and understanding over the years have been a wellspring of ongoing support. Walid Sadek and Samar Kanafani were delightful interlocutors as well. And Ahmad Dallal's uncommon kindness and scholarly commitments made the American University of Beirut a second intellectual home.

Among the many Syrians whose thinking helped shape my own are Hala Mohammed, Haitham Hakki, Amal Mohammed, Orwa Nyrabia, Mouaffaq Nyrabia, Cherif Kiwan, Khaled Khalifa, Rosa Yassin Hassan, and the late Omar Amiralay. My dear friend, the brilliant filmmaker Ossama Mohammed, and his equally amazing wife, the opera singer and composer Noma Omran, are like family to me. Their unfaltering friendship and love — and their beautiful minds — make every day I am on this planet a gift. And their art has allowed me to think in new and fresh ways, as I hope proved apparent in chapter 4. I am forever indebted to them for their trust, insights, and fidelity to my project. In that category are also my comrade for life Osama Esber; his wife, Maha Atfeh; and their two children, Mariam and Aliyah — whom I have had the privilege of watching grow up, first in Damascus, later in Chicago, and now in California. I miss their presence in Chicago every day. Osama Esber's careful reading of the manuscript, his help with the translations and transliterations, and his belief in me have made this book possible. So too have the lively conversations with Yahya al-'Abdallah, whose knowledge of Syria, particularly of Aleppo, and his keen sense of popular culture have enhanced my work immeasurably. There are others who are mentioned in footnotes or who I have chosen not to invoke due to their preferences or prevailing circumstances, but they should know that they are deeply appreciated.

Many people have earned my gratitude for their intellectual support. Thanks are owed to my colleagues at the University of Chicago for their critical engagement with my work. I am grateful to my friends and comrades at the Chicago Center for Contemporary Theory — especially Lauren Berlant, Bill Brown, Andreas Glaeser, Rochona Majumdar, Joe Masco, William Mazzarella, William H. Sewell Jr., and Kaushik Sunder Rajan — for their careful readings of part or all of the manuscript. In political science, I want to thank my former colleagues Patchen Markell, John Patty, and Dan Slater, as well as my current interlocutors in comparative politics and political theory, Michael Albertus, Gary Herrigel, Demetra Kasimis, Benjamin Lessing, John McCormick, Monika Nalepa, Paul Staniland, and the recently returned Susan Stokes, for their comments on parts of the manuscript. I am especially indebted to Jim Chandler for teaching me how to understand film as a particular visual medium — and for watching a number of Syrian films with me. As should be obvious from reading the book, my work is deeply influenced by Lauren Berlant's imaginative thinking about comedy, melodrama, sentimentality, and nonsovereignty. I had the pleasure and the privilege of taking one of her courses on comedy during a sabbatical year in 2016. My work has also benefited immensely from conversations about judgment with Linda Zerilli, whose love and friendship are a source of ongoing delight. Jennifer Pitts is my writing partner. Without her, this book would never have seen the light of day. Her intelligence, conscientiousness, sense of solidarity, interpretive generosity, and unfathomable patience—not to mention her line-by-line editing—have made the process of writing the book remarkably rewarding.

Earlier versions of chapters were presented at Columbia University, the CUNY Graduate Center, Georgetown University, George Washington University's Project on Middle East Political Science, Harvard University, Johns Hopkins University, Marquette University, the Massachusetts Institute of Technology, New York University, Northwestern University, Princeton University, UCLA, the University of Minnesota, the University of Texas at Austin, the University of Toronto, the University of Washington, Washington University in St. Louis, Yale University, and multiple American Political Science Association conventions. I also had the opportunity to present my work at the American Academy in Berlin, the American University of Beirut, CEMAT-AIMS (the American Institute of Maghrebi Studies in Tunisia), the Central European University, the École Normale Supérieure, Lund University, Makerere Institute of Social Research, Sciences Po, the University of Chicago's Center in Delhi, the University of Copenhagen, the University of Exeter, and the University of Marburg. I would especially like to thank Nadia Abu El-Haj, Lina Sergie Attar, Asli Bali, Carles Boix, Melani Cammett, Steven Caton, Laryssa Chomiak, William Connolly, Omar Dahi, Donatella Della Ratta, Noura Erakat, Michael Gilsenan, Bassam Haddad, Steven Heydemann, Jeffrey Isaac, Amaney Jamal, Resat Kasaba, Adria Lawrence, Zachary Lockman, Ellen Lust, Marc Lynch, Mahmood Mamdani, Kevin Mazur, Anne-Marie McManus, Robert Meister, Brinkley Messick, Timothy Mitchell, Rosalind Morris, Sarah Parkinson, Wendy Pearlman, Danny Postel, Christa Salamandra, David Samuels, Jillian Schwedler, James C. Scott, Max Weiss, Gary Wilder, and Elisabeth Wood for their comments.

Students and former students (not mentioned above) have also been crucial interlocutors for this book. Thanks are owed to Daragh Grant, Tania Islas, Steven Klein, Taylor Lowe, Emma Stone Mackinnon, Yasmeen Mekawy, Tejas Parasher, Dina Rashed, Omar Safadi, Jeremy Siegman—

and especially to the phenomenal Yuna Blajer de la Garza, who has read more drafts of this book than either of us would care to count. Sofia Fenner's extraordinary research assistance in the early years of the project and her data collection for and writing of the book's appendix speak to her exceptional talents. Rachel Schine's help with transliterations at the end was of inestimable value as well.

I would also like to thank the staff at the former Danish Institute in Damascus. The captioning of the television comedy skits discussed in chapter 2 was funded by a National Science Foundation grant and required the collaboration of the production company, Sama Art International. Additional funding was provided by the University of Chicago and Marquette University. Thanks are owed to Colin Elman and Diana Kapiszewski for spearheading the NSF grant writing. Although we have our disagreements about the Data and Research Transparency initiative, I am delighted to make these comedies available (with Sebastian Karcher's technical assistance) to an English-speaking audience. And because of our disagreement, I was also introduced to wonderful new friends in political science — Nancy Hirschmann, Mala Htun, Jane Mansbridge, Kathleen Thelen, and Elisabeth Wood. I feel so lucky to have these fabulous women in my life.

Recognition is also due to the reviewers at the University of Chicago Press. Two have revealed themselves to me: Elliot Colla and Jessica Winegar offered exceptionally wise comments and criticisms. The third, anonymous reader did as well. I have my editor, Priya Nelson, to thank for choosing such astute reviewers of my manuscript. The reviewers' suggestions made the prose much better than it otherwise would have been, as did Priya's own incisive interventions. Christine Schwab, Sandra Hazel, and Dylan Montanari were also indispensable to converting the manuscript into a book.

For their devotion and friendship over many years, I would like to thank, some for a second or even third time, Nadia Abu El-Haj, Betsy Andrews, Lauren Berlant, Dipesh Chakrabarty, Laryssa Chomiak, Osama Esber, John McCormick, Jennifer Pitts, Jillian Schwedler, and Linda Zerilli. Nadia Abu El-Haj's partner, Amer Bisat, whose fiction recommendations have kept me sane, deserves special mention. Nadia, Amer, and their daughter Aya welcomed me into their family; words cannot express how much that has meant to me. My own parents died while I was writing this book. Their failing health was terrible to witness—and a source of sorrow and exhaustion independent of the aching sadness of Syria's conflict. I am sorry that they are not here to experience the appearance of this third book. I am very appreciative of my sister, Laura Wedeen, for her caretaking and organizational skills during that gloomy time. Our reconnection has been a silver lining. I am also profoundly grateful to Jennifer Cole and Rochona Majumdar for their commitment to the everyday-ness of attachment. The constancy of their companionship and the shared language it enables anchor my world. Annie Padrid and Katherine Billingham deserve my heartfelt gratitude as well. They keep me healthy—and as happy as a thinking person can be.

My husband, Don Reneau, and my son, Zack Reneau-Wedeen, remain the lights of my life. Don's humor, his amazing editorial skills, and his irrepressible patience with me helped make our third decade of marriage the most wonderful yet. And Zack's wisdom, emotional honesty, wry wit, mathematical intelligence, and fearless displays of self-confidence fill me with wonder every day.

While I was working on this book, my friend and colleague Saba Mahmood passed away. Saba was a ferocious intellect, a demanding teacher, and a playful, passionate, witty friend. I miss her laughter, her warmth, and what became, in the face of her illness, an exemplary grace.

This book is dedicated to Jean Comaroff and John Comaroff because they taught me how to be a colleague. Their camaraderie, devotion to scholarship, playfulness, energy, sizzling intellects, political and philosophical commitments, and unwavering affection—their ability to "show up" for me (and for others)—remind me why I chose my peculiar form of political theory as my vocation.

Appendix

SOFIA FENNER

The figures in this appendix demonstrate that simple economic measures are extremely weak predictors of mobilization during the first eleven months of the Syrian uprising. A cross-province analysis reveals little to no consistent relationship between mobilization (as proxied by deaths) between March 2011 and January 2012 and any of three economic measures—household expenditures, inflation, or relative inflation—in the years leading up to the uprising.

DEATH TOLLS AND MOBILIZATION

All six figures use civilian[1] death tolls as a proxy for the intensity of mobilization. We envision at least two ways in which the geographic distribution of deaths during the first year of the conflict might serve as a proxy (though admittedly an imperfect one) for anti-regime protest. First, areas with more intense anti-regime protests might have seen deadlier state repression in response. Second, areas of intense protest may have militarized earlier, producing conflict deaths among regime forces, rebel combatants, and civilians caught in the crossfire during the first year of the uprising (Homs is the exemplar of this process). Death tolls might also capture the willingness or capacity of regime forces to crush opposition; without a direct measure of protest (see below), and given the empirical patterns we observe, it is simply not possible to separate the regime's ability to repress from the existence of a militarized opposition on which to crack down. Regime forces might well have been more willing to fire on protesters in Homs than in Damascus, for example, but relatively low levels of mobilization in Damascus meant that they were rarely faced with such a choice. In all, the death tolls reported here probably reflect some combination of all these factors—the intensity of protest, the earliness of militarization, and the regime's willingness to squelch unrest in a particular area—and perhaps even others.

Deaths are an imperfect proxy, and we are wary of treating human casualties as "mere" statistics—a practice this book actively fights against. Countless individuals have, however, taken great risks to produce casualty counts; the lists of names they have compiled can tell us something about the conflict even in their aggregated, de-identified form. From a practical standpoint, moreover, there are few workable alternatives. Some scholars[2] have created event counts from diverse media sources, but none of these media sources were solely focused on counting each and every event during the uprising's early days. By contrast, multiple organizations—the Violations Documentation Center, the Syrian Observatory for Human Rights, and the March 15 group, among others—have dedicated significant efforts to counting deaths as accurately as possible. A deaths measure, therefore, is likely to be a more complete account of all deaths than an event measure would be of all events. Moreover, the data on deaths accord broadly with observed patterns of mobilization, showing peaks where and when a close observer of the uprising would expect (March 2011 in Dar'a and June 2011 in Idlib, for example).

Crucially, we recognize that death tolls become an increasingly poor proxy for protest over time. As the conflict militarized, death tolls increasingly included rebel fighters and civilians caught in the crossfire of disproportionate regime retaliation. By late 2011, a range of rebel groups were carrying out armed attacks on regime personnel or installations, often provoking massive air assaults in response (as in Homs and Hama in February 2012). In a militarized conflict, death tolls come to represent changing front lines, balances of power, and strategic considerations rather than state repression of predominantly peaceful demonstrations.[3]

By ending the quantitative analysis in January 2012, we speak directly to the claims of chapter 1. Rebel attacks in Damascus (and much more so its suburbs) began to occur in late 2011, but the city's casualty counts do not spike until July 2012, in the aftermath of a rebel attack on the National Security headquarters. Similarly, deaths in Aleppo rise sharply in response to bombings of regime installations on February 10, 2012, but not beforehand. In both cities, death tolls began to increase dramatically only after major military developments (rebel attacks and regime counteroffensives)—not as a result of intensified protest. As the war continued, Aleppo eventually became a key center of conflict, and parts of Damascus saw considerable violence (although the downtown area has remained relatively unscathed). The point of this appendix, however, is to demonstrate two key points: first, that Damascus and Aleppo remained relatively quiescent during the first, largely peaceful eleven months of the uprising; and second, that simple economic explanations struggle to account for why Damascus and Aleppo did not mobilize *during those crucial initial months*.

THE FIGURES

Figures A.1, A.3, and A.5 use total death tolls calculated from the database of the Violations Documentation Center (VDC).[4] The VDC is aligned with the opposition (specifically, with the Local Coordinating Committees). In 2011–12, the organization was headquartered in the Syrian town of Duma in Rif Dimashq, though it claimed to draw from sources throughout the country. A 2013 statistical analysis commissioned by the United Nations High Commissioner for Refugees found that the death tolls provided by the VDC were broadly consistent with three other opposition-linked databases: the Syrian Observatory for Human Rights (SOHR), the Syrian Martyrs database (SM), and the Syrian Network for Human Rights (SNHR).[5] SOHR and SNHR do not make their data publicly available, nor do they provide summaries of casualties by province over time. SM does make its data available; re-creating the figures here with SM death tolls yielded similar results.[6] While the Syrian regime did collect some casualty data throughout 2011, the patterns of deaths in state data do not at all resemble those in the four mutually consistent opposition totals.[7]

Figures A.2, A.4, and A.6 place total deaths in the context of overall provincial population. To do this, VDC totals were calculated per one thousand people residing in each province. The most recent province-level population data come from Syria's 2004 census, which may not capture the influx of Iraqi refugees in 2003 or displacements due to drought throughout the decade. Nevertheless, even assuming some demographic change, Damascus and Aleppo were two of the country's most populous provinces—making their low death totals even more striking.

Figures A.1 and A.2 consider the relationship between mobilization (proxied by total deaths in figure A.1 and deaths per one thousand residents in figure A.2) and wealth (proxied by average household expenditures in 2009, measured in 2009 Syrian pounds). As both figures demonstrate, provinces with higher household expenditures were not systematically less likely to mobilize, nor were provinces with lower expenditures systematically more likely to mobilize. While wealthy areas like Lattakia, Tartus, and Aleppo saw few deaths, Damascus and Homs have relatively similar household average expenditures but sharply different death tolls. Similarly, al-Hasaka, al-Suwayda', and Hama all look similarly poor from the data, but Hama was a site of major mobilization while al-Hasaka and al-Suwayda' remained largely quiescent. Whereas a history of rebellion might help explain Hama, it does not explain Aleppo's nonparticipation.

In figures A.1 and A.2, the data points for al-Hasaka partially obscure those for al-Suwayda' as a result of the two provinces' similar expenditure levels and similar (that is, extremely low) death tolls.

Figures A.3 and A.4 consider a different sort of potential economic pressure: inflation. Perhaps areas that had recently experienced high inflation were more likely to mobilize, regardless of their overall levels of household expenditure. To capture rising prices in the years leading up to the uprising, we calculated inflation between 2005 and 2010 using the consumer price index for all goods. Inflation is expressed as a percentage of 2005 prices. Figures A.3 and A.4 suggest no clear relationship between inflation and deaths: consider the pairs of Homs and Lattakia, Hama and al-Hasaka, and Dar'a and Aleppo. In each pair, provinces with very similar levels of inflation saw sharply different levels of mobilization.

In figures A.3 and A.4, the two sparsely populated southern provinces of al-Qunaytra and al-Suwayda' have nearly identical x-values (inflation levels) and very similar death tolls. In figure A.3, al-Qunaytra is completely obscured by al-Suwayda'. In figure A.4, al-Qunaytra is represented by the slightly higher data point; al-Suwayda' by the lower one.

Finally, figures A.5 and A.6 consider *relative* levels of inflation among the different provinces. We used the inflation data from figures A.3 and A.4 to calculate each province's 2005–10 inflation as a percentage of the national average. Yet again, no clear relationship with mobilization is visible in the graphs. Several provinces with high relative inflation also saw serious mobilization, especially Dar'a and Hama.

The similar economic, demographic, and mobilizational profiles of al-Qunaytra and al-Suwayda' are relevant in these two last figures as well. As in figure A.3, in figure A.5 al-Suwayda' completely hides al-Qunaytra. And as in figure A.4, in figure A.6 al-Qunaytra is the point with the slightly higher y-value, while al-Suwayda' is the lower.

SOURCES AND DATA COLLECTION

All economic and population data come from the Syrian Central Bureau of Statistics (CBS), a government agency. These data were published between 2004 and 2010, and therefore fully predate the uprising; they were downloaded in 2015. The CBS website is no longer active. Scholars of Syria and Syrian professionals involved in economic planning have tended to treat CBS data as reliable.

Death toll data were collected in July 2018 from the online databases of the Violations Documentation Center (http://www.vdc-sy.info/index.php/en/martyrs) and the Syrian Martyrs group (http://syrianshuhada.com/?a=st&st=20).

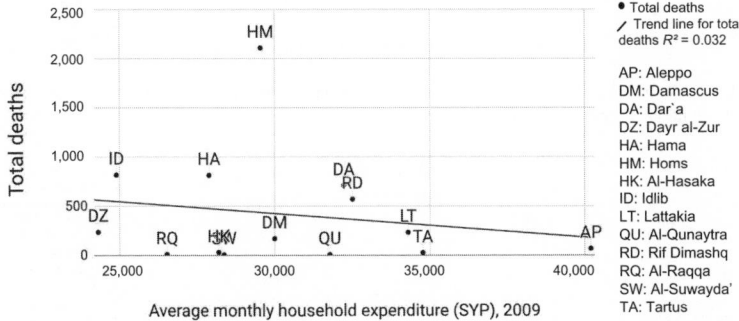

FIGURE A.1. Average monthly household expenditure (2009) vs. total deaths (3/2011–2/2012). SYP denotes Syrian pounds.

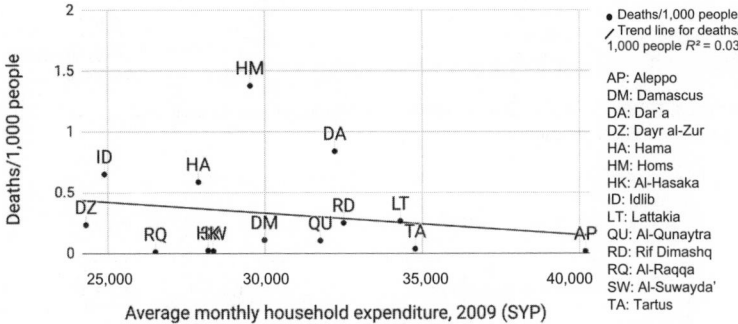

FIGURE A.2. Average monthly household expenditure (2009) vs. deaths per 1,000 people (3/2011–1/2012). SYP denotes Syrian pounds.

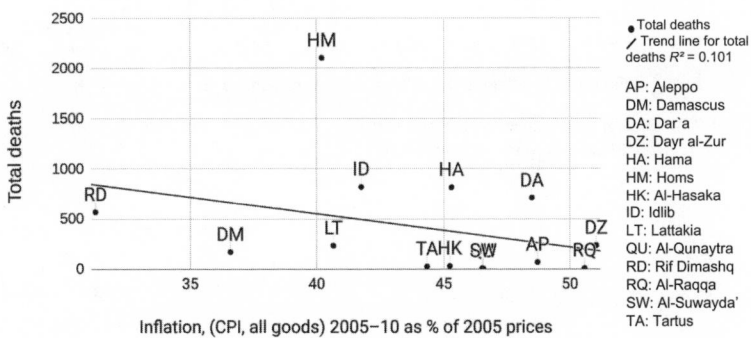

FIGURE A.3. Inflation (2005–10) vs. total deaths (3/2011–1/2012). CPI denotes consumer price index.

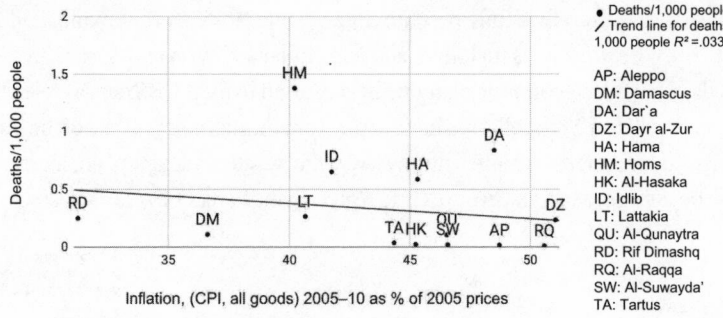

FIGURE A.4. Inflation (2005–10) vs. deaths per 1,000 people (3/2011–1/2012). VDC denotes Violations Documentation Center; CPI denotes consumer price index.

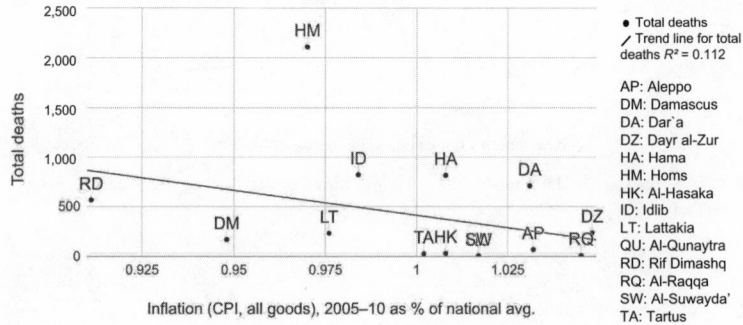

FIGURE A.5. Inflation (2005–10) as a percentage of the national average vs. total deaths (3/2011–1/2012). CPI denotes consumer price index.

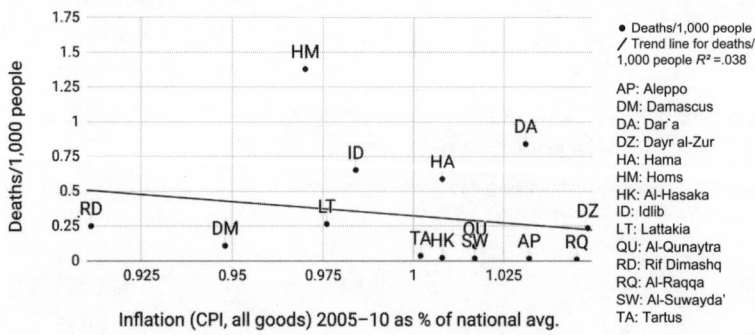

FIGURE A.6. Inflation (2005–10) as a percentage of the national average vs. deaths/1,000 people (3/2011–1/2012). CPI denotes consumer price index.

Notes

PREFACE

1 See *Ambiguities of Domination: Politics, Rhetoric, and Symbols in Contemporary Syria* (Chicago: University of Chicago Press, 1999). Note that the passages here are snippets from the account provided in "Conceptualizing Culture: Possibilities for Political Science," *American Political Science Review* 96, no. 4 (December 2002): 724. The notion that compliance is what counts politically is taken from Slavoj Žižek's *The Sublime Object of Ideology* (London: Verso, [1989] 2009), discussed at length in *Ambiguities of Domination*, 154–55.

2 See the new preface to Wedeen, *Ambiguities of Domination* (2015).

3 Louis Althusser, "Ideology and Ideological State Apparatuses (Notes towards an Investigation)," in *Lenin and Philosophy, and Other Essays*, trans. Ben Brewster (New York: Monthly Review Press, 1971), 127–86.

4 Althusser, 168.

5 The phrase was introduced to me by Lauren Berlant's invocation in *Cruel Optimism* (Durham, NC: Duke University Press, 2011), 13. She takes the phrase from Adorno's essay "Commitment," where the actual passage reads literally from the German as "it should be otherwise." See Theodor Adorno, "Commitment," trans. Francis McDonagh, *New Left Review* 87 (September 1974): 89.

6 Hannah Arendt, *Between Past and Future: Eight Exercises in Political Thought*, trans. Jerome Kohn (New York: Penguin Classics, 2006).

7 This statement was from an early draft of Kaushik Sunder Rajan's *Pharmocracy: Value, Politics, and Knowledge in Global Biomedicine* (Durham, NC: Duke University Press, 2017). It did not make it into the final version of the book, but I have permission from the author to quote. Personal correspondence, September 2017.

8 Hisham Matar, *The Return: Fathers, Sons and the Land in Between* (New York: Random House, 2017), 150, Kindle edition.

9   It is possible to understand even seemingly petty complaints like those about electricity cutoffs and high prices as ways of expressing grief, as Omar Safadi has invited me to consider and as chapter 4 suggests.

10 Matar, *The Return*, 143.

11 Rania Abouzeid, *No Turning Back: Life, Loss, and Hope in Wartime Syria* (New York: W. W. Norton, 2018); Alia Malek, *The Home That Was Our Country: A Memoir of Syria* (New York: Nation Books, 2017); Yassin al-Haj Saleh, *Impossible Revolution: Making Sense of the Syrian Tragedy*, trans. Ibtihal Mahmood (London: Hurst, 2017); Samar Yazbek, *The Crossing: My Journey to the Shattered Heart of Syria* (London: Ebury Press, 2016); and Robin Yassin-Kassab and Leila Al-Shami, *Burning Country: Syrians in Revolution and War* (London: Pluto Press, 2016). Wendy Pearlman's is a scholarly curation of Syrian voices: *We Crossed a Bridge and It Trembled: Voices from Syria* (New York: Harper Collins, 2017). Others — scholars, activists, and fellow artists — have chosen to focus on artistic production in this vein: Malu Halasa, Zaher Omareen, and Nawara Mahfoud, eds., *Syria Speaks: Art and Culture from the Frontline* (London: Saqi Books, 2014); Joshka Wessels, *Documenting Syria: Filmmaking, Video Activism and Revolution* (London: I. B. Tauris, forthcoming 2019); and Donatella Della Ratta, *Shooting a Revolution: Visual Media and Warfare in Syria* (London: Pluto Press, 2018). Throughout the manuscript, I cite Della Ratta's previous work. Her now-published book, read in haste as I was copyediting my own, offers some important clarifications and revisions to her articles. Her knowledge of Syria and her long-standing commitments to its cultural production, social media activism, and the uprising are worthy of note.

12 Anthony Marra, *The Constellation of Vital Phenomena* (New York: Hogarth, 2013).

INTRODUCTION

1   See for instance Milan W. Svolik's work: "The Foundations of Limited Authoritarian Government: Institutions, Commitment, and Power-Sharing in Dictatorships" (with Carles Boix), *Journal of Politics* 75, no. 2 (April 2013): 300–316; "Contracting on Violence: The Moral Hazard in Authoritarian Repression and Military Intervention in Politics," *Journal of Conflict Resolution* 57, no. 5 (2013): 765–94; or "Power-Sharing and Leadership Dynamics in Authoritarian Regimes," *American Journal of Political Science* 53, no. 2 (1999): 477–94. This is not an exhaustive list, but consider the game-theoretic models offered by Milan W. Svolik to understand both elite and mass incentives in his *The Politics of Authoritarian Rule* (New York: Cambridge University Press, 2012); and Daron Acemoglu and James A. Robinson, *Economic Origins of Dictatorship and Democracy* (New York: Cambridge University Press, 2006), the latter beholden to Barrington Moore's influential *Social Origins of Dictatorship and Democracy: Lord and Peasant in the Making of the Modern World* (Boston: Beacon Press, 1967 [paperback]). Other works inspired by Moore's structural analysis of relations among elites (often via Theda Skocpol and with an emphasis on political parties or class relations) include the following: Dan Slater, *Ordering Power: Contentious Politics and Authoritarian Leviathans in Southeast Asia* (New York: Cambridge University Press, 2010); and Michael Albertus, *Autocracy and Redistribution: The Politics of Land Reform* (New York: Cambridge University Press, 2015). For a discussion of phony elections, see Beatriz Magaloni, *Voting for Autocracy: Hegemonic Party Survival and Its Demise in Mexico* (New York: Cambridge University Press, 2006); and Alberto Simpser,

Why Governments and Parties Manipulate Elections: Theory, Practice, and Implications (New York: Cambridge University Press, 2014). See as well Steven Levitsky and Lucan A. Way, *Competitive Authoritarianism: Hybrid Regimes after the Cold War* (New York: Cambridge University Press, 2010); Sheena C. Greitens, *Dictators and Their Secret Police: Coercive Institutions and State Violence* (Cambridge: Cambridge University Press, 2016); and Stephan Haggard and Marcus Noland, *Hard Target: Sanctions, Inducements, and the Case of North Korea* (Palo Alto, CA: Stanford University Press, 2017). On the Middle East, see Eva R. Bellin, "The Robustness of Authoritarianism in the Middle East: Exceptionalism in Comparative Perspective," *Comparative Politics* 36, no. 2 (2004): 139–57, and "Reconsidering the Robustness of Authoritarianism in the Middle East: Lessons from the Arab Spring," *Comparative Politics* 44, no. 2 (2012): 127–49; Lisa Blaydes, *Elections and Distributive Politics in Mubarak's Egypt* (New York: Cambridge University Press, 2010); Jason Brownlee, *Authoritarianism in an Age of Democratization* (New York: Cambridge University Press, 2007); Sofia Fenner, "Life after Co-optation" (PhD diss., University of Chicago, 2016); Ellen Lust-Okar, *Structuring Conflict in the Arab World: Incumbents, Opponents, and Institutions* (Cambridge: Cambridge University Press, 2007); and Dina Rashed, "Authoritarianism and the Civilianization of Force: Police Power in Militarized Regimes" (PhD diss., University of Chicago, 2017).

2   For an overview of game-theoretic models of authoritarianism, see Scott Gehlbach, Konstantin Sonin, and Milan W. Svolik, "Formal Models of Authoritarian Politics," *Annual Review of Political Science* 19 (2016): 565–84. For an account of the ways in which politically "polarized" populations are attracted to dictators, see Svolik's "When Polarization Trumps Civic Virtue: Partisan Conflict and the Subversion of Democracy by Incumbents" (unpublished manuscript, last modified August 2018; https://tinyurl.com/ybtw2vc6, accessed November 25, 2018), PDF document.

3   To be sure, there were small political gatherings in Damascus in the weeks leading up to the March demonstrations, and a significant crowd of fifteen hundred that converged near the main marketplace to protest a policeman's ill-treatment of a local shopkeeper. But it is generally acknowledged that Syria's uprising gained considerable momentum nationwide after the events in Darʿa.

4   See Reinoud Leenders, "'Oh Buthaina, Oh Shaʿban—the Hawrani Is Not Hungry, We Want Freedom!': Revolutionary Framing and Mobilization at the Onset of the Syrian Uprising," in *Social Movements, Mobilization, and Contestation in the Middle East and North Africa*, ed. Joel Beinin and Frédéric Vairel (2nd ed., Palo Alto, CA: Stanford University Press, 2013), 248–49.

5   In *Suriya: Darb al-alam nahwa al-hurriyya; Muhawala fi al-tarikh al-rahin* (Doha, Qatar: al-Markaz al-ʿArabi lil-Abhath wa Dirasat al-Siyasat, 2013), ʿAzmi Bishara claims that this dominant narrative about the children of Darʿa lacks compelling evidence. But most disagree with Bishara's assessment.

6   Leenders, "'Oh Buthaina, Oh Shaʿban.'"

7   See notes 34 and 70 of chapter 1 about the drought. In fact, most of the work claiming a correlation between the drought and the uprising relies on the very same IRIN reports, which are themselves problematic.

8   The children were ultimately released. As violence escalated, other citizens, including some children, became iconic figures (for the opposition) of a dissenting public's vulnerability and the regime's cruelty.

9   As an important aside: for game theorists, ambivalence gets modeled as
    indifference. But this is a problematic version of what ambivalence connotes.
    Indifference bears a family resemblance to apathy or withdrawal; ambivalence
    connotes tension, contradiction, being pulled in competing directions. It is this
    appreciation of internal struggle—both affective and cognitive—that a theory of
    ideological interpellation enables us to grasp. Thanks are owed to John Patty for
    discussions of this matter.

10 There is an important literature on ideology in the Marxist tradition, including
    Antonio Gramsci's notions of hegemony in *Selections from the Prison Notebooks of
    Antonio Gramsci*, ed. and trans. Quintin Hoare and Geoffrey Nowell Smith (New
    York: International Publishers, 1971); Fredric Jameson, *The Political Unconscious:
    Narrative as a Socially Symbolic Act* (Ithaca, NY: Cornell University Press, 1981);
    Raymond Williams, *Marxism and Literature* (Oxford: Oxford University Press,
    1977); Terry Eagleton, *The Meaning of Life* (Oxford: Oxford University Press,
    2007); Althusser, "Ideology and Ideological State Apparatuses," quoted above;
    and, by Pierre Bourdieu, *Outline of a Theory of Practice*, trans. Richard Nice
    (Cambridge: Cambridge University Press 1977), *Distinction: A Social Critique of
    the Judgement of Taste*, trans. Richard Nice (Cambridge, MA: Harvard University
    Press, 1984), and *The Logic of Practice*, trans. Richard Nice (Palo Alto, CA: Stan-
    ford University Press, 1990), to name some obvious examples. For an excellent
    introduction to this literature and the stakes involved in distinguishing ideology
    from hegemony and culture, see Jean Comaroff and John Comaroff, *Of Revelation
    and Revolution*, vol. 1, *Christianity, Colonialism, and Consciousness in South Africa*
    (Chicago: University of Chicago Press, 1991).

11 Contemporary theorists, thinkers associated with "late liberalism" in particular,
    often shy away from using the term *ideology* on the grounds that it is too logo-
    centric, ignores the value of affect, carries with it the baggage of "false conscious-
    ness," or somehow fails to incorporate the intricacies of the "later Marx." On late
    liberalism, see Elizabeth Povinelli, *The Cunning of Recognition: Indigenous Alteri-
    ties and the Making of Australian Multiculturalism* (Durham, NC: Duke University
    Press, 2002). For a discussion of value, refer to Kaushik Sunder Rajan, *Pharmoc-
    racy: Value, Politics, and Knowledge in Global Biomedicine* (Durham, NC: Duke
    University Press, 2017). The sophisticated account of ideology in Marx comes in
    his discussion of commodity fetishism in *Capital*, vol. 1, in which the commodity
    form is the depository of value as self-valorizing.

12 Žižek writes, "It is the same with commodities: the real problem is not to pen-
    etrate the 'hidden kernel' of the commodity—the determination of its value by
    the quantity of the work consumed in its production—but to explain why work
    assumed the form of the value of a commodity, why it can affirm its social charac-
    ter only in the commodity-form of its product" (in *The Sublime Object of Ideology*
    [New York: Verso, 2009], 3–4). The "essential constitution of [the] dream is thus
    not its 'latent thought' but this work (the mechanisms of displacement and con-
    densation, the figuration of the contents of words or syllables) which confers on it
    the form of a dream" (Žižek, 5).

13 For examples of the strain of thinking about the concept of ideology I draw from
    in this book, see Althusser, "Ideology and Ideological State Apparatuses," quoted
    above. Also Louis Althusser, Étienne Balibar, Roger Establet, et al., *Reading
    Capital: The Complete Edition*, trans. Ben Brewster and David Fernbach (London:
    Verso, 2015). And Jameson, *The Political Unconscious* (1981), especially chapter
    6. For a recent effort to draw attention to Althusser's "aleatory materialism,"
    see Banu Bargu's "In the Theater of Politics: Althusser's Aleatory Materialism

and Aesthetics," *Diacritics* 40, no. 3 (2012): 86–113. See as well the introduction to Rosalind C. Morris and Daniel Leonard, *The Returns of Fetishism: Charles de Brosses's "The Worship of Fetish Gods" and Its Legacies* (Chicago: University of Chicago Press, 2017).

14 Fredric Jameson, "Reification and Utopia in Mass Culture," *Social Text* 1 (Winter 1979): 141.

15 Žižek, *The Sublime Object of Ideology*, 27.

16 I take this version of ideology to be consonant with Foucault's insight that "political and economic conditions of existence are not a veil or an obstacle for the subject of knowledge but the means by which subjects of knowledge are formed." See "Truth and Juridical Forms," in *Power*, ed. James D. Faubion and trans. Robert Hurley et al. (New York: New Press, 2000), 15. Foucault rightly criticizes "traditional" Marxist views of ideology for, among other things, their insistence on false consciousness. As I hope to have demonstrated here, a repurposing of the concept, drawing from Berlant, Comaroff and Comaroff, Jameson, Mazzarella, and Žižek, helps eliminate these problems while maintaining a rich understanding of practices of interpellation and the complexities they illuminate for our analyses of uptake, attachment, belief, and knowledge. Foucault's move toward power/ knowledge, with an emphasis on juridical forms, truth claims, and the power of the human sciences, while salutary, is in many respects more limiting than the concept of ideology (with all its admitted baggage) subscribed to here. See also Foucault's critique of ideology in *On the Government of the Living: Lectures at the Collège de France*, trans. Graham Burchell (New York: Palgrave-MacMillan, 2014), 11.

17 Slavoj Žižek, "Denial: The Liberal Utopia," available at https://tinyurl.com /yzewpw2, accessed December 1, 2018.

18 Author's email correspondence with Jean Comaroff, May 26, 2013.

19 Terry Eagleton, *Ideology: An Introduction* (London: Verso, [1991] 2007).

20 Timur Kuran, *Private Truths, Public Lies: The Social Consequences of Preference Falsification* (Cambridge, MA: Harvard University Press, 1995); and William Mazzarella, "Totalitarian Tears: Does the Crowd Really Mean It?," *Cultural Anthropology* 30, no. 1 (2015): 91–112.

21 Lisa Wedeen, *Ambiguities of Domination: Politics, Rhetoric, and Symbols in Contemporary Syria* (Chicago: University of Chicago Press, 1999). Or, and this is another possibility, performing an act repeatedly might lead to conviction (as religious acts such as turning the Buddhist prayer wheel are supposed to do). Other examples of belief's complexity (which Žižek helpfully invokes) are canned laughter used on sitcoms or professional weepers attending funerals, which relieve the audience or mourners of the obligation to register publicly their delight or their grief without the structure of the situation itself being undermined by their reticence to do so.

22 Žižek, *The Sublime Object of Ideology*, 33.

23 Žižek, 35.

24 Thanks are owed to William Mazzarella and Lauren Berlant here. The latter's attention to incoherence and attachment is an obvious influence.

25 "*Je sais bien, mais quand même . . .*" (I know very well, yet nevertheless) is the title of Octave Mannoni's essay on fetishism and ambivalence that speaks to the

structure of disavowal (*Clefs pour l'imaginaire ou l'Autre Scène* [Paris: Seuil, 1985], 9–33). See also Slavoj Žižek's *Looking Awry: An Introduction to Jacques Lacan through Popular Culture* (Boston: MIT Press, 1991).

26 William Mazzarella, email correspondence with the author, August 2017.

27 Louis Althusser, "Ideology and Ideological State Apparatuses (Notes towards an Investigation)," in *Lenin and Philosophy, and Other Essays*, trans. Ben Brewster (New York: Monthly Review Press, 1971), 127–86.

28 Lisa Wedeen, "Ideology and Humor in Dark Times: Notes from Syria," *Critical Inquiry* 39 (Winter 2013): 841–73.

29 Michel Pêcheux, *Language, Semantics and Ideology*, trans. Harbans Nagpal (London: MacMillan, 1982), cited in Žižek, *The Sublime Object of Ideology*, xxv.

30 This conscience is a "turning back upon oneself in the sense that Nietzsche described" in *The Genealogy of Morality* (in Judith Butler, *The Psychic Life of Power: Theories in Subjection* [Palo Alto, CA: Stanford University Press, 1997], 109). For a critique of Butler's reading of Althusser, see Michael Lampert's "Resisting Ideology: On Butler's Critique of Althusser," *Diacritics* 43, no. 2 (2015): 124–47. I am less concerned with whether she gets Althusser "right" (and to be fair to Lampert, his *main* concern is not that either) than how her engagement facilitates thinking about our entanglements in power relations. Lampert claims that Butler's account is ultimately "politically demotivating," but I think her account is less deflating than that. A key point consistent with her view is that interpellation both assumes and constitutes "the subject" through a process of recursive naming that "supplies the linguistic guarantee of existence." Subject formation thus entails a readiness to respond to being hailed, which, as Butler puts it, "suggests that one is, as it were, already in relation to the voice before the response, already implicated in the terms of the animating misrecognition by an authority to which one subsequently yields. . . . In this sense, the scene with the police is a belated and redoubled scene, one which renders explicit a founding submission for which no such scene would prove adequate" (Butler, *The Psychic Life of Power*, 111).

31 Butler, 112.

32 The stakes of the debate over ideology and subject formation are multiple. For Butler, this ability to recognize yourself as a subject before or in the moment of becoming a subject is bound up with a prior guilt and thus with conscience. For the Lacanian Mladen Dolar, whereas the symbolic encompasses communicable speech and social ties, the fundamentally distinct "psychic" register entails a Lacanian-inspired account of a "remainder," that thing or "kernel of the real" outside social life. As William Mazzarella nicely puts it, for Lacanians "the trigger for our joyously constitutive (but also perpetually frustrated) engagements with the imaginary and symbolic orders through which we come to experience ourselves as subjects with identities and desires is our distinctively human *lack*. Like Kant and Hegel before him, Jacques Lacan understood the congenital incompleteness of human beings to be both the origin of our bondage and the gateway to our freedom" (William Mazzarella, *The Mana of Mass Society* [Chicago: University of Chicago Press, 2017], 151). In *The Mana of Mass Society*, Mazzarella opts instead for Peter Sloterdijk's account of "biunity," which "proposes the human universality of an early experience of relationality (*not* merger) that is pre-subjective and non-objectifying" (Mazzarella, 151). It is not the purpose of this book to commit to Butler's conscience or any other definitive position among a host of ones providing deep-seated universally applicable psychological reasons for why people recognize themselves as addressees (and thereby become "themselves") in

moments of ideological interpellation. I therefore remain agnostic about the list of plausible psychic drivers.

33 Thanks are owed to Ghassan Hage for pushing me to elaborate this point while delivering a talk in Sydney, Australia. Judith Butler notes that Althusser's use of the example of religious authority, invoking the uppercase *S* to indicate the grand subject or God, "inadvertently assimilates social interpellation to the divine performative," where subject formation "depends upon a passionate pursuit of recognition which, within the terms of the religious example, is inseparable from a condemnation" (*The Psychic Life of Power*, 110, 113). In other words, Althusser's argument seems to be premised on a deistic/paternal model of recognition and punishment, which invites us to consider nonresponse as a kind of response—a *Deus absconditus*, to borrow Mazzarella's formulation of my claim. Mazzarella has also pointed out that in some instances the addresser may come to recognize that role only in the context of a response. Of course, my use of the allegory is not meant to imply that all instances of interpellation are deliberate or self-conscious, as the following chapters make clear.

34 Thanks to Steven Heydemann for encouraging me to think through this example.

35 Bourdieu, *Distinction*, 95.

36 For a discussion of activists' personal and collective transformation in the events leading up to and during protests calling for *karama* in Jordan, see Yazan Doughan, "Corruption, Authority, and the Discursive Production of Reform and Revolution in Jordan" (PhD diss. submitted to the University of Chicago's Department of Anthropology, June 2018). As Doughan rightly notes, *karameh* (*karama* in Fusha Arabic) used to refer to "what one received in acts of generosity (*karam*). More specifically, various kinds of saints (Christian: *qiddisin*; Muslim, *awliya'*) were said to have *karama*: Divinely bestowed powers to perform marvelous deeds. *Karamat* (pl.) were given to saints in acts of Divine grace that were simultaneously acts of honoring (*takrim*)—to be generous to someone is to honor that person as an indication of love and respect, and *vice versa*" (97). By contrast, "modern uses of *karāmah* refer to an innate human quality that all humans have and can exhibit by virtue of being human (*karamat al-insan*)," a version that seems to have its origins in the second half of the nineteenth century and was popularized by anticolonial and anti-imperial nationalists to denote both individual and collective dignity (96–97). Doughan also correctly notes that the word *nizam* (for "regime") was not used frequently before the uprisings—a point also made by a number of Syrian activists and ordinary observers in the context of my fieldwork.

37 Susan Sontag, *Regarding the Pain of Others* (New York: Picador, 2003); Luc Boltanski, *Distant Suffering: Morality, Media and Politics*, trans. Graham D. Burchell (Cambridge: Cambridge University Press, 1999); Andrea Muehlebach, *The Moral Neoliberal: Welfare and Citizenship in Italy* (Chicago: University of Chicago Press, 2012); and Mazzarella, *The Mana of Mass Society*.

38 Raymond Williams, "Structures of Feeling," in *Marxism and Literature* (Oxford: Oxford University Press, 1977), 128–35. See also Lauren Berlant, "Structures of Unfeeling: Mysterious Skin," *International Journal of Politics, Culture, and Society* 8, no. 3 (2015): 191–213. For an updated version, see her "Humorlessness (Three Monologues and a Hairpiece)," *Critical Inquiry* 43, no. 2 (2017): 305–40. Also cited in chapter 5.

39 Melissa Gregg and Gregory Seigworth, "Introduction: An Inventory of Shimmers," in *The Affect Theory Reader*, ed. Gregg and Seigworth (Durham, NC: Duke

University Press, 2010), 9–10. Also cited in Shannon L. Mariotti, *Adorno and Democracy: The American Years* (Lexington: University Press of Kentucky, 2016), location 1387, Kindle. For the dangers of comedy, especially satire, see Alexei Yurchak, *Everything Was Forever until It Was No More: The Last Soviet Generation* (Princeton, NJ: Princeton University Press, 2005).

CHAPTER ONE

1   At mediaMe.com/country/Syria.happynings. The site is defunct as of December 1, 2018.

2   *Happynings*, January 2011, 46, also 41.

3   Husayn al-Dik [also transliterated Hussein al-Deek], "Natir Bint al-Madarseh," video, 5:25, YouTube, September 26, 2013, https://youtu.be/bAwxij1-PHI.

4   Milan Svolik in a personal conversation (September 2017) pointed out that it is unusual for the capital city to avoid being the focal point of protest in authoritarian contexts, making quiescence in Damascus especially puzzling. Stathis Kalyvas reiterated this point to me (June 2018).

5   See Lauren Berlant's pathbreaking *Cruel Optimism* (Durham, NC: Duke University Press, 2011).

6   By *multicultural* here, I mean the way in which experiences of difference among Syrians, such as those produced by sectarian organizations or by distinct regional practices, were rendered "cultural" and thereby unthreatening in the official discourse. The concept of culture operates as a celebratory term to denote good, conflict-free, folkloric variety, unlike sect, which conjures up *fitna* (discord), suggesting dangerous, destabilizing forms of societal contestation.

7   *Neoliberal autocracy* is my term and could easily be applied to other places as well, such as China, Vietnam, Singapore, and a host of Middle Eastern regimes, as I note in the text.

8   This notion of freedom, in theory, relates open markets and volunteer ("free") labor to individual rights and personal liberties. But in the actual workings of neoliberalism, and perhaps particularly in the "odd" but now all-too-familiar "coupling" of neoliberalism with autocracy, open markets become opportunities for the intensification of patronage networks (see John Comaroff and Jean Comaroff, eds., "Millennial Capitalism and the Culture of Neoliberalism," special issue, *Public Culture* 12, no. 2 [2000]; the issue was printed as a book in 2001). "Citizen solidarity" does not disappear in the neoliberal era but is reduced to a conceptualization of national subjects as dutiful and "co-responsible for the public good"; see Andrea Muehlebach, *The Moral Neoliberal: Welfare and Citizenship in Italy* (Chicago: University of Chicago Press, 2012), 11–12.
      Whereas anthropological and political theory texts in the 1990s and 2000s emphasized neoliberalism's resilience, in scientific domains of political science, the term *neoliberal* is arguably still pejorative and its use indicative of a scholar's presumed leftist affiliations. Examples from political and social theory of crucial contributions to our thinking about neoliberalism include Wendy Brown's *Undoing the Demos*, where she makes the compelling argument that neoliberalism is "a peculiar form of reason that configures all aspects of existence in economic terms"; it "economizes spheres of activity" (in *Undoing the Demos: Neoliberalism's Stealth Revolution* [New York: Zone Books, 2015], 17 and 21). See also Koray Çalışkan and Michel Callon, "Economization, Part 1: Shifting Attention from

the Economy towards Processes of Economization," *Economy and Society* 38, no. 3 (2009): 369–98; Bernard Harcourt, *The Illusion of Free Markets: Punishment and the Myth of Natural Order* (Cambridge, MA: Harvard University Press, 2012); and Timothy Mitchell's *Rule of Experts: Egypt, Techno-Politics, Modernity* (Berkeley: University of California Press, 2002), *Carbon Democracy: Political Power in the Age of Oil* (New York: Verso, 2011), and "Dreamland: The Neoliberalism of Your Desires," *Middle East Report* 29 (1999), available at https://tinyurl.com/y8s5u2yd.

Political scientists, by contrast, have tended to underemphasize neoliberalism and focus on authoritarian retrenchment. See for example Eva Bellin, "The Robustness of Authoritarianism in the Middle East: Exceptionalism in Comparative Perspective," *Comparative Politics* 36, no. 2 (2004): 139–57. For her updated version of the argument: Bellin, "Reconsidering the Robustness of Authoritarianism in the Middle East: Lessons from the Arab Spring," *Comparative Politics* 44, no. 2 (2012): 127–49. Other examples include Jason Brownlee, *Authoritarianism in an Age of Democratization* (New York: Cambridge University Press, 2007); Jennifer Gandhi, *Political Institutions under Dictatorship* (New York: Cambridge University Press, 2008); Barbara Geddes, "What Do We Know about Democratization after Twenty Years?," *Annual Review of Political Science* 2 (1999): 115–44; Kenneth F. Greene, *Why Dominant Parties Lose: Mexico's Democratization in Comparative Perspective* (New York: Cambridge University Press, 2007); Steven Heydemann, ed., *Upgrading Authoritarianism in the Arab World* (Washington, DC: Saban Center for Middle East Policy, Brookings Institution, 2007); Beatriz Magaloni, *Voting for Autocracy: Hegemonic Party Survival and Its Demise in Mexico* (New York: Cambridge University Press, 2006); and Dan Slater, *Ordering Power: Contentious Politics and Authoritarian Leviathans in Southeast Asia* (New York: Cambridge University Press, 2010).

My book is an effort to put together the contributions of each in order to understand the phenomenon I am calling neoliberal autocracy.

9   Thanks are owed to Lauren Berlant here.

10 Heydemann, *Upgrading Authoritarianism in the Arab World.*

11 See for example Joseph Daher, "Syria: The Social Origins of the Uprising," Rosa Luxemburg Stiftung, n.d., available at https://tinyurl.com/ybyjvdnh, accessed December 2, 2018; various articles in Raymond Hinnebusch, ed., *Syria: From Authoritarian Upgrading to Revolution?* (Syracuse, NY: Syracuse University Press, 2015); Gilbert Achcar, *The People Want: A Radical Exploration of the Arab Uprisings* (Berkeley: University of California Press, 2013); Adam Baczko, Gilles Dorronsoro, and Arthur Quesnay, *Syrie: Anatomie d'une guerre civile* (Paris: CNRS Édition, 2016); Nabil Marzuq (Marzouq), "Al-tanmiyya al-mafquda fi Suriya," in *Khalfiyyat al-thawra, dirasat suriyya,* ed. A. Bishara (Doha, Qatar: Arab Center for Research and Policy Studies, 2013), 35–70; Linda Matar, *The Political Economy of Investment in Syria* (Hampshire, UK: Palgrave Macmillan, 2016); and Samir Seifan, "Siyasat tawziʿ al-dakhl wa dawrha fi al-infijar al-ijtimaʿi fi Suriya," in *Khalfiyyat al-thawra, dirasat suriyya,* ed. A. Bishara (Doha, Qatar: Arab Center for Research and Policy Studies, 2013), 95–146. For thoughtful Marxist orientations toward the political economy of the uprising in English, see Adam Hanieh, *Lineages of Revolt: Issues of Contemporary Capitalism in the Middle East* (Chicago: Haymarket Books, 2013); and John Chalcraft, *Popular Politics in the Making of the Modern Middle East* (Cambridge: Cambridge University Press, 2016).

12 João Biehl, *Vita: Life in a Zone of Social Abandonment* (Berkeley: University of California Press, 2005).

13 The term *al-ramadiyyin* precedes the uprising, but was generally limited in its use to intellectual circles. Its deployment as a political descriptor seems to originate with the uprising and becomes increasingly popularized as a category to describe various kinds of ambivalence. In 2012–13, it became a prevalent derogatory label, used by activists as a way of indicating the moral deficiency of those on the fence. At the time of this writing, the term has arguably become less pejorative—as some of the dimensions of being undecided or not brave, or even indifferent, can seem like a warranted prudence in retrospect. Thanks are owed to Yahya al-ʿAbdallah and Osama Esber for illuminating discussions on this matter. See also a pertinent issue of the United Arab Emirates daily newspaper the *Union* at http://www.alittihad.ae/wajhatdetails.php?id=55395, accessed December 1, 2018.

14 Fieldwork, January–May 2011 in Damascus. Also refer to my introduction, where I discuss Bourdieu's insights on the cultivation of taste and status rather than simply economic class. Pierre Bourdieu, *Distinction: A Social Critique of the Judgement of Taste*, trans. Richard Nice (Cambridge, MA: Harvard University Press, 1984).

15 Fieldwork, January–May 2011 in Damascus.

16 Jean Comaroff, email correspondence with the author, May 26, 2013. The language here also harkens back to Marx's discussion in *Capital*, vol. 1, pt. 1, "Section 4: The Fetishism of Commodities and the Secret Thereof." Marx writes, "Hence, when we bring the products of our labour into relation with each other as values, it is not because we see in these articles the material receptacles of homogenous human labor. Quite the contrary: whenever, by an exchange, we equate as values our different products, by that very act, we also equate, as human labour, the different kinds of labour expended upon them. We are not aware of this, nevertheless we do it. Value, therefore, does not stalk about with a label describing what it is. It is value, rather, that converts every product into a social hieroglyphic." Quoted from *The Marx-Engels Reader: Second Edition*, ed. Robert C. Tucker (New York: W. W. Norton, 1978), 322.

17 See Kheder Khaddour and Kevin Mazur's data set of Syrian towns before the 2011 uprising. It uses the 2004 national census as well as newly collected data on ethnic identity: https://dataverse.harvard.edu/dataset.xhtml?persistentId=doi:10.7910/DVN/YQQ07L, accessed December 18, 2018. Issues arise about how sect/ethnic identifications are coded or whether quantitative data best capture people's experiences of affiliation, but this data set is one important effort to get at regional variation. Noura Hourani and Avery Edelman, "After the Idlib City Council Refuses to Hand Over Administrative Control, HTS Takes It by Force," *Syria Direct*, August 29, 2017, https://tinyurl.com/y7rld8ud; and Thomas Joscelyn, "Al Nusrah Front Leader Preaches Jihadist Unity in Idlib," *FDD's Long War Journal*, April 2, 2015, https://tinyurl.com/yddgmtfb, give readers a sense of the challenges Idlib faced as a battleground for various militias. For some specifics on Darʿa especially, see Reinoud Leenders and Steven Heydemann, "Popular Mobilization in Syria: Opportunity and Threat, and the Social Networks of the Early Risers," *Mediterranean Politics* 17, no. 2 (2012): 139–59. On Hama: Raphaël Lefèvre, *Ashes of Hama: The Muslim Brotherhood in Syria* (Cary, NC: Oxford University Press, 2014); and Patrick Seale, *Asad: The Struggle for the Middle East* (Berkeley: University of California Press, 1989). On Homs, see notes 27, 28, and 29 in this chapter. Thomas Pierret, *Religion and State in Syria: The Sunni Ulema under the Baʿth* (New York: Cambridge University Press, 2013), is helpful in illuminating the loyalty of the clergy in Aleppo and Damascus relative to other areas.

18 Mohammed Jamal Barout, *Al-Taqrir al-watani al-istishrafi al-asasi al-awwal li-mashru'a Suriya 2025: Al-mihwar al-sukkani wa al-majali* (Damascus: UNDP and the Syrian Arab Republic, 2007), 232.

19 Mohammed Jamal Barout, *Al-'Aqd al-akhir fi tarikh Suriya: Jadaliyyat al-Jumud wa al-Islah* (Beirut: al-Markaz al-'Arabi lil-Abhath wa Dirasat al-Siyasat, 2012), 224.

20 Kevin Mazur, "Social Categories, Patronage, and the State: Variation in the Syria Uprising" (unpublished manuscript in preparation, May 21, 2018), 196.

21 See Kheder Khaddour, "The Coast in Conflict: Migration, Sectarianism, and Decentralization in Syria's Latakia and Tartus Governorates," Carnegie Middle East Center, July 28, 2016, https://tinyurl.com/y754ayg8; or his work with Kevin Mazur, "The Struggle for Syria's Regions," *Middle East Report* 269 (2013): 2–11, https://tinyurl.com/yc52bsvq. See also Khaddour and Mazur, https://dataverse.harvard.edu/dataset.xhtml?persistentId=doi:10.7910/DVN/YQQ07L, accessed December 18, 2018.

22 For example, Mazur rightly notes in his revised dissertation, "Social Categories, Patronage, and the State" (2018), that Hama, Syria's fourth-largest city and site of the regime's brutal attack on the Muslim Brotherhood in the early 1980s, sustained some of the largest peaceful protests in the country. Aleppo, another historical area of contention, showed few signs of joining the fray. Barout (*Al-'Aqd al-akhir fi tarikh Suriya*, 262) estimates that six hundred residents of the town of Kafranbel in the Jabal Zawiya region were arrested in the 1980s, affecting the majority of the town's families. But Kafranbel became an area of peaceful resistance—producing striking caricatures of regime brutality that became a globally recognized phenomenon. Many other such examples could be named. See Barout's *Al-'Aqd al-akhir fi tarikh Suriya* and the following by Kheder Khaddour: "The Alawite Dilemma (Homs 2013)," in *Playing the Sectarian Card: Identities and Affiliations of Local Communities in Syria*, ed. Friederike Stolleis (Beirut: Friedrich-Ebert-Stiftung, 2015), 11–26, http://library.fes.de/pdf-files/bueros/beirut/12320.pdf; "The Coast in Conflict: Migration, Sectarianism, and Decentralization in Syria's Latakia and Tartus Governorates," Carnegie Middle East Center, July 28, 2016, https://tinyurl.com/y754ayg8; and "Consumed by War: The End of Aleppo and Northern Syria's Political Order" (Berlin: Friedrich-Ebert-Stiftung, October 2017), http://library.fes.de/pdf-files/iez/13783.pdf. See as well Khaddour's work with Kevin Mazur, "The Struggle for Syria's Regions."

23 My own argument is not about what caused the uprising but about why its uptake remains consequentially limited. The political scientists Stathis N. Kalyvas and Ignacio Sánchez-Cuenca underscore the importance of studying absence or non-events in "Killing without Dying? The Absence of Suicide Missions," in *Making Sense of Suicide Missions*, ed. Diego Gambetta (Oxford: Oxford University Press, 2005), 209–32.

24 See Lisa Wedeen, *Peripheral Visions: Publics, Power, and Performance in Yemen* (Chicago: University of Chicago Press, 2008).

25 For example, while neoliberalism is often associated with intensified means of exploitation, in Latin America the imposition of macroeconomic stabilization policies in the 1990s seems to have benefitted the poor, who had experienced a dramatic erosion of their meager salaries and savings during the hyperinflation crisis of the previous decade. For a key volume on the local and translocal dimensions of neoliberalism, see Jean Comaroff and John L. Comaroff, eds., *Millennial Capitalism and the Culture of Neoliberalism* (Durham, NC: Duke University

Press, 2001). An anthropological study that grapples productively with the social and political theory literatures on neoliberalism, abandonment, and exhaustion in "late liberalism" is Elizabeth Povinelli's *Economies of Abandonment: Social Belonging and Endurance in Late Liberalism* (Durham, NC: Duke University Press, 2011). Fewer works by those who are rightly critical of neoliberalism are devoted to its seductions, that is, the affective investments in this version of the good life despite its cruelties. A partial exception is Nigel Thrift, "Understanding the Material Practices of Glamour," in *The Affect Theory Reader*, ed. Melissa Gregg and Gregory J. Seigworth (Durham, NC: Duke University Press, 2010), 289–308.

Much of the literature on globalization and neoliberalism overlaps or discusses similar phenomena, such as the growth of international trade, the proliferation of financial flows and instruments, and the integration of nation-states previously understood as more autonomous or bounded. For example, see Saskia Sassen, *Globalization and Its Discontents: Essays on the New Mobility of People and Money* (New York: New Press, 1999), as well as *The Global City: New York, London, Tokyo* (Princeton, NJ: Princeton University Press, 1991). In sorting out these arguments, helpful basic studies include David Harvey, *A Brief History of Neoliberalism* (Oxford: Oxford University Press, 2005); and Robert Gilpin, *The Challenge of Global Capitalism: The World Economy in the 21st Century* (Princeton, NJ: Princeton University Press, 2000). Eric Hobsbawm, *The Age of Extremes: A History of the World, 1914–1991* (New York: Vintage Books, 1994), helped me grasp the importance of the breakdown of Bretton Woods in the 1970s. For an illuminating discussion of the concept, see Peter Evans and William H. Sewell, Jr., "Neoliberalism: Policy Regimes, International Regimes, and Social Effects," in *Social Resilience in the Neoliberal Era*, ed. Peter Hall and Michele Lamont (New York: Cambridge University Press, 2013), 35–68. Thomas Piketty, *Capital in the Twenty-First Century*, trans. Arthur Goldhammer (Cambridge, MA: Harvard University Press, 2014), specifies in rich historical detail shifts in the concentration of income and wealth, tracking the changes in patterns of inequality since the Industrial Revolution and capturing the dynamics of wealth accumulation that have characterized the neoliberal age, a term he tends not to use. See also Leo Panitch and Sam Gindin, *The Making of Global Capitalism: The Political Economy of American Empire* (New York: Verso, 2012). For an important attention to race under neoliberalism, see Michael C. Dawson, "The Hollow Shell: Loïc Wacquant's Vision of State, Race and Economics," *Review of Racial and Ethnic Studies* 37, no. 10 (2014): 1767–75; Michael C. Dawson and Megan Ming Francis, "Black Politics and the Neoliberal Racial Order," *Public Culture* 28, no. 1 (2016): 23–62; Cedric Johnson, ed., *The Neoliberal Deluge: Hurricane Katrina, Late Capitalism, and the Remaking of New Orleans* (Minneapolis: University of Minnesota Press, 2011); and Loïc Wacquant, *Punishing the Poor: The Neoliberal Government of Social Insecurity* (Durham, NC: Duke University Press, 2009). Michael C. Dawson, *Not in Our Lifetimes: The Future of Black Politics* (Chicago: University of Chicago Press, 2011), chronicles the effects of neoliberalism on race, inequality, and ideological reorientations in the United States. I am grateful to him and to earlier conversations with the political economist Carles Boix.

26 Syria's Deputy Prime Minister of Economic Affairs, 'Abdallah Dardari, termed this economic liberalization "social market" reform. For an overview of some of the literature on Syria's economy under Bashar al-Asad, and on Dardari's influence in particular, see Shana R. Marshall, "Syria and the Financial Crisis: Prospects for Reform?," *Middle East Policy* 16, no. 2 (2009): 106–15, https://tinyurl .com/y8j8cc6e; Bassam Haddad, "The Formation and Development of Economic Networks in Syria: Implications for Economic and Fiscal Reforms, 1986–2000,"

in *Networks of Privilege in the Middle East: The Politics of Economic Reform Revisited*, ed. Steven Heydemann (London: Palgrave-MacMillan, 2004), 37–76; and more recently, Bassam Haddad, *Business Networks in Syria: The Political Economy of Authoritarian Resilience* (Palo Alto, CA: Stanford University Press, 2012). Also: Barout, *Al-'Aqd al-akhir fi tarikh Suriya*. See as well Omar S. Dahi and Yasser Munif, "Revolts in Syria: Tracking the Convergence between Authoritarianism and Neoliberalism," *Journal of African and Asian Studies* 47, no. 4 (2012): 323–32; and Omar S. Dahi, "The Political Economy of the Egyptian and Arab Revolt," *IDS Bulletin* 43, no. 1 (2012): 47–53.

27   Haddad, *Business Networks in Syria*, especially chapters 4, 5, 6, and the conclusion. The president's cousin Rami Makhluf has the nickname Mr. Five Percent, speaking to his alleged penchant for skimming 5 percent, if not more, from every investment deal made in Syria. Some people, perhaps more accurately, call him Mr. Sixty Percent. See as well Achcar, *The People Want*.

28   See Michel Foucault, *The Birth of Biopolitics: Lectures at the Collège de France, 1978–79*, trans. Graham Burchell, ed. François Ewald and Alessandro Fontana (New York: Picador, 2010), 13. For an extension of Foucault's argument, see Nikolas Rose's *Governing the Soul: The Shaping of the Private Self* (London: Free Association Books, 1999). For cogent efforts to understand neoliberalism as a process, as "neoliberalization," see Neil Brenner, Jamie Peck, and Nik Theodore's jointly authored works, especially "After Neoliberalization?," *Globalizations* 27 (2010): 327–45. See also Çalışkan and Callon, "Economization, Part 1," quoted above, and Wendy Brown, "American Nightmare: Neoliberalism, Neoconservatism and Democratization," *Political Theory* 34, no. 6 (2006): 690–714.

29   This is a paraphrase of a definition I can no longer find on Wikipedia, but which I liked for its concision.

30   Jean Comaroff, email correspondence with the author, May 26, 2013. See also Jean Comaroff and John L. Comaroff, "Law and Disorder in the Postcolony: An Introduction," in *Law and Disorder in the Postcolony*, ed. Jean Comaroff and John L. Comaroff (Chicago: University of Chicago Press, 2006), 1–56.

31   For excellent, general political economy accounts of Syria in English (primarily written in the 1990s), see the following by Steven Heydemann: "The Political Logic of Economic Rationality: Selective Stabilization in Syria," in *The Politics of Economic Stabilization Programs in the Middle East*, ed. Henri J. Barkey (New York: Saint Martin's Press, 1992), 11–39; "Taxation without Representation," in *Rules and Rights in the Middle East: Democracy, Law, and Society*, ed. Resat Kasaba et al. (Seattle: University of Washington Press, 1993), 96–97; and, as editor, *Networks of Privilege in the Middle East* (New York: Palgrave-MacMillan, 2004). See also Haddad, *Business Networks in Syria*; Volker Perthes, *The Political Economy of Syria under Asad* (London: I. B. Tauris, 1995); Perthes, "The Private Sector, Economic Liberalization, and the Prospects of Democratization: The Case of Syria and Some Other Arab Countries," in *Democracy without Democrats? The Renewal of Politics in the Muslim World*, ed. Ghassan Salame (London: I. B. Tauris, 1994), 243–69; and Perthes, "Stages of Economic and Political Liberalization," in *Contemporary Syria: Liberalization between Cold War and Cold Peace*, ed. Eberard Kienle (London: I. B. Tauris, 1994), 44–71. Writings in the 2000s include Samir Seifan, "The Road to Economic Reform in Syria," *St. Andrews Papers on Contemporary Syria*, 2011; and Amanda Patricia Terc, "Syria's New Neoliberal Elite: English Usage, Linguistic Practices and Group Boundaries" (PhD diss., University of Michigan, 2011).

32　According to political economists, these reforms came in part as a response to dwindling oil and gas reserves. See Haddad, *Business Networks in Syria*; Seifan, "The Road to Economic Reform in Syria"; Andrew Tabler, "Squaring the Circle?," *Syria Today*, June 6, 2006, https://tinyurl.com/yapv6luk; and Muhammad Dibo, "I'adat al-i'mar: Bayn mu'assasat al-niolibraliyya wal istibdad," Syria Untold, February 1, 2015, https://tinyurl.com/ydhlgnqr.

33　Pierret, *Religion and State in Syria*.

34　Statistics are notoriously inaccurate in authoritarian regimes, and Syria's is no exception. Even bracketing our skepticism, however, the economic picture remains intriguingly complicated in ways that simple political economic assertions of inequality or the drought *causing* the uprising do not capture. For a sophisticated account of the problems with such arguments, see Omar S. Dahi, Jan Selby, et al., "Climate Change and the Syrian Civil War Revisited," *Political Geography* 60 (2017): 232–44. Worth consulting, despite problems with reporting, are the data from the Central Bureau of Statistics of the Syrian Arab Republic, at http://www.cbssyr.sy/index-EN.htm, accessed December 2, 2018. For more recent data in English and Arabic which include the years 2010 and 2011, see http://www.cbssyr.sy/CPI/inflation_years_2013.htm, accessed December 2, 2018. For annual growth rates, see http://www.tradingeconomics.com/syria/gdp -growth-annual (derived from the Central Bureau of Statistics, the Syrian Arab Republic), accessed December 2, 2018. For inflation, see http://www.trading economics.com/syria/inflation-cpi, accessed December 2, 2018. See also the appendix to this book, quantitative data compiled and explanation of methodological choices written by Sofia Fenner. Thanks are owed to her and to Amer Bisat for helping me understand what these numbers do and do not reveal.

35　The element of personalization, or what some political scientists refer to as patrimonial rule, is important symbolically. Attention to the person of the leader (or in this case, the couple) provides an embodied and ritual focus for what is otherwise—to use Eric Santner's terms—the "excarnation of sovereignty," one that makes apparent the dangers of "the people" or the unwieldy excesses of "the masses." Thanks are owed to William Mazzarella here. See Eric L. Santner, *The Royal Remains: The People's Two Bodies and the Endgames of Sovereignty* (Chicago: University of Chicago Press, 2011).

36　Even people in the advertising profession—some who supported the president, others who imagined that the regime could reform under pressure, and still others who while writing off the president continued to admire the first lady— acknowledged that the timing was wrong for such a piece, and its claims of democratic openness woefully exaggerated.

37　Joan Buck, "Asma' al-Assad: A Rose in the Desert," *Gawker*, June 9, 2013, http:// gawker.com/asma-al-assad-a-rose-in-the-desert-1265002284. The *Gawker* article is a republication of the original *Vogue* article of March 2011. The Syrian regime hired an international public relations firm, Brown Lloyd James, which reportedly was paid five thousand dollars per month to arrange and manage the *Vogue* article; see "PR Firm Worked with Syria in Controversial Photoshoot," *Hill*, August 3, 2011, https://tinyurl.com/428cgcv; and "The Only Remaining Online Copy of *Vogue*'s Asma' al-Assad Profile," *Atlantic*, January 3, 2012, https://tinyurl.com /yafj8mpc.

38　Recall the famous scene in Milan Kundera's *The Book of Laughter and Forgetting* in which a discredited comrade is airbrushed out of the picture ([New York: Harper Perennial Classics, 1999], 3–4).

39 Syrian directors were overwhelmingly negative about the film, with one published critique on the online site all4syria likening it to "bad television"; http://www.all4syria.info/Archive/430274 (link broken as of December 12, 2018). All4syria is best accessed via Facebook and Twitter these days, but the claim was hardly controversial.

40 Thanks are owed to Rasha Salti for conversations about this film and its relationship to the regime official Ghazzi Kan'an's purported suicide.

41 Of course, as William Mazzarella notes, the camera eye implies an additional surveillance vantage point, one of which Majd must remain unaware.

42 Fieldwork, January–May 2011.

43 See Michael Burawoy, *Manufacturing Consent: Changes in the Labor Process under Monopoly Capitalism* (Chicago: University of Chicago Press, 1979). For a contrasting view, see Adam Przeworski, *Capitalism and Social Democracy* (New York: Cambridge University Press, 1986).

44 See Andrea Muehlebach's *The Moral Neoliberal*. The third sector as an "affective and ethical field" is taken from Nikolas Rose, "Community, Citizenship, and the Third Way," *American Behavioral Scientist* 43, no. 9 (2000): 1395–1411; cited in Muehlebach, 37.

45 Cultlike practices centered on the deceased president Hafiz al-Asad continued to be prevalent especially in the army, where hagiographic images were circulated and excerpts from his speeches routinely read aloud—and to a lesser extent (and with less discipline) in schools.

46 Fieldwork, April–May 2011.

47 See Christa Salamandra, *A New Old Damascus: Authenticity and Distinction in Urban Syria* (Bloomington: Indiana University Press, 2004).

48 Bouthaina Shaaban, "Shape of the Things to Come," *Forward Magazine*, March 2011, 64, https://issuu.com/haykalmedia/docs/forwardsyria0311. The proper IJMES transliteration is Buthayna Sha'ban, but her first name is almost always rendered Bouthaina. Her last name is spelled variously. I have preferred to keep the letter 'ayn for her last name. The double *aa* generally indicates the letter alif in Arabic and is therefore misleading.

49 Field notes, February–May 2011.

50 The support of television stars for neoliberal autocracy is a region-wide phenomenon.

51 Al-Dunya television, May 6, 2012, "Silsilat al-Khawna al-Suriyyin, Khamsat Fannanin Khawna," video, 9:56, YouTube, May 22, 2011, https://tinyurl.com/y8wd5mhe.

52 Author's interviews with Syrian citizens, March and April 2011 in Damascus.

53 Al-Jazeera Arabic, "Bashshar al-Asad Yaltaqi bi 'Adad min Fannanin al-Drama al-Suriyya," video, 4:59, YouTube, May 16, 2011, https://youtu.be/Vd3WPzvuEWA. The middle-ground group issued two statements in the early days of the uprising, the second one a quasi retraction of the first in which signatories' support for reforms pursued in moderation was tempered by declarations of fidelity to the president.

54 William Mazzarella, *Censorium: Cinema and the Open Edge of Mass Publicity* (Durham, NC: Duke University Press, 2013), 156.

55 I am grateful to a Syrian advertising executive for alerting me to this connection. See also Donatella Della Ratta's "Irony, Satire, and Humor in the Battle for Syria," Muftah, February 13, 2012 (at https://tinyurl.com/y7pbotql), in which she notes that on a Facebook page from Homs (called Kulluna Jarathim [We Are All Germs]; https://www.facebook.com/syria.germs?sk=wall, accessed December 2, 2018), Bashar al-Asad is called Doctor Dettol. Anthony Shadid notes that protesters from Hama responded to Bashar al-Asad's drawing an analogy between citizens and germs by claiming that the speech was "sponsored by Dettol" (Anthony Shadid, "Rejecting Offer of Dialogue by Syrian President, Protesters Return to the Streets," *New York Times*, June 24, 2011, https://tinyurl.com/yce378zh). For a theoretical take in a different context, see (in addition to Mazzarella, *Censorium*) Anne McClintock, "Soft Soaping Empire," in *Imperial Leather: Race, Gender, and Sexuality in the Colonial Contest* (New York: Routledge, 1995), 207–31; and of course Roland Barthes's famous essay on the French laundry detergent Omo, "Saponides and Detergents," in *Mythologies*, trans. Annette Lavers and Richard Howard (New York: Hill and Wang, 2013), 32–34.

56 This is a perfect illustration of what one might call meta-interpellation, i.e., being interpellated by the message of interpellation itself. Thanks are owed to Mazzarella here.

57 Berlant, *Cruel Optimism*. Della Ratta details some of the parodic slogans poking fun at the "I am with the law" and like-minded campaigns in "Irony, Satire, and Humor in the Battle for Syria." See also an updated version in *Shooting a Revolution: Visual Media and Warfare in Syria* (London: Pluto Press, 2018).

58 This is not to argue that all members of minorities (such as Christian communities or 'Alawi ones) identify with the regime or are prosperous.

59 Author's conversations with Syrian citizens, August 2012, Beirut.

60 The "two faces of American freedom," borrowing from a persuasive book on settler colonialism's comportment with liberalism, is only one obvious case in point. See Aziz Rana, *Two Faces of American Freedom* (Cambridge, MA: Harvard University Press, 2010). For a discussion of Enlightenment thinkers' continued justification of both freedom and colonialism, see Jennifer Pitts, *A Turn to Empire: The Rise of Imperial Liberalism in Britain and France* (Princeton, NJ: Princeton University Press, 2005); and Uday Singh Mehta, *Liberalism and Empire: A Study in Nineteenth-Century British Liberal Thought* (Chicago: University of Chicago Press, 2000).

61 See Omar Safadi, "Apolitical Citizenship and Authoritarian Survival: A Damascene Experience of the Syrian Civil War," BA thesis, University of Chicago, April 2016.

62 Thanks are owed to Robert Meister for helping me think through this argument.

63 Jean Comaroff and John L. Comaroff, *Law and Disorder in the Postcolony* (Chicago: University of Chicago Press, 2006), 48.

64 Fredric Jameson, "Reification and Utopia in Mass Culture," *Social Text* 1 (Winter 1979): 130–48.

65 For a document from the Al-Jazeera website describing the precautions taken to prevent protesters from occupying the main squares in Damascus, see https://tinyurl.com/ybbjou79, accessed December 2, 2018. That so many regime infiltrators were able to succeed in Aleppo before the onset of violent war there, for example, raises the question of why this was the case in Aleppo and not else-

where. As is well known, the regime outsourced some of its security work to the notorious Birri clan, whose leader's execution was broadcast publicly by opposition militia in a YouTube video criticized by human rights groups and regime supporters alike. The event did dramatize how collaborative arrangements that once offered clear benefits were becoming costly, and quickly.

66 Protesters have shown remarkable creativity at times. For example, some of the small demonstrations that occurred in downtown Damascus, even in the first year of rebellion, featured savvy young people using contemporary tactics like flash mobs (in one instance, twenty or so protesters all appeared dressed in white). In another memorable move, young activists released hundreds of Ping-Pong balls marked Depart and Democracy, which rolled down from the area of Muhajireen on Mount Qasiyun into the city center of Damascus. These stories were relayed to me in October 2011 and later were chronicled in English in Elleke Bal's humorously titled "A Man with Balls," *Intelligent Optimist* (January–February 2014), https://tinyurl.com/yabcnmt8.

Anonymous denouncements of the regime were also broadcast from a remote-controlled loudspeaker positioned strategically in a downtown square, and a famous anti-regime song could also be heard from inside a municipal building. People's reactions, including frantic attempts on the part of security agents to locate the source of the music, were filmed and uploaded to YouTube. These instances of creativity are important, but their impact has been limited. For a chronicle of some of these actions, see Donatella Della Ratta's works, including "Creative Resistance Challenges Syria's Regime," Al-Jazeera, December 25, 2011, https://tinyurl.com/c8llnzy; "Irony, Satire, and Humor in the Battle for Syria," Muftah, February 13, 2012, https://tinyurl.com/y7pbotql; "Syria: The Virtue of Civil Disobedience," Al-Jazeera, April 6, 2012, https://tinyurl.com/bpxh9ee; and "Dramas of the Authoritarian State," *Middle East Report Online*, February 2012, https://www.merip.org/mero/interventions/dramas-authoritarian-state, which focuses on the entanglements between Syrian television producers and the regime. In this latter piece she also highlights attempts to "work the weaknesses" of the system (to borrow Judith Butler's felicitous phrase).

67 At the height of protests in Yemen, for example, 25 percent of the population was estimated to have taken to the streets.

68 Thanks are owed to Kevin Mazur for his question at an earlier presentation at Princeton University in November 2011, which pressed me to consider in more detail the economic geographies of protest.

69 Author's conversations with activists from Damascus and Aleppo, February 2012 in Beirut.

70 Articles suggesting a strong correlation between the drought and the uprising or that note the force of the argument include Francesco Femia and Caitlin Werrell, "Syria: Climate Change, Drought, and Social Unrest," *Brief No. 11* (2012), https://tinyurl.com/yc4bl5jj, accessed December 1, 2018; also their 2013 article "Climate Change before and after the Arab Awakening: The Cases of Syria and Libya," in *The Arab Spring and Climate Change*, ed. Caitlin E. Werrell and Francesco Femia (Washington, DC: Center for American Progress, 2013), 23–32. See also Jessica Barnes, "Managing the Waters of Ba'th Country: The Politics of Water Scarcity in Syria," *Geopolitics* 17 (2009): 510–30; Hannu Juusola, "The Internal Dimensions of Water Security: The Drought Crisis in Northeastern Syria," in *Managing Blue Gold: New Perspectives on Water Security in the Levantine Middle East*, ed. Mari Luomi (Helsinki: Finnish Institute of International Affairs, 2012), 21–34; Thomas L. Friedman, "The Other Arab Spring," *New York Times*, April 7, 2012,

https://tinyurl.com/y8993x8a; Shahrzad Mohtadi, "Climate Change and the Syrian Uprising," *Bulletin of the Atomic Scientists*, August 16, 2012, 1–4; Anne-Marie Slaughter, preface to Werrell and Femia, *The Arab Spring and Climate Change*, 1–6; Jeannie Sowers and John Waterbury, "Did Drought Trigger the Crisis in Syria?," Footnote, September 12, 2013, https://tinyurl.com/ycfqzfyo; IRIN Middle East, "Syria: Act Now to Stop Desertification, Says FAO," ReliefWeb, June 15, 2010, https://tinyurl.com/ycewjcz8 (heavily reliant on other flawed IRIN reports); and Leenders and Heydemann, "Popular Mobilization in Syria."

71 See the appendix. Sofia Fenner gathered the quantitative data, made the charts, and wrote the text explaining them. The aggregated data on economic conditions (2005–10) and of conflict deaths by province (2011–12) are available at the Qualitative Data Repository: https://doi.org/10.5064/F63776W4.

72 In addition to the data provided in the appendix, it is worth noting that according to the political economist Omar S. Dahi, inflation rates in Syria were "driven by local production, government subsidies, quota or supported goods, and prices of internationally traded commodities" as well as by "regular market fluctuation" (email correspondence with the author, April 25, 2016). Because of widespread income tax evasion—only public sector employees directly taxed by the government through payroll "complied"—Syria's tax system relied on indirect taxes, such as stamps purchased for official papers signed by various bureaucrats, customs taxes, and sales taxes on what were in the 2000s a proliferating number of luxury items. Of course, the ability to purchase these luxury items, as well as their desirability, varied by region. In the second half of the 2000s, the tax system was in the process of being streamlined—in the context of a number of market-associated reforms. Basic staples such as rice, bulgur, sugar, and salt remained heavily subsidized, however. Energy was as well until what has become the famous lifting of those subsidies and the consequent rise of energy prices in 2009—which did hurt farmers and the urban poor. But if the withdrawal of energy subsidies generated discontent, the connection to an uprising two years later is by no means clear or straightforward. And interestingly, the lifting of the energy subsidy was accompanied by a spurt in economic growth in 2009—in the wake of a major global recession. The spike seems to be largely reflective of increasing foreign direct investment, which may have been encouraged by the regime's vigorous (and reassuring to capital) public relations campaigns of glamorous authoritarianism whose addressees were both local and global.

73 For a list of the most common slogans in Arabic, see the website of the Beirut-based media company Raseef22 at https://tinyurl.com/y8ka9mug, accessed December 2, 2018. See also this YouTube video (2:39, March 18, 2015), which compiled common slogans: https://www.youtube.com/watch?v=Imf-n8ZrQeY. Notably, slogans based on "bread" or economic deprivation were rare—which arguably is one of the distinctions between Syria's uprising and Egypt's. This article in the newspaper *Al-Akhbar* typifies those that recognize the absence of such slogans but argue that the underlying reasons for the uprising were nonetheless economic: https://www.al-akhbar.com/Opinion/93204, accessed December 2, 2018. My own analysis presumes that human actions are ultimately "dual," composed both of what "the outside observer can see and of the actors' understandings of what they are doing," to borrow Hanna Pitkin's words in *Wittgenstein and Justice: On the Significance of Ludwig Wittgenstein for Social and Political Thought* (Berkeley: University of California Press, 1993), 242.

74 For a discussion of this slogan and similar ones being chanted in Dar'a, the heartland of defiance, see Reinoud Leenders's "'Oh Buthaina, Oh Sha'ban.'"

75 The price of housing and rent was heavily controlled under a 2004 rent law in response to the influx of Iraqi refugees. This law was a boon to landlords and squeezed renters. But what counted as a landlord was also changing as real estate speculation soared, also as a result of the American-initiated war in Iraq. Syria's multitiered system of exchange rates was also being unified and streamlined, which may have made FDI investment more attractive, although these measures could not fully offset the challenges of doing business in what remained a kleptocracy.

76 For a detailed discussion of Aleppo's neighborhoods, see Yahya al-'Abdallah's pathbreaking account, currently in preparation.

77 For a vivid account of memories of the violence in Hama in 1982, see Salwa Ismail, *The Rule of Violence: Subjectivity, Memory and Government in Syria* (Cambridge: Cambridge University Press, 2018), especially 131–58. Ismail rightly points out that social memory-making need not require citizens to have actually experienced the events firsthand. But the difference between those who grew up in the 1980s and those born in the late 1990s and early 2000s was apparent.

78 According to numerous sources, university protests in Aleppo were composed primarily of residents in the dormitories, making it important to note that these were students whose families resided in areas under siege and not in Aleppo. Residents of Aleppo tended to live at home.

79 Rif'at and his Defense Brigades are widely understood to have led the assault on Hama in 1982, although who has ultimate responsibility for the massacre continues to be debated. Also claimed by residents of Mu'addamiyya was land occupied by the Mezze military airport.

80 Further details cannot be disclosed in the interest of protecting human subjects, but the general claim circulated widely in 2012 and 2013.

81 Yasin al-Hajj Salih, "Fi al-Shabbiha wa al-Tashbih wa Dawlathima," *Kalamon* (Winter 2012), http://www.kalamonreview.org/articles-details-122#axzz5YOTQs Wao, accessed December 2, 2018, is one well-informed example of a growing number of discussions of pro-regime thugs called *shabbiha*. See chapter 5 for an in-depth account.

82 Anthony Shadid, "Syrian Elite to Fight Protests to 'the End,'" *New York Times*, May 10, 2011, https://tinyurl.com/y95oyb9k.

83 The widespread story is that Hamza 'Ali al-Khateeb had his genitals removed while detained, a move that some regime-oriented commentators preposterously justified by claiming that the boy was a terrorist and even a rapist. He was detained on April 29 and died at the end of May 2011. He became an early icon of revolutionary righteousness and, for activists, of the insupportability of a regime capable of carrying out and justifying such capricious cruelty. An instance in English of the kind of vitriol by regime supporters that flooded the internet in reference to al-Khateeb was the following: *The Truth about Syria* (blog), "Western and Arabic Media Honor the Rapists and Ignore the Real Innocent Victims," January 23, 2012, https://tinyurl.com/yb55r8wn. The opposition website, Orient News, provided a summary of official Syrian media attempts to undermine al-Khateeb's character and his parents' and activists' accounts of his death: Orient News, "Fabrications of Syrian Television: From 'Hamza' the Rapist to 'Sha'ban' the Murderer," October 12, 2013, https://tinyurl.com/yampsdjq.

CHAPTER TWO

1 Henri Bergson, *Laughter: An Essay on the Meaning of the Comic*, trans. Cloudesley Brereton and Fred Rothwell (Mineola, NY: Dover Publications, 2005).

2 These comedies are all in colloquial Arabic and are translated by me—unless otherwise noted. With *Day'a daay'a*, I had significant help, given the difficulties of the dialect. Thanks are owed to Osama Esber and staff from the production company, Sama Art International, for their assistance with this dimension of the chapter. The video clips from *A Forgotten Village* and *Hope—There Isn't Any* captioned by us in English as well as a list of archived links are available at the Qualitative Data Repository: https://doi.org/10.5064/F63776W4.

3 Bergson, *Laughter*, 3.

4 Lauren Berlant and Sianne Ngai, "Comedy Has Issues," *Critical Inquiry* 43, no. 2 (Winter 2017): 233–49. They cite Simon Critchley, *On Humour (Thinking in Action)* (New York: Routledge, 2002), 18.

5 For Lacanians, comedy allows us to endure the shame and pleasure of *jouissance*, or enjoyment, collectively. The solidarity-inducing aspects of comedy have been widely remarked on. For some examples, see Glenda Carpio's *Laughing Fit to Kill: Black Humor in the Fictions of Slavery* (New York: Oxford University Press, 2008); Joseph Litvak, *The Un-Americans: Jews, the Blacklist, and Stoolpigeon Culture* (Durham, NC: Duke University Press, 2009); Alexei Yurchak, *Everything Was Forever until It Was No More: The Last Soviet Generation* (Princeton, NJ: Princeton University Press, 2005); Alan Dundes, *Cracking Jokes: Studies of Sick Humor Cycles and Stereotypes* (Berkeley: Ten Speed Press, 1987); and Berlant and Ngai's "Comedy Has Issues."

6 Most of the humor discussed here is political satire that takes the form of parody. Some parodies have more observational irony than others, as we shall see. Many are prone to hyperbole and exaggeration, but only *A Forgotten Village* relies on the clowning-like gestures of slapstick.

7 This argument is modified from my *Ambiguities of Domination: Politics, Rhetoric, and Symbols in Contemporary Syria* (Chicago: University of Chicago Press, 1999; new preface 2015). But in Hafiz al-Asad's era, the time period the *Ambiguities* book tracks, that sense of solidarity was based on counteracting a politics of public dissimulation by recognizing conditions of unbelief. Solidarity can also be premised on experiences other than shared unbelief, of course, such as grievance or ambivalence or the recognition of contradictorily felt interests, to name a few possibilities.

8 Slavoj Žižek, *The Sublime Object of Ideology* (London: Verso, 1989), 37. Cited in Wedeen, *Ambiguities of Domination*, 73.

9 Mladen Dolar, "The Comic Mimesis," *Critical Inquiry* 43, no. 2 (Winter 2017): 580.

10 Rebecca Joubin, "Resistance amid Co-optation on the Syrian Television Series *Buq'a Daw'* 2001–2012," *Middle East Journal* 61, no. 1 (2014): 9–32; Marlin Dick, "Syria under the Spotlight: Television Satire That Is Revolutionary in Form, Reformist in Content," *Arab and Media Society*, October 1, 2007, https://tinyurl.com/yad6llcx; and Christa Salamandra's "Prelude to an Uprising: Syrian Fictional Television and Socio-Political Critique," *Jadaliyya*, May 17, 2012, https://tinyurl.com/y7z48w55, as well as her chapter "Syria's Drama Outpouring: Between Complicity and Critique," in *Syria from Reform to Revolt*, vol. 2, *Culture,*

Society and Religion, ed. Salamandra and Leif Stenberg (Syracuse, NY: Syracuse University Press, 2015), 36–52. My interviews with Allayth Hajju took place throughout 2011–12 and during the summer of 2013 in Damascus, Chicago, and Beirut.

11 Author's interviews with the director Allayth Hajju, 2011–12, Damascus, Chicago, and Beirut. See also Salamandra, "Prelude to an Uprising," and Dick, "Syria under the Spotlight."

12 Ghawwar al-Tushi, played by Durayd Lahham in the 1970s and 1980s, functioned as a jester figure. See Wedeen, *Ambiguities of Domination*, chap. 4. Also see Lisa Wedeen, "Ideology and Humor in Dark Times," *Critical Inquiry* 39 (Winter 2013): 841–73. On the open secret, see especially Jodi Dean, *Publicity's Secret: How Technoculture Capitalizes on Democracy* (Ithaca, NY: Cornell University Press, 2002); Gregory J. Seigworth and Matthew Tiessen, "Mobile Affects, Open Secrets, and Global Illiquidity: Pockets, Pools, and Plasma," *Theory, Culture, and Society* 29, no. 6 (2012): 47–77; Lauren Berlant, "Structures of Unfeeling: Mysterious Skin," *International Journal of Politics, Culture, and Society* 28, no. 3 (2015): 191–213; and Demetra Kasimis, *The Perpetual Immigrant and the Limits of Athenian Democracy* (Cambridge: Cambridge University Press, 2018).

13 See also Christa Salamandra and Leif Stenberg, "Introduction: A Legacy of Raised Expectations," in Salamandra and Stenberg, *Syria from Reform to Revolt*, vol. 2, *Culture, Society and Religion* (Syracuse, NY: Syracuse University Press, 2015), 1–15; and Salamandra, "Syria's Drama Outpouring: Between Complicity and Critique" in the same volume. Her "Prelude to an Uprising" is also relevant. Chapter 4 in my *Ambiguities of Domination* covers in greater depth some of what is a vast literature on humor. My work here is also in conversation with Peter Sloterdijk's work in *Critique of Cynical Reason*, trans. Michael Eldred (Minneapolis: University of Minnesota Press, 1988).

14 Salamandra, "Prelude to an Uprising."

15 Hajju also directed a dramatic series entitled *al-Intizar* (Waiting), perhaps his most critically acclaimed, aesthetically inventive *drama*. That series offered a pointed critique of growing inequalities and pervasive corruption, but it operated as well within the regime's conventional confines of acceptable criticism.

16 See also Wedeen, *Ambiguities of Domination*, 146, which draws from Louis Marin's *Portrait of the King* (New York: Palgrave-MacMillan, 1988); and James C. Scott's *Domination and the Arts of Resistance: Hidden Transcripts* (New Haven, CT: Yale University Press, 1990).

17 This episode was written by Hajju's younger brother, thirteen years his junior.

18 See Salamandra's description, in "Prelude to an Uprising."

19 Cited in Salamandra. "Push comes to shove" could also be translated as "ultimately" or "when the going gets tough."

20 Thanks are owed to Christa Salamandra for making this point. I had not initially noticed the change of mise-en-scène (as described in Salamandra, "Prelude to an Uprising"). See also Nadine Elali's interview with members of the With You collective in which they distance themselves from what they consider to be Hajju's superficial treatment of the issues. See "The Syrian Revolution in Sketches," *Now Lebanon*, July 19, 2011, https://tinyurl.com/y8dxdswh. For especially keenly observed skits by With You that try to transform the political resignation of *Hope—There Isn't Any* into an affirmative politics: http://podcastarabia.net

/programmes/freedomwobas/5TCoJ-R56Ro ("The Puppet Theater"), June 22, 2011; https://www.youtube.com/watch?v=1coqjAzpEuo ("The Resistance"), August 30, 2011; and https://www.youtube.com/watch?v=St5dzQTwRfU ("Liar, Liar"), August 30, 2011.

21 *A Forgotten Village* is Hajju's sustained collaboration with the comedic screenwriter Mamduh Hamada, who also collaborated on some episodes of *Hope—There Isn't Any*. Hajju's own corpus is wide-ranging, with a string of melodramatic, socially pedagogical "soap operas" in addition to comedic fare. I am also indebted to the work of Donatella Della Ratta, including her dissertation, "Dramas of the Authoritarian State: The Politics of Syrian TV Serials in the Pan Arab Market" (PhD diss., University of Copenhagen, April 2013), and her various articles on the subject, among which are the following: "Making Real-Time Drama: The Political Economy of Cultural Production in Syria's Uprising" (PARGC paper, Pennsylvania University, Fall 2014, https://tinyurl.com/y7tnoqs6); "Dramas of the Authoritarian State," *Middle East Report Online*, February 2012, https://www.merip.org/mero/interventions/dramas-authoritarian-state; and "The 'Whisper Strategy': How Syrian Drama Makers Shape Television Fiction in the Context of Authoritarianism and Commodification," in *Syria from Reform to Revolt*, vol. 2, *Culture, Society and Religion*, ed. Salamandra and Leif Stenberg (Syracuse, NY: Syracuse University Press, 2015), 53–76.

  Khirba (*Ruins*), the follow-up comedy series to *A Forgotten Village* that Hajju directed, again with writer Mamduh Hamada, in 2011, was already being shot as the uprising got underway. It covers similar themes, with a greater emphasis on generation, but without the freshness or critical acclaim that defined *A Forgotten Village*. The flatness of this series is largely the result of the difference in political times separating 2010 from 2011, but it may also have to do with the risks for creativity involved in relying on what had become a comedic formula.

22 Cited in Miriam Bratu Hansen, *Cinema and Experience: Sigfried Kracauer, Walter Benjamin, and Theodor W. Adorno* (Berkeley: University of California Press, 2012), 181.

23 Cited in Hansen, 168.

24 See Hansen. Thanks are owed to Bill Brown for his suggestion that I look at Hansen's discussion of the exchange between Walter Benjamin and Theodor Adorno on Mickey Mouse.

25 The reviews and comments are simply too numerous to cite. The popularity of the series was also confirmed by Syrian students and in the advertising agencies where I spent time in winter 2011. Also worthy of note are both pro-regime and opposition appropriations of lines and images from episodes from 2011 to the present.

26 Importantly, many of the characters' accents are more typical of the poor Sunni area of Slaybeh in Lattakia (al-Ladhiqiyya), and the character whose 'Alawi dialect is particularly pronounced is the smuggler. The chief secret-police agent who occasionally visits the village to check in on how things are being managed and berate the police for their incompetence wears the conventional leather jacket of someone of his ilk. Named "Hummalali," colloquial for someone in the security forces known to inflict especially painful torture, his accent is from the Hawran, an area in the southern interior near Jordan whose inhabitants before the uprising were disproportionately members of the ruling Ba'th Party. Dar'a, the site of the schoolchildren's arrest and the subsequent protest, is in the Hawran.

27   The poem is available at http://www.sobe3.com/vb//showthread.php?t=18596, accessed December 2, 2018. Thanks are owed to Allayth Hajju for this reference.

28   I am grateful to Lauren Berlant for our ongoing conversations on comedy and world-affirming practices, as well as for her specific insights in *Cruel Optimism* (Durham, NC: Duke University Press, 2011).

29   Berlant.

30   Della Ratta, "Dramas of the Authoritarian State" and "The 'Whisper Strategy,'" cited above.

31   Author's interviews with Allayth Hajju, March 2011, August 2011, and June 2012 in Damascus, Chicago, and Beirut respectively. See also Della Ratta, "Dramas of the Authoritarian State."

32   Alenka Zupančič, *The Odd One In: On Comedy* (Boston: MIT Press, 2008).

33   Edward Ziter's email interview of a member of Masasit Mati, December 10, 2012, cited in *Political Performance in Syria: From the Six-Day War to the Syrian Uprising* (New York: Palgrave-MacMillan, 2015), 26. See also miriam cooke, *Dancing in Damascus: Creativity, Resilience, and the Syrian Revolution* (New York: Routledge, 2016), 43; and Marwan M. Kraidy, *The Naked Blogger of Cairo: Creative Insurgency in the Arab World* (Cambridge, MA: Harvard University Press, 2016), 132–40.

34   While the song urging Syrians not to be afraid repeats and Shabih exits the stage, Beeshu says in a panic that he'll have to talk to Iran's President Ahmadinejad and flee to that country. This theme of Iranian support for an increasingly unpopular domestic regime became a staple of activist fare, with the YouTube cartoon channel Wikisham, for example, featuring *Qasr al-Sha'b*, a show lampooning not only the president, his brother, his corrupt cousin, and the adviser Bouthaina Sha'ban but also Ahmadinejad and Ayatollah Ali Khamenei. See *Qasr al-Sha'b* (2011), YouTube channel, https://www.youtube.com/user/wikisham, accessed December 12, 2018.

35   Two members of the troupe left after the first season, in part because they no longer agreed with the group's commitment to peaceful resistance. My interviews took place in February 2012 in Paris. The two members' departure is also cited in Ziter, *Political Performance in Syria*, 46.

36   For the classic discussion of the political import of inversion, see Mikhail Bakhtin, *Rabelais and His World*, trans. Helene Iswolsky (Bloomington: Indiana University Press, [1965] 1984).

37   Ziter, *Political Performance in Syria*, 48.

38   Bergson, *Laughter*, 18 and 19.

39   Zupančič, *The Odd One In*, 118.

40   Zupančič, 118.

41   Berlant and Ngai, "Comedy Has Issues," 234.

42   Berlant and Ngai, 39.

43   *Jadaliyya*, "The Strong Heroes of Moscow," video, 3:25, YouTube, June 25, 2011, https://youtu.be/LThziRgKzTQ.

44   Dolar, "The Comic Mimesis," 581.

45 Author's discussions with two of the three primary creators in 2012, 2013, and 2014.

46 Dolar, "The Comic Mimesis," 581–82; and Sigmund Freud, *Totem and Taboo: Some Points of Agreement between the Mental Lives of Savages and Neurotics*, ed. and trans. James Strachey (New York: W. W. Norton, 1990), 103–4.

47 Sumar Barish, *Little Poke* [*Nakzeh*]: episode "Gray People" [Al-Ramadiyyin], video, 6:24, Lamba Production/YouTube, September 4, 2016, https://youtu.be /BAbfMSP0DN4.

48 *Nakzeh* is produced by Lamba Production, a group of activists who come primarily from Aleppo. The Lamba group became famous when it created a television series called *Umm 'Abdu al-Halabiyya*, using children in eastern Aleppo to depict a family under siege in that city. Focused on daily life, the show went on for a few seasons until a main character was killed in Aleppo.

49 Enab Baladi, *Min Fawq al-Asatih* [*Over the Roofs*], video, 4:44, YouTube, March 20, 2017, https://youtu.be/6bLVQjmKgYI.

50 Zupančič, *The Odd One In*, 133.

51 For Zupančič, "the discrepancy that constitutes the motor of comedy lies not in the fact that satisfaction can never really meet demand, but rather that the demand can never really meet (some unexpectedly produced surplus satisfaction)" (131).

52 Zupančič, 132.

53 Berlant and Ngai, "Comedy Has Issues," 236.

54 The "it should have been otherwise" from Adorno is slightly but salutarily altered to be "it could have been otherwise" in Berlant's *Cruel Optimism*, 13. See Theodor Adorno, "Commitment," trans. Francis McDonagh, *New Left Review* 87 (1974): 87–88.

55 Bergson, *Laughter*, 98.

56 Author's text conversation with Lauren Berlant. Reproduced with permission.

CHAPTER THREE

1 Michael Pizzi, "The Syrian Opposition Is Disappearing from Facebook," *Atlantic*, February 4, 2014, https://tinyurl.com/y8ekoc9x.

2 Pizzi.

3 Pizzi.

4 Denial of climate change, for example, is often based on the attempt to dispel the scientific evidence of climate change while paying formulaic obeisance to science.

5 Pagan Kennedy, "How to Destroy the Business Model of Breitbart and Fake News," *New York Times*, January 7, 2017, https://tinyurl.com/yc2sm9qc.

6 For example, Cass R. Sunstein, "A Case Study in Group Polarization (with Warnings for the Future)," in *Aftermath: The Clinton Impeachment and the Presidency in the Age of Political Spectacle*, ed. Leonard V. Kaplan and Beverly I. Moran (New York: New York University Press, 2001), 11–21.

7   Errol Morris, *Believing Is Seeing: Observations on the Mysteries of Photography* (London: Penguin Books, 2014).

8   The online organizer Eli Pariser calls this phenomenon the "filter bubble." For him, the problem lies less with consumers and more with web companies that tailor their services, including news and search results, to personal predilections, limiting exposure to alternative ways of seeing the world. Eli Pariser, *The Filter Bubble: How the New Personalized Web Is Changing What We Read and How We Think* (New York: Penguin Books, 2012).

9   Brian Massumi, "The Future Birth of the Affective Fact," in *The Affect Theory Reader*, ed. Melissa Gregg and Gregory J. Seigworth (Durham, NC: Duke University Press, 2010), 52–70; quotation is on p. 60.

10 For some striking parallels in another authoritarian context, see Laura-Zoe Humphreys, "Symptomologies of the State: Cuba's 'Email War' and the Paranoid Public Sphere," in *Digital Cultures and the Politics of Emotion: Feelings, Affect, and Technological Change*, ed. Athina Karatzogianni and Adi Kuntsman (Hampshire, UK: Palgrave MacMillan, 2012), 197–213.

11 A recent article by Gary King, Jennifer Pan, and Margaret E. Roberts (2017) showcases how the Chinese government "fabricates social media posts" to distract readers from substantive engagement with political concerns ("How the Chinese Government Fabricates Social Media Posts for Strategic Distraction, Not Engaged Argument," unpublished manuscript, PDF format, last modified April 9, 2017, at https://tinyurl.com/y89pddet, accessed December 2, 2018); and a spate of journalistic articles have focused on Russia's use of "disinformation." See for example Neil MacFarquhar, "A Powerful Russian Weapon: The Spread of False Stories," *New York Times*, August 28, 2016, https://tinyurl.com/y7smamnv; and Arkady Ostrovsky's op-ed on Putin's use of disinformation, "For Putin, Disinformation Is Power," *New York Times*, August 5, 2016, https://tinyurl.com/y75kc7cg.

12 A young Syrian American calling himself Omar Offendum was catapulted into the limelight in 2011 by a music video, "#Jan25," honoring the large-scale demonstrations in Egypt. His subsequent tribute to the Syrian uprising was uploaded on March 19, 2012, capturing the initial heady days of Syria's protests. In that widely circulated video, Offendum lays his own voice over the voice attributed to what was then thought to be a popular singer by the name of Ibrahim Qashush, evidently paying tribute to the local singer's memory.

13 See Elie Abdo, "The Impact of the Arts on the Syrian Revolution," Heinrich-Böll-Stiftung Middle East, February 28, 2013, https://tinyurl.com/y7n6ocrc.

14 In some articles in English, Qashush is transliterated as Qashoush.

15 An article, "Suriya: Ibrahim al-Qashush al-mughani al-haqiqi ma zal hayyan" (Syria: Ibrahim Qashush, the Real Singer Is Still Alive), published in October 2013 by Huna Sawtak, an Amsterdam-based online media platform covering news from the Middle East in Al-Jazeera-like style, sheds new light on the murky circumstances of Qashush's death. The article explained that the actual singer was not Qashush but 'Abd al-Rahman Farhud (Rahmani), who organized a troupe with Qutaybat Na'san, a backup singer. Qashush, in this version, was a retired officer and the band's drummer. The point of the article was not to suggest that Qashush himself was still alive—the account seems to concur with the news of his death—but to establish that the actual singers were very much alive and had joined the Free Syrian Army. Their story, moreover, was that Qashush had been

killed by the regime, despite loyalist claims to the contrary: "Many Hama activists and Syrians know the real story of Qashush, but powerful propaganda around his murder prevented them from revealing it." Available at https://tinyurl.com /y9efxsyc, accessed December 2, 2018. The Facebook page from that same time period, however, in purportedly depicting Qashush himself in Ghaziantep, Turkey, lends a different meaning to the title "The Real Singer Is Still Alive." The *GQ* article by James Harkin discussed in the text supports some key assertions of this earlier but generally unknown or ignored Huna Sawtak report.

16   James Harkin, "The Incredible Story behind the Syrian Protest Singer Everyone Thought Was Dead," *GQ*, December 7, 2016, https://tinyurl.com/ycyer6f4. And here is an Arabic-language piece reporting on the *GQ* article: Syrian Press Center, "What Is the Degree of Truth about the Nightingale of the Syrian Revolution Being Alive," December 29, 2016, https://tinyurl.com/y889bbu2.

17   Harkin, "The Incredible Story behind the Syrian Protest Singer Everyone Thought Was Dead."

18   "The Truth about Ibrahim Qashoush (Qashush)," video, 1:24, YouTube, February 8, 2012, https://www.youtube.com/watch?v=M4roioLitdA.

19   "One of the Arms of Terrorism: The Terrorist Fadi Zurayq," video, 19:45, YouTube, October 9, 2011, https://tinyurl.com/ydap4xyq. This coupling of Saudi Arabia and Israel was easily recognizable to most Syrians. And although Americans might be tempted to dismiss such allegations as preposterous, there are plenty of times when Saudi and Israeli foreign policy have been aligned, and meetings between the two countries' diplomatic representatives have occurred. The two countries also share the same superpower backer, of course, in the United States. Yet these remarks are not meant to suggest that any concrete evidence is available in this particular instance to support such a conspiracy theory, only that for some Syrian addressees, the coupling would be credible; for others, a cynical effort to undermine the uprising; but for all, familiar enough.

20   Author's email correspondence with a Syrian analyst-activist, July 12, 2016. Slightly edited for clarity.

21   Email correspondence, July 12, 2016.

22   See Slavoj Žižek's discussion of Stalinist show trials and the important difference between Stalinism and Nazism: "The Two Totalitarianisms," *London Review of Books* 27, no. 6 (March 17, 2005), 8, https://tinyurl.com/ybknv4hl.

23   In a subsequent English-language article in 2012, "The Truth about Ibrahim Qashoush, the Alleged Singer and Composer of the So-Called 'Syrian Revolution'" (by *The Truth about Syria* [blog], February 18, 2012, https://tinyurl.com /y7c6rbsw), the author's citational practices, for those in the know, index the regime's Arabic-language television program and make specific reference to "the terrorist" Zurayq, reproducing the young man's orchestrated confession as proof of opposition malfeasance. The blog's aim is "to reveal the truth about the Syrian crisis . . . to expose the media misleading against Syria . . . to show the world that Syria is fighting terrorism . . . to prove that the dirty fingers of radical Islamic fundamentalism are behind the bloodshed in Syria." The piece explicitly positions itself as writing in opposition to the "Zionist-Wahhabi" media. It oscillates between a didactic effort to instruct readers on how to interpret opposition and Western news—with snapshots and references to prior reports—and a stridency that undercuts any journalistic claims to evidentiary logic. For example, "in every lie related to the Syrian Revolution, the Western and Arabic media behaved like

ruminants, and the case of Qashoush is no exception. What is really disgusting is that Barbara Walters raised this issue in the interview with president Bashar al-Assad, accompanied of course with the other very widespread lie about the rapist Hamza al-Khateeb." Recall that Hamza al-Khateeb was a thirteen-year-old boy who died under torture in the early days of Dar'a, having had his genitals removed before his death.

By "ruminants," the author presumably means those who ruminate, and in Arabic as in English, the connotation is arguably especially derogatory — conjuring up images of masticating beasts. The links are provided, the moral outrage at Western bias and gullibility registered, and an appeal to common knowledge made: "We all know who kills the people by cutting their throats, we have already seen dozens of videos in Iraq of such crimes. It is not the Syrian intelligence or military style, it is the Wahhabi and al-Qaeda style, so let them stop accusing the Syrian security of this murder." Who the "we" is remains unclear; but despite the vituperative language, patently false allegations (such as the one about Hamza al-Khateeb), and wealth of malapropisms, even — or perhaps especially — an article like this was able to contribute to the overall atmosphere of epistemic and affective insecurity, calling into question the widely publicized original story as well as the various oppositional positions that maintained its veracity.

24 See also William Mazzarella's discussion of Durkheim in *The Mana of Mass Society* (Chicago: University of Chicago Press, 2017) in which the "collective plenitude" of mass participation is viewed as an "actualization of the mimetic archive" (43).

25 The "outside" in regime-speak was generally understood to mean "religiously" minded nation-states and their Western allies, such as the United States.

26 See Žižek's "The Two Totalitarianisms."

27 Ludwig Wittgenstein, *On Certainty*, trans. Denis Paul and G. E. M. Anscombe and ed. G. E. M. Anscombe and G. H. von Wright (New York: Harper Torchbooks, 1969), 12e, para. 83; emphases in the original.

28 Kathleen Stewart, *Ordinary Affects* (Durham, NC: Duke University Press, 2007), 20. Conjuring up Walter Benjamin, Stewart notes that "potentiality is a thing immanent to fragments of sensory experience and dreams of presence. A layer, or layering to the ordinary, it engenders attachments or systems of investment in the unfolding of things" (21).

29 Phone conversation with Yahya al-'Abdallah, July 2016.

30 A more detailed time line looks like this: On March 19, 2013, a chemical attack occurred in the Khan al-'Asal area of Aleppo in which between twenty and twenty-six people are known to have died. By "known" I mean that both opposition and regime sources agree that an attack happened, and some such number of people perished. The weapon was allegedly a rocket armed with the chemical warfare agent sarin. Among the dead, and complicating the task of determining what actually happened, were regime soldiers, which prompted the Syrian regime to call for a United Nations investigation. Two days after the attack, on March 21, UN secretary-general Ban Ki-moon established the UN Mission to Investigate Allegations of the Use of Chemical Weapons in the Syrian Arab Republic. That mission was delayed, arriving only five months later, so that by that time it had a total of twelve attacks under its mandate. According to a number of sources, the time lag between the March attack and the mission's implementation stemmed from disagreements about the extent of the UN mandate. Oddly enough, the Syrian government's own report on Khan al-'Asal was released on August 20,

2013, one day before the al-Ghouta attacks. Sites under investigation included the following:

October 17, 2012, Salqin
December 23, 2012, Homs
March 13, 2013, Darayya
March 9, 2013, Khan al-ʿAsal
March 19, 2013, Utayba
March 24, 2013, Adra
April 12–14, 2013, Jubar
April 13, 2013, Shaykh Maqsud
April 25, 2013, Darayya
April 29, 2013, Saraqib
May 14, 2013, Qasr Abu Samra
May 23, 2013, Adra

The investigation was eventually expanded to include the following subsequent alleged chemical weapons incidents as well:

August 21, 2013, Al-Ghouta
August 22, 2013, Bahariyya
August 24, 2013, Jubar
August 25, 2013, Ashrafiyya Sahnaya

Thanks are owed to Sofia Fenner for her excellent research assistance here.

31   The text is available here: John Kerry, "Remarks on Syria," Press Briefing Room, Washington, DC, August 26, 2013, US Department of State archive, https:// tinyurl.com/y8pp9rcd.

32   Christopher Reuter, "Asad's Cold Calculations: The Poisonous Gas War on Syrians," *Al-Jumhuriya*, August 31, 2013, https://www.aljumhuriya.net/16517; and Human Rights Watch's report: "Attacks on Ghouta: Analysis of the Alleged Use of Chemical Weapons in Syria," September 10, 2013, https://www.hrw.org/report /2013/09/10/attacks-ghouta/analysis-alleged-use-chemical-weapons-syria#.
     The Syrian Observatory for Human Rights is a watchdog website for the opposition based in London but with a number of eyewitnesses inside Syria. The list of reports it produced is extensive, but here are some examples: "The Results of the Search for the Chemical Massacre," August 17, 2015, https://tinyurl.com /ycanjc9q; "The Office for Documenting the Syrian Chemical Attack: The Regime Has Not Handed Over Any Shipments in a Month," April 3, 2014, https://tinyurl .com/yddl2x8m; and "The Russian Campaign in the Security Council to Change the Story of the Chemical [Attack]," December 17, 2013, https://tinyurl.com /y7wjuf26. An article a year later reiterates these findings: Orient News, August 17, 2014, http://www.orient-news.net/ar/news_show/80599. A comprehensive list with short introductions to most of the reports/articles/videos and images accusing the Asad regime is available at "Al-Asad Yartakib Jarima Ibada Jamaʿiyya wa Yaqtal 635 Shakhsan bil-Ghazat al-Sama" [Al-Asad Perpetrates Genocidal Crime, Killing 635 People with Poison Gas], https://tinyurl .com/y7ttkf74, accessed December 4, 2018. For official responses to the attack from various sides, see "Rudud al-Faʿl ʿala Qasf ʿIsabat al-Asad Halab bil-Kimawi" [Response to the Chemical Bombing of Aleppo by Asad's Troops], https://tinyurl .com/ycduff4m, accessed December 4, 2018.

The Violations Documentation Center, a human rights website well regarded by opposition activists, produced a report on August 22, one day after the attacks. This circulated vigorously among Syrian- and Arabic-language global activists on social media outlets, and is available here: Center for Documentation of Violations in Syria, *A Special Report on the Use of Chemical Weapons in the Province of Rural Damascus, Eastern Ghouta*, August 22, 2013, https://tinyurl.com /y9nmmz98. An archive of videos and commentary from human rights activists, as well as some comments accusing both parties of the atrocity, formerly at http://the-syrian.com/archives/102020, is available through the Internet Archive, https://web.archive.org/web/20160917170322/http://the-syrian.com/archives /102020, accessed December 11, 2018.

33   Phil Sands, "Syrian Chemical Attack Spurs Finger-Pointing inside Assad Regime," *The National*, August 26, 2013, https://tinyurl.com/y7zwab09.

34   Noah Shachtman, "Exclusive: Intercepted Calls Prove Syrian Army Used Nerve Gas, U.S. Spies Say," *Foreign Policy*, August 17, 2013, https://tinyurl.com/q9otn9g.

35   Three years later, in 2016, a regime-oriented publication summarized the many stories focused on the opposition's capacity to launch a chemical weapons attack, including the possibility that the attack was tied to the disappearance of the Syrian human rights lawyer Razzan Zaytuna, widely believed to be kidnapped by the late Zahran 'Alloush's Jaysh al-Islam. See "Al-Ghouta Chemical Weapons: How Three Armed Factions Came into Possession of Chemical Weapons," *Almersad*, October 31, 2013, https://tinyurl.com/y9p75emt. For a similar but less detailed account, see "Three Years after the Chemical Attack on al-Ghouta: The Secrets of the Massacre," *Ad-Diyar*, August 23, 2016, https://tinyurl.com/y7qrxnaz.

36   'Adnan 'Ali, "Chemical Attack: From Denial to Fabrication," Al-Araby, August 21, 2016, https://tinyurl.com/y7mexgyj.

37   Dale Gavlak and Yahya Ababneh, "Syrians in Ghouta Claim Saudi-Supplied Rebels behind Chemical Attack," *MPN News*, August 29, 2013, https://tinyurl .com/nbrykrr.

38   Madhi Darius Nazemroaya, "Is Prince Bandar behind the Chemical Attacks in Syria?" Global Research, September 17, 2013, https://tinyurl.com/y7qfa35d.

39   *Brown Moses Blog*, "Statement by Dale Gavlak on the Mint Press Article 'Syrians in Ghouta Claim Saudi-Supplied Rebels behind Chemical Attack,'" September 20, 2013, https://tinyurl.com/y87dhbym; and Robert MacKey, "Reporter Denies Writing Article That Linked Syrian Rebels to Chemical Attack," *New York Times*, September 21, 2013, https://tinyurl.com/y8h7fg3d. For a fascinating investigative follow-up, see Brian Whitaker's efforts to get to the bottom of the mystery of who wrote the MintPress story (and on what authority): "Yahya Ababneh Exposed," *Al-bab*, September 22, 2013, http://al-bab.com/blog/2013/09/yahya-ababneh -exposed.

40   Fieldwork in Turkey, Lebanon, and France, 2013–14. See also the Arabic-language news website Breaking News: "Analysts of the CIA: The Ghouta Chemical Attack Was Carried Out by the Opposition by Order of Saudi Arabia," September 10, 2013, http://breakingnews.sy/ar/article/25147.html, which cites the US news and opinion website WorldNetDaily in support of the argument that even US intelligence knew that the Syrian regime was not behind the attack. Rather, the piece suggests that the likely culprits are Saudi Arabia and Turkey. And the Israelis are also implicated. The unifying motive lies with none of these countries wanting to see stability in Syria.

41 See https://tinyurl.com/y9de7mwe, last accessed successfully in November 2014. This link is, interestingly, defunct as of December 4, 2018. My claims here are also based on ongoing conversations with Syrians in exile from August 2013 through December 2018.

42 William J. Broad, "Rockets in Syrian Attack Carried Large Payload of Gas, Experts Say," *New York Times*, September 4, 2013, https://tinyurl.com/lfnjcuw.

43 The quote is from Broad's *New York Times* article of September 4, 2013; the original report seems to be available only as a PowerPoint presentation.

44 Broad, "Rockets in Syrian Attack Carried Large Payload of Gas, Experts Say."

45 C. J. Chivers, "New Study Refines View of Sarin Attack in Syria," *New York Times*, December 28, 2013, https://tinyurl.com/noh3fm9.

46 Sky News, "Syria: US 'Using Lies to Justify Strikes,'" September 4, 2013, https://tinyurl.com/y8w4cc6h.

47 The *Brown Moses Blog* released on September 16, 2013, "a look at the open source evidence of who is responsible . . . evidence that's freely available for anyone to examine." Its author, Eliot Higgins, argues that no opposition force possesses the specific types of munitions used in the attacks, and that there is significant evidence dating back to January 2013 that the regime *does* have those types of munitions, and has used them in conventional as well as chemical attacks. Higgins notes the mystery surrounding the UMLACA, or Unidentified Munition Linked to Alleged Chemical Attack, which, he argues, has "never been seen in any other conflict . . . [which] has led some people to claim the munition could have been constructed by the opposition." He argues that the consistency and complexity with which the UMLACA is constructed is "beyond anything the opposition has manufactured themselves, indicating this is something that's been manufactured by the Syrian military, or one of it's [*sic*] allies." "Who Was Responsible for the August 21st Attack?," *Brown Moses Blog*, September 16, 2013, https://tinyurl.com /ybbarngd.
    That same day, the UN Mission to Investigate Allegations of the Use of Chemical Weapons in the Syrian Arab Republic released its first report, which focuses on al-Ghouta. This report was intended to establish that chemical weapons were in fact used, and made no explicit statement about who might have been responsible for their use. However, the report's conclusion that the rockets used in the attack were fired from a government-controlled area—specifically, Mount Qasiyun in Damascus—did seem to implicate the regime. Human Rights Watch, in its evidence-based report produced in both English and Arabic, also holds the Syrian regime responsible. The Arabic version is at https://www.hrw.org/ar/report /2013/09/10/256469, accessed December 4, 2018 (also cited above). Subsequent articles in newspapers, on television and radio, and on internet sites likewise implicate the regime. This one from Al-Jazeera is typical: "Ghouta: The Planned Attack," August 23, 2014, https://tinyurl.com/y9sho8z7.

48 Vladimir V. Putin, "A Plea for Caution from Russia," *New York Times*, September 11, 2013, https://tinyurl.com/or5vtco.

49 Subrata Ghoshroy, "Serious Questions about the Integrity of the UN Report," *21st Century Wire*, September 26, 2013, https://tinyurl.com/l835ygp.

50 Ghoshroy. The UN Mission released its final report on December 13, addressing wider claims of chemical weapons use. The report determined that chemical weapons were used in al-Ghouta on August 21, 2013; it also noted that there was "credible information that corroborates the allegations that chemical weapons

were used in Khan Al-ʿAsal on March 19, 2013 against soldiers and civilians"; the mission had "collected evidence consistent with the probable use of chemical weapons in Jubar on August 24, 2013, on a relatively small scale against soldiers" and "collected evidence that suggests that chemical weapons were used in Saraqueb [*sic*] on 24 August 2013 on a small scale, also against civilians"; and similarly, it had "collected evidence that suggests that chemical weapons were used in Ashrafiyah Sahnaya [*sic*] on 25 August 2013 on a small scale against soldiers." In the latter three cases, Jubar, Saraqib, and Ashrafiyya Sahnaya, the mission "could not establish the link" between the victims, the precise place and time, and the alleged event. The mission could not "corroborate the allegation" of chemical weapons use in either Bahariyya or Sheikh (Shaykh) Maqsud. For a PDF of the final report: United Nations, "United Nations Mission to Investigate Allegations of the Use of Chemical Weapons in the Syrian Arab Republic," December 2013, https://tinyurl.com/pkzrbey. For a list of all the cases under scrutiny, see note 31.

51 Seymour M. Hersh, "Whose Sarin?," *London Review of Books* 35, no. 24 (December 19, 2013), https://tinyurl.com/kkwkn3p.

52 Seymour M. Hersh, "The Red Line and the Rat Line," *London Review of Books* 36, no. 8 (April 17, 2014), https://tinyurl.com/kmelblf.

53 Hersh's April 2014 article "The Red Line and the Rat Line," translated into Arabic and published by an international daily, was initially here: http://www .awsatnews.net/?p=127436 (link broken as of December 4, 2018); an account of Hersh's accusations, also from April 2014, formerly at http://breakingnews.sy /ar/article/36785.html, is now available through the Internet Archive: https:// web.archive.org/web/20140412151825/http://breakingnews.sy/ar/article/36785 .html, accessed December 18, 2018. There were also recent follow-up investigative reports in English by like-minded anti-imperialist journalists. See for example Robert Parry's 2016 account: "Evidence That Syria's Chemical Attacks Were Staged by Jihadists," Global Research, September 9, 2016, https://tinyurl .com/y9vc39kr. People identified with the opposition recalled the third anniversary of the chemical attacks with articles presuming regime culpability. See the well-known intellectual Yasin al-Hajj Salih's piece, "The Day Clothed in Shame: Its Sponsors and Its World," August 21, 2016, on *Al-Jumhuriya*'s website: http:// aljumhuriya.net/35465; also the Syrian writer Najati Tayara's intervention at https://tinyurl.com/yazajo9l (no longer available as of December 2, 2018). For an article in 2016 documenting famous tweets and posts about the incident: Arab 48, "The Chemical [Attack] of al-Asad: The Third Anniversary of the Ghouta Massacre," August 21, 2016, https://tinyurl.com/grh88wv.

54 See for example from France 24, the state-owned international news and current affairs television network based in Paris: "Bashar al-Asad: The Khan Shaykhun Chemical Attack Was Fabricated 100 Percent," April 13, 2017, https://tinyurl.com /ybcd297p. See also Asad's interview claiming that the attack was a conspiracy against his regime: Presidency Syria, "President Asad Interview with the French Press," video, 23:28, YouTube, April 13, 2017, https://tinyurl.com/kxd8wkz (no longer available as of September 2018). Putin's statement about the attack, reported in Arabic in the newspaper *Al-Ghad*, May 30, 2017: https://tinyurl.com /y8gfdxed.

    Additional Arabic-language articles from *Russia Today*, in its typical short format: Arabic RT, "A Former US Intelligence Officer Determines Who Is Responsible for the Khan Shaykhun Chemical Attack," April 20, 2017, https://tinyurl.com /y9c3y8yd. This *Russia Today* article is based on information from a supposed "CIA expert": Arabic RT, "CIA Director: We've Gathered Compelling Evidence on Khan Shaykhun in One Day!," July 12, 2017, https://tinyurl.com/ybbrrfrp. See also a recent UN report accusing the Asad regime of responsibility (in Arabic): Enab Baladi, "The United Nations Confirms That the Regime Is Responsible for the Massacre at Khan Khaykhun," September 6, 2017, https://www.enabbaladi .net/archives/171441.

55   Refer for instance to "Russia Says Syria Gas Incident Caused by Rebels' Own Chemical Arsenal," Reuters, April 5, 2017, https://tinyurl.com/yb3kcppf; Martin Chulov and Kareem Shaheen, "Syria Chemical Weapons Attack Toll Rises to 70 as Russian Narrative Is Dismissed," *Guardian*, US edition, April 5, 2017, https:// tinyurl.com/m9lh8q8; Ole Solvang, "Russia's Claim on Alleged Chemical Attack in Syria," Human Rights Watch, April 6, 2017, https://tinyurl.com/yb6mkmge; Danielle Ryan, "Why Is US Media Ignoring All Dissenting Expert Voices on the Khan Sheikhoun Attack?," *RT*, April 20, 2017, https://tinyurl.com/y9gp3hre; and Ammar Abdullah, "Chemical Incident in Khan Shaykhun Deliberately Staged by Militants, Syrian Probe Finds," *RT*, August 17, 2017, https://tinyurl .com/y7rlby93. Accounts of the attack that place the onus on an aerial bombardment include well-regarded opposition sites: an article from the online bulletin all4syria is available through the Internet Archive, https://web.archive.org/web /20171029112408/http://www.all4syria.info/Archive/400043, accessed January 28, 2019; another is Step News Agency, "Hundreds of Victims without Blood in a Chemical Bombing on Khan Shaykhun," April 4, 2017, https://tinyurl.com /yce4wxzv. There was also horrifying video about the same brutal event: Assi Press, "Scenes from the Chemical Massacre in the City of Khan Shaykhun Caused by the Regime's Aircraft by Targeting the City with Chemical Gases," video, 0:40, YouTube, April 4, 2017, https://tinyurl.com/y6wafjhc. Some videos chronicled the death of an entire family: Assi Press, "The Martyrdom of a Whole Family, Most of Whom Are Children in Khan Shaykhun, as a Result of the Regime's Aircraft Targeting with Chemical Gases," video, 0:51, YouTube, April 3, 2017, https:// tinyurl.com/y83s76wr. A helpful time line was produced by Eliot Higgins: "Summary of Claims surrounding the Khan Sheikhoun Chemical Attack," *Bellingcat*, July 4, 2017, https://tinyurl.com/y94gadfc. Higgins refuted Hersh's efforts to sow doubt about this attack, claiming that he had been hoodwinked: "Will Get Fooled Again — Seymour Hersh, Welt, and the Khan Sheikhoun Chemical Attack," *Bellingcat*, June 25, 2017, https://tinyurl.com/ybaxukm2.

56   Richard Hofstadter, "The Paranoid Style in American Politics," *Harper's Magazine*, November 1964, 77–86, https://tinyurl.com/y83yfzt5.

57   Samir Saliha, "Who Provided Hersh with the Information?," Al-Arabiya, April 16, 2014, https://tinyurl.com/ybaff92h.

58   Hofstadter, "The Paranoid Style"; and David Harper, "The Politics of Paranoia: Paranoid Positioning and Conspiratorial Narratives in the Surveillance Society," *Surveillance and Society* 5, no. 1 (2008): 1–32. Harper argues, much like James Scott, that conspiracy theories and rumors are "weapons of the weak." See Scott's *Weapons of the Weak: Everyday Forms of Peasant Resistance* (New Haven, CT: Yale University Press, 1985). But Michael Rogin's early work on the McCarthy era, as well as his subsequent analysis of political "demonology" in the American context, suggests otherwise. See Michael Rogin, *The Intellectuals and McCarthy: The Radical Specter* (Boston: MIT Press, 1967), and *Ronald Reagan the Movie: And Other Episodes in Political Demonology* (Los Angeles: University of California Press, 1988). For recent work in this vein, see Joseph Masco's *The Theater of Operations: The National Security State from the Cold War to the War on Terror* (Durham, NC: Duke University Press, 2014).

59 The essay was originally published as Hannah Arendt, "Truth and Politics," *New Yorker*, February 25, 1967.

60 Linda Zerilli, *A Democratic Theory of Judgment* (Chicago: University of Chicago Press, 2016), 135.

61 For a discussion of the difference between Arendt's and Wittgenstein's views and Jürgen Habermas's notion of communicative rationality or reason, see Zerilli, *A Democratic Theory of Judgment.*

62 Abounaddara, Vimeo profile, https://vimeo.com/user6924378; see *The Trajectory of an Unknown Soldier* [Abu Naddara, *Masirat al-jundi al-majhul*], video, 1:56, Vimeo, November 23, 2012, https://vimeo.com/54135942.

63 Abounaddara, *In the Name of the Father* [Abu Naddara, *Bi-ism al-ab*], video, 2:13, Vimeo, May 24, 2013, https://vimeo.com/66891077.

64 See Lisa Wedeen, *Ambiguities of Domination* (Chicago: University of Chicago Press, 1999).

65 Freud originally used the term *family romance* to refer to a boy's neurotic fantasy of "getting free from the parents of whom he now has a low opinion and of replacing them by others, who, as a rule, are of higher social standing." "Family Romances," in *Standard Edition of the Complete Psychological Works of Sigmund Freud*, trans. James Strachey (London: Hogarth Press, 1959), 9:238–39. The scholars Lynn Hunt and Michael Rogin extended that idea of the family romance beyond the individual psyche to public action and politics. Lynn Hunt, *The Family Romance in the French Revolution* (Berkeley: University of California Press, 1992), xiii; see also Michael Rogin, *Fathers and Children: Andrew Jackson and the Subjugation of the American Indian* (New York: Alfred A. Knopf, 1975). I discuss the use of the family romance in the context of Hafiz al-Asad's cult of personality in Wedeen, *Ambiguities of Domination*, 50. Here the young woman is also reproducing a presumption of the liberal public sphere: by straining toward impersonal truths—i.e., by transcending our selfish inclinations—we "grow up" and are thereby less likely to fall victim to tyrants.

66 Abounaddara, *The Trajectory of an Unknown Soldier* [Abu Naddara, *Masirat al-jundi al-majhul*], video, 1:56, Vimeo, November 23, 2012, https://vimeo.com/54135942.

67 Thanks are owed to Nadia Abu El-Haj for rich conversations about the US context.

68 Hannah Arendt, *The Human Condition* (Chicago: University of Chicago Press, 1958), 175.

69 Wittgenstein, *On Certainty*, 12e, para. 83.

70 Abounaddara, *Aïcha* [Abu Naddara, *'A'isha*], video, 3:29, Vimeo, October 3, 2014, https://vimeo.com/107948804. See Lisa Wedeen, "Ideology and Humor in Dark Times: Notes from Syria," *Critical Inquiry* 39 (Winter 2013): 841–73.

71 This position is discussed in greater length in relation to national sentimentality in the following chapter.

72 See Yahya al-'Abdallah's two-part documentary on the *dumari* living in Istanbul: "We Don't Stay in Camps," video, 26:33, 2014, available at http://www.educationalleaderswithoutborders.com/, accessed December 4, 2018; and "Water," video, 18:55, YouTube, November 12, 2015, https://youtu.be/8d44oIi woSE.

73 Cited from Edward Ziter's presentation at the New School's Vera List Center on the occasion of honoring the collective, Abounaddara, "Abounaddara: The Right to the Image," lecture, Vera List Center for Art and Politics, New School, New York City, October 22, 2015.

74 Ziter, "Abounaddara."

75 Others such as the site Ta'kkad (Verify) are attempting anew to produce journalism with acceptable standards of objectivity. Motivated by committed activists in the opposition who became disillusioned with both the regime's and the opposition's penchant for bending the truth, these citizen journalists have tried to reanchor the world of facts by operating as a watchdog unit, one that follows up on assertions about events that transpired and the images that are purportedly connected to those events. Their work has generated some important retractions, including from BBC Arabic.

76 Max D. Weiss, "Slow Witnessing: Syrian War Literature in Real Time," Lecture, Chicago Center for Contemporary Theory (CCCT), University of Chicago, October 7, 2016.

CHAPTER FOUR

1 As the political theorist Linda Zerilli notes, for Arendt, "judging is an activity, and judgment is not political because it is about political things that are prior, independent, and external to it; it is political because it is a judgment that is arrived at politically—that is to say, with Arendt's Kant, 'by thinking in the place of everybody else'" (in Linda Zerilli, *A Democratic Theory of Judgment* [Chicago: University of Chicago Press, 2016], 8). Zerilli also points out that Arendt's understanding of judgment is not simply a mental exercise but requires ongoing political engagement. For an argument that understands Arendt's judgment to be primarily aesthetic, see George Kateb's essay "The Judgment of Arendt," in *Judgment, Imagination, and Politics: Themes from Kant and Arendt*, ed. Ronald Beiner and Jennifer Nedelsky (Lanham, MD: Rowman and Littlefield, 2001), 121–38. The volume more generally attempts to think through the role of imagination in judgment, using Kant's *Critique of Judgment*, trans. Werner S. Pluhar (Indianapolis: Hackett Classics, 1987) and Arendt's *Lectures on Kant's Political Philosophy* to do so (the latter is edited with an interpretive essay by Ronald Beiner [Chicago: University of Chicago Press, 1989]). For further discussion of judgment, see my invocation of Arendt's "representative thinking" in relation to Syrian films in this chapter. My own interest is less in who got Arendt right than in the promising notions of the political and of judgment—by way of an engagement with Syrian aesthetic projects—that "representative thinking" enables.

2 Allayth Hajju, dir., *We'll Return Shortly* (2013). See Bassem Mroue's "Syrian War Takes Center Stage on Ramadan TV Series," *Arab News*, July 30, 2013, http://www.arabnews.com/news/459811. Other discussions of the series include Muhammad al-Najjar, "The Syrian Crisis Is Present in Drama during Ramadan," Al-Jazeera, July 14, 2013, https://tinyurl.com/yazsrr2v; *DPNews* at https://tinyurl.com/y74xyjb5 (link broken as of December 4, 2018); *Syria Truth* at https://tinyurl.com/yackwpln (link broken as of December 4, 2018); and *Safahat Suriya*, "The Syrian Critic 'Ali Safar: Syrian Drama Suffers like Everything Else in Syria," August 11, 2013, https://tinyurl.com/y7dja8ca.

3 Rasha Sharbaji, dir., *Birth from the Waist, Part Three* (2013). For a discussion of this television drama, see Donatella Della Ratta's 2014 paper, "Making Real-

Time Drama: The Political Economy of Cultural Production in Syria's Uprising," PARGC paper, Pennsylvania University, Fall 2014, https://tinyurl.com/y7tnoqs6.

4   Kai Ryssdal and Maria Hollenhorst, "Why Ramadan Is a Big Deal for Arab TV Networks," *Marketplace*, May 26, 2017, https://tinyurl.com/yadtv2uw.

5   Ryssdal and Hollenhorst. Also, author's email correspondence from 2013 and discussions in Beirut, Lebanon, with various Syrians—both viewers and cultural producers in the aftermath of the shows' airing during Ramadan 2013.

6   Author's email correspondence with Rasha Salti, August 22, 2013. Reprinted with Salti's permission.

7   See James Chandler, *An Archaeology of Sympathy: The Sentimental Mode in Literature and Cinema* (Chicago: University of Chicago Press, 2013), 223.

8   Author's conversations in Beirut and Chicago, 2013.

9   Quoted in Earl McCabe, "Depressive Realism: An Interview with Lauren Berlant," *Hypocrite Reader* 5 (June 2011), http://hypocritereader.com/5/depressive-realism.

10   See for example Ravi Vasudevan's *The Melodramatic Public: Film Form and Spectatorship in Indian Cinema* (New York: Palgrave, 2011).

11   In the Middle East context, see especially Lila Abu-Lughod's *Dramas of Nationhood: The Politics of Television in Egypt* (Chicago: University of Chicago Press, 2004). For a discussion of Syrian drama in the context of ongoing discussions of love, sexuality, and nationalism, see Rebecca Joubin's *The Politics of Love: Sexuality, Gender, and Marriage in Syrian Television Drama* (Lanham, MD: Lexington Books, 2015).

12   Peter Brooks, *The Melodramatic Imagination: Balzac, Henry James, Melodrama, and the Mode of Excess* (New Haven, CT: Yale University Press, 1976; new preface, 1995), 21. Cited also in Abu-Lughod, *Dramas of Nationhood*, 112.

13   Brooks, *The Melodramatic Imagination*, xiii.

14   Ben Singer, *Melodrama and Modernity: Early Sensational Cinema and Its Contexts* (New York: Columbia University Press, 2001), 44–45.

15   Henry James Smith, "The Melodrama," *Atlantic Monthly* 99 (March 1907): 320–28, cited in Singer, *Melodrama and Modernity*, 47. See also Lea Jacobs, "The Woman's Picture and the Poetics of Melodrama," *Camera Obscura* 11 (1993): 120–47. For a discussion of melodrama as a genre of political discourse with special emphasis on US politics, see Elisabeth R. Anker, *Orgies of Feeling: Melodrama and the Politics of Freedom* (Durham, NC: Duke University Press, 2014).

16   Singer, *Melodrama and Modernity*, 46.

17   Singer, 49. John G. Cawelti describes this synthesis of melodrama with a detailed account of social setting as "social melodrama," which combines the "emotional satisfactions of melodrama with the interest inherent in a detailed, intimate, and realistic analysis of major social or historical phenomena . . . the appeal of this synthesis combines the escapist satisfactions of melodrama—in particular its fantasy of a moral universe following conventional social values—with the pleasurable feeling that we are learning something important about reality." John G. Cawelti, *Adventure, Mystery, and Romance: Formula Stories as Art and Popular Culture* (Chicago: University of Chicago Press, 1976), 261.

18 Ethnographic work in Lebanon, 2013. See also Della Ratta, "Making Real-Time Drama"; and Yasmin Hannawi's piece, "We Are Its Heroes and the Events Are Our Story (*We Will Return Shortly*): The Television Series of One Hundred Years," Al-Jaras, October 7, 2013, https://tinyurl.com/y8hlv3vw. Given that many of the dramatis personae were drawn from the regime in Syria, the serial was interpreted by viewers identified with the opposition as testimony to an ongoing and disappointing complicity between the Syrian drama community and the regime.

19 And the presumption underpinning this expectation was that there was a "we" who could agree on what the genre of reality was.

20 The regime's efforts are not unlike what Jacques Rancière calls "the distribution of the sensible" (*le partage du sensible*), referring both to the "existence of something in common and the delimitations that define the respective parts and positions within it," the forms of partition and exclusion that are intrinsic to group-making and the "historical regimes of identification" that authorize some political positions, art, feelings, and judgments while demeaning or ignoring others. Jacques Rancière, *The Politics of Aesthetics*, trans. Gabriel Rockhill (London: Bloomsbury, 2004), 7 and 48. The "partage du sensible" is also found in elaborated form in Rancière's *Dissensus: On Politics and Aesthetics*, ed. and trans. Steve Corcoran (London: Continuum Books, 2010).

21 There were subsequently many clips available from the video, some with this title, some with English subtitles, and some searchable by Googling 'Id al-umm, Asma' al-Asad 2013. https://www.youtube.com/watch?v=y1PvEg98Z9Y; https://youtu .be/y-eIktOiKP4.

22 Ethnographic work in Beirut, July 2013. For an effort to grasp literary reception and reading practices through fieldwork and surveys, see Janice A. Radway's classic *Reading the Romance: Women, Patriarchy, and Popular Literature* (Durham: University of North Carolina Press, [1984] 1991). Radway makes the important point, now largely accepted in literary theory, that genre-based theories of interpretation are more compelling than encoding-decoding ones.

23 A translation into English in a 2014 version is followed by an explanation for English-speaking audiences, which was not part of the original untranslated version of 2013: "Damascus is the city of Jasmines [*sic*]." It is also the capital of Syria and the heart of the regime's urban power base.

24 See the discussion in Lisa Wedeen, *Ambiguities of Domination* (Chicago: University of Chicago Press, 1999), 55–60, for the way various terms are used, and issues of translation with the word *nation*. There are other words for "nation" and "the national" in Arabic as well—but the connection between motherhood and Syria as national mother is explicit here, even when *watan*, as "nation" or "nation-state," is used instead.

25 Elizabeth Povinelli, *The Cunning of Recognition: Indigenous Alterities and the Making of Australian Multiculturalism* (Durham, NC: Duke University Press, 2012), 27.

26 The semantic shades distinguishing *watan* from *umma* are complex. For a discussion of *umma* in Ba'thist rhetoric, see Wedeen, *Ambiguities of Domination*, 55–60. To put it simply, *umma* tends to refer to a pan-Arab nationalist project, whereas *watan* gets associated with existing nation-states. The latter is also more masculine, muscular, pragmatic, and part of an actual geopolitics, in contrast with *umma*, which comes from *umm* (mother). The term *umma* can also refer to the community of Muslims, and hence in that instance to a version of collective imagining different from a nationalist one. See Talal Asad's discussion of the *umma* in

Formations of the Secular: Christianity, Islam, Modernity (Palo Alto, CA: Stanford University Press, 2003), 197.

27   Lauren Berlant, *Cruel Optimism* (Durham, NC: Duke University Press, 2011).

28   Jacques Rancière, *The Emancipated Spectator*, trans. Gregory Elliott (London: Verso, 2011), 14.

29   Berlant, *Cruel Optimism.*

30   The documentary can be found here: Enab Baladi, *Asma' al-Akhras without Body-guards: A Documentary Film, Russian Production*, video produced by Moscow-based channel Russia-24, October 23, 2016, https://tinyurl.com/yap9lqvl (no longer available as of December 12, 2018). The thirty-minute interview with Asma' al-Asad is the first and only thus far: Thishreen, "Asma' Assad Interview with Russia Channel 24," video, 33:20, YouTube, October 18, 2016, https://tinyurl.com /y9m3yxg8. The interview was translated into Arabic on the YouTube account of the presidency (Presidency Syria), which was terminated in September 2018.

31   In a subsequent interview with 'Umran's father, conducted by a reporter known for both her vulgarity and her unwavering identification with the regime, the father claims that 'Umran's photo was taken without parental permission and was used exploitatively by the opposition to suggest regime culpability. His own position raises doubts that the violence was a result of the regime's aerial bombardment, as was initially alleged when the civilian rescuers, the White Helmets, extricated the boy from his crumbled home. See Enab Baladi, "The First Appearance of the Child 'Umran Daqnaysh on Syrian Regime Media Outlets," June 5, 2017, https://www.enabbaladi.net/archives/154229; and CNN Arabic, "For the Syrian Child 'Umran . . . under the Spotlight Again," video, 2:58, September 6, 2017, https://tinyurl.com/ycvghwpa.

32   Al-Jazeera's Faisal Al-Qasim juxtaposes Bashar al-Asad's statements to his wife's: video, 1:26, Facebook, October 21, 2016, https://tinyurl.com/yb3u5scm. An interview with Bashar al-Asad can be found here: Super Storm Wave, "President Assad's Interview with Swiss TV," video, 20:54, YouTube, October 19, 2016, https://tinyurl.com/yag5mxw6, accessed January 25, 2019. A second interview, formerly at the YouTube channel Presidency Syria, https://www.youtube.com /watch?v=9H9LE9bfsHQ, is no longer available.

33   Her preachy remarks on the difference between being distinguished and being superior are a prime example of this moral superiority, as is her celebration of graduating distinguished students with the admonition that Syria can graduate more than just the thirty-three attending this year's ceremony. Refer, for instance, to the Facebook page for the National Center for Distinguished [Students], launched in 2009: https://tinyurl.com/ybubpwcm. Here is the full video of the speech: JP News, "Asma' al-Asad: After the Graduation Ceremony of the Students of the Academic Programs of the National Center for Distinguished Students," video, 7:01, September 7, 2016, https://jpnews-sy.com/ar/news.php?id =109067. See Al-Jazeera, "YouTube Shuts Down Pro-Syrian Government Channels," September 10, 2018, https://tinyurl.com/ycb45wte. See also the regime's news outlet SANA (Syrian Arab News Agency), "The Graduation of 33 Students from the Academic Programs Sponsored by the Organization of Excellence and Creativity," September 8, 2016, https://www.sana.sy/?p=427957. Most of the students graduating with distinction, unsurprisingly, come from regions where regime loyalists reside in large numbers: the data from September 19, 2016, are at https://syrianpc.com/archives/146360, accessed December 4, 2018.

34 An important scholarly account of Syrian war fiction is Max D. Weiss, "Slow Witnessing: Syrian War Literature in Real Time," lecture, Chicago Center for Contemporary Theory, University of Chicago, October 7, 2016; on Syrian artists' images of ruin and desolation, see Anne-Marie McManus's "On the Ruins of What's to Come, I Stand: Time and Devastation in Syrian Cultural Production since 2011," *Critical Inquiry*, forthcoming.

35 Thanks are owed here to Lauren Berlant for our discussions of melodrama.

36 Lauren Berlant, *The Anatomy of National Fantasy: Hawthorne, Utopia, and Everyday Life* (Chicago: University of Chicago Press, 1991).

37 Khalid 'Abd al-Wahid, *Tuj*, video, 2:14, Vimeo, 2012, https://vimeo.com/610972 42, accessed December 15, 2018.

38 Khalid 'Abd al-Wahid, *Shaqq fi Dhakira* [*Slot in Memory*], video, 2:25, Vimeo, 2012, https://vimeo.com/61093429, accessed December 15, 2018

39 In one version, the director dedicates *Slot in Memory* to the "children of Sabra and Shatila and of Syria," making common cause between Palestinian and Syrian children, so many of whom have ended up in Palestinian refugee camps in Lebanon. In another version, the dedication was removed, so that viewers who have not seen the original can imagine children of war *tout court*. Author's interview with the artist, Khaled 'Abd al-Wahid, August 2014, Berlin. The current version on Vimeo retains the dedication to Palestinian and Syrian children.

40 Ziad Kalthum, dir., *The Immortal Sergeant* [*Al-Raqib al-Khalid*], Crystal Films, Beirut, 2014 (filmed 2012–13).

41 Recall from chapter 3 Hannah Arendt's use of Isak Dinesen to underscore how storytelling works similarly, enabling otherwise unbearable sorrows to be borne.

42 Hannah Arendt, "Truth and Politics," in *Between Past and Future: Eight Exercises in Political Thought* (New York: Penguin, [1961] 2006), 233–34.

43 In Lauren Berlant, *The Female Complaint: The Unfinished Business of Sentimentality* (Durham, NC: Duke University Press, 2008).

44 Kalthum's ethnographic sensibility and his self-declared embrace of the role of participant-observer recalls Sigmund Freud's analysis in his 1917 "Mourning and Melancholia" (in *Collected Papers*, trans. James Strachey, vol. 4 [New York: Hogarth Press, 1953]). Freud argues there that a crucial part of the work of mourning involves the "testing of reality," whereby "reality passes its verdict—that the object no longer exists—upon each single one of the memories and hopes through which the libido was attached to the lost object, and the ego, confronted as it were with the decision whether it will share this fate, is persuaded by the sum of its narcissistic satisfaction in being alive to sever its attachment to the non-existent object" (Freud, 166). This severance is slow and gradual, Freud notes, and "the expenditure of energy necessary for it becomes somehow dissipated by the time the task is carried through" (Freud, 166).

Melanie Klein cites these insights to call attention to the close connection between this "testing of reality" in adult mourning and early childhood states of mind. For Klein, in fact, adult mourning "revives" these infantile processes in which the lost "object" was originally the mother's breast and all the feelings associated with it—nourishment, security, love, kindness, etc. This loss produces complicated feelings of distress, "phantasies" of aggression, guilt, and fear. The baby is often in conflict with itself, having incorporated its mother (and soon its father) into a world of unconscious phantasies living within the child's body—

its "inner objects"—which interact with anxieties connected to the "external" mother. The two mother objects—the internal and the external—are bound up with each other, with the internal one undergoing changes through encounters with the external one and "through the very process of internalization." For Klein, what she calls the "depressive position" is a failure of integration in which persecutory fears of a destroyed ego by internal persecutors (bad objects) are linked to feelings of sorrow—a "pining" for the loved (good) object. When the "depressive position arises," writes Klein, "the ego is forced (in addition to earlier defences) to develop methods of defence which are essentially directed against the 'pining' for the loved object," what Klein identifies as "the manic position" (in Melanie Klein, "Mourning and Its Relation to Manic-Depressive States," *International Journal of Psycho-Analysis* 21 [1940]: 130). All children go through this struggle, according to Klein, and "omnipotence, denial, and idealization, closely bound up with ambivalence, enable the early ego to assert itself to a certain degree against its internal persecutors and against a slavish and perilous dependence upon its loved objects" (Klein, 131). Patterns associated with this depressive position are triggered anew when adults experience loss, and Klein keenly observes the experiences of ambivalence, of the guilt and rage tied up with love. The point here is not to digress into a detailed account of Klein's object relations theory, nor to superimpose psychoanalytic insights drawn from the specific familial relations of nineteenth- and twentieth-century Europe onto twenty-first-century Syria, but to highlight the conflictual, ambivalent guilt/rage-inflected defenses that are observed to come to the fore in the work of mourning. See as well Freud, *Collected Papers*, 4:163 and 166.

45 Rohit Goel offers a particularly thought-provoking account of Lebanon as an object cause of desire in his dissertation proposal and various talks. See for example "War and Peace in Lebanon," https://www.lebtivity.com/event/lebanon -as-object-cause-of-desire-a-public-talk-by-rohit-goel-in-conversation-with-walid -sadek; and http://www.jp-india.org/uploads/newsletters/pdfs/41_pdf.pdf, both accessed December 26, 2018. As William Mazzarella has rightly pointed out, all community is, to some extent, premised on this constitutive lack. But there is something especially charged, I would argue, about nationalism's version of this object cause of desire, the nation form's persistence over time, and the concept's ability to stand in for both intimate and abstract attachments that make it a particularly dramatic, pressing example. As Étienne Balibar notes, the nation form's specificity is tied to its peculiar structural demand that it refer to a past that "has never been present and will never be." In "The Nation Form: History and Ideology," trans. Chris Turner, chap. 5 in *Race, Nation, Class: Ambiguous Identities*, ed. Étienne Balibar and Immanuel Wallerstein (New York: Verso, 1990), 86–106.

46 Ossama Mohammed/Usama Muhammad, dir., *Ma' al-Fidda* [*Silvered Water, Syria Self-Portrait*], film, 2014, Les Films d'Ici, Paris, and Proaction Films, Damascus.

47 See also *Khutwa, Khutwa* [*Step by Step* (1979)], an experimental work Mohammed completed for his MA at Moscow's Gerasimov Institute of Cinematography (VGIK), as well as the magisterial tragicomedy *Nujum al-Nahar* [*Stars in Broad Daylight* (1988)] and *Sunduq al-Dunya* [*Sacrifices* or, more aptly, *Camera Obscura* (2002)]. The contemporary resonance for young filmmakers of his oldest, *Khutwa, Khutwa* (1979), has partly to do with his agile blurring of the conventional boundaries between documentary and fiction, producing a poetic tour de force whose aesthetic and political sensibilities have continued to inspire new generations of Syrian filmmakers—especially once the uprising got underway. Mohammed's attention to the juxtaposition of beauty to violence in everyday life also finds expression in *Sunduq al-Dunya*, another account of familial conflict in

Syria's coastal countryside. Less overtly political than *Nujum al-Nahar, Sunduq al-Dunya* focuses on a grandfather who wants to bestow his name on one of his three grandchildren but dies before fulfilling his wish, consigning the children to a life of namelessness. Each grandchild finds meaning and pleasure in different ways over the course of a quasi-allegorical tale of human frailty, political power, and the seductions of violence. The first child practices restraint and composure, the second, love, and the third, cruelty and caprice. Again we see power corrupting, even as the countryside, the filmmaker, and the audience bear witness to life's beauty and brutality. Symbols of fecundity and openness suggest the power of regeneration while simultaneously producing a sense of being boxed in, not unlike an actual camera obscura, in which light from an external scene passes through the aperture into an enclosure, generating an inverted image. Ossama Mohammed/Usama Muhammad, dir., *Sunduq al-Dunya* [*Sacrifices*], film, 2002, AMIP, Arte France Cinéma, Ministère de la Culture de la République Française, National Film Organization (all from Paris); Syria, various locations.

48   *Nujum al-Nahar* [*Stars in Broad Daylight* (1988)] is perhaps the most politically critical film ever to have been made in Syria. An insightful and revelatory critique, its plot is a thinly disguised metaphor for political power and for the now-deceased president Hafiz al-Asad's "cult" of personality. In the film, Mohammed depicts the moral crisis of a rural 'Alawi family, some of whose members have moved to the city and succumbed to urban life and corrupt officialdom. As characters, they represent the regime's vulgarity and brutality. The main male protagonist—who looks uncannily like the former ruler—is the controlling, manipulative, stingy brother and de facto patriarch of the family, an association that explicitly connects patriarchal family life to martial rule and political violence. Drawing from his intimate knowledge of sectarian and regional specificities, Mohammed parodies the emptiness and tedium of official discourse, at the same time lamenting the beautiful but ultimately unlivable countryside. Overrun with petty familial disputes and patriarchal violence, rural life offers no refuge, even while collective fantasies of national belonging have themselves been reduced to vapid slogans—devoid of the hope or sense of community that animated the early days of postcolonial rule. Ossama Mohammed/Usama Muhammad, dir., *Nujum al-Nahar* [*Stars in Broad Daylight*], film, 1988, National Film Organization, Damascus. See also my *Ambiguities of Domination* (1999).

   This endnote passage is excerpted from my laudation for Ossama Mohammed (Usama Muhammad) when he received a Prince Claus Award in Amsterdam in 2015.

49   See Rashid 'Isa, "Did *Silvered Water* Reach the Cannes Festival with the Power of Cinema or the Power of Politics? How the Story of Wiam Bedirxan Was Confiscated," *Al-Quds Al-Arabi*, September 29, 2014, https://tinyurl.com/y9ecd26n. A philosophical piece, which, as Yahya al-'Abdallah points out, is in the same style as the one used by Ossama Mohammed in narrating the film, is Yusuf Raybir, "The Film *Silvered Water*: The Poeticizing of Death," n.d., on the website of the journal *Maaber*: https://tinyurl.com/y9f42azl, accessed December 1, 2018. A thorough complementary discussion by a Syrian critic that underscores the film's revolutionary spirit is Randa al-Rahuni, "*Silvered Water*: The Creative Documentation of the Ugliness of the Syrian Revolution; The Film of Usama Muhammad and Simav Bedirxan," *Arab Cinema Magazine* 2 (Spring 2015), https://tinyurl.com /y97wsuzj. See also Salah Hashim, "*Silvered Water*: The Fish Is Demonstrating Underwater and Demanding the Toppling of the Regime," Elwatan News, May 21, 2014, https://tinyurl.com/y7gdoqav. For an important discussion defending the

use of grotesque images that begins with Ossama Mohammed's film, see Yasin al-Hajj Salih, "Staring at the Face of the Horror," *Al-Jumhuriya*, May 29, 2015, http://aljumhuriya.net/33487.

50 This latter question recalls the film theorist André Bazin's essays, *Qu'est-ce que le cinéma?* The English version of the text is available as *What Is Cinema?*, trans. Hugh Gray (Berkeley: University of California Press, 1967).

51 Patchen Markell, *Bound by Recognition* (Princeton, NJ: Princeton University Press, 2003), 13; see also Hannah Arendt, *The Human Condition* (Chicago: University of Chicago Press, 1958), 184.

52 Enormous gratitude is owed to James Chandler for watching the film with me and for helping me understand film's formal properties. His insightful observations here have been crucial to my thinking.

53 Ossama Mohammed, conversation via email with me, October 2016. My reading of Mohammed's work is a product of and remains indebted to a long and close connection to him and his work—since 1996. I have been privileged to watch the film with him on a number of occasions and to discuss it at length from 2014 onward. I also helped, in a rushed and unsatisfactory (to me) way, with the English subtitles.

54 Berlant, *The Female Complaint*, 41. See also Elaine Scarry, *The Body in Pain: The Making and Unmaking of the World* (Oxford: Oxford University Press, 1987).

55 Lauren Berlant, "Structures of Unfeeling: Mysterious Skin," *International Journal of Politics, Culture, and Society* 28, no. 3 (2015): 211.

56 Berlant, 211.

57 Berlant, 209, which is about flat affect.

58 Robert Meister, *After Evil: A Politics of Human Rights* (New York: Columbia University Press, 2010).

59 Hannah Arendt, *The Human Condition* (Chicago: University of Chicago Press, [1958]; 2nd ed., with an introduction by Margaret Canovan, 1998), 84.

60 Arendt, "Truth and Politics," 237.

61 Arendt, 237; my emphasis.

62 Linda Zerilli, *Feminism and the Abyss of Freedom* (Chicago: University of Chicago Press, 2005), 175. In her *A Democratic Theory of Judgment*, Zerilli points compellingly to Arendt as offering a profound and valuable alternative to liberal forms of judgment—both in the Habermasian sense of being rule-bound and in the Rawlsian quest for a decontextualized "original position."

63 Ludwig Wittgenstein, *Lectures and Conversations on Aesthetics, Psychology and Religious Belief*, ed. Cyril Barrett (Berkeley: University of California Press, 1967), 28, quoted in Zerilli, *A Democratic Theory of Judgment*, 78.

64 To modify an insight from the film theorist André Bazin (*What Is Cinema?*, 28).

65 Hannah Arendt, *Eichmann in Jerusalem: A Report on the Banality of Evil* (New York: Penguin Books, [1963] 1977).

66 See Hanna Pitkin, *Wittgenstein and Justice: On the Significance of Ludwig Wittgenstein for Social and Political Thought* (Berkeley: University of California Press, 1993), 216; Arendt, *The Human Condition*, 52.

67 I owe a tremendous debt to Jennifer Pitts here for helping me with this language and with the chapter's arguments about judgment throughout.

CHAPTER FIVE

1   Recall that the ʿAlawi sect is an offshoot of Shiʿa Islam, which is disproportionately represented in regime circles.

2   Author's conversations in May 2011 in Damascus, July 2012 in Beirut, and multiple occasions from October 2012 through August 2015 in Chicago. Versions of this or similar stories also circulated on the internet, although unfortunately they are no longer available and I lacked the foresight at the time to preserve them. The point remains the same—that the story in all its variations raises issues of anticipatory fear, disavowal, and displacement, as I describe them here. I am grateful to one Syrian artist in particular for his telling of the story and our subsequent discussions.

3   Raymond Williams, *Marxism and Literature* (Oxford: Oxford University Press, 1977), especially 121–35.

4   See ʿAzmi Bishara, *Suriya: Darb al-alam nahwa al-hurriyya; Muhawala fi al-tarikh al-rahin* (Doha, Qatar: al-Markaz al-ʿArabi lil-Abhath wa Dirasat al-Siyasat, 2013), for an argument that emphasizes the regime's techniques of rule and how they reproduce social structures. See also Mohammed Abu Hajar, "Our Sectarianism: Not Just the Regime's Creation," Syria Untold, June 14, 2018, http://syria untold.com/2018/06/our-sectarianism-not-just-the-regimes-creation/. Thanks are owed to Kevin Mazur for inviting me to clarify my argument.

5   Brian Massumi, "The Future Birth of the Affective Fact," in *The Affect Theory Reader*, ed. Melissa Gregg and Gregory J. Seigworth (Durham, NC: Duke University Press, 2010), 53. See also Sofia A. Fenner, "Life after Co-optation" (PhD diss., University of Chicago, 2016).

6   Massumi, "The Future Birth of the Affective Fact," 54.

7   Michael Taussig, *The Nervous System* (New York: Routledge, 1992).

8   Massumi, "The Future Birth of the Affective Fact," 53.

9   Massumi, 63.

10 Massumi, repeatedly throughout the article, 52–70.

11 René Girard, *The One by Whom Scandal Comes*, trans. Malcom B. DeBevoise, Studies in Violence, Mimesis and Culture (East Lansing: Michigan State University, 2014), 30.

12 See René Girard, *Violence and the Sacred*, trans. Patrick Gregory (Baltimore: John Hopkins University Press, 1979).

13 Lisa Wedeen, *Ambiguities of Domination: Politics, Rhetoric, and Symbols in Contemporary Syria* (Chicago: University of Chicago Press, 1999).

14 Thanks are owed to Daragh Grant for pressing me on this point.

15 Joseph Masco, *The Theater of Operations: The National Security State from the Cold War to the War on Terror* (Durham, NC: Duke University Press, 2014), 12.

16 Yasin al-Hajj Salih's article "Fi al-Shabbiha wa al-Tashbih wa Dawlathima," in *Kalamon* (Winter 2012), http://www.kalamonreview.org/articles-details-122

#axzz5YOTQsWao, is one well-informed example of what became a growing number of discussions about pro-regime thugs called *shabbiha* in Syria. See also https://en.wikipedia.org/wiki/Shabiha (accessed December 4, 2018) for a brief history of this organization, which is said to have been established as a smuggling ring in the 1980s by a member of the Asad clan. The term has evolved in the context of ongoing violence, and is now used by both regime and opposition members as a general pejorative (in both noun and verb forms) to indicate thuggish behavior.

17 See Aziz Nakkash, "The Alawite Dilemma in Homs: Survival, Solidarity, and the Making of a Community" (Berlin: Friedrich-Ebert-Stiftung, March 2013), http://library.fes.de/pdf-files/iez/09825.pdf.

18 Shabbiha also extended their businesses to areas that had previously been off limits, setting up small stalls proffering contraband tobacco and fashionable clothing in places like wealthy western Aleppo.

19 Fieldwork, March–May 2011. For a discussion of the "baltagi effect" as a way of theorizing the production of counterrevolution in Egypt, see Paul Amar's *The Security Archipelago* (Durham, NC: Duke University Press, 2013). Dara Kay Cohen's *Rape during Civil War* (Ithaca, NY: Cornell University Press, 2016) emphasizes rape's importance for cultivating trust and solidarity among soldiers who previously did not know one another. I am not discussing rape, and most members of shabbiha formations know each other well; but Cohen's attention to male camaraderie gets at the solidarity central to what I think needs to be understood as libidinal energy. See Rosalind Morris on war's general "libidinization." Her own analysis is of American soldiers at Abu Ghraib in "The War Drive: IMAGE FILES CORRUPTED," *Social Text* 25, no. 2 (Summer 2007): 103–42, https://doi.org/10.1215/01642472-2006-029.

20 For example, see "Suhayl al-Hasan to the Governor of Homs: You Have a Quarter of an Hour, If You Don't Appear Here Consider Yourself Wanted by All the Security Agencies," video, 1:37, YouTube, May 3, 2016, https://tinyurl.com/y768ruxp. Refer as well to the following Facebook page devoted to the Syrian Army: https://tinyurl.com/yddrwo9h, accessed December 3, 2018. Specifically on the Tiger, see https://tinyurl.com/yak2vqrj, accessed December 4, 2018. The following YouTube videos (in Arabic) are also on point: "The Journalist Shadi Hulwa and the Tiger's Poem," video, 1:58, YouTube, June 14, 2014, https://tinyurl.com/yd53vv7d; "Interview with Colonel Suhayl al-Hasan, Commander of the Military Operation in the Eastern Neighborhoods of Aleppo," video, 7:45, YouTube, December 25, 2016, https://tinyurl.com/y94pvvbo; Salim Darwish, "Song of Yellow Air, Dedicated to Colonel Suhayl al-Hasan, the Tiger," video, 8:06, YouTube, October 19, 2014, https://tinyurl.com/ycybl6z2; and Sulayman Nasra, "Colonel Suhayl al-Hasan." video, 2:17, YouTube, May 29, 2015, https://tinyurl.com/yaq787lo.

21 See for instance the following four videos (in Arabic) posted on Facebook: 0:55, December 15, 2016, https://tinyurl.com/y72990jy; 3:28, December 17, 2016, https://tinyurl.com/ya9qr59h; 0:37, December 27, 2016 (to the tune of "The Pink Panther Theme"), https://tinyurl.com/ybwdgsmd; 3:23, April 26, 2017, https://tinyurl.com/yb8l7rch.

22 The video containing this song, "Kalimat ra'is al-lajna al-amaniyya bi-Hamah lil-'aqid Suhayl al-Hassan ba'd tahrir madinat Murak bi-rif Hamah" (in Arabic), is available here: Qamhana News Network, video, 1:31, YouTube, October 25, 2014, https://www.youtube.com/watch?v=eQSm7OOo9pE.

23 On shabbiha tattoos, see (in Arabic) Hala Nasralla, "Sectarianism in Tattoos," Al-Hurra, October 6, 2017, https://www.alhurra.com/a/lebanon-sectarianism-tatto/395996.html.

24 Thanks are owed to Yuna Blajer de la Garza for this point.

25 Lauren Berlant, "Structures of Unfeeling: Mysterious Skin," *International Journal of Politics, Culture, and Society* 8, no. 3 (2015): 191–213. For an updated version, see her "Humorlessness (Three Monologues and a Hairpiece)," *Critical Inquiry* 43, no. 2 (2017): 305–40.

26 Raymond Williams, *Marxism and Literature*, 132.

27 Williams, 132.

28 Williams, 133.

29 Williams, 122.

30 Williams, 135 and 126.

31 Some scholars emphasize the importance of external forces such as "modernization," colonial occupation, and/or foreign intervention in the creation of sectarian solidarities and difference. But as Max Weiss helpfully puts it, "Sectarianism in the modern Middle East neither emerged out of whole cloth nor was it neatly imposed from without. Sectarianism, like other sociological categories and markers of affiliation, has depended and continues to depend upon routinized forms of cultural and social practice." This calls for analysis of its evolution and diffusion by going into the "nooks and crannies of everyday life," such as we see here with the creation and circulation of rumors. Max D. Weiss, *In the Shadow of Sectarianism: Law, Shi'ism, and the Making of Modern Lebanon* (Cambridge, MA: Harvard University Press, 2010), 15.

32 Rogers Brubaker, *Ethnicity without Groups* (Cambridge, MA: Harvard University Press, 2004), 43; Rogers Brubaker and Frederick Cooper, "Beyond 'Identity,'" *Theory and Society* 29 (2000): 1–47; Elizabeth Povinelli, *The Cunning of Recognition: Indigenous Alterities and the Making of Australian Multiculturalism* (Durham, NC: Duke University Press, 2002); Virginia R. Dominguez, *White by Definition: Social Classification in Creole Louisiana* (New Brunswick, NJ: Rutgers University Press, 1997); and Timothy Mitchell, *Rule of Experts: Egypt, Techno-Politics, Modernity* (Berkeley: University of California Press, 2002). In *Peripheral Visions: Publics, Power, and Performance in Yemen* (Chicago: University of Chicago Press, 2008), I drew on this scholarship to emphasize how organizations, dramatic events, and regime strategies conditioned, and at times were even crucial, in "making" people and groups (in Ian Hacking's phrase). Scholars of Islamic jurisprudence, such as the anthropologist Brinkley Messick, have also underscored the importance of conceiving categories like the ones related to sect as "relational in nature," existing in interpretive worlds constituted by other interpretive worlds. As a result, as the historian Ussama Makdisi shows in the context of Lebanon's confessional system, "sectarianisms" are also "multiple," with overlapping significations and manifestations. Ussama Makdisi, *The Culture of Sectarianism: Community, History, and Violence in Nineteenth-Century Ottoman Lebanon* (Berkeley: University of California Press, 2000). Makdisi demonstrates how Maronite and Druze affiliations were produced in nineteenth-century Ottoman Mount Lebanon in the context of Ottoman reforms and European interventions, which together undermined local status distinctions and revamped the relationship between local religious allegiances and an emergent

"modernity" (Makdisi, 6). See also Weiss's discussion (*In the Shadow of Sectarianism*, 16).

33 Brubaker, *Ethnicity without Groups*, 16.

34 Williams, 129.

35 For an overview of the rise of 'Alawis in Syria's public and military sectors during the French mandate, see Hanna Batatu, *Syria's Peasantry, the Descendants of Its Lesser Rural Notables, and Their Politics* (Princeton, NJ: Princeton University Press, 1999), 155–58; Patrick Seale, *Asad: The Struggle for the Middle East* (Berkeley: University of California Press, 1989), 14–23; Nikolaos Van Dam, *The Struggle for Power in Syria: Politics and Society under Asad and the Baʻth Party* (London: I. B. Tauris, [1979] 2011), 26–27; Nazih N. Ayubi, *Over-Stating the Arab State: Politics and Society in the Middle East* (London: I. B. Tauris, 1995), 90–91; Ayse Tekdal Fildis, "Roots of Alawite-Sunni Rivalry in Syria," *Middle East Policy* 19, no. 2 (Summer 2012), https://tinyurl.com/ybjz94z4; and Ayse Tekdal Fildis, "The Troubles in Syria: Spawned by French Divide and Rule," *Middle East Policy* 18, no. 4 (Winter 2011), https://www.mepc.org/troubles-syria-spawned-french-divide-and-rule. See also Chris Zambelis, who rightly notes that the regime still enjoys support from important sectors of the Sunni population, and that 'Alawis are not as privileged as they are sometimes made out to be: "Syria's Sunnis and the Regime's Resilience," *Politikan*, June 17, 2015, https://tinyurl.com/y7hyvodm.

36 Charles Lister and Dominic Nelson, "All the President's Militias: Assad's Militiafication of Syria," Middle East Institute, December 14, 2017, https://tinyurl.com/ya79ol93.

37 Muhammad al-ʻAttar's interview with Fawwaz Traboulsi, February 20, 2013. The English version of the interview is available at Heinrich-Böll-Stiftung Middle East, Fawwaz Traboulsi interview by Muhammad al-ʻAttar in "Syrian Revolutionaries Owe Nobody an Apology," *Conflict and International Politics*, posted on March 3, 2014, https://tinyurl.com/yd3kw9m4. The original Arabic version is available here: https://www.bidayatmag.com/node/349, accessed December 16, 2018.

38 See Vicente L. Rafael, "Anticipating Nationhood," *Diaspora: A Journal of Transnational Studies* 1, no. 1 (1991): 67–82; and Lauren H. Derby, *The Dictator's Seduction: Politics and the Popular Imagination in the Era of Trujillo* (Durham, NC: Duke University Press, 2009), 141.

39 Compare these two videos: one is from YouthFreeSyria (via Islam4TV), "Demonstrations against Bashar al-Asad and His Criminals," video, 6:02, YouTube, February 21, 2011, https://tinyurl.com/y7td7yc2; the other is from, *Razan's Closet*, the blog of a well-known Syrian feminist activist: video, 4:55, February 17, 2011, https://tinyurl.com/y82xtf3e.

40 Thanks are owed to Kevin Mazur and Yahya al-ʻAbdallah here for inviting me to clarify my position—and Dima's. For evidence of this sectarian language occurring in other regions of Syria as early as March 2011, see Mohammed Jamal Barout, *Al-ʻAqd al-akhir fi tarikh Suriya: Jadaliyyat al-Jumud wa al-Islah* (Beirut: al-Markaz al-ʻArabi lil-Abhath wa Dirasat al-Siyasat, 2012); Bishara, *Suriya* (2013).

41 Thanks are owed to Tejas Parasher for urging me to discuss the post-9/11 regional situation and for his invocation of Hobbes.

42 See for example Robin Yassin-Kassab and Leila Al-Shami's *Burning Country: Syrians in Revolution and War* (New York: Pluto Press, 2016).

43 Fieldwork in Syria, March 2011.

44 Alia Malek, *The Home That Was Our Country: A Memoir of Syria* (New York: Nation Books, 2017), 231.

45 Salafis are those who claim to emulate the "pious predecessors," *al-salaf al-salih*, from the first three generations of Muslims. But here the term is used as a pejorative to indicate Muslim extremism without much attention to Sunni doctrinal differences.

46 Malek, *The Home That Was Our Country*, 229.

47 Malek, 330.

48 For example, James D. Fearon and David D. Laitin in their debate-inspiring account contend that "ethnic differences are too common to help distinguish the countries and years that see civil wars." James D. Fearon and David D. Laitin, "Ethnicity, Insurgency, and Civil War," *American Political Science Review* 97, no. 1 (2003): 75–90; quotation is from p. 81. Recent research has challenged this analysis by looking at the robust relationship between civil war onset and the exclusion of ethnic groups from access to power. See for example Andreas Wimmer, Lars-Erik Cederman, and Brian Min, "Ethnic Politics and Armed Conflict: A Configurational Analysis of a New Global Data Set," *American Sociological Review* 74 no. 2 (2009): 316–37; Lars-Erik Cederman, Kristian Skrede Gleditsch, and Halvard Buhaug, *Inequality, Grievances, and Civil War* (New York: Cambridge University Press, 2013); and Philip Roessler, *Ethnic Politics and State Power in Africa: The Logic of the Coup–Civil War Trap* (Cambridge: Cambridge University Press, 2016). These latter authors, despite their lip service to social constructivism, end up writing in ways that reproduce a cultural essentialism they purport to disavow. For a discussion of this literature and its relation to the Syrian case, see Kevin Mazur, "Social Categories, Patronage, and the State: Variation in the Syria Uprising" (unpublished manuscript in preparation, May 21, 2018).

CONCLUSION

1 Fredric Jameson, "Reification and Utopia in Mass Culture," *Social Text* 1 (Winter 1979): 144.

APPENDIX

Sofia Fenner is assistant professor of political science at Bryn Mawr College.

1 The Violations Documentation Center and other opposition-linked organizations monitoring deaths in the conflict claim to be counting civilian deaths. Some of these civilians may have been armed, even during the early months of the conflict. Certain border areas, such as Zabadani, have had armed opposition since nearly the beginning of the uprising; in many other areas, debates about arming in the face of regime violence were raging as early as late spring 2011. Since we aim to use deaths as a proxy for anti-regime mobilization, we are not particularly concerned with the civilian-combatant distinction here.

2 Kevin Mazur, "Social Categories, Patronage, and the State: Variation in the Syria Uprising" (unpublished manuscript in preparation, May 21, 2018).

3 This is not to say that peaceful protests entirely ceased; activists in many areas of the country have continued to hold demonstrations and other symbolic actions

throughout the conflict. Our suggestion is simply that state repression of these actions is, as the conflict wears on, increasingly unlikely to account for a large proportion of deaths.

4   The VDC database is available at http://www.vdc-sy.net, accessed December 12, 2018.

5   Megan Price, Jeff Klingner, and Patrick Ball, "Preliminary Statistical Analysis of Documentation of Killings in the Syrian Arab Republic" (Benetech Human Rights Program, commissioned by the United Nations Office of the High Commissioner for Human Rights, 2013).

6   As Price, Klingner, and Ball note, a relatively high proportion of the deaths recorded by SM are unidentified—that is, they do not include a full name for the deceased person (7). For the purposes of comparison with VDC totals, we removed all unidentified records from the SM counts.

7   Price, Klingner, and Ball, 6.

Bibliography

PRIMARY SOURCES

Primary sources include newspaper and magazine articles, opinion pieces, videos, data, and official statements, as well as TV series and films. When available, a link to each item has been provided. Additionally, many of these materials have been uploaded to the Qualitative Data Repository, where they can be accessed: https://doi.org/10.5064/F63776W4.

JOURNALISTIC ARTICLES AND REPORTS

In English

Abdullah, Ammar. "Chemical Incident in Khan Shaykhun Deliberately Staged by Militants, Syrian Probe Finds." *RT*, August 17, 2017. https://tinyurl.com/y7rlby93.

Abu Hajar, Mohammed. "Our Sectarianism: Not Just the Regime's Creation." Syria Untold, June 14, 2018. http://syriauntold.com/2018/06/our-sectarian-ism-not-just-the-regimes-creation/.

Associated Press. "Syrian War Takes Center Stage on Ramadan TV Series." *Arab News*, July 30, 2013. http://www.arabnews.com/news/459811.

Bal, Elleke. "A Man with Balls." *Intelligent Optimist*, January–February 2014. https://tinyurl.com/yabcnmt8.

Broad, William. "Rockets in Syrian Attack Carried Large Payload of Gas, Experts Say." *New York Times*, September 4, 2013. https://tinyurl.com/lfnjcuw.

Brown Moses Blog. "Statement by Dale Gavlak on the Mint Press Article 'Syrians in Ghouta Claim Saudi-Supplied Rebels behind Chemical Attack.'" September 20, 2013. https://tinyurl.com/y87dhbym.

Brown Moses Blog. "Who Was Responsible for the August 21st Attack?" September 16, 2013. https://tinyurl.com/ybbarngd.

Buck, Joan. "Asma' al-Assad: A Rose in the Desert." *Gawker,* June 9, 2013. http://gawker.com/asma-al-assad-a-rose-in-the-desert-1265002284.

Chivers, C. J. "New Study Refines View of Sarin Attack in Syria." *New York Times,* December 28, 2013. https://tinyurl.com/noh3fm9.

Chulov, Martin, and Kareem Shaheen. "Syria Chemical Weapons Attack Toll Rises to 70 as Russian Narrative Is Dismissed." *Guardian,* US edition, April 5, 2017. https://tinyurl.com/m9lh8q8.

Elali, Nadine. "The Syrian Revolution in Sketches." *Now Lebanon,* July 19, 2011. https://tinyurl.com/y8dxdswh.

Gavlak, Dale, and Yahya Ababneh. "Syrians in Ghouta Claim Saudi-Supplied Rebels behind Chemical Attack." MPN News, August 29, 2013. https://tinyurl.com/nbrykrr.

Ghoshroy, Subrata. "Serious Questions about the Integrity of the UN Report." *21st Century Wire,* September 26, 2013. https://tinyurl.com/l835ygp.

Happynings (monthly magazine). January 2011. mediaMe.com/country/Syria.happynings. The site is defunct as of December 1, 2018.

Harkin, James. "The Incredible Story behind the Syrian Protest Singer Everyone Thought Was Dead." *GQ,* December 7, 2016. https://tinyurl.com/ycyer6f4.

Higgins, Eliot. "Summary of Claims surrounding the Khan Sheikhoun Chemical Attack." *Bellｿngcat,* July 4, 2017. https://tinyurl.com/y94gadfc.

Higgins, Eliot. "Will Get Fooled Again—Seymour Hersh, Welt, and the Khan Sheikhoun Chemical Attack." *Bellｿngcat,* June 25, 2017. https://tinyurl.com/ybaxukm2.

Hourani, Noura, and Avery Edelman. "After the Idlib City Council Refuses to Hand Over Administrative Control, HTS Takes It by Force." *Syria Direct,* August 29, 2017. https://tinyurl.com/y7rld8ud.

Human Rights Watch. "Attacks on Ghouta: Analysis of the Alleged Use of Chemical Weapons in Syria." September 10, 2013. https://www.hrw.org/report/2013/09/10/attacks-ghouta/analysis-alleged-use-chemical-weapons-syria#.

IRIN Middle East. "Syria: Act Now to Stop Desertification, says FAO." ReliefWeb, June 15, 2010. https://tinyurl.com/ycewjcz8.

Joscelyn, Thomas. "Al Nusrah Front Leader Preaches Jihadist Unity in Idlib." *FDD's Long War Journal,* April 2, 2015. https://tinyurl.com/yddgmtfb.

Kennedy, Pagan. "How to Destroy the Business Model of Breitbart and Fake News." *New York Times,* January 7, 2017. https://tinyurl.com/yc2sm9qc.

Kerry, John. "Remarks on Syria." Press Briefing Room, Washington, DC, August 26, 2013. US Department of State archive, https://tinyurl.com/y8pp9rcd.

MacFarquhar, Neil. "A Powerful Russian Weapon: The Spread of False Stories." *New York Times,* August 28, 2016. https://tinyurl.com/y7smamnv.

MacKey, Robert. "Reporter Denies Writing Article That Linked Syrian Rebels to Chemical Attack." *New York Times*, September 21, 2013. https://tinyurl.com/y8h7fg3d.

Ostrovsky, Arkady. "For Putin, Disinformation Is Power." Op-ed, *New York Times*, August 5, 2016. https://tinyurl.com/y75kc7cg.

Parry, Robert. "Evidence That Syria's Chemical Attacks Were Staged by Jihadists." Global Research, September 9, 2016. https://tinyurl.com/y9vc39kr.

Pizzi, Michael. "The Syrian Opposition Is Disappearing from Facebook." *Atlantic*, February 4, 2014. https://tinyurl.com/y8ekoc9x.

Putin, Vladimir V. "A Plea for Caution from Russia." *New York Times*, September 11, 2013. https://tinyurl.com/or5vtco.

Reuters. "Russia Says Syria Gas Incident Caused by Rebels' Own Chemical Arsenal." April 5, 2017. https://tinyurl.com/yb3kcppf.

Ryan, Danielle. "Why Is US Media Ignoring All Dissenting Expert Voices on the Khan Sheikhoun Attack?" *RT*, April 20, 2017. https://tinyurl.com/y9gp3hre.

Ryssdal, Kai, and Maria Hollenhorst. "Why Ramadan Is a Big Deal for Arab TV Networks." *Marketplace*, May 26, 2017. https://tinyurl.com/yadtv2uw.

Sands, Phil. "Syrian Chemical Attack Spurs Finger-Pointing inside Assad Regime." *The National*, August 26, 2013. https://tinyurl.com/y7zwabo9.

Shaaban, Bouthaina. "Shape of the Things to Come." *Forward Magazine*, March 2011, 64. https://issuu.com/haykalmedia/docs/forwardsyria0311.

Shachtman, Noah. "Exclusive: Intercepted Calls Prove Syrian Army Used Nerve Gas, U.S. Spies Say." *Foreign Policy*, August 17, 2013. https://tinyurl.com/q9otn9g.

Shadid, Anthony. "Rejecting Offer of Dialogue by Syrian President, Protesters Return to the Streets." *New York Times*, June 24, 2011. https://tinyurl.com/yce378zh.

Shadid, Anthony. "Syrian Elite to Fight Protests to 'the End.'" *New York Times*, May 10, 2011. https://tinyurl.com/y95oyb9k.

Solvang, Ole. "Russia's Claim on Alleged Chemical Attack in Syria." Human Rights Watch, April 6, 2017. https://tinyurl.com/yb6mkmge.

Sowers, Jeannie, and John Waterbury. "Did Drought Trigger the Crisis in Syria?" Footnote, September 12, 2013. https://tinyurl.com/ycfqzfyo.

Tabler, Andrew. "Squaring the Circle?" *Syria Today*, June 6, 2006. https://tinyurl.com/yapv6luk.

The Truth about Syria (blog). "The Truth about Ibrahim Qashoush, the Alleged Singer and Composer of the So-Called 'Syrian Revolution.'" February 18, 2012. https://tinyurl.com/y7c6rbsw.

The Truth about Syria (blog). "Western and Arabic Media Honor the Rapists and Ignore the Real Innocent Victims." January 23, 2012. https://tinyurl.com/yb55r8wn.

United Nations. "United Nations Mission to Investigate Allegations of the Use of Chemical Weapons in the Syrian Arab Republic." December 2013. https://tinyurl.com/pkzrbey.

Whitaker, Brian. "Yahya Ababneh Exposed." *Al-bab*, September 22, 2013. http://
al-bab.com/blog/2013/09/yahya-ababneh-exposed.

In Arabic (Titles Given in English)

Abbas, Hassan. "The Slogans That Syrians Should Overcome." Raseef22, March
17, 2015. https://tinyurl.com/y8ka9mug.
Ad-Diyar. "Three Years after the Chemical Attack on al-Ghouta: The Secrets of
the Massacre." August 23, 2016. https://tinyurl.com/y7qrxnaz.
'Ali, 'Adnan. "Chemical Attack: From Denial to Fabrication." Al-Araby, August 21,
2016. https://tinyurl.com/y7mexgyj.
Al-Jazeera. "Al-Jazeera Documents Reveal Plans to Divide Damascus." March 18,
2012. https://tinyurl.com/ybbjou79.
Al-Jazeera. "Ghouta: The Planned Attack." August 23, 2014. https://tinyurl.com
/y9sho8z7.
Al-Jazeera. "YouTube Shuts Down Pro-Syrian Government Channels." Septem-
ber 10, 2018. https://tinyurl.com/ycb45wte.
Almersad. "Al-Ghouta Chemical Weapons: How Three Armed Factions Came
into Possession of Chemical Weapons." October 31, 2013. https://tinyurl
.com/y9p75emt.
Arab 48. "The Chemical [Attack] of al-Asad: The Third Anniversary of the
Ghouta Massacre." August 21, 2016. https://tinyurl.com/grh88wv.
Arabic RT. "CIA Director: We've Gathered Compelling Evidence on Khan
Shaykhun in One Day!" July 12, 2017. https://tinyurl.com/ybbrrfrp.
Arabic RT. "A Former US Intelligence Officer Determines Who Is Responsible
for the Khan Shaykhun Chemical Attack." April 20, 2017. https://tinyurl.com
/y9c3y8yd.
Arab Orient Center. "Reactions to al-Asad's Gang Bombing of Aleppo with
Chemical Weapons." March 20, 2013. http://www.asharqalarabi.org.uk/barq
/b-qiraat-1376.htm.
Breaking News. "Analysts of the CIA: The Ghouta Chemical Attack Was Carried
Out by the Opposition by Order of Saudi Arabia." Breaking News, September
10, 2013. http://breakingnews.sy/ar/article/25147.html.
Center for Documentation of Violations in Syria. *A Special Report on the Use
of Chemical Weapons in the Province of Rural Damascus, Eastern Ghouta.*
August 22, 2013. https://tinyurl.com/y9nmmz98.
Dayub, 'Ammar. "The Syrian Revolution: The Uprising of Bread and Freedom."
Al-Akhbar, August 18, 2011. https://www.al-akhbar.com/Opinion/93204.
Dibo, Muhammad. "Reconstruction: Between Neoliberal Institutions and Despo-
tism." Syria Untold, February 1, 2015. https://tinyurl.com/ydhlgnqr.
Enab Baladi. "The First Appearance of the Child 'Umran Daqnaysh on Syrian
Regime Media Outlets." June 5, 2017. https://www.enabbaladi.net/archives
/154229.
Enab Baladi. "The United Nations Confirms That the Regime Is Responsible for

the Massacre at Khan Khaykhun." September 6, 2017. https://www.enabbaladi
.net/archives/171441.

France 24. "Bashar al-Asad: The Khan Shaykhun Chemical Attack Was Fabricated
100 Percent." April 13, 2017. https://tinyurl.com/ybcd297p.

Hajj Salih, Yasin al-. "The Day Clothed in Shame: Its Sponsors and Its World." *Al-
Jumhuriya*, August 21, 2016. http://aljumhuriya.net/35465.

Hajj Salih, Yasin al-. "On Thugs and Thuggery and Their Two States." *Kalamon*
(Winter 2012). http://www.kalamonreview.org/articles-details-122
#axzz5YOTQsWao. Accessed December 2, 2018.

Hajj Salih, Yasin al-. "Staring at the Face of the Horror." *Al-Jumhuriya*, May 29,
2015. http://aljumhuriya.net/33487.

Hannawi, Yasmin. "We Are Its Heroes and the Events Are Our Story (*We Will
Return Shortly*): The Television Series of One Hundred Years." Al-Jaras, October 7, 2013. https://tinyurl.com/y8hlv3vw.

Hashim, Salah. "*Silvered Water*: The Fish Is Demonstrating Underwater and
Demanding the Toppling of the Regime." Elwatan News, May 21, 2014.
https://tinyurl.com/y7gdoqav.

Heinrich-Böll-Stiftung Middle East. Fawwaz Traboulsi interview by Muhammad al-'Attar in "Syrian Revolutionaries Owe Nobody an Apology." *Conflict
and International Politics*, February 20, 2013. https://tinyurl.com/yd3kw9m4
(English version, posted March 3, 2014). Original Arabic version available at
https://www.bidayatmag.com/node/349, accessed December 16, 2018.

Huna Sawtak. "Syria: Ibrahim Qashush, the Real Singer Is Still Alive." October
2013. https://tinyurl.com/y9efxsyc.

'Isa, Rashid. "Did *Silvered Water* Reach the Cannes Festival with the Power of
Cinema or the Power of Politics? How the Story of Wiam Bedirxan Was
Confiscated." *Al-Quds Al-Arabi*, September 29, 2014. https://tinyurl.com
/y9ecd26n.

Mari, 'Aisha al-. "The Gray Person!" *Al-Ittihad*, October 18, 2010. http://www
.alittihad.ae/wajhatdetails.php?id=55395.

Najjar, Muhammad al-. "The Syrian Crisis Is Present in Drama during Ramadan."
Al-Jazeera, July 14, 2013. https://tinyurl.com/yazsrr2v.

Nasrallah, Hala. "Sectarianism in Tattoos." Al-Hurra, October 6, 2017. https://
www.alhurra.com/a/lebanon-sectarianism-tatto/395996.html.

Nazemroaya, Mahdi Darius. "Is Prince Bandar behind the Chemical Attacks in
Syria?" Global Research, September 17, 2013. https://tinyurl.com/y7qfa35d.

Orient News. "Fabrications of Syrian Television: From 'Hamza' the Rapist to
'Sha'ban' the Murderer." October 12, 2013. https://tinyurl.com/yampsdjq.

Rahuni, Randa al-. "*Silvered Water*: The Creative Documentation of the
Ugliness of the Syrian Revolution; The Film of Usama Muhammad and
Simav Bedirxan." *Arab Cinema Magazine* 2 (Spring 2015). https://tinyurl
.com/y97wsuzj.

Raybir, Yusuf. "The Film *Silvered Water*: The Poeticizing of Death." *Maaber*, n.d.
https://tinyurl.com/y9f42azl. Accessed December 1, 2018.

Reuter, Christopher. "Asad's Cold Calculations: The Poisonous Gas War on Syrians." *Al-Jumhuriya*, August 31, 2013. https://www.aljumhuriya.net/16517.

Safahat Suriya. "The Syrian Critic 'Ali Safar: Syrian Drama Suffers like Everything Else in Syria." August 11, 2013. https://tinyurl.com/y7dja8ca.

Saliha, Samir. "Who Provided Hersh with the Information?" Al-Arabiya, April 16, 2014. https://tinyurl.com/ybaff92h.

Sky News. "Syria: US 'Using Lies to Justify Strikes.'" September 4, 2013. https://tinyurl.com/y8w4cc6h.

Step News Agency. "Hundreds of Victims without Blood in a Chemical Bombing on Khan Shaykhun." April 4, 2017. https://tinyurl.com/yce4wxzv.

Syrian Arab News Agency. "The Graduation of 33 Students from the Academic Programs Sponsored by the Organization of Excellence and Creativity." September 8, 2016. https://www.sana.sy/?p=427957.

Syrian Observatory for Human Rights. "The Office for Documenting the Syrian Chemical Attack: The Regime Has Not Handed Over Any Shipments in a Month." April 3, 2014. https://tinyurl.com/yddl2x8m.

Syrian Observatory for Human Rights. "The Results of the Search for the Chemical Massacre." August 17, 2015. https://tinyurl.com/ycanjc9q.

Syrian Observatory for Human Rights. "The Russian Campaign in the Security Council to Change the Story of the Chemical [Attack]." December 17, 2013. https://tinyurl.com/y7wjuf26.

Syrian Press Center. "What Is the Degree of Truth about the Nightingale of the Syrian Revolution Being Alive." December 29, 2016. https://tinyurl.com/y889bbu2.

Tumaer. "The Regime Forces Began a Large-Scale Military Offensive at Dawn." August 21, 2013. http://www.tumaer.com/vb/archive/index.php/t-114514.html. (Tumaer appears to be a site that compiles various news sources.)

TV SERIES, COMEDY SKITS, FILMS, SONGS

Abounaddara. *Aïcha* ['A'isha]. Video, 3:29. Vimeo, 2014. https://vimeo.com/107948804.

Abounaddara. *In the Name of the Father* [Bi-ism al-ab]. Video, 2:13. Vimeo, May 24, 2013. https://vimeo.com/66891077.

Abounaddara. *The Trajectory of an Unknown Soldier* [Masirat al-jundi al-majhul]. Video, 1:56. Vimeo, November 23, 2012. https://vimeo.com/54135942.

Barish, Sumar, director. *Little Poke* [Nakzeh]: episode "Gray People" [Al-Ramadiyyin]. Video, 6:24. Lamba Production/YouTube, September 4, 2016. https://youtu.be/BAbfMSPoDN4.

Darwish, Salim. "Song of Yellow Air, Dedicated to Colonel Suhayl al-Hasan, the Tiger." Video, 8:06. YouTube, October 19, 2014. https://tinyurl.com/ycybl6z2.

Dik, Husayn al-. "Waiting for the Schoolgirl" [Natir Bint al-Madarseh]. Video, 5:25. YouTube, September 26, 3013. https://youtu.be/bAwxiji-PHI.

Enab Baladi. *Min Fawq al-Asatih* [Over the Roofs]. Video, 4:44. YouTube, March 20, 2017. https://youtu.be/6bLVQjmKgYI.

Hajju, Allayth, director
  A Forgotten Village [*Day'a daay'a*]. Sama Art International, 2008, 2010.
    Episode "In the Pitch-Dark of Night, the Full Moon Is Missed" [Fi laylat al-zalma', yuftaqad al-badr]. Sama Art International, 2010.
    Episode "The Night of the Arrest" [Laylat al-qabd]. Sama Art International, 2008.
    Episode "Sucking Up" [Tamalluq]. Sama Art International, 2010.
  Hope—There Isn't Any [*Amal—ma fi*]. Sama Art International, 2004.
    Episode "Ali Baba and the 400 Thieves" ['Ali Baba wa al-arba' mit harami]
    Episode "The Democratic Imperative" [Dimuqratiyya ilzamiyya]
    Episode "Malignancies" [Awram khabitha]
    Episode "Pulse of the Street" [Nabd al-Shari']
    Episode "Revolution" [Thawra]
  Ruins [*al-Khirba*]. Syrian Art Production International, Damascus, 2011.
  Spotlight [*Buq'a daw'*]. Syrian Art Production International, Damascus, 2001–.
  Waiting [*al-Intizar*]. Al-'Arabiyya, Damascus, 2006.
  We'll Return Shortly [*Sana'ud ba'd qalil*]. Clacket Media, Abu Dhabi and Damascus, 2013.
Jadaliyya. "The Strong Heroes of Moscow." Video, 3:25. YouTube, June 25, 2011. https://youtu.be/LThziRgKzTQ.
Kalthum, Ziad, director. *The Immortal Sergeant* [*Al-Raqib al-Khalid*]. Crystal Films, Beirut, 2014 (filmed 2012–13).
Masasit Mati. *Top Goon: Diaries of a Little Dictator* [*Al-Shabbih al-Awwal, Yawmiyyat Diktatur Saghir*]. Season 1, 2011.
    Episode "Beeshu's Nightmares" [Kawabis Bishu]. https://www.youtube.com/watch?v=W5RifYxWr-4.
    Episode "Beeshu's Reforms" [Islahat Bishu]. https://www.youtube.com/watch?v=Gn2MF-XLZ5A.
    Episode "Dracula" [Drakula]. https://www.youtube.com/watch?v=Ijdx JitecaI.
    Episode "Last Days in Hell" [al-Fasl al-akhir fi al-jahim]. https://www.youtube.com/watch?v=YGTOvUvmYAk.
    Episode "Prostitute Media" [al-I'lam al-'ahir]. https://www.youtube.com/watch?v=72qAlyeCzH8&t=90s.
    Episode "Who Wants to Kill a Million?" [Man sayaqtul al-milyun?]. https://www.youtube.com/watch?v=7AobG4vsszo.
Mohammed, Ossama, director
  Khutwa, Khutwa [*Step by Step*]. MA film project. National Superior Institute of Cinematography (VGIK), Moscow, 1979.
  Ma' al-Fidda [*Silvered Water, Syria Self-Portrait*]. Film. Les Films d'Ici, Paris, and Proaction Films, Damascus, 2014.
  Nujum al-Nahar [*Stars in Broad Daylight*]. Film. National Film Organization, Damascus, 1988.
  Sunduq al-Dunya [*Sacrifices* or, more aptly, *Camera Obscura*]. Film. AMIP,

Arte France Cinéma, Ministère de la Culture de la République Française, National Film Organization, Paris, 2002.

Nasra, Sulayman. "Colonel Suhayl al-Hasan." Video, 2:17. YouTube, May 29, 2015. https://tinyurl.com/yaq787lo.

Qamhana News Network. "Words of the Head of the Security Force in Hama to Colonel Suhayl al-Hasan after the Liberation of Murak in Hama's Environs." Video, 1:31. YouTube, October 25, 2014. https://www.youtube.com/watch?v=eQSm7OOo9pE.

Sharbaji, Rasha, director. *Birth from the Waist* [*Wilada min al-Khasira*]. Film, 2013.

Wahid, Khalid 'Abd al-, director
  Qanadil al-Bahr [*Jellyfish*]. Unreleased film, 2014–16.
  Shaqq fi Dhakira [*Slot in Memory*]. Video, 2:25. Vimeo, 2012. https://vimeo.com/61093429. Accessed December 15, 2018.
  Tuj [an onomatopoeia for the sound of something banging against a wall]. Video, 2:14. Vimeo, 2012. https://vimeo.com/61097242. Accessed December 15, 2018.

Wikisham. *Qasr al-Sha'b* [*The Presidential Palace*]. YouTube channel. https://www.youtube.com/user/wikisham. Accessed December 12, 2018.

With You collective. *Hurriyya wa Bas* [*Freedom and Nothing But*]; skit examples of *Hope—There Isn't Any*, remixed:
  http://podcastarabia.net/programmes/freedomwobas/5TCoJ-R56Ro [The Puppet Theater]. Video, 2:40. Podcast Arabia, June 22, 2011.
  https://www.youtube.com/watch?v=St5dzQTwRfU [Liar, Liar]. Video, 2:23. YouTube, August 30, 2011.
  https://www.youtube.com/watch?v=1coqjAzpEuo [The Resistance]. Video, 2:57. YouTube, August 30, 2011.

ONLINE VIDEOS (MOSTLY IN ARABIC)

'Abdallah, Yahya al-. "Water." Video, 18:55. YouTube, November 12, 2015. https://youtu.be/8d44OIiwoSE.

'Abdallah, Yahya al-. "We Don't Stay in Camps." Video, 26:33. 2014. http://www.educationalleaderswithoutborders.com/documentaries.html. Accessed December 4, 2018.

Al-Dik, Husayn. "Natir Bint al-Madarseh." Video, 5:25. YouTube, September 26, 2013. https://youtu.be/bAwxij1-PHI.

Al-Dunya television. "The Series of Syrian Traitors, Five Treacherous Artists." Video, 9:56. YouTube, May 22, 2011. https://tinyurl.com/y8wd5mhe.

Al-Jazeera Arabic. "Bashar al-Asad Meets with a Number of Artists from Syrian Drama." Video, 4:59. YouTube, May 16, 2011. https://youtu.be/Vd3WPzvuEWA.

Assi ('Asi) Press. "The Martyrdom of a Whole Family, Most of Whom Are Children in Khan Shaykhun, as a Result of the Regime's Aircraft Targeting with

Chemical Gases." Video, 0:51. YouTube, April 3, 2017. https://tinyurl.com
/y83s76wr.

Assi ('Asi) Press. "Scenes from the Chemical Massacre in the City of Khan
Shaykhun Caused by the Regime's Aircraft by Targeting the City with
Chemical Gases." Video, 0:40. YouTube, April 4, 2017. https://tinyurl.com/
y6wafjhc.

CNN Arabic. "For the Syrian Child 'Umran . . . under the Spotlight Again." Video,
2:58. September 6, 2017. https://tinyurl.com/ycvghwpa.

Enab Baladi. *Asma' al-Akhras without Bodyguards: A Documentary Film, Russian
Production.* Documentary on Asma' al-Asad produced by Russia-24, Moscow,
October 23, 2016. https://tinyurl.com/yap9lqvl. (No longer available as of
December 12, 2018.)

"Interview with Colonel Suhayl al-Hasan, Commander of the Military Operation
in the Eastern Neighborhoods of Aleppo." Video, 7:45. YouTube, December 25, 2016. https://tinyurl.com/y94pvvbo.

"The Journalist Shadi Hulwa and the Tiger's Poem." Video, 1:58. YouTube,
June 14, 2014. https://tinyurl.com/yd53vv7d.

JP News. "Asma' al-Asad: After the Graduation Ceremony of the Students of
the Academic Programs of the National Center for Distinguished Students."
Video, 7:25. September 7, 2016. https://jpnews-sy.com/ar/news.php?id
=109067.

National Center for Distinguished [Students]. Facebook page, created in 2009.
https://tinyurl.com/ybubpwcm.

"One of the Arms of Terrorism: The Terrorist Fadi Zurayq." Video, 19:45.
YouTube, October 9, 2011. https://tinyurl.com/ydap4xyq.

Opposition-oriented videos of the Tiger (all in Arabic), on Facebook:
Video, 0:55, December 15, 2016. https://tinyurl.com/y72990jy.
Video, 3:28, December 17, 2016. https://tinyurl.com/ya9qr59h.
Video, 0:37, December 27, 2016. https://tinyurl.com/ybwdgsmd.
Video, 3:23, April 26, 2017. https://tinyurl.com/yb8l7rch.

Presidency Syria. "President Asad Interview with the French Press." Video,
23:38. YouTube, April 13, 2017. https://www.youtube.com/watch?v
=Bnpy7mrGMSo. (The account was terminated in September 2018.)

Qasim, Faisal al-. Video, 1:26. Facebook, October 21, 2016. https://tinyurl.com
/yb3u5scm.

"The Slogans of the Syrian Revolution." Video, 2:39. YouTube, March 18, 2015.
https://www.youtube.com/watch?v=Imf-n8ZrQeY.

"Suhayl al-Hasan to the Governor of Homs: You Have a Quarter of an Hour, If
You Don't Appear Here Consider Yourself Wanted by All the Security Agencies." Video, 1:37. YouTube, May 3, 2016. https://tinyurl.com/y768ruxp.

Super Storm Wave. "President Assad's Interview with Swiss TV." Video, 20:54.
YouTube, October 19, 2016. https://tinyurl.com/yag5mxw6.

Thishreen. "Asma' Assad Interview with Russia Channel 24." Video, 33:20.
YouTube, October 18, 2016. https://tinyurl.com/y9m3yxg8.

"The Truth about Ibrahim Qashoush (Qashush)." Video, 1:24. YouTube, February 8, 2012. https://www.youtube.com/watch?v=M4roioLitdA.

YouthFreeSyria (from Islam4TV). "Demonstrations against Bashar al-Asad and His Criminals." Video, 6:02. YouTube, February 21, 2011. https://tinyurl.com/y7td7yc2. Compare the video posted on *Razan's Closet*, the Tumblr blog by a well-known Syrian feminist activist: 4:55, February 17, 2011, https://tinyurl.com/y82xtf3e.

We Are All Germs [Kulluna Jarathim]. Facebook page. https://www.facebook.com/syria.germs?sk=wall, accessed December 2, 2018.

DATA

Central Bureau of Statistics of the Syrian Arab Republic. http://www.cbssyr.sy/index-EN.htm. Accessed December 2, 2018.

Khaddour, Kheder, and Kevin Mazur. Syria Town Database. https://dataverse.harvard.edu/dataset.xhtml?persistentId=doi:10.7910/DVN/YQQo7L. Accessed December 18, 2018.

Qualitative Data Repository. https://doi.org/10.5064/F63776W4. Additional data, in the form of video clips captioned in English from *A Forgotten Village* and *Hope—There Isn't Any*, the aggregated data on economic conditions (2005–10) and conflict deaths (2011–12) by province collected by Sofia Fenner to construct the graphs in the appendix, and a list of archived links from this book, are available from the Qualitative Data Repository.

Syrian Martyrs Group. http://syrianshuhada.com/?a=st&st=20. Accessed December 4, 2018.

Syrian Press Center. Data on the Students Graduating from National Center for Distinguished Students. https://syrianpc.com/archives/146360. Accessed December 4, 2018.

Trading Economics. "Syria GDP Annual Growth Rate, 1971–2018." http://www.tradingeconomics.com/syria/gdp-growth-annual. Accessed December 2, 2018.

Trading Economics. "Syria Inflation Rate." http://www.tradingeconomics.com/syria/inflation-cpi. Accessed December 2, 2018.

Violations Documentation Center. http://www.vdc-sy.info/index.php/en/martyrs, accessed December 4, 2018; http://www.vdc-sy.net, accessed December 12, 2018.

SECONDARY SOURCES

Abdo, Elie. "The Impact of the Arts on the Syrian Revolution." Heinrich-Böll-Stiftung Middle East, February 28, 2013. https://tinyurl.com/y7n6ocrc.

Abouzeid, Rania. *No Turning Back: Life, Loss, and Hope in Wartime Syria*. New York: W. W. Norton, 2018.

Abu-Lughod, Lila. *Dramas of Nationhood: The Politics of Television in Egypt*. Chicago: University of Chicago Press, 2004.

Acemoglu, Daron, and James A. Robinson. *Economic Origins of Dictatorship and Democracy*. New York: Cambridge University Press, 2006.

Achcar, Gilbert. *The People Want: A Radical Exploration of the Arab Uprisings*. Berkeley: University of California Press, 2013.

Adorno, Theodor. "Commitment." Translated by Francis McDonagh. *New Left Review* 87 (September 1974): 75–89.

Albertus, Michael. *Autocracy and Redistribution: The Politics of Land Reform*. New York: Cambridge University Press, 2015.

Althusser, Louis. "Ideology and Ideological State Apparatuses (Notes towards an Investigation)." In *Lenin and Philosophy, and Other Essays*, translated by Ben Brewster, 127–86. New York: Monthly Review Press, 1971.

Althusser, Louis, Étienne Balibar, Roger Establet, et al. *Reading Capital: The Complete Edition*. Translated by Ben Brewster and David Fernbach. London: Verso, 2015.

Amar, Paul. *The Security Archipelago*. Durham, NC: Duke University Press, 2013.

Anker, Elisabeth R. *Orgies of Feeling: Melodrama and the Politics of Freedom*. Durham, NC: Duke University Press, 2014.

Arendt, Hannah. *Between Past and Future: Eight Exercises in Political Thought*. Translated by Jerome Kohn. New York: Penguin Classics, 2006.

Arendt, Hannah. *Eichmann in Jerusalem: A Report on the Banality of Evil*. New York: Penguin Books, [1963] 1977.

Arendt, Hannah. *The Human Condition*. Chicago: University of Chicago Press, 1958.

Arendt, Hannah. *Lectures on Kant's Political Philosophy*. Edited by Ronald Beiner. Chicago: University of Chicago Press, 1989.

Arendt, Hannah. "Truth and Politics." In *Between Past and Future: Eight Exercises in Political Thought*, 223–59. New York: Penguin, [1961] 2006. References are to the 2006 edition.

Asad, Talal. *Formations of the Secular: Christianity, Islam, Modernity*. Palo Alto, CA: Stanford University Press, 2003.

Ayubi, Nazih N. *Over-Stating the Arab State: Politics and Society in the Middle East*. London: I. B. Tauris, 1995.

Baczko, Adam, Gilles Dorronsoro, and Arthur Quesnay. *Syrie: Anatomie d'une guerre civile*. Paris: CNRS Éditions, 2016.

Bakhtin, Mikhail. *Rabelais and His World*. Translated by Helene Iswolsky. Bloomington: Indiana University Press, [1965] 1984.

Balibar, Étienne. "The Nation Form: History and Ideology." Translated by Chris Turner. In *Race, Nation, Class: Ambiguous Identities*, edited by Étienne Balibar and Immanuel Wallerstein, 86–106. New York: Verso, 1990.

Bargu, Banu. "In the Theater of Politics: Althusser's Aleatory Materialism and Aesthetics." *Diacritics* 40, no. 3 (2012): 86–113.

Barnes, Jessica. "Managing the Waters of Ba'th Country: The Politics of Water Scarcity in Syria." *Geopolitics* 17 (2009): 510–30.

Barout, Mohammed Jamal. *Al-'Aqd al-akhir fi tarikh Suriya: Jadaliyyat al-Jumud wa al-Islah* [The Last Decade in Syria's History: Dialectic of Stagnation and Reform]. Beirut: al-Markaz al-'Arabi lil-Abhath wa Dirasat al-Siyasat, 2012.

Barout, Mohammed Jamal. *Al-Taqrir al-watani al-istishrafi al-asasi al-awwal li-mashru'a Suriya 2025: Al-mihwar al-sukkani wa al-majali* [The First National, Predictive, Basic Report on the Project of Syria 2025: The Axis of Population and Space]. Damascus: UNDP and the Syrian Arab Republic, 2007.

Barthes, Roland. "Saponides and Detergents." In *Mythologies*, translated by Annette Lavers and Richard Howard, 32–34. New York: Hill and Wang, 2013.

Batatu, Hanna. *Syria's Peasantry, the Descendants of Its Lesser Rural Notables, and Their Politics.* Princeton, NJ: Princeton University Press, 1999.

Bazin, André. *What Is Cinema?* Translated by Hugh Gray. Berkeley: University of California Press, 1967.

Bellin, Eva R. "Reconsidering the Robustness of Authoritarianism in the Middle East: Lessons from the Arab Spring." *Comparative Politics* 44, no. 2 (2012): 127–49.

Bellin, Eva R. "The Robustness of Authoritarianism in the Middle East: Exceptionalism in Comparative Perspective." *Comparative Politics* 36, no. 2 (2004): 139–57.

Bergson, Henri. *Laughter: An Essay on the Meaning of the Comic.* Translated by Cloudesley Brereton and Fred Rothwell. Mineola, NY: Dover, 2005.

Berlant, Lauren. *The Anatomy of National Fantasy: Hawthorne, Utopia, and Everyday Life.* Chicago: University of Chicago Press, 1991.

Berlant, Lauren. *Cruel Optimism.* Durham, NC: Duke University Press, 2011.

Berlant, Lauren. *The Female Complaint: The Unfinished Business of Sentimentality.* Durham, NC: Duke University Press, 2008.

Berlant, Lauren. "Humorlessness (Three Monologues and a Hairpiece)." *Critical Inquiry* 43, no. 2 (2017): 305–40.

Berlant, Lauren. "Structures of Unfeeling: Mysterious Skin." *International Journal of Politics, Culture, and Society* 8, no. 3 (2015): 191–213.

Berlant, Lauren, and Sianne Ngai. "Comedy Has Issues." *Critical Inquiry* 43, no. 2 (Winter 2017): 233–49.

Biehl, João. *Vita: Life in a Zone of Social Abandonment.* Berkeley: University of California Press, 2005.

Bishara, 'Azmi. *Suriya: Darb al-alam nahwa al-hurriyya; Muhawala fi al-tarikh al-rahin* [The Road of Pain toward Freedom: An Effort (to Study) Present History]. Doha, Qatar: al-Markaz al-'Arabi lil-Abhath wa Dirasat al-Siyasat, 2013.

Blaydes, Lisa. *Elections and Distributive Politics in Mubarak's Egypt.* New York: Cambridge University Press, 2010.

Boltanski, Luc. *Distant Suffering: Morality, Media and Politics.* Translated by Graham D. Burchell. Cambridge: Cambridge University Press, 1999.

Bourdieu, Pierre. *Distinction: A Social Critique of the Judgement of Taste.* Translated by Richard Nice. Cambridge, MA: Harvard University Press, 1984.

Bourdieu, Pierre. *The Logic of Practice*. Translated by Richard Nice. Palo Alto, CA: Stanford University Press, 1990.

Bourdieu, Pierre. *Outline of a Theory of Practice*. Translated by Richard Nice. Cambridge: Cambridge University Press, 1977.

Brenner, Neil, Jamie Peck, and Nik Theodore. "After Neoliberalization?" *Globalizations* 27 (2010): 327–45.

Brooks, Peter. *The Melodramatic Imagination: Balzac, Henry James, Melodrama, and the Mode of Excess*. New Haven, CT: Yale University Press, [1976] 1995. References are to the 1995 edition.

Brown, Wendy. "American Nightmare: Neoliberalism, Neoconservatism and De-democratization." *Political Theory* 34, no. 6 (2006): 690–714.

Brown, Wendy. *Undoing the Demos: Neoliberalism's Stealth Revolution*. New York: Zone Books, 2015.

Brownlee, Jason. *Authoritarianism in an Age of Democratization*. New York: Cambridge University Press, 2007.

Brubaker, Rogers. *Ethnicity without Groups*. Cambridge, MA: Harvard University Press, 2004.

Brubaker, Rogers, and Frederick Cooper. "Beyond 'Identity.'" *Theory and Society* 29 (2000): 1–47.

Burawoy, Michael. *Manufacturing Consent: Changes in the Labor Process under Monopoly Capitalism*. Chicago: University of Chicago Press, 1979.

Butler, Judith. *The Psychic Life of Power: Theories in Subjection*. Palo Alto, CA: Stanford University Press, 1997.

Çalışkan, Koray, and Michel Callon. "Economization, Part 1: Shifting Attention from the Economy towards Processes of Economization." *Economy and Society* 38, no. 3 (2009): 369–98.

Carpio, Glenda. *Laughing Fit to Kill: Black Humor in the Fictions of Slavery*. New York: Oxford University Press, 2008.

Cawelti, John G. *Adventure, Mystery, and Romance: Formula Stories as Art and Popular Culture*. Chicago: University of Chicago Press, 1976.

Cederman, Lars-Erik, Kristian Skrede Gleditsch, and Halvard Buhaug. *Inequality, Grievances, and Civil War*. New York: Cambridge University Press, 2013.

Chalcraft, John. *Popular Politics in the Making of the Modern Middle East*. Cambridge: Cambridge University Press, 2016.

Chandler, James. *An Archaeology of Sympathy: The Sentimental Mode in Literature and Cinema*. Chicago: University of Chicago Press, 2013.

Cohen, Dara Kay. *Rape during Civil War*. Ithaca, NY: Cornell University Press, 2016.

Comaroff, Jean, and John L. Comaroff, eds. *Law and Disorder in the Postcolony*. Chicago: University of Chicago Press, 2006.

Comaroff, Jean, and John L. Comaroff. "Law and Disorder in the Postcolony: An Introduction." In *Law and Disorder in the Postcolony*, edited by Jean Comaroff and John L. Comaroff, 1–56. Chicago: University of Chicago Press, 2006.

Comaroff, Jean, and John Comaroff, eds. *Millennial Capitalism and the Culture of Neoliberalism*. Durham, NC: Duke University Press, 2001.

Comaroff, Jean, and John Comaroff. *Of Revelation and Revolution.* Vol. 1, *Christianity, Colonialism, and Consciousness in South Africa.* Chicago: University of Chicago Press, 1991.

Comaroff, John, and Jean Comaroff, eds. "Millennial Capitalism and the Culture of Neoliberalism." Special issue, *Public Culture* 12, no. 2 (2000).

cooke, miriam. *Dancing in Damascus: Creativity, Resilience, and the Syrian Revolution.* New York: Routledge, 2016.

Critchley, Simon. *On Humour (Thinking in Action).* New York: Routledge, 2002. Page 18 cited in Berlant and Ngai, "Comedy Has Issues."

Daher, Joseph. "Syria: The Social Origins of the Uprising." Rosa Luxemburg Stiftung, n.d. https://tinyurl.com/ybyjvdnh. Accessed December 2, 2018.

Dahi, Omar S. "The Political Economy of the Egyptian and Arab Revolt." *IDS Bulletin* 43, no. 1 (2012): 47–53.

Dahi, Omar S., and Yasser Munif. "Revolts in Syria: Tracking the Convergence between Authoritarianism and Neoliberalism." *Journal of African and Asian Studies* 47, no. 4 (2012): 323–32.

Dahi, Omar S., Jan Selby, et al. "Climate Change and the Syrian Civil War Revisited." *Political Geography* 60 (2017): 232–44.

Dawson, Michael C. "The Hollow Shell: Loïc Wacquant's Vision of State, Race and Economics." *Review of Racial and Ethnic Studies* 37, no. 10 (2014): 1767–75.

Dawson, Michael C. *Not in Our Lifetimes: The Future of Black Politics.* Chicago: University of Chicago Press, 2011.

Dawson, Michael C., and Megan Ming Francis. "Black Politics and the Neoliberal Racial Order." *Public Culture* 28, no. 1 (2016): 23–62.

Dean, Jodi. *Publicity's Secret: How Technoculture Capitalizes on Democracy.* Ithaca, NY: Cornell University Press, 2002.

Della Ratta, Donatella. "Creative Resistance Challenges Syria's Regime." Al-Jazeera, December 25, 2011. https://tinyurl.com/c8llnzy.

Della Ratta, Donatella. "Dramas of the Authoritarian State." *Middle East Report Online*, February 2012. https://www.merip.org/mero/interventions/dramas-authoritarian-state.

Della Ratta, Donatella. "Dramas of the Authoritarian State: The Politics of Syrian TV Serials in the Pan Arab Market." PhD diss., University of Copenhagen, April 2013.

Della Ratta, Donatella. "Irony, Satire, and Humor in the Battle for Syria." Muftah, February 13, 2012. https://tinyurl.com/y7pbotql.

Della Ratta, Donatella. "Making Real-Time Drama: The Political Economy of Cultural Production in Syria's Uprising." PARGC paper, Pennsylvania University, fall 2014. https://tinyurl.com/y7tnoqs6.

Della Ratta, Donatella. *Shooting a Revolution: Visual Media and Warfare in Syria.* London: Pluto Press, 2018.

Della Ratta, Donatella. "Syria: The Virtue of Civil Disobedience." Al-Jazeera, April 6, 2012. https://tinyurl.com/bpxh9ee.

Della Ratta, Donatella. "The 'Whisper Strategy': How Syrian Drama Makers Shape Television Fiction in the Context of Authoritarianism and Commodification." In *Syria from Reform to Revolt*. Vol. 2, *Culture, Society and Religion*, edited by Christa Salamandra and Leif Stenberg, 53–76. Syracuse, NY: Syracuse University Press, 2015.

Derby, Lauren H. *The Dictator's Seduction: Politics and the Popular Imagination in the Era of Trujillo*. Durham, NC: Duke University Press, 2009.

Dick, Marlin. "Syria under the Spotlight: Television Satire That Is Revolutionary in Form, Reformist in Content." *Arab and Media Society* (2007). https://tinyurl.com/yad6llcx.

Dolar, Mladen. "The Comic Mimesis." *Critical Inquiry* 43, no. 2 (Winter 2017): 570–89.

Dominguez, Virginia R. *White by Definition: Social Classification in Creole Louisiana*. New Brunswick, NJ: Rutgers University Press, 1997.

Doughan, Yazan. "Corruption, Authority, and the Discursive Production of Reform and Revolution in Jordan." PhD diss., University of Chicago, 2018.

Dundes, Alan. *Cracking Jokes: Studies of Sick Humor Cycles and Stereotypes*. Berkeley, CA: Ten Speed Press, 1987.

Eagleton, Terry. *Ideology: An Introduction*. London: Verso, [1991] 2007.

Eagleton, Terry. *The Meaning of Life*. Oxford: Oxford University Press, 2007.

Evans, Peter, and William H. Sewell, Jr. "Neoliberalism: Policy Regimes, International Regimes, and Social Effects." In *Social Resilience in the Neoliberal Era*, edited by Peter Hall and Michele Lamont, 35–68. New York: Cambridge University Press, 2013.

Fearon, James D., and David D. Laitin. "Ethnicity, Insurgency, and Civil War." *American Political Science Review* 97, no. 1 (2003): 75–90.

Femia, Francesco, and Caitlin Werrell. "Climate Change before and after the Arab Awakening: The Cases of Syria and Libya." In *The Arab Spring and Climate Change*, edited by Caitlyn E. Werrell and Francesco Femia, 23–32. Washington, DC: Center for American Progress, 2013.

Femia, Francesco, and Caitlin Werrell. "Syria: Climate Change, Drought, and Social Unrest." *Brief No. 11* (2012). https://tinyurl.com/yc4bl5jj, accessed December 1, 2018.

Fenner, Sofia A. "Life after Co-optation." PhD diss., University of Chicago, 2016.

Fildis, Ayse Tekdal. "Roots of Alawite-Sunni Rivalry in Syria." *Middle East Policy Council* 19, no. 2 (Summer 2012). https://tinyurl.com/ybjz94z4.

Fildis, Ayse Tekdal. "The Troubles in Syria: Spawned by French Divide and Rule." *Middle East Policy Council* 18, no. 4 (Winter 2011). https://www.mepc.org/troubles-syria-spawned-french-divide-and-rule.

Foucault, Michel. *The Birth of Biopolitics: Lectures at the Collège de France, 1978–79*. Translated by Graham Burchell and edited by François Ewald and Alessandro Fontana. New York: Picador, 2010.

Foucault, Michel. *On the Government of the Living: Lectures at the Collège de France*. Translated by Graham Burchell. New York: Palgrave MacMillan, 2014.

Foucault, Michel. "Truth and Juridical Forms." In *Power*, edited by James D. Faubion and translated by Robert Hurley et al., 1–89. New York: New Press, 2000.

Freud, Sigmund. *Collected Papers*. Translated by James Strachey. Vol. 4. New York: Hogarth Press, 1953.

Freud, Sigmund. "Family Romances." In *Standard Edition of the Complete Psychological Works of Sigmund Freud*, translated by James Strachey, 9:238–39. London: Hogarth Press, 1959.

Freud, Sigmund. *Totem and Taboo: Some Points of Agreement between the Mental Lives of Savages and Neurotics*. Edited and translated by James Strachey. New York: W. W. Norton, 1990.

Friedman, Thomas L. "The Other Arab Spring." *New York Times*, April 7, 2012. https://tinyurl.com/y8993x8a.

Gandhi, Jennifer. *Political Institutions under Dictatorship*. New York: Cambridge University Press, 2008.

Geddes, Barbara. "What Do We Know about Democratization after Twenty Years?" *Annual Review of Political Science* 2 (1999): 115–44.

Gehlbach, Scott, Konstantin Sonin, and Milan W. Svolik. "Formal Models of Authoritarian Politics." *Annual Review of Political Science* 19 (2016): 565–84.

Gilpin, Robert. *The Challenge of Global Capitalism: The World Economy in the 21st Century*. Princeton, NJ: Princeton University Press, 2000.

Girard, René. *The One by Whom Scandal Comes*. Translated by Malcom B. DeBevoise. Studies in Violence, Mimesis, and Culture. East Lansing: Michigan State University Press, 2014.

Girard, René. *Violence and the Sacred*. Translated by Patrick Gregory. Baltimore: Johns Hopkins University Press, 1979.

Goel, Rohit. "War and Peace in Lebanon." Talks given in Beirut and Mumbai. https://www.lebtivity.com/event/lebanon-as-object-cause-of-desire-a-public -talk-by-rohit-goel-in-conversation-with-walid-sadek; http://www.jp-india .org/uploads/newsletters/pdfs/41_pdf.pdf. Both accessed December 26, 2018.

Gramsci, Antonio. *Selections from the Prison Notebooks of Antonio Gramsci*. Edited and translated by Quintin Hoare and Geoffrey Nowell Smith. New York: International Publishers, 1971.

Greene, Kenneth F. *Why Dominant Parties Lose: Mexico's Democratization in Comparative Perspective*. New York: Cambridge University Press, 2007.

Gregg, Melissa, and Gregory Seigworth, eds. *The Affect Theory Reader*. Durham, NC: Duke University Press, 2010.

Gregg, Melissa, and Gregory Seigworth. "Introduction: An Inventory of Shimmers." In *The Affect Theory Reader*, edited by Gregg and Seigworth, 1–28. Durham, NC: Duke University Press, 2010.

Greitens, Sheena C. *Dictators and Their Secret Police: Coercive Institutions and State Violence*. Cambridge: Cambridge University Press, 2016.

Haddad, Bassam. *Business Networks in Syria: The Political Economy of Authoritarian Resilience*. Palo Alto, CA: Stanford University Press, 2012.

Haddad, Bassam. "The Formation and Development of Economic Networks in

Syria: Implications for Economic and Fiscal Reforms, 1986–2000." In *Networks of Privilege in the Middle East: The Politics of Economic Reform Revisited*, edited by Steven Heydemann, 37–76. London: Palgrave MacMillan, 2004.

Haggard, Stephan, and Marcus Noland. *Hard Target: Sanctions, Inducements, and the Case of North Korea*. Palo Alto, CA: Stanford University Press, 2017.

Haj Saleh, Yassin al-. *Impossible Revolution: Making Sense of the Syrian Tragedy*. Translated by Ibtihal Mahmood. London: Hurst Publishers, 2017.

Halasa, Malu, Zaher Omareen, and Nawara Mahfoud, eds. *Syria Speaks: Art and Culture from the Frontline*. London: Saqi Books, 2014.

Hanieh, Adam. *Lineages of Revolt: Issues of Contemporary Capitalism in the Middle East*. Chicago: Haymarket Books, 2013.

Hansen, Miriam Bratu. *Cinema and Experience: Sigfried Kracauer, Walter Benjamin, and Theodor W. Adorno*. Berkeley: University of California Press, 2012.

Harcourt, Bernard. *The Illusion of Free Markets: Punishment and the Myth of Natural Order*. Cambridge, MA: Harvard University Press, 2012.

Harper, David. "The Politics of Paranoia: Paranoid Positioning and Conspiratorial Narratives in the Surveillance Society." *Surveillance and Society* 5, no. 1 (2008): 1–32.

Harvey, David. *A Brief History of Neoliberalism*. Oxford: Oxford University Press, 2005.

Hersh, Seymour M. "The Red Line and the Rat Line." *London Review of Books* 36, no. 8 (April 17, 2014). https://tinyurl.com/kmelblf.

Hersh, Seymour M. "Whose Sarin?" *London Review of Books* 35, no. 24 (December 19, 2013). https://tinyurl.com/kkwkn3p.

Heydemann, Steven, ed. *Networks of Privilege in the Middle East*. New York: Palgrave MacMillan, 2004.

Heydemann, Steven. "The Political Logic of Economic Rationality: Selective Stabilization in Syria." In *The Politics of Economic Stabilization Programs in the Middle East*, edited by Henri J. Barkey, 11–39. New York: Saint Martin's Press, 1992.

Heydemann, Steven. "Taxation without Representation." In *Rules and Rights in the Middle East: Democracy, Law, and Society*, edited by Resat Kasaba et al., 96–97. Seattle: University of Washington Press, 1993.

Heydemann, Steven. *Upgrading Authoritarianism in the Arab World*. Washington, DC: Saban Center for Middle East Policy, Brookings Institution, 2007.

Hinnebusch, Raymond, ed. *Syria: From Authoritarian Upgrading to Revolution?* Syracuse, NY: Syracuse University Press, 2015.

Hobsbawm, Eric. *The Age of Extremes: A History of the World, 1914–1991*. New York: Vintage Books, 1994.

Hofstadter, Richard. "The Paranoid Style in American Politics." *Harper's Magazine*, November 1964, 77–86. https://tinyurl.com/y83yfzt5.

Humphreys, Laura-Zoe. "Symptomologies of the State: Cuba's 'Email War' and the Paranoid Public Sphere." In *Digital Cultures and the Politics of Emotion: Feelings, Affect, and Technological Change*, edited by Athina Karatzogianni and Adi Kuntsman, 197–213. Hampshire, UK: Palgrave MacMillan, 2012.

Hunt, Lynn. *The Family Romance in the French Revolution.* Berkeley: University of California Press, 1992.

Ismail, Salwa. *The Rule of Violence: Subjectivity, Memory and Government in Syria.* Cambridge: Cambridge University Press, 2018.

Jacobs, Lea. "The Woman's Picture and the Poetics of Melodrama." *Camera Obscura* 11 (1993): 120–47.

Jameson, Fredric. *The Political Unconscious: Narrative as a Socially Symbolic Act.* Ithaca, NY: Cornell University Press, 1981.

Jameson, Fredric. "Reification and Utopia in Mass Culture." *Social Text* 1 (Winter 1979): 130–48.

Johnson, Cedric, ed. *The Neoliberal Deluge: Hurricane Katrina, Late Capitalism, and the Remaking of New Orleans.* Minneapolis: University of Minnesota Press, 2011.

Joubin, Rebecca. *The Politics of Love: Sexuality, Gender, and Marriage in Syrian Television Drama.* Lanham, MD: Lexington Books, 2015.

Joubin, Rebecca. "Resistance amid Co-optation on the Syrian Television Series *Buq'a Daw'* 2001–2012." *Middle East Journal* 61, no. 1 (2014): 9–32.

Juusola, Hannu. "The Internal Dimensions of Water Security: The Drought Crisis in Northeastern Syria." In *Managing Blue Gold: New Perspectives on Water Security in the Levantine Middle East,* edited by Mari Luomi, 21–34. Helsinki: Finnish Institute of International Affairs, 2012.

Kalyvas, Stathis N., and Ignacio Sánchez-Cuenca. "Killing without Dying? The Absence of Suicide Missions." In *Making Sense of Suicide Missions,* edited by Diego Gambetta, 209–32. Oxford: Oxford University Press, 2005.

Kant, Immanuel. *Critique of Judgment.* Translated by Werner S. Pluhar. Indianapolis: Hackett Classics, 1987.

Kasimis, Demetra. *The Perpetual Immigrant and the Limits of Athenian Democracy.* Cambridge: Cambridge University Press, 2018.

Kateb, George. "The Judgment of Arendt." In *Judgment, Imagination, and Politics: Themes from Kant and Arendt,* edited by Ronald Beiner and Jennifer Nedelsky, 121–38. Lanham, MD: Rowman and Littlefield, 2001.

Khaddour, Kheder. "The Alawite Dilemma (Homs 2013)." In *Playing the Sectarian Card: Identities and Affiliations of Local Communities in Syria,* edited by Friederike Stolleis, 11–26. Beirut: Friedrich-Ebert-Stiftung, 2015. http://library.fes.de/pdf-files/bueros/beirut/12320.pdf.

Khaddour, Kheder. "Assad's Officer Ghetto: Why the Syrian Army Remains Loyal." Beirut: Carnegie Endowment for International Peace, 2015. https://tinyurl.com/yc577bqf.

Khaddour, Kheder. "The Coast in Conflict: Migration, Sectarianism, and Decentralization in Syria's Latakia and Tartus Governorates." Carnegie Middle East Center, July 28, 2016. https://tinyurl.com/y754ayg8.

Khaddour, Kheder. "Consumed by War: The End of Aleppo and Northern Syria's Political Order." Berlin: Friedrich-Ebert-Stiftung, October 2017. http://library.fes.de/pdf-files/iez/13783.pdf.

Khaddour, Kheder, and Kevin Mazur. "The Struggle for Syria's Regions." *Middle East Report* 269 (2013): 2–11. https://tinyurl.com/yc52bsvq.

King, Gary, Jennifer Pan, and Margaret E. Roberts. "How the Chinese Government Fabricates Social Media Posts for Strategic Distraction, Not Engaged Argument." Unpublished manuscript, PDF format, last modified April 9, 2017. Available at https://tinyurl.com/y89pddet. Accessed December 2, 2018.

Klein, Melanie. "Mourning and Its Relation to Manic-Depressive States." *International Journal of Psycho-Analysis* 21 (1940): 125–53.

Kraidy, Marwan M. *The Naked Blogger of Cairo: Creative Insurgency in the Arab World*. Cambridge, MA: Harvard University Press, 2016.

Kundera, Milan. *The Book of Laughter and Forgetting*. Translated by Aaron Asher. New York: Perennial Classics, [1979] 1999. References are to the 1999 edition.

Kuran, Timur. *Private Truths, Public Lies: The Social Consequences of Preference Falsification*. Cambridge, MA: Harvard University Press, 1995.

Lampert, Michael. "Resisting Ideology: On Butler's Critique of Althusser." *Diacritics* 43, no. 2 (2015): 124–47.

Leenders, Reinoud. "'Oh Buthaina, Oh Sha'ban—the Hawrani Is Not Hungry, We Want Freedom!': Revolutionary Framing and Mobilization at the Onset of the Syrian Uprising." In *Social Movements, Mobilization, and Contestation in the Middle East and North Africa*, edited by Joel Beinin and Frédéric Vairel, 246–64. 2nd ed. Palo Alto, CA: Stanford University Press, 2013.

Leenders, Reinoud, and Steven Heydemann. "Popular Mobilization in Syria: Opportunity and Threat, and the Social Networks of the Early Risers." *Mediterranean Politics* 17, no. 2 (2012): 139–59.

Lefèvre, Raphaël. *Ashes of Hama: The Muslim Brotherhood in Syria*. New York: Oxford University Press, 2013.

Levitsky, Steven, and Lucan A. Way. *Competitive Authoritarianism: Hybrid Regimes after the Cold War*. New York: Cambridge University Press, 2010.

Lister, Charles, and Dominic Nelson. "All the President's Militias: Assad's Militiafication of Syria." Middle East Institute, December 14, 2017. https://tinyurl.com/ya79ol93.

Litvak, Joseph. *The Un-Americans: Jews, the Blacklist, and Stoolpigeon Culture*. Durham, NC: Duke University Press, 2009.

Lust-Okar, Ellen. *Structuring Conflict in the Arab World: Incumbents, Opponents, and Institutions*. Cambridge: Cambridge University Press, 2007.

Magaloni, Beatriz. *Voting for Autocracy: Hegemonic Party Survival and Its Demise in Mexico*. New York: Cambridge University Press, 2006.

Makdisi, Ussama. *The Culture of Sectarianism: Community, History, and Violence in Nineteenth-Century Ottoman Lebanon*. Berkeley: University of California Press, 2000.

Malek, Alia. *The Home That Was Our Country: A Memoir of Syria*. New York: Nation Books, 2017.

Mannoni, Octave. *Clefs pour l'imaginaire ou l'Autre Scène*. Paris: Seuil, 1985.

Marin, Louis. *Portrait of the King*. New York: Palgrave MacMillan, 1988.

Mariotti, Shannon L. *Adorno and Democracy: The American Years*. Lexington: University Press of Kentucky, 2016.

Markell, Patchen. *Bound by Recognition*. Princeton, NJ: Princeton University Press, 2003.

Marra, Anthony. *The Constellation of Vital Phenomena*. New York: Hogarth, 2013.

Marshall, Shana R. "Syria and the Financial Crisis: Prospects for Reform?" *Middle East Policy* 16, no. 2 (2009): 106–15. https://tinyurl.com/y8j8cc6e.

Marx, Karl. *The Marx-Engels Reader: Second Edition*. Edited by Robert C. Tucker. New York: W. W. Norton, 1978.

Marzuq (Marzouq), Nabil. "Al-tanmiyya al-mafquda fi Suriya" [Lost Development in Syria]. In *Khalfiyyat al-thawra, dirasat suriyya* [Backgrounds of the Revolution, Syrian Studies], edited by A. Bishara, 35–70. Doha, Qatar: Arab Center for Research and Policy Studies, 2013.

Masco, Joseph. *The Theater of Operations: The National Security State from the Cold War to the War on Terror*. Durham, NC: Duke University Press, 2014.

Massumi, Brian. "The Future Birth of the Affective Fact." In Gregg and Seigworth, *The Affect Theory Reader*, 52–70.

Matar, Hisham. *The Return: Fathers, Sons and the Land in Between*. New York: Random House, 2017.

Matar, Linda. *The Political Economy of Investment in Syria*. Hampshire, UK: Palgrave Macmillan, 2016.

Mazur, Kevin. "Social Categories, Patronage, and the State: Variation in the Syria Uprising." Unpublished manuscript in preparation, May 21, 2018.

Mazzarella, William. *Censorium: Cinema and the Open Edge of Mass Publicity*. Durham, NC: Duke University Press, 2013.

Mazzarella, William. *The Mana of Mass Society*. Chicago: University of Chicago Press, 2017.

Mazzarella, William. "Totalitarian Tears: Does the Crowd Really Mean It?" *Cultural Anthropology* 30, no. 1 (2015): 91–112.

McCabe, Earl. "Depressive Realism: An Interview with Lauren Berlant." *Hypocrite Reader* 5 (June 2011). http://hypocritereader.com/5/depressive-realism.

McClintock, Anne. "Soft Soaping Empire." In *Imperial Leather: Race, Gender, and Sexuality in the Colonial Contest*, 207–31. New York: Routledge, 1995.

McManus, Anne-Marie. "On the Ruins of What's to Come, I Stand: Time and Devastation in Syrian Cultural Production since 2011." *Critical Inquiry*, forthcoming.

Mehta, Uday Singh. *Liberalism and Empire: A Study in Nineteenth-Century British Liberal Thought*. Chicago: University of Chicago Press, 2000.

Meister, Robert. *After Evil: A Politics of Human Rights*. New York: Columbia University Press, 2010.

Mitchell, Timothy. *Carbon Democracy: Political Power in the Age of Oil*. New York: Verso, 2011.

Mitchell, Timothy. "Dreamland: The Neoliberalism of Your Desires." *Middle East Report* 29 (1999). https://tinyurl.com/y8s5u2yd.

Mitchell, Timothy. *Rule of Experts: Egypt, Techno-Politics, Modernity.* Berkeley: University of California Press, 2002.

Mohtadi, Shahrzad. "Climate Change and the Syrian Uprising." *Bulletin of the Atomic Scientists,* August 16, 2012, 1–4.

Moore, Barrington. *Social Origins of Dictatorship and Democracy: Lord and Peasant in the Making of the Modern World.* Paperback ed. Boston: Beacon Press, 1967.

Morris, Errol. *Believing Is Seeing: Observations on the Mysteries of Photography.* London: Penguin Books, 2014.

Morris, Rosalind C. "The War Drive: IMAGE FILES CORRUPTED." *Social Text* 25, no. 2 (Summer 2007): 103–42. https://doi.org/10.1215/01642472-2006-029.

Morris, Rosalind C., and Daniel Leonard. *The Returns of Fetishism: Charles de Brosses's "The Worship of Fetish Gods" and Its Legacies.* Chicago: University of Chicago Press, 2017.

Muehlebach, Andrea. *The Moral Neoliberal: Welfare and Citizenship in Italy.* Chicago: University of Chicago Press, 2012.

Nakkash, Aziz. "The Alawite Dilemma in Homs: Survival, Solidarity and the Making of a Community." Berlin: Friedrich-Ebert-Stiftung, March 2013. http://library.fes.de/pdf-files/iez/09825.pdf.

Panitch, Leo, and Sam Gindin. *The Making of Global Capitalism: The Political Economy of American Empire.* New York: Verso, 2012.

Pariser, Eli. *The Filter Bubble: How the New Personalized Web Is Changing What We Read and How We Think.* New York: Penguin Books, 2012.

Pearlman, Wendy. *We Crossed a Bridge and It Trembled: Voices from Syria.* New York: Harper Collins, 2017.

Pêcheux, Michel. *Language, Semantics and Ideology.* Translated by Harbans Nagpal. London: MacMillan, 1982. Cited in Žižek, *The Sublime Object of Ideology,* xxv.

Perthes, Volker. *The Political Economy of Syria under Asad.* London: I. B. Tauris, 1995.

Perthes, Volker. "The Private Sector, Economic Liberalization, and the Prospects of Democratization: The Case of Syria and Some Other Arab Countries." In *Democracy without Democrats? The Renewal of Politics in the Muslim World,* edited by Ghassan Salame, 243–69. London: I. B. Tauris, 1994.

Perthes, Volker. "Stages of Economic and Political Liberalization." In *Contemporary Syria: Liberalization between Cold War and Cold Peace,* edited by Eberard Kienle, 44–71. London: I. B. Tauris, 1994.

Pierret, Thomas. *Religion and State in Syria: The Sunni Ulema under the Ba'th.* New York: Cambridge University Press, 2013.

Piketty, Thomas. *Capital in the Twenty-First Century.* Translated by Arthur Goldhammer. Cambridge, MA: Harvard University Press, 2014.

Pitkin, Hanna Fenichel. *Wittgenstein and Justice: On the Significance of Ludwig*

Wittgenstein for Social and Political Thought. Berkeley: University of California Press, 1993.

Pitts, Jennifer. *A Turn to Empire: The Rise of Imperial Liberalism in Britain and France*. Princeton, NJ: Princeton University Press, 2005.

Povinelli, Elizabeth. *The Cunning of Recognition: Indigenous Alterities and the Making of Australian Multiculturalism*. Durham, NC: Duke University Press, 2002.

Povinelli, Elizabeth. *Economies of Abandonment: Social Belonging and Endurance in Late Liberalism*. Durham, NC: Duke University Press, 2011.

Przeworski, Adam. *Capitalism and Social Democracy*. New York: Cambridge University Press, 1986.

Radway, Janice A. *Reading the Romance: Women, Patriarchy, and Popular Literature*. Chapel Hill: University of North Carolina Press, [1984] 1991.

Rafael, Vicente L. "Anticipating Nationhood." *Diaspora: A Journal of Transnational Studies* 1, no. 1 (1991): 67–82.

Rajan, Kaushik Sunder. *Pharmocracy: Value, Politics, and Knowledge in Global Biomedicine*. Durham, NC: Duke University Press, 2017.

Rana, Aziz. *Two Faces of American Freedom*. Cambridge, MA: Harvard University Press, 2010.

Ranci, Constanzo. "Democracy at Work: Social Participation and the 'Third Sector' in Italy." *Daedalus* 130, no. 3 (2001): 73–84. Cited in Muehlebach, *The Moral Neoliberal*, 37.

Rancière, Jacques. *Dissensus: On Politics and Aesthetics*. Edited and translated by Steve Corcoran. London: Continuum Books, 2010.

Rancière, Jacques. *The Emancipated Spectator*. Translated by Gregory Elliott. London: Verso, 2011.

Rancière, Jacques. *The Politics of Aesthetics*. Translated by Gabriel Rockhill. London: Bloomsbury, 2004.

Rashed, Dina. "Authoritarianism and the Civilianization of Force: Police Power in Militarized Regimes." PhD diss., University of Chicago, 2017.

Roessler, Philip. *Ethnic Politics and State Power in Africa: The Logic of the Coup–Civil War Trap*. Cambridge: Cambridge University Press, 2016.

Rogin, Michael. *Fathers and Children: Andrew Jackson and the Subjugation of the American Indian*. New York: Alfred A. Knopf, 1975.

Rogin, Michael. *The Intellectuals and McCarthy: The Radical Specter*. Boston: MIT Press, 1967.

Rogin, Michael. *Ronald Reagan the Movie: And Other Episodes in Political Demonology*. Berkeley: University of California Press, 1988.

Rose, Nikolas. "Community, Citizenship, and the Third Way." *American Behavioral Scientist* 43, no. 9 (2000): 1395–1411. Cited in Muehlebach, *The Moral Neoliberal*, 37.

Rose, Nikolas. *Governing the Soul: The Shaping of the Private Self*. London: Free Association Books, 1999.

Safadi, Omar. "Apolitical Citizenship and Authoritarian Survival: A Damascene Experience of the Syrian Civil War." BA thesis, University of Chicago, April 2016.

Salamandra, Christa. *A New Old Damascus: Authenticity and Distinction in Urban Syria*. Bloomington: Indiana University Press, 2004.

Salamandra, Christa. "Prelude to an Uprising: Syrian Fictional Television and Socio-Political Critique." *Jadaliyya*, May 17, 2012. https://tinyurl.com /y7z48w55.

Salamandra, Christa. "Syria's Drama Outpouring: Between Complicity and Critique." In *Syria from Reform to Revolt*. Vol. 2, *Culture, Society and Religion*, edited by Christa Salamandra and Leif Stenberg, 36–52. Syracuse, NY: Syracuse University Press, 2015.

Salamandra, Christa, and Leif Stenberg. "Introduction: A Legacy of Raised Expectations." In *Syria from Reform to Revolt*. Vol. 2, *Culture, Society and Religion*, edited by Salamandra and Stenberg, 1–15. Syracuse, NY: Syracuse University Press, 2015.

Santner, Eric L. *The Royal Remains: The People's Two Bodies and the Endgames of Sovereignty*. Chicago: University of Chicago Press, 2011.

Sassen, Saskia. *The Global City: New York, London, Tokyo*. Princeton, NJ: Princeton University Press, 1991.

Sassen, Saskia. *Globalization and Its Discontents: Essays on the New Mobility of People and Money*. New York: New Press, 1999.

Scarry, Elaine. *The Body in Pain: The Making and Unmaking of the World*. Oxford: Oxford University Press, 1987.

Schwab, Gabriele. *Imaginary Ethnographies: Literature, Culture, and Subjectivity*. New York: Columbia University Press, 2012.

Scott, James C. *Domination and the Arts of Resistance: Hidden Transcripts*. New Haven, CT: Yale University Press, 1990.

Scott, James C. *Weapons of the Weak: Everyday Forms of Peasant Resistance*. New Haven, CT: Yale University Press, 1985.

Seale, Patrick. *Asad: The Struggle for the Middle East*. Berkeley: University of California Press, 1989.

Seifan, Samir. "The Road to Economic Reform in Syria." *St. Andrews Papers on Contemporary Syria*, 2011.

Seifan, Samir. "Siyasat tawzi' al-dakhl wa dawrha fi al-infijar al-ijtima'i fi Suriya" [The Politics of Income Distribution and Its Role in the Social Explosion in Syria]. In *Khalfiyyat al-thawra, dirasat suriyya* [Backgrounds of the Revolution, Syrian Studies], edited by A. Bishara, 95–146. Doha, Qatar: Arab Center for Research and Policy Studies, 2013.

Seigworth, Gregory J., and Matthew Tiessen. "Mobile Affects, Open Secrets, and Global Illiquidity: Pockets, Pools, and Plasma." *Theory, Culture, and Society* 29, no. 6 (2012): 47–77.

Shami, Leila al-, and Robin Yassin-Kassab. *Burning Country: Syrians in Revolution and War*. New York: Pluto Press, 2016.

Simpser, Alberto. *Why Governments and Parties Manipulate Elections: Theory, Practice, and Implications*. New York: Cambridge University Press, 2014.

Singer, Ben. *Melodrama and Modernity: Early Sensational Cinema and Its Contexts*. New York: Columbia University Press, 2001.

Slater, Dan. *Ordering Power: Contentious Politics and Authoritarian Leviathans in Southeast Asia*. New York: Cambridge University Press, 2010.

Slaughter, Anne-Marie. Preface to *The Arab Spring and Climate Change*, edited by Caitlin E. Werrell and Francesco Femia, 1–6. Washington, DC: Center for American Progress, 2013.

Sloterdijk, Peter. *Critique of Cynical Reason*. Translated by Michael Eldred. Minneapolis: University of Minnesota Press, 1988.

Smith, Henry James. "The Melodrama." *Atlantic Monthly* 99 (March 1907): 320–28. Cited in Singer, *Melodrama and Modernity*, 47.

Sontag, Susan. *Regarding the Pain of Others*. New York: Picador, 2003.

Stewart, Kathleen. *Ordinary Affects*. Durham, NC: Duke University Press, 2007.

Sunstein, Cass R. "A Case Study in Group Polarization (with Warnings for the Future)." In *Aftermath: The Clinton Impeachment and the Presidency in the Age of Political Spectacle*, edited by Leonard V. Kaplan and Beverly I. Moran, 11–21. New York: New York University Press, 2001.

Svolik, Milan W. "Contracting on Violence: The Moral Hazard in Authoritarian Repression and Military Intervention in Politics." *Journal of Conflict Resolution* 57, no. 5 (2013): 765–94.

Svolik, Milan W. *The Politics of Authoritarian Rule*. New York: Cambridge University Press, 2012.

Svolik, Milan W. "Power-Sharing and Leadership Dynamics in Authoritarian Regimes." *American Journal of Political Science* 53, no. 2 (1999): 477–94.

Svolik, Milan W. "When Polarization Trumps Civic Virtue: Partisan Conflict and the Subversion of Democracy by Incumbents." Unpublished manuscript, PDF format, last modified August 2018. https://tinyurl.com/ybtw2vc6. Accessed November 25, 2018.

Svolik, Milan W., and Carles Boix. "The Foundations of Limited Authoritarian Government: Institutions, Commitment, and Power-Sharing in Dictatorships." *Journal of Politics* 75, no. 2 (April 2013): 300–316.

Taussig, Michael. *The Nervous System*. New York: Routledge, 1992.

Terc, Amanda Patricia. "Syria's New Neoliberal Elite: English Usage, Linguistic Practices and Group Boundaries." PhD diss., University of Michigan, 2011.

Thrift, Nigel. "Understanding the Material Practices of Glamour." In Gregg and Seigworth, *The Affect Theory Reader*, 289–308.

Van Dam, Nikolaos. *The Struggle for Power in Syria: Politics and Society under Asad and the Ba'th Party*. London, New York: I. B. Tauris, [1979] 2011. References are to the 2011 edition.

Vasudevan, Ravi. *The Melodramatic Public: Film Form and Spectatorship in Indian Cinema*. New York: Palgrave, 2011.

Wacquant, Loïc. *Punishing the Poor: The Neoliberal Government of Social Insecurity*. Durham, NC: Duke University Press, 2009.

Wedeen, Lisa. *Ambiguities of Domination: Politics, Rhetoric, and Symbols in Contemporary Syria*. Chicago: University of Chicago Press, 1999.

Wedeen, Lisa. "Conceptualizing Culture: Possibilities for Political Science." *American Political Science Review* 96, no. 4 (December 2002): 713–28.

Wedeen, Lisa. "Ideology and Humor in Dark Times: Notes from Syria." *Critical Inquiry* 39 (2013): 841–73.

Wedeen, Lisa. *Peripheral Visions: Publics, Power, and Performance in Yemen.* Chicago: University of Chicago Press, 2008.

Weiss, Max D. *In the Shadow of Sectarianism: Law, Shi'ism, and the Making of Modern Lebanon.* Cambridge, MA: Harvard University Press, 2010.

Weiss, Max D. "Slow Witnessing: Syrian War Literature in Real Time." Lecture, Chicago Center for Contemporary Theory (CCCT), University of Chicago, October 7, 2016.

Wessels, Joshka. *Documenting Syria: Filmmaking, Video Activism and Revolution.* London: I. B. Tauris, 2019.

Williams, Raymond. *Marxism and Literature.* Oxford: Oxford University Press, 1977.

Wimmer, Andreas, Lars-Erik Cederman, and Brian Min. "Ethnic Politics and Armed Conflict: A Configurational Analysis of a New Global Data Set." *American Sociological Review* 74, no. 2 (2009): 316–37.

Wittgenstein, Ludwig. *Lectures and Conversations on Aesthetics, Psychology and Religious Belief.* Edited by Cyril Barrett. Berkeley: University of California Press, 1967. Quoted in Zerilli, *A Democratic Theory of Judgment*, 78.

Wittgenstein, Ludwig. *On Certainty.* Translated by Denis Paul and G. E. M. Anscombe and edited by G. E. M. Anscombe and G. H. von Wright. New York: Harper Torchbooks, 1969.

Yassin-Kassab, Robin, and Leila al-Shami. *Burning Country: Syrians in Revolution and War.* London: Pluto Press, 2016.

Yazbek, Samar. *The Crossing: My Journey to the Shattered Heart of Syria.* London: Ebury Press, 2016.

Yurchak, Alexei. *Everything Was Forever until It Was No More: The Last Soviet Generation.* Princeton, NJ: Princeton University Press, 2005.

Zambelis, Chris. "Syria's Sunnis and the Regime's Resilience." *Politikan*, June 17, 2015. https://tinyurl.com/y7hyvodm.

Zerilli, Linda. *A Democratic Theory of Judgment.* Chicago: University of Chicago Press, 2016.

Zerilli, Linda. *Feminism and the Abyss of Freedom.* Chicago: University of Chicago Press, 2005.

Ziter, Edward. "Abounaddara: The Right to the Image." Lecture, Vera List Center for Art and Politics, New School, New York City, October 22, 2015.

Ziter, Edward. *Political Performance in Syria: From the Six-Day War to the Syrian Uprising.* New York: Palgrave MacMillan, 2015.

Žižek, Slavoj. "Denial: The Liberal Utopia." Available at https://tinyurl.com/yzewpw2. Accessed December 1, 2018.

Žižek, Slavoj. *Looking Awry: An Introduction to Jacques Lacan through Popular Culture.* Boston: MIT Press, 1991.

Žižek, Slavoj. *The Sublime Object of Ideology*. London: Verso, [1989] 2009. References are to the 2009 edition.

Žižek, Slavoj. "The Two Totalitarianisms." *London Review of Books* 27, no. 6 (March 17, 2005). https://tinyurl.com/ybknv4hl.

Zupančič, Alenka. *The Odd One In: On Comedy*. Boston: MIT Press, 2008.

Index

Ababneh, Yahya, 90

'Abdallah, Yahya al-, 168, 188n13, 197n76, 205n29, 211n72, 218n49, 223n40

Abounaddara, 14, 82, 97, 99, 101–5, 122–23, 136, 166, 211nn62–63, 211n66, 211n70, 212n73; *Aïcha*, 102–3; *In the Name of the Father*, 97; and representative thinking, 166; *The Trajectory of an Unknown Soldier*, 99, 104–5, 123, 129, 211n62, 211n66

Adorno, Theodor, x, 55, 109, 179n5, 200n24, 202n54

advertising, ix, 9, 22, 27, 29, 35, 37–39, 52, 119, 165, 192n36, 194n55, 200n25, plate 4

affect, 4–8, 11, 13–16, 21, 25, 32, 35, 40, 45, 47, 51, 75, 81, 95, 107–8, 110–12, 122, 127, 134, 141, 143–47, 150, 152, 154–55, 161, 182n11, 189–90n25, 193n44, 204–5n23, 219n57

affective attachment, 3, 6, 7, 16, 29, 32, 47, 51, 123, 153, 161–62, 184n32; and advertising, 38; and ambivalence, 51; and ideology, 35

Al-Arabiya, 96

Aleppo, 20, 22, 24, 26, 33–34, 39, 40–44, 62–63, 108, 128, 164, 168, 174, 178, 194n65, 195n69, 197n76, 197n78, 202n48, 205n30, 221n18; political quiescence of, 40–42, 62; violence in, 174–75

al-Ghouta (chemical attack), 13, 71, 81, 87, 90–91, 93–94, 108, 205–6n30, 208n47

al-Hariqa market, 2011 protest in, 156

'Ali, 'Adnan, 89

Al-Jazeera, 36, 96, 194n65, 208n47

Al-Qa'ida, 94, 160–61

Althusser, Louis, ix, x, 2, 6–10, 43, 59, 182n13, 184n30, 185n33

Ambiguities of Domination (Wedeen), viii, ix, 6, 7, 145, 179n1–2, 183n21, 198n7, 199n13, 211n65, 214n24, 214n26, 218n48

ambivalence, viii, x, xii, 3, 5–7, 12–13, 21–25, 28, 31, 35, 37–38, 40–41, 49, 51, 64–65, 70, 80, 82, 85, 94, 99, 105, 108, 111, 113, 121, 127, 135, 137, 146–47, 158, 163, 165, 183n25, 188n13, 198n7, 216–17n44

Arab League, 161

Arendt, Hannah, x, 4, 13, 15, 78, 81, 96–97, 102, 104, 108, 127, 132, 135, 137, 211n61, 212n1, 216n41, 219n62; political judgment, 108, 135, 137, 212n1; representative thinking, 4, 135–36

armed opposition, 42, 67, 84, 143, 165, 174, 224n1. *See also* civil war; violence

'Ar'ur, 'Adnan, 158

Asad, Asma' al-, 16, 20, 27, 29, 32, 64, 84, 114–21. *See also* first family

Asad, Bashar al-, vii, 3, 4, 12, 19, 20, 27, 37, 40, 49–52, 54, 60–61, 70, 120, 126, 128, 146, 150, 163, 194n55, 204–5n23, 209n54, 215n32, plate 1, plate 6, plate 7, plate 10, plate 11, plate 12; promises reform, 29, 31, 36, 64. *See also* first family

Asad, Hafiz al-, vii, viii, ix, x, 2, 27, 30, 33–34, 37, 44, 71, 82, 84, 99, 148, 193n45, 198n7, 211n65, 218n48, plate 10

Asad, Maher al-, 82, plate 10

Asad, Rif'at al-, 44–45

as if, acting, viii, 4, 6–7, 27, 50, 145, 161
atmospherics of doubt, 80, 82, 96, 105
atomization, 50
authoritarianism, x, xii, 1, 33, 72
autocracy, 13, 25, 32, 80; kinder, gentler, vii, 2, 38, 46, 51, 79, 149, 163. *See also* neoliberal autocracy
Ayesha, Abu, 90

Bahrain, vii, 2, 39
Ban Ki-moon, 88, 205n30
Barish, Sumar, 70–71, 202n47
Barout, Mohammed Jamal, 23, 189n22, plate 8
Ba'th Party, ix, 32, 72, 118, 120, 126–27, 152, 200n26, 214n26, plate 11, plate 12
Beckett, Samuel, 52
Bedirxan, Wiam Simav. *See* Simav (Wiam Simav Bedirxan)
Benjamin, Walter, 55, 200n24, 205n28
Bergson, Henri, 49, 65–66, 73, 75
Berlant, Lauren, 20, 38, 49, 52, 66–67, 74, 111, 119, 128, 134, 150, 168–69, 179n5, 183n16, 183n24, 185n38, 187n9, 201n28, 202n54, 202n56, 216n35, 219n57
Bin Jiddu, Ghassan, 37
bin Sultan Al Saud, Bandar, 90
Birth from the Waist, Part Three (TV series), 109, 112, 212
Bourdieu, Pierre, 11, 188n14
branding, 28–29, 39, 79
Brecht, Bertolt, 49
Brooks, Peter, 112
Brown, Wendy, 186n8
Brown Moses. *See* Higgins, Eliot (Brown Moses)
Brubaker, Rogers, 151
Buck, Joan Juliet, 28
Butler, Judith, 9, 10, 184n30, 184n32, 185n33

café culture, 10, 11, 34
Chandler, James, 110, 168, 219n52
children: Aylan, 120; as stand-in for nation, 47, 123; 'Umran, 120
China, 16, 39
Chivers, C. J., 91
civil war, 11–12, 94, 96, 107–8, 117, 161, 221n19, 224n48
Clausewitz, Carl von, 96
clergy ('*ulama*), 26, 62, 188n17
CNN, 96
Colbert, Stephen, 67
Comaroff, Jean, 5, 23, 26, 171, 183n16, 183n18, 188n16, 189n25, 191n30
Comaroff, John, 171, 183n16
comedy, ix, xi, 8, 13, 16, 49–75, 122, 166, 169–70, 185–86n39, 198n2, 198n5, 200n21, 202n51, 217n47
Communist Party, 23, 44, 165
conspiracy, 19, 36–37, 46, 67–68, 78, 85, 89–90, 94, 109, 204n19, 209n54, 210n58

cultural producers, x, 15, 35, 40, 57, 60, 80, 108, 213n5

Damascus, 10, 20, 22–24, 26–27, 29–30, 33, 35, 36–37, 39–45, 52, 63, 87–89, 109, 114, 123, 128, 156–57, 160–61, 167–68, 174–78, 181n3, 188nn14–15, 193n52, 195n66, 201n31, 208n47, 214n23, 220n2, plate 4, plate 5; political quiescence of, 20–24, 39–42, 156–57, 174–78, 181n3, 186n4, 195n66; violence in, 175
Dar'a, 2–4, 23, 36, 47, 67, 132, 174, 176, 181n3, 181n5
Day'a daay'a (TV series). *See* Hajju, Allayth
Dayr al-Zur, 2, 43, 177–78
Della Ratta, Donatella, 60, 180n11, 194n55, 194n57, 195n66, 200n21, 212n3, plate 5
democratic activists, 155–57, 162, 165
De Niro, Robert, 72
"digital revolution," 80
Dik, Husayn al-, 3, 19, 186n3
Din Al-Ayyubi, 'Ala' Al-, 85
Dinesen, Isak, 102, 104, 216
disavowal, 7–8, 12, 22, 29, 38, 41, 90, 96, 105, 141, 144–45, 164, 183–84n25, 220n2
displacement, 5, 29–30, 32, 35, 51, 103, 109, 114, 119, 129, 141–42, 146, 159, 162, 164, 175, 182n12, 220n2
Doctors without Borders, 87–88
Dolar, Mladen, 9, 66–67, 184n32
drama community, 27, 165, 214n18
Durkheim, Émile, 85, 205n24

Eagleton, Terry, 6
Egypt, vii, 2, 24, 35, 39, 42, 47, 118, 125, 156, 161, 196n73, 203n12, 221n19
Facebook, 38, 44, 61, 77–78, 81, 83, 112, 119–20, 130, 149, 155, 193n39, 203–4n15, 215n33, 221n20, 221n21
fake news, 8, 77–78, 107, 166
Farzat, 'Ali, plate 6
fashion, 9, 29, 31, 75
fear, 2–4, 14, 20–21, 29, 34, 41, 46, 50, 55–56, 61, 74, 79, 98, 124, 129, 131, 141–62, 164–65, 216n44, 220n2; anticipatory, 141, 142–44, 154, 158, 162, 220n2
fetishism, 4, 23, 26, 182n11, 183n25, 188n16
first family, ix, 20, 27–29, 43, 46–47, 51, 82, 99, 114, 137, 164; mimesis, 20, 99
Fisk, Robert, 159
fitna (discord), 37, 155, 186n6, plate 4
flag pre-Ba'thist, 16, 38
Flayhan, Rima, 36
Forgotten Village, A (TV series). *See* Hajju, Allayth
Foucault, Michel, 26, 143, 151, 183n16, 191n28
frames of reference, 8, 86–87, 89, 97
France, 12, 159, 207n40, 209n54
freedom, 1–2, 20–21, 24, 31, 33, 42, 44, 55, 60, 65, 68, 71, 74, 97, 99, 133, 135, 165, 184n32, 186n8, 194n60

Malek, Alia, 160–61
Malick, Terrence, 132
Mannoni, Octave, 41, 141, 183n25
March 15 group, 174
Markell, Patchen, 132, 168
Marra, Anthony, xii
Marx, Karl, x, 4–5, 182n10, 182n11, 183n16, 187n11, 188n16
Masasit Mati, 61, 201n33; *Top Goon*, 61, 63, 65, 67, 69, 73–74, plate 7
Masco, Joseph, 146, 168, 210n58
Massumi, Brian, 80, 142–43
Matar, Hisham, xii
Mazur, Kevin, 24, 169, 188n17, 189n22, 195n68, 220n4, 223n40, 224n48
Mazzarella, William, 6, 37, 168, 183n16, 183n24, 185n33, 192n35, 194n56, 205n24, 217n45
melodrama, 14, 103, 107, 111, 112–13, 115–18, 120–22, 127, 131, 135, 138, 164, 169, 200n21, 213n15, 213n17, 216n35
Min Fawq al-Asatih (*Over the Roofs*), 71, 202n49
minorities, 1, 31, 35, 46, 60, 143, 152–53, 156, 158, 160–61, 163, 194n58; 'Alawi, 45–46, 56, 91, 101, 141, 143–44, 146–48, 153–58, 160, 194n58, 200n26, 218n48, 220n1, 223n35; Christian, 6, 30, 34, 46, 160–61, 188n17
MintPress News, 89, 90, 207n39
mobilization, 3, 55, 80, 173–76, 181n3, 224n1
Mohammed, Ossama, 14, 107, 129–38, 166, 168, 217nn46–47, 219n53; on film, 132; *Silvered Water, Syria Self-Portrait* (*Ma' al-Fidda*), 129–31, 134, 137, 166, 217n46, 218n49
moral neoliberalism, 27, 32, 186n8
Morris, Errol, 79, 93
Mother's Day film. See *With Your Soul You Protect the Jasmine* (film)
mourning, xii, 4, 8, 107, 111, 115–16, 121, 125–26, 128–29, 138, 164, 216n44
Mu'addamiyya, 44–46, 197n79
Mubarak, Husni, 2, 35, 161
Muehlebach, Andrea, 32, 186n8, 193n44
multicultural accommodation, 20, 31, 38, 52, 56, 102, 112, 118, 142, 149, 153, 160, 186n6
Muslim Brotherhood, 85, 160–61, 189n22

Nakzeh (*Little Poke*), 70, 202n48
Nasir, Gamal 'Abd al-, 125
nationalism, 14, 107–39, 150, 153, 159, 213n11, 217n45
national unity, 38, 85, 148, 151–52
Nelson, Dominic, 153
neoliberal autocracy, 10, 12–13, 19–47, 50, 80, 105, 142, 147–49, 151, 164–65, 186n7, 186–87n8, 193n50
neoliberalism, 15, 21, 25, 32, 39–40, 74, 186n7, 186–87n7, 189n25, 191n28
"nervous system," Syrian, 143, 154–56, 159, 162
Network for Human Rights, 175
Ngai, Sianne, 49, 66–67, 74

nonjudgment, 80, 82, 104, 162
nonsovereignty, 119, 132, 138–39, 148, 155, 160, 169

Obama, Barack, 92, 94–95
opposition. *See* armed opposition; protest
Othering, 8, 14, 37, 43, 68, 102, 135, 138, 143–44, 151, 155, 159, 164–65
Ottoman reforms, 152, 222n32
Over the Roofs. See *Min Fawq al-Asatih* (*Over the Roofs*)

Parry, Robert, 159, 209n53
Pêcheux, Michel, 9
Pitkin, Hanna, 196n73
Pizzi, Michael, 77
Police in the Service of the People, The, 85
political agency, 166
popular committees, 46
Postol, Theodore A., 90–93, 105
protest, 2–3, 9, 12, 16, 20–24, 26, 33–34, 36, 39–40, 42–44, 46–47, 61–63, 80, 83, 85, 96, 102, 109, 130, 143, 146–47, 156–58, 173–74, 181n3, 189n22, 194n55, 194n65, 195nn66–68, 197n78, 200n26, 203n12; calls for dignity (*karama*), 2, 11, 42, 47, 51, 57, 84, 102, 147, 165, 185n36; economic geography of, 42; ideological geography of, 43; and sectarianism, 156
public dissimulation, politics of, 6–8, 27, 97, 120–21, 145. See also *as if*, acting
Putin, Vladimir, 92–93, 149, 203n11, 209n54, plate 11

Qashush, Ibrahim, 83–84, 86–87, 105, 203n12, 203nn14–15
Qatar, 85, 158, 165

Rahman Farhud, 'Abd al-, 83, 203n15
Ramadan television dramas, 109–12, 212n2, 213n5
Rancière, Jacques, 119, 214n20
reform: economic, 26–27, 192n32; market, 46, 190n26, 196n72; neoliberal, 9, 33; opposition, 7, 31, 36, 40, 47, 57, 156, 193n53; political, 2, 13; promises of, 31, 40, 47, 51–52, 64
regime, support for: clergy, 26, 62, 188n17; loyalists, 12, 16, 33, 35, 37, 43, 45, 70, 72, 85, 89, 94–95, 99, 113, 124, 142, 146, 148, 150, 153, 158, 163, 203–4n15, 215n33, plate 9; minorities and, 35, 46, 143, 158, 160–61, 194n58; professional managerial elite, viii, ix, 10, 26–27, 31, 35, 40, 46, 58, 60, 63, 71, 80, 165; regime-oriented image-makers, 37
representative thinking, 102, 108, 135–38, 166, 212n1
Resnais, Alain, 133
revolution, 53–55, 64, 71, 73, 80, 83–85, 95, 98, 105, 109, 121, 130, 132–33, 144, 166, 197n83, 204n23
Rif Dimashq (outskirts of Damascus), 10, 23, 42, 44, 63, 71, 87, 108, 133, 175, 177–78